D0760396

GERMANS TO THE FRONT

DAVID CLAY LARGE

GERMANS
TO THE FRONT

WEST

GERMAN

REARMAMENT

IN THE

ADENAUER

ERA

THE UNIVERSITY OF NORTH CAROLINA PRESS

CHAPEL HILL & LONDON

The paper in this book meets the guidelines for permanence and durability of
the Committee on Production Guidelines for Book Longevity of the Council
on Library Resources.

Library of Congress Cataloging-in-Publication Data
Large, David Clay.
Germans to the front : West German rearmament in the Adenauer era / by
David Clay Large.
      p.   cm.
Includes bibliographical references and index.
ISBN 0-8078-2235-3 (alk. paper).—ISBN 0-8078-4539-6 (pbk. : alk. paper)
    1. Germany (West)—Defenses.   2. Germany (West)—Politics and gov-
ernment.   Germany (West)—Foreign relations.   I. Title.
UA710.L27   1995
355'.033043'09045—dc20   95-5401
                                                                   CIP

David Clay Large is professor of history at Montana State University.

oo 99 98 97 96   5 4 3 2 1

To Josh

CONTENTS

ACKNOWLEDGMENTS

This book has taken longer to complete than it took to rearm West Germany. During the seemingly eternal process of researching and writing it I have become indebted to the institutions that helped finance my work. I thank Yale University for a Morse Faculty Fellowship; the American Philosophical Society for a Penrose Fund grant; the German Academic Exchange Service for a summer study grant to the Federal Republic; Montana State University for a Research-Creativity grant; and the German Marshall Fund of the United States for a Research Fellowship in 1990–91. I am grateful to both Yale and Montana State Universities for allowing me generous leaves of absence to pursue this project.

During the initial phase of my research, I enjoyed the hospitality and assistance of the Militärgeschichtliches Forschungsamt in Freiburg. The scholars and staff at that institution are models of professional competence, but, to their credit, they also take time out for tea or a beer. My headquarters in Bonn was the Deutsche Gesellschaft für Auswärtige Politik, whose archive and library are a treasure trove to students of modern German foreign policy. My thanks to Professor Dr. Karl Kaiser for the invitation to work there. I owe thanks as well to the (now long departed) denizens of the Burschenschaft Alemannia in Bonn, who allowed me to live in their splendid house on the Rhine without making me duel.

In addition to the resources of the Forschungsamt and the Gesellschaft, I drew on the relevant holdings of the following archives and libraries, whose staffs I thank: Archiv für Christlich-Demokratische Politik, St. Augustine; Bundesarchiv-Militärarchiv, Freiburg; Universitätsbibliothek Freiburg; Bundesarchiv, Koblenz; Friedrich Ebert Stiftung, Bonn; Friedrich Naumann Stiftung/Heuss Akademie, Gummersbach; Konrad Adenauer Haus, Rhöndorf; Parlamentsarchiv, Bonn; Presse- und Informationsamt der Bundesregierung, Bonn; Institut für Zeitgeschichte, Munich; Bayerische Staatsbibliothek, Munich; Public Records Office, London; British Library, London; Bibliothèque Nationale, Paris; National Archives, Washington, D.C.; Doe Library, University of California, Berkeley; Greene Library, Stanford University, Hoover Institution, Stanford; Renne Library, Montana State University, Sterling Library, Yale University; Suzzalo Library, University of Washington; Widener Library, Harvard University.

Friends and colleagues read parts of the manuscript and discussed problems connected to it with me. Without holding them responsible for what finally resulted, I would like to thank them for their help. They include Donald Abenheim, Johannes Bähr, Arnulf Baring, Karl Baumgart, Maarten

Brands, Karl-Dietrich Bracher, David Carlton, Mark Cioc, James Diehl, Jürgen Förster, Dieter Gosewinkel, Wolfgang Krieger, Klaus Maier, Georg Meyer, Pierce Mullen, Jeffrey Safford, Thomas Schwartz, Fritz Stern, Henry Turner, and Bernd Wegner. Karl Baumgart was very helpful in sending me materials from Germany when I was unable to go there myself.

Three of the "founding fathers" of the Bundeswehr—Wolf Graf von Baudissin, Johann Graf von Kielmansegg, and Heinz Karst—granted me interviews when I embarked on this project in the early 1980s. I am grateful for the personal insights they provided on a process to which they contributed so significantly.

My greatest debt of gratitude, however, is owed to my wife, Margaret, for she had to live with me while I wrote this book.

DCL
San Francisco, California

ABBREVIATIONS

The following abbreviations are used in the text.

ACC	Allied Control Council
AHC	Allied High Commission
BHE	Bund der Heimatvertriebenen und Entrechteten
BPA	Bundespresseamt
CCS	Combined Chiefs of Staff
CDU	Christian Democratic Union
CSU	Christian Social Union
DGB	Deutsche Gewerkschaftsbund
DP	Deutsche Partei
DRP	Deutsche Rechtspartei
DVP	Deutsche Volkspartei
EDC	European Defense Community
EKD	Evangelische Kirche Deutschlands
EUCOM	European Command (United States)
EVG	Europäische Verteidigungsgemeinschaft
EWG	Europäische Wirtschaftsgemeinschaft
FDP	Freie Demokratische Partei
FRG	Federal Republic of Germany
GDR	German Democratic Republic
GVP	Gesamtdeutsche Volkspartei
JCS	Joint Chiefs of Staff
KPD	Kommunistische Partei Deutschlands
MRP	Mouvement Républicain Populaire
NATO	North Atlantic Treaty Organization
NSC	National Security Council
OMGUS	Office of Military Government, United States
SACEUR	Supreme Allied Commander Europe
SFIO	Section Française de l'Internationale ouvrière
SHAEF	Supreme Headquarters Allied Expeditionary Force
SHAPE	Supreme Headquarters Allied Powers Europe
SMAD	Sowjetische Militäradministration in Deutschland
SPD	Sozialdemokratische Partei Deutschlands
SRP	Sozialistische Reichspartei
VdS	Verband deutscher Soldaten
WEU	Western European Union

GERMANS TO THE FRONT

INTRODUCTION

On 22 June 1900, as an international expeditionary force prepared to storm Fort Hsiku during the Boxer Rebellion in China, Lord Edward Hobart Seymour, the expedition's British commander, ordered the German contingent to the front. The command was natural enough, for the Germans were regarded as the best-trained and most enthusiastic soldiers in the world. Their sponsor, Kaiser Wilhelm II, had excitedly referred to them as "Huns" when he sent them off to Peking to help rescue the besieged European legations. The German troops behaved as everyone knew they would—efficiently and with grim relish. Their exploits were later memorialized in a famous battle painting, *Germans to the Front*, which made this phrase famous throughout the world.

A half century later, the order "Germans to the Front" went out again, but this time the context was far different: now the front was the Iron Curtain and the Germans in question had been thoroughly demilitarized following their defeat, for the second time in the twentieth century, in a devastating world war. The Germans responded unquestioningly to that first order to the front in 1900, but they did not do so at mid-century; on the contrary, many of them resisted the call to arms with the cry "*Ohne Mich!*" (Leave Me Out). The Western Allies who issued the appeal were by no means unanimously or unambiguously certain that entrusting the Germans with military responsibility was a good idea. After the rearmament question had been tentatively and informally raised in 1947–48, it took some six years of wearisome negotiations to get the West Germans into uniform. And even when the new West German army, the Bundeswehr, finally appeared in 1956, many in the West still thought it was far too early.

Although both German states of the postwar era, the Federal Republic of Germany (FRG) and the German Democratic Republic (GDR), were armed by their respective Great Power sponsors, this book focuses on the international effort to integrate the new Bonn Republic into the Western alliance system. Developments in East Germany are assessed here, too, but only to the extent that they affected the rearmament debate in the West. (An up-to-date, full-scale study of East German rearmament is needed, and it is now more feasible after Eastern archives have been opened following the collapse of the GDR and the Soviet Union.) This book concludes with the difficult birth of the Bundeswehr in the mid-1950s. Though I do not follow the later evolution of that organization, I propose that some of the difficulties that the Bundeswehr encountered as it became established in German society and in the Atlantic alliance were rooted in the new army's troubled origins.

The story of West German rearmament must be told on several levels, for it was at once a crucial chapter in the history of the Cold War; a major bone of contention among the victorious Western powers; a demanding rite of passage for the young Federal Republic; a—or better, *the*—primary question in West German domestic politics of the early 1950s; a bold new departure in German military affairs; and finally a moral challenge harboring profound implications for postwar Germany's relationship with its problematic past and uncertain future. No other single issue contains within it so many dimensions of the "German Question" in its post-1945 variant, as the hot war against the Nazis segued into the Cold War with the Soviets.

To be understood in its full significance, the rearmament process has to be examined not only against the backdrop of the West's changing strategic policies in the early Cold War era but also within the broader continuum of German statecraft and military politics in the twentieth century. To this end, frequent comparisons with earlier policies and practices will be made. Additionally, because rearmament was a moral and cultural dilemma as well as a political one, I will look at the ways in which the debate became enmeshed in questions of the new state's "spiritual direction" and cultural identity.

Part I follows the progress of events from an ambitiously far-reaching demilitarization of the shattered German Reich, through the opening discussions of a possible remilitarization, to the formal decision to pursue the development of a West German contribution to the Western alliance. I suggest that the disintegration of the draconian demilitarization program resulted not only from the dawning East-West split but also from design flaws in Allied disarmament policy. Stripping western Germany of its entire military potential proved to be impossible without making it dependent on its conquerors for everything from soda ash to police protection. Nevertheless, strict demilitarization remained officially in place even though a few voices in the Allied camp, citing the threat to Western security posed by Moscow's emergent East European empire and vast armies, began to raise the possibility of putting the West Germans back into uniform.

Official reluctance to abandon the demilitarization policy should remind us that when the Cold War began, Germany was still seen as a major threat to world peace—albeit one significantly crippled by the devastation visited upon it in World War II. Thus the first tentative calls to put Germans on the Cold War front caused considerable consternation even in the West, where political leaders were quick to disavow them. The Germans, most policy makers averred, would have to prove that they were fully reformed, that their militaristic affliction was in total remission, before they could be allowed to maintain armed forces of any kind.

Trepidation about rearming West Germany, however, competed early on with concerns that the new state was not only vulnerable to aggression from the Soviets but perhaps in danger of "drifting to the East" on its own accord unless it was made more confident of its Western connections and integrated more firmly into the Western community. Given the strong pro-Western inclinations of Bonn's first chancellor, Konrad Adenauer, this worry may seem exaggerated; yet it was by no means clear that "Der Alte," who was seventy-three years old and a relatively unknown quantity when he assumed the chancellorship, would turn out to be as dominant or decisive as he became.

Many of the Western politicians and military men who pushed for rapid German rearmament assumed that doing so would not be terribly difficult. After all, were not the Germans inveterate lovers of things military? (The assumption that they were was, of course, the prime justification for the initial determination to keep them thoroughly demilitarized.) Moreover, even if some Germans should prove reluctant to take up arms again so soon after their devastating defeat, they appeared to have little choice in the matter. The new Federal Republic possessed only limited sovereignty and no control over its external security. As an occupied nation, Bonn could be expected to do the bidding of its occupiers.

Yet virtually from the outset, the West Germans proved considerably less tractable than their conquerors-cum-allies might have wished. Although West German leaders appreciated their dependence on the West (especially America), they were determined to define and articulate their own political interests, even at the risk of irritating the occupation powers. Chancellor Adenauer actually anticipated the Allies' formal request for a military contribution to the Western alliance by making a defense offer of his own, albeit one embedded in far-reaching political "conditions." In essence, Adenauer offered to trade a military contribution to the alliance for increased German sovereignty, political rehabilitation, and full membership in the Western community of states.

Though many in the Western camp were willing enough to welcome Bonn to the "Western Club," few were prepared to do so on terms of complete equality. Thus the international effort to get Germans to the front eventually engendered a complicated contest between Bonn and the Western powers over the precise conditions under which the Federal Republic might rearm. The stakes were very high, involving nothing less than determining how "free" the Germans would be, how heavy a defense burden they would carry, and how their role in the Western community would be defined. The answers to these questions ultimately shaped the evolution of Germany's foreign and security policy in the second half of the twentieth century.

The rearmament issue had been raised and debated, but by no means firmly decided upon, when the Korean War broke out in June 1950. Though many in the West drew ominous analogies between the Korean situation and that of divided Germany, the Far Eastern conflict only gradually convinced

America, the West's lone superpower, to adopt West German rearmament as its official policy. Once that happened, however, this goal became the key to Washington's vision for Germany and Europe. In addition to shaping America's policy toward Bonn, it dramatically affected relations among the three Western allies. Indeed, the German rearmament question quickly emerged as the first major test of the new North Atlantic Treaty Organization (NATO) alliance.

The alliance was strained because Washington's enthusiasm for rearming the Germans was not equally shared by Great Britain and France. Both, of course, had been severely tested by the Germans in two world wars, and both were anything but sanguine about the revival of Germany's martial potential. Though, with some cajoling, London eventually came around to the American line, France proved determined to prevent, or at the very least to delay, the military revival of its old enemy. Its vehement opposition ensured that the initial Allied decision to pursue German rearmament, taken at the NATO Foreign Ministers Conference in Brussels in December 1950, would not produce any German armed forces in the immediate future.

The next phase of the German rearmament debate evolved within the context of the abortive European Defense Community (EDC) scheme, which is the subject of Part II of this study. The EDC initiative was a modification of the so-called Pleven Plan, which arose from French efforts to ensure that if Bonn ever *was* allowed to field armed forces, they would be tightly controlled through their integration in a common "European army" format. This ideal of keeping Bonn in line through extensive integration in the European-Atlantic political and security system became a constant theme in Germany's relations with the West for the next half century.

The EDC project seemed to take on added viability when the United States, which had initially scoffed at the plan, became an avid sponsor and champion of it. My assessment of Washington's volte-face on this matter affords insights into America's perception of its postwar role in European security. Unlike its disgruntled retreat into isolationism after World War I, Washington would stay actively involved in European affairs, even maintaining a significant military presence in Britain and on the Continent. Yet America's leaders also hoped that the Europeans could take on more of the defense burden themselves; the EDC, they believed, offered the best means to this objective.

Like Washington, Bonn eventually embraced the EDC project after strong initial misgivings. Adenauer himself became an energetic partisan, eventually touting the plan as the last, best hope for the free world. Rhetoric aside, there was good reason for Bonn's conversion: in addition to enhanced military security, integration into "Europe" seemed to offer the FRG the best route to political rehabilitation and added sovereignty. It was a testament to Bonn's uniqueness in the Western community that its road to genuine nationhood was paved with internationalist intentions.

At the same time, however, Bonn was unprepared to accept uncontested the many features of the EDC plan that discriminated against West Germany and denied it even the pretense of equality with the other European states. I examine at some length the largely successful campaign by Bonn's negotiators to scale back the "anti-German" dimensions of the project. In pursuing this effort, Bonn showed that even at this early stage in its history, it was by no means a meek or docile supplicant, prepared simply to accept whatever role its senior partners assigned it. Bonn's fight for its rights in the EDC arena constituted an important early round in its larger struggle for a respectable place in the postwar community of nations.

Success, however, had its price. The West Germans' ability to curtail some of the discriminatory features inherent in the original EDC scheme was one of the reasons why France, the plan's main author, killed the project in August 1954. In its revised form, the EDC seemed to give Bonn far too long a leash for French tastes. A European army also seemed less urgent in the wake of Josef Stalin's death in 1953 and in light of the increasing nuclearization of Western defense strategy. But perhaps the most important reason for the EDC's rejection is that traditional notions of national sovereignty were reasserted in Paris. West Germany might have everything to gain and little to lose by integrating its future armed forces in a common European military, but France ultimately saw itself in a different position: even the desire to control Germany had to take a back seat to the retention of military sovereignty and dignity as a Great Power. The failure of the EDC initiative cast a long shadow over the further evolution of "United Europe" because it left the emerging economic ties without a security component and blunted early efforts toward a common European foreign policy.

Though the EDC never came to fruition, it figures prominently in this book because the protracted effort to realize it tells us much about how Germans, other Western Europeans, and Americans hoped to reorder the postwar world. The powers were forced to think not only about West Germany's place in this world but also about the shape of the new "United Europe" into which the Federal Republic was to be politically and militarily integrated. How much national sovereignty were the European powers willing to sacrifice to create this new Europe? How much authority would the projected common institutions, including the common army, possess? What were Europe's fundamental values, and which countries legitimately belonged to this community? What was Europe's proper relationship to Atlantic powers such as America and Britain? Obviously, such questions retained their relevance long after the demise of the EDC project, and they became particularly urgent when belated efforts were made in the late 1980s and early 1990s to strengthen Europe's economic unity and to define a common foreign and security policy. The EDC negotiations may have taken place forty years ago, but they can still instruct us regarding the difficulties inherent in overcoming the pull of nationalist sentiments.

While European and American diplomats were negotiating over the EDC and the terms of German rearmament, citizens of the infant West German state were engaged in their own fierce debate over whether they should agree to rearm at all. Their reputation as insatiable militarists notwithstanding, many Germans in the postwar era were inclined to believe that they, and perhaps the rest of the world, were better off without a German army. Some argued, as had the Allies in their original demilitarization edicts, that Germany simply could not be trusted with military arms. They implied that in this domain they were like recovering alcoholics, for whom even the slightest relapse might occasion a full-scale plunge into the old addiction. Others insisted that the horrible wounds of World War II were far too fresh for Germans to contemplate taking up weapons of destruction again. Still others stressed the dangers that a standing army might pose to West Germany's fledgling democracy. For many Germans the central problem was that rearmament within the Western alliance was likely to deepen the division between the two new German states, rendering reunification unlikely if not impossible.

Though a variety of groups embraced some or all of these reservations, the campaign against rearmament was led chiefly by the powerful Social Democratic Party (SPD). The first half decade of the Federal Republic's history thus witnessed a crucial struggle between the SPD and the Adenauer government over the fundamentals of German security and foreign policy. Just as in the international arena, this domestic debate helped define political roles and relationships for years to come. Through his masterful, though often imperious, handling of security questions, Adenauer ensured that the executive branch would retain the dominant voice in this debate. By challenging the chancellor on the principles, and then on the procedures, of rearmament, however, Adenauer's critics in parliament helped gain a participatory role for the legislature in the making of defense policy. Indeed, in a more general sense, West Germany's parliamentary-democratic system underwent an accelerated maturation process because of the demands placed on it by this test. The debate over rearmament, I will argue, did much to define the political culture of the Federal Republic in the crucial formative years of its history.

Political culture, of course, comprises more than just the workings of political institutions; it also involves the articulation of national values and collective self-images derived from history. For the citizens of the new FRG, heirs (along with their East German counterparts) of both the failed Weimar Republic and the Third Reich, the cultivation of national self-esteem and historical identity could hardly be taken for granted. Yet every nation needs a "usable past" with which it can validate its present and inspire faith in its future. This was especially true of the two new German states, neither of which enjoyed full sovereignty or diplomatic recognition outside its own sphere.

In Bonn's search for validating traditions, questions of military reconstruction inevitably figured prominently. If West Germany was obliged to field an army, what historical legacies might it attempt to appropriate? Which traditions might be carried over? Could "healthy" elements from the past be retrieved while eschewing the principles and practices that had previously made German armies such potent barriers to effective parliamentary government? And if such were possible, what would that army look like and how would it compare with its partners in the Western alliance?

The agency charged with developing a German contribution to the Western alliance, the so-called Dienststelle or Amt Blank, eventually drew up plans for a new military structure that departed significantly from past models, whether defined by the imperial armies, the Reichswehr of the Weimar Republic, or the Wehrmacht of the Third Reich. The new military was to be tightly integrated into the Federal Republic's pluralistic and democratic society and reflective of that society through its own "democratic" structure. Tellingly, the defining slogan for the new enterprise was *Bürger in Uniform* (Citizens in Uniform), with emphasis on the word "citizens."

As one might imagine, this project did not find much favor with Germany's still-sizable contingent of military traditionalists; nor did it reassure the antimilitary skeptics. A passionate debate about the "spirit" and structure of the new German army quickly succeeded the larger debate about whether West Germany should rearm at all. The discussion drew in representatives of all the major political parties as well as wide segments of the public. Much of the discussion was ill-informed, inflammatory, or self-serving. Nevertheless, there was at least broad understanding that this was a crucial undertaking— one that would allow, for the first time in history, a German army to be made not just of the people but also by and for the people.

Like the original decision to rearm, however, the nature of Bonn's future army was not strictly a German concern, for the West German forces were to function as part of the common European army. As they took part in the international discussions aimed at shaping that army, Bonn's planners discovered just how radically liberal their own conceptions really were. Bonn's partners got their first glimpse of a resolutely reformed Germany, eager to turn a new page in its military history. Soon the Reich's conquerors found themselves wondering what had happened to the aggressive militarists they had just defeated: had they gone soft, lost their martial zeal? Anxieties about a revival of German militarism now gave way to concerns that Germany's new armed forces might not be as formidable or as efficient as their predecessors. In their scorn for the projected German reforms, some Western military men became positively nostalgic for their old foes, for those "Huns" who had always seemed so anxious to rush to the front.

The third and concluding section of this study examines Bonn's integration into NATO and the appearance, at long last, of the Bundeswehr.

Although Adenauer called NATO an "ersatz solution" to the question of German rearmament, he—and his American backers—had pushed for direct German participation in the Atlantic alliance before their conversion to the EDC. The EDC had not long been buried before the powers returned to the NATO option, aware that it could serve many of the same functions promised by the European army. It too could serve as a vehicle for Bonn's "entangling integration" into the Western European and Atlantic community, simultaneously providing security for Germany and guarantees against Bonn's going its own way. Moreover, it had the advantage of tying Germany closer than ever to the main protector of the postwar order, the United States.

Yet because Bonn's forces would be under stricter control than other NATO armies and because adherence to the alliance seemed to doom chances for German reunification, various groups in the FRG (Socialists as well as assorted nationalists of the Right) objected fiercely to the NATO arrangement. The passage of the Paris Treaties through Bonn's parliamentary system occasioned impassioned debates about the direction of West German foreign policy and the status of the new state in the Western community. These debates were accompanied by an extraparliamentary protest movement, the so-called Paulskirche initiative, which sought to mobilize grassroots opposition to the treaties. This effort failed. Its failure was important not only for the immediate fate of rearmament but also for the long-term political evolution of the FRG because it helped confirm the primacy of parliament over plebiscitary movements in the marshaling of public sentiment. Here was another early indication that the Bonn democracy was indeed different from its Weimar predecessor.

The final shaping of the Bundeswehr in 1955–56 also augured well for the future of Bonn's parliamentary system. In a narrow sense, the laws that allowed the appearance of the first West German soldiers constituted a significant victory of parliament over attempts by the chancellor to hurry the rearmament process and to avoid extensive legal preparations. More broadly and fundamentally, parliament went on to draft a "military constitution" that thoroughly anchored the new army in the laws of the land. My examination of the legal foundation of the Bundeswehr will show that Bonn ultimately took good advantage of the fact that the creation of new democratic institutions preceded the existence of armed forces, if only barely. Here too Bonn differed happily from Weimar.

By early 1956 West German forces were finally on the front, but many West Germans questioned their necessity or usefulness at a time when the alliance of which they were a part was switching to a greater reliance on nuclear weapons. Would not Bonn's forces amount to little more than "atomic cannon fodder"? it was asked. The Adenauer government responded that Germany's conventional forces were needed now more than ever, for they would help to ensure that no nuclear war ever broke out. Nonetheless, partly to allay ongoing public criticism of his security policy, Adenauer summarily cut the length of time draftees would serve. Meanwhile, Bonn's pugnacious new defense minister, Franz Josef Strauss, announced that the Bundeswehr's buildup would proceed much more slowly than originally promised.

This renewed display of West German assertiveness caused NATO's leaders to worry about how well their newest member would fit into the alliance and perform its obligations. "How reliable is Bonn?" they asked. Like so many aspects of the long rearmament debate, this question would remain relevant even as the FRG evolved into a strong and stable partner in the Atlantic alliance and the European Community.

In addressing the manifold problems of German rearmament in the Adenauer era, *Germans to the Front* follows a conventional chronological format, for this seemed the most effective way to tell this complex story. This tactic allows for a gradual unfolding of the central issues, letting the reader see them arise as the contemporary actors did, though I also take care to examine the problems within the larger context that hindsight affords. Throughout the narrative, I quote extensively from the contemporary record, published and unpublished. Deconstructionist debunking of the "text" notwithstanding, what people actually said made a difference, and a great many small revelations are to be discovered in precise choices of words and turns of phrase.

German rearmament is not, alas, one of those topics that has been "strangely neglected" by scholars. There are studies on the subject, ranging from specialized monographs on specific dimensions of the problem to the vast *Anfänge westdeutscher Sicherheitspolitik*, a multivolume, team-authored compendium produced by the Militärgeschichtliches Forschungsamt (the historical research agency of the German Ministry of Defense). In contrast both to this last work and to the various monographs, *Germans to the Front* attempts to bring together the key issues relating to the rearmament question in a single volume of manageable size and broad accessibility. No doubt this means that certain aspects of the problem will be treated in less detail than some specialists might wish. I remain confident, however, that most readers will learn as much—if not more—than they wanted to about West German rearmament from this book. In designing and writing it, I have been guided by the principle that it is generally better to bite off more than one can chew than (as was once said of Henry James) to chew more than one has bitten off.

PART

1

THE

REARMAMENT

DECISION

1

GERMANY

DISARMED Often during World War II, the leaders of the Big Three Allied powers—Winston Churchill, Franklin Roosevelt, and Josef Stalin—claimed that they had learned the lessons of World War I: this time, after defeating Germany, they would so thoroughly demilitarize the country that it would never again disturb the peace of the world. Once the postwar military occupation had begun, the Allied Control Council (ACC), in which France was also represented, began issuing directives designed to accomplish this goal. But though this policy seemed straightforward enough, it was understood in quite different ways by the conquering powers. The primary problem was that the disarmament effort had meaning only within a broader context of political and economic reorganization in which a welter of ambiguities produced extensive quarreling. Thus the business of disarming the Reich soon became enmeshed in the tangle of postwar disputes that eventually led to the bifurcation of Germany and Europe.

Another problem was that the victors, especially the Americans, tended to oversimplify the issues they were dealing with. They tended to see the German war machine as the culmination of three hundred years of Prusso-German military history. In this view, the Nazis were the heirs of a unilinear tradition beginning with the Great Elector in the mid-seventeenth century; Hitler's attempt to conquer all of Europe was the "latest stage of Prussian militarism."[1] American policy makers believed that the only way to end this pattern of "militaristic aggression" was to insist upon a thorough "demilitarization of the German mind." The notion that there was a militarized German mind was in itself dubious; and in any event the demilitarization project soon proved unworkable because of the complexity of historical legacies and contemporary challenges faced by the World War II victors in the postwar era.

WARTIME DISSONANCES

Intimations of future difficulties were evident in some of the earliest wartime pronouncements on German disarmament. Winston Churchill and Franklin

Roosevelt could agree in the Atlantic Charter (14 August 1941) that "perennial disturbers of the peace" like Germany and Japan must be deprived of their capacity to wage future wars. But Josef Stalin, who was not a party to the charter, declared on 6 November 1942 that the Soviets did not envisage "any such endeavor as the destruction of all organized military power in Germany," for that was "neither possible nor in the best interests of the victor." Moscow's only enemy was the "National Socialist system."[2]

Stalin made this declaration to encourage aspirations for an armistice among his German adversaries at a time when the war was going badly for the Soviet Union. In January 1943, at the Casablanca Conference, Stalin joined the Western allies in calling for unconditional surrender, but a few months later Moscow established the National Committee for a Free Germany, composed of prominent German prisoners of war, to propagandize against Hitler and the German war effort. This initiative contradicted the declared policy of unconditional surrender because the committee's leaders were promised that if Hitler were overthrown and the war terminated, Germany would be allowed to retain its borders of 1937.[3] Here demilitarization was subordinated to the larger goals of foreign policy, as indeed it would often be in the future, and not only by the Soviets.

When the three Allied leaders gathered in Teheran in December 1943, they were again unanimous in their professed determination to demilitarize Germany, but they did not see eye to eye on the all-important question of economic disarmament. The statesmen agreed that Germany's "war industry" must be destroyed and that it must pay reparations, but they had trouble defining these terms and establishing their scope. Stalin set the tone for future Soviet policy when he noted that furniture factories and clock works ought to be considered war industries because they could be converted into aircraft plants or bomb-fuse facilities. The Germans, he reminded his colleagues, were a "very talented people [who] could easily revive within fifteen or twenty years and again become a threat to the world" unless held firmly in check by their conquerors.[4]

With these innocuous-sounding phrases the Soviet leader was hinting at another crucial dimension of Moscow's emerging demilitarization policy—the notion that removing Germany as a military threat would mean dramatically altering its socioeconomic structure, which was allegedly at the root of the militarist evil. More specifically, in the Soviet perspective demilitarization would soon come to mean "liquidation of the Junkers as a class" and the "destruction of German monopoly-capital." Once these goals were accomplished, Germany could presumably be entrusted with military forces of some sort. Indeed, even before the war was over, Moscow was developing plans for a "people's militia" in "liberated Germany." Of course, Stalin could not discuss such notions with his wartime allies, but even his broad definition of war industry ran counter to the Western policy of that time, which said that defeated Germany should be allowed to maintain its "economic independence," a goal hardly compatible with the destruction or confiscation of its entire industrial capacity.

The battles over disarmament policy advanced across the diplomatic landscape as the German armies retreated over the battered physical terrain of Europe. The British and American armies needed guidance on how to administer enemy territories once they had overrun them. They were given a directive by the Supreme Headquarters Allied Expeditionary Force (SHAEF), known as CCS 551, which urged the "normalization" of conditions so as not to impede the conduct of the war. Military administration was to be "as just and humane with respect to the civilian population . . . as [was] consistent with strict military requirements"; local agriculture and industry were to be kept functioning "to prevent a breakdown in the economy."[5] Surrendering soldiers might be herded into "internment areas," rather than confined in prisoner of war camps, as was required by the Geneva Convention. Justifying this decision, the British and Americans insisted that adhering to the Geneva rules would have imposed an "unbearable" burden on their limited resources. Besides, they added, it was "politically out of the question to pamper Germans . . . when their victims, the liberated populations [of Europe], were in desperate want."[6]

The Soviets, having agreed with their Western allies to sidestep the Geneva Convention, were nonetheless very suspicious of their partners' tactics. They rejected the Anglo-American provisions for the German economy as too generous, while complaining that the Western treatment of German troops, far from pampering the enemy, was all too "tender to German fascism and militarism."[7] The West's internment of German troops, though also practiced by the Red Army, awakened old Soviet fears that the British and Americans might make common cause with the Germans against the USSR. Certainly the comments of General George Patton, who favored "pushing on to Moscow," and of Field Marshal Bernard Montgomery, who advocated the immediate establishment of a "flank facing east," did much to exacerbate Soviet anxieties.[8]

The Soviets were not the only ones who were unhappy with Anglo-American occupation policy as expressed in CCS 551 or in SHAEF's *Occupation Handbook*. Within the American camp, Secretary of the Treasury Henry Morgenthau was incensed over what he regarded as coddling of the enemy. He thought harsh control and economic deprivation were just what these people deserved. He favored summarily executing Nazi war criminals; dividing Germany into northern and southern states; and ceding the Saar to France, Silesia to Poland, and East Prussia to the Soviet Union. There was considerable irony in this territorial proposition, for if, as Morgenthau (like so many American policy makers) believed, "Prussia" was at the heart of German militarism, putting the core Prussian lands in the Soviet orbit was perhaps not the wisest idea. Equally bizarre was Morgenthau's long-term solution to the problem of German aggression: the entire nation should be turned into a patchwork of small pastoral enclaves, like Denmark. "As a farmer myself," he wrote, "I knew that people who lived close to the land tended to tranquil and peaceloving lives, [so] why not make Germany a nation predominantly of small farmers?"[9]

In mid-1944 Morgenthau presented his views to FDR, who was likewise convinced that the Germans were inherently aggressive. At a cabinet meeting the president expressed his displeasure with the "lack of severity" in the *Occupation Handbook*, arguing that a system of "army soup kitchens" would be adequate to sustain life for the German population. In a memorandum to Secretary of War Henry Stimson, he fumed that the handbook "gives me the impression that Germany is to be restored just as much as the Netherlands or Belgium, and the people of Germany brought back as quickly as possible to their pre-war estate. [But] it is of the utmost importance that every person in Germany should realize that this time Germany is a defeated nation."[10]

FDR's agreement with Morgenthau was evident also at the second Quebec Conference (September 1944), where the president proposed to Churchill that "we have to castrate the German people or . . . treat them in such a manner so they can't just go on reproducing people who want to continue the way they have in the past."[11] Against the advice of Stimson and Secretary of State Cordell Hull, FDR pressed for a disarmament program that included dismantling the industries of the Ruhr and the Saar.

Churchill had come to Quebec prepared to oppose this proposal. He had been advised by his Foreign Office that these measures would substantially complicate the occupation by producing economic chaos. The Allies, argued the Foreign Office, would be forced to support a starving population, and their attempts to establish a democratic government would be undermined— as the Weimar government had been undercut—by popular association with economic collapse and deprivation. Impressed by these arguments, Churchill argued vehemently against Morgenthau's plan, declaring with characteristic pith that he did "not want to be chained to a dead German." Within hours, however, he reversed his position, explaining that he now saw the American scheme as "beneficial" to Britain.[12] Apparently he had been convinced by Morgenthau that British coal and steel production would substantially profit from the curtailment of German competition. Morgenthau had also proposed that Washington grant Britain financial credits totaling some $6.5 billion. As Cordell Hull quipped in his memoirs: "This might suggest to some the *quid pro quo* with which the Secretary of the Treasury was able to get Mr. Churchill's adherence to his cataclysmic plan for Germany."[13]

the captured German units to remain intact with their weapons. German arms already captured by the British were to be stockpiled for possible "emergency use."[25] Churchill later boasted (apparently after several whiskeys) that he had issued these orders to warn the Soviets that if they tried to continue their march westward, Britain would team up with the Wehrmacht to turn them around.[26]

Churchill tried to persuade Eisenhower to adopt similar measures and to push as far eastward as possible regardless of agreements with the Russians. The American commander, however, still regarded Germany, not the Soviet Union, as his primary enemy. Revolted by the sight of the concentration camps his troops were liberating, he ordered that all Wehrmacht and Waffen-SS units be disarmed immediately—an order that some GIs interpreted liberally enough to allow the confiscation of pocketknives and even wristwatches. (Later, when the Americans began pressing for German rearmament, a German cartoon showed a former Wehrmacht soldier asking a GI if he would get his wristwatch back if he put on a uniform again.) Unlike most of Britain's prisoners, America's were crowded into very primitive enclosures with little shelter beyond their army blankets.[27] Some were beaten and denied adequate food, water, and medical care. It is not the case, however, as has recently been argued,[28] that Eisenhower deliberately starved to death hundreds of thousands of German prisoners.

Especially worrisome to American military officials was the huge German officer corps, which the Office of the Military Government, United States (OMGUS) saw as a historic evil with plenty of potential for future trouble-making. The Americans feared that thousands of embittered German officers might—as they had after World War I—flock to antidemocratic organizations and thwart efforts to stabilize the shattered country. It was imperative, they thought, that these dangerous men not be dumped en masse onto the rubble heap of postwar German society. But what to do with them? An OMGUS study of August 1945 proposed three possible alternatives. One was exiling the lot of them to some distant penal colony, dubbed the "St. Helena solution," in honor of Napoleon's last exile in the distant South Atlantic.[29] (The British also briefly entertained this possibility, proposing the Falkland Islands as a suitable home for the German General Staff.[30]) OMGUS realized, however, that this approach was likely to make martyrs out of the officers, just as the St. Helena exile had made a martyr out of Napoleon. Another option was to disperse the officers among Allied-controlled enclaves throughout the world. But this gambit had the disadvantage of potentially infecting the entire globe with the virus of German militarism. Finally, as a third alternative, the Allies could keep much of the officer corps "under severe restrictive measures" in Germany itself. Logistically, this was the most the US practical measure and provided "a fitting disposition of these persons before the eyes of other Germans."[31] Though this option was finally chosen, it too would prove full of difficulties for its executors.

While American army officials were rounding up German military personnel, Civil Affairs detachments carried out a thorough disarmament of the civilian population. Civilians were ordered to turn in not just weapons and explosives but "cameras, radio equipment, and other means of communication, including pigeons." To ensure compliance, the Americans undertook house-to-house searches that "frequently turned up sizable collections of arms that the civilians had not turned in, probably more out of fear than malice."[32]

Meanwhile, on the diplomatic front, America was encountering what some of its leaders saw as genuine malice from the Soviets. The new American president, Harry Truman, shared Churchill's anxieties about Moscow's intentions in Eastern Europe, especially in Poland. Though not yet the thoroughgoing Cold Warrior he was soon to become, Truman embarked upon his presidency convinced that the USSR was acting like a "World Bully." He was encouraged in this conviction by some of his advisers—most notably Navy Secretary James Forrestal and Admiral William Leahy—though his secretary of war, Henry Stimson, suggested that the Russians were perhaps "being more realistic than we in regard to their own security."[33] Stimson's assistant, John McCloy, later to become high commissioner in Germany, also cautioned that the difficulties of administering that defeated and crippled country would require maintaining "a practical relationship with the Russians," along with "the highest talents, tolerance, and wisdom." Similar views were expressed by Generals Dwight D. Eisenhower and Lucius Clay, who worried that the State Department was being too quick to find fault with the Russians.[34] Despite such warnings, America's leaders, like those of Britain, were coming to regard their erstwhile Russian ally with almost as much suspicion as their defeated German enemy. It would not be long before pundits in Washington would heartily echo Churchill's famous postwar quip, "My God, we've slaughtered the wrong pig!"[35]

FROM POTSDAM TO BIZONIA

In the meantime, Allied leaders gathered in Potsdam for their first conference after the German surrender. When debating occupation policy, they quickly agreed on certain fundamental principles, such as joint administration of Germany by Allied commanders in chief; "uniform treatment of the German population"; and (again) "complete disarmament and demilitarization of

Germany and elimination or control of all German industry that could be used for military production."[36]

For a time it seemed that the Potsdam agreements might indeed provide a viable instrument for governing postwar Germany. That they ultimately did not resulted in part from the deceptiveness of the initial agreement. The discussions at Potsdam had revealed many disagreements, but the chief demand of the hour—securing Russian support for the conclusion of the war against Japan—required at least a modicum of unanimity. Thus the leaders had papered over their differences in a final protocol full of ambiguous language.

As in previous encounters, one of the disputes concerned reparations. The Soviet delegation was divided over what kind of reparations to demand, but Stalin made clear that the settlement must be geared to the needs of the victors, among whom the USSR had the greatest need. The Western leaders did not disagree, but they opposed drawing reparations from current production, which would undermine Germany's ability to pay for imports. This "First-Charge" principle made good sense to the Americans, who would be doing most of the exporting to Germany, but it struck Stalin as added proof of Washington's insensitivity to the Soviet Union's wartime sacrifices. The Soviet leader could not understand why the "Wall Street bankers" should be paid before the pressing needs of the Russian people were satisfied.[37]

Truman, however, had been observing Soviet dismantling activities around Berlin with great misgivings. He saw them as part of a broader scheme to weaken Germany so that it would become an easy prey for a Communist takeover. He left the conference convinced that the Soviets were "not in earnest" about a peace settlement.[38] Of course, he also left Potsdam with an ace up his sleeve: the atomic bomb. If force was all the Russians understood, America's sole possession of the bomb might make them behave. Perhaps this was the grandest illusion of all to come out of the Potsdam Conference.

Another deficiency was the exclusion of the French. France saw its absence as more evidence of the Allies' determination to minimize its role in the postwar order. Even more than the Soviets, the French believed they were being relegated to the status of a second-class power, a fate to which they were unprepared to reconcile themselves. With respect to their relationship with Germany, moreover, they shared the Russians' deep-seated animosities and insecurities: France, after all, had been invaded by the Germans three times in seven decades and with the exception of 1914 had not managed to keep the hated *Boche* out of their capital.

France therefore not only embraced the commitment to total demilitarization, but—in time-honored French tradition—pursued the physical dismemberment of Germany and the occupation of its westernmost territories. General De Gaulle justified these policies by noting that at Potsdam "Germany was amputated in the East but not in the West," which would turn "the current of German vitality westwards." Because "one day German aggressiveness might face westwards too," there had to be "a settlement in the West counterbalancing that in the East."[39]

De Gaulle tried to generate international support for this "French Thesis" by playing on fears not only of the Germans but also of a possible Soviet drive to the west with the help of the Germans. He warned Truman in August 1945 that a weakened Germany was in danger of becoming "a political instrument of other [i.e., Soviet] powers."[40] From this assessment one might have concluded (as the Anglo-Americans eventually did) that Germany should be made stronger so as to deter any Soviet ambitions east of the Elbe. De Gaulle's conclusion, however, was just the opposite: the present power vacuum in Central Europe should be filled not with a revived Germany but with strong French influence, backed by American financial and military might.

The new Labour government in Britain was not much more favorably disposed toward the defeated Germans than were the French. Prime Minister Clement Attlee and his foreign minister, Ernest Bevin, fully shared French fears of a revived, centralized Germany. Hugh Dalton, the cabinet's most rabid Germanophobe, wanted to Balkanize Germany and to keep the inhabitants on short rations. He declared more than once that he was unprepared to see Britain make sacrifices for the Germans at a time of hardship and shortages at home.[41] His views reflected profound popular animosities toward the Germans in postwar Britain, where many people doubted that Germany could ever become a truly trustworthy member of the world community.

Yet the Attlee government was also under severe pressure to minimize the costs of occupation by allowing the Germans to revive their economy and shoulder some of the burdens of administration. Also, instead of sending food to its occupation forces, Britain hoped to have them draw on local supplies. Attlee and his colleagues, moreover, soon found it hard to get along with their fellow "socialists" in Moscow, as had Churchill. Initially inclined to regard the Germans as a far greater threat than the Russians, Attlee's government soon swung around to the American position on the immediacy of the Soviet menace. Attlee was pushed in this direction by the British Chiefs of Staff, who in 1946 identified Soviet Russia as a "much more dangerous potential enemy than Germany." The Chiefs proposed that "our long term policy with regard to Germany . . . cannot be shaped solely from the point of view of preventing a revival of a threat from Germany."[42] Foreign Minister Bevin became a mainstay of this new view. By 1946, gloated Dean Acheson (soon to become American secretary of state), the British statesman had come to "understand the full significance of the Soviet aggressive policy."[43]

Disagreement over disarmament policy, pervasive as it was, did not prevent the ACC from handing down a host of regulations that confirmed the most draconian of the earlier disarmament pronouncements. Between August 1945 and December 1946, the agency prohibited Germans from wearing their old military uniforms of field gray or sky-blue (*"färben oder sterben"*—"dye or die"—was the word of the day); displaying military rank, medals, and insignia; belonging to any veterans' organizations, regimental associations, or sport groups with a military character; possessing weapons, munitions, or explosives; planning, constructing, or maintaining military facilities of any kind; conducting scientific or historical research of a military nature; maintaining commemorative plaques, monuments, statues, buildings, or street designations that might keep alive the German military tradition; and operating exhibitions or museums focusing on German military history since 1914. Libraries and educational institutions were ordered to purge their collections of any materials that might be used for the preservation of Germany's war-making potential.[44] ACC Law 34 (20 August 1946) officially dissolved the Wehrmacht along with all the legal and economic rights of its former members and their dependents. Thus Germany's former soldiers (or their widows and families) would receive no pension payments at a time when many veterans found it impossible to find regular employment in the shattered postwar economy.[45]

The German people's response to these draconian regulations and to the concurrent dismantling of war-related industries varied widely, depending on their political outlook, age, and the degree to which they were personally affected. Though (as we shall see in more detail below), most Germans were happy enough to see the disappearance of the Wehrmacht, which they held largely responsible for their miserable plight, they regarded many of the demilitarization measures as petty, vindictive, and stupid. Librarians, for example, were appalled at the orders to purge their holdings of military histories and biographies; museum directors rebelled against closing exhibits on World War I. Industrial dismantling, because it threw many out of work and often curtailed the production of goods that people desperately needed, generated profound resentment. The citizens of Duisberg, for example, could not understand how the British could shut down the Mathes and Weber soda plant when soda was necessary to produce washing powder. Hamburgers were up in arms over the dynamiting of their cherished ship-building firms. Anger over these policies fed into the vivid sense of aggrievement left over from the "terror bombing" of German cities.[46]

Although frustration and resentment may have been widespread, no group felt more maltreated than the former officers of the Wehrmacht, who saw themselves persecuted and slandered for "just doing our duty." Their sudden loss of power and status was hard to swallow. A "hungry looking" former officer, who hid his old uniform under his bed, told an American visitor: "I commanded a tank squadron at Tula. Now, I am a neurotic student, rotting in a miserable Germany. I cannot bear it forever."[47] At times such self-pity could reach obscene proportions. Certainly this was true of the former general who insisted that the plight of the former soldiers was worse than that of the Jews under Nazism because the veterans had no one to help them, whereas the Jews "could count on the support of world-wide Jewry."[48]

On the whole, the Allies were not much moved by the former officers' complaints, but they could not help but take notice when some of the demilitarization regulations began causing difficulties for themselves as well as for the Germans. The result was that some of the rules were conveniently neglected, while others were modified to suit the conquerors.

The confiscation of arms and ammunition, for example, meant that German farmers were unable to control wild game that preyed on orchards and crops. Eventually Allied officials turned a blind eye when natives dug out old rifles from closets and haylofts and went hunting. A more pressing problem was predatory people. Postwar Germany, especially its western parts, was overrun by refugees and displaced persons, some of whom, like the liberated Russian prisoners of war in the British zone, "roamed the countryside at will, raiding isolated farms for food, valuables, and women."[49] German expellees from eastern Germany and Eastern Europe also posed a security problem, for they arrived hungry and destitute in areas where food and housing were already critically scarce. Though many were taken in by local residents, many others had to fend for themselves, with predictably anarchic consequences.

Because there were not enough Allied troops to maintain law and order everywhere, the occupation authorities were forced to turn to the Germans for help: they not only allowed, but ordered, Germans to rebuild local police forces. But once they had begun to do this, the Germans complained that their ragtag forces lacked the authority and hardware to deal effectively with the meandering refugees and displaced persons, "especially the Poles and Jews." Again the Allies were forced to show flexibility: German police forces in the western zones were armed with pistols and allowed to arrest natives and unruly foreigners.[50]

The Allied ban on German military research posed another difficulty. The Americans were anxious to make use of German expertise in writing a first-hand account of the war in Western Europe. In late 1946 they expanded this task to include the Eastern front, where the German experience was seen as especially instructive.[51] For these studies they recruited former General Staff officers—the same men they had recently condemned as inveterate militarists. This operation was conducted in secrecy not only because it violated the Allies' own disarmament regulations but also because publicity about it would have caused problems at home. Thus former general Reinhard Gehlen, who had headed the Abteilung Fremde-Heere Ost (the General

Staff's military agency dealing with Soviet and other Eastern European armed forces), was clandestinely flown to Washington for consultations. He was told that the reason for such precautions was that "one had to wait until [American] public opinion over Germany calmed down and turned negative toward the Russians."[52] Shortly thereafter, Gehlen was entrusted by the Office of Strategic Services with the formation of a new intelligence operation focused on the East; this "Organization Gehlen" was the nucleus of West Germany's future intelligence agency, the Bundesnachrichten Dienst.[53]

The Allied effort to deal with the implications of total disarmament was complicated not only by the victors' ambitious regulations but also by procedural variations from zone to zone. This was particularly evident in the administration of native police forces. The Americans divided their police apparatus between municipal forces, *Länder*-based structures, and Grenzpolizei (Border Police). The British rebuilt the police in their zone on a regional basis, ensuring that no district except Hamburg had more than two thousand men. The French instituted a centralized system rigorously controlled from Paris. Throughout the Western zones, there was an effort to prevent native police from taking on paramilitary qualities; their armaments were limited and their authority closely circumscribed.[54]

The Soviets followed a different policy from the outset. They paid great attention to police and other security forces, for they regarded control of these agencies as vital to the consolidation of their power. In spring 1945 Moscow employed native Communists in Berlin to establish a Communist-dominated police force in the Reich capital. Moscow's main German agent in Berlin, Walter Ulbricht, ordered his aides to ensure that "a totally reliable comrade" took charge of each police district in the city. Armed forces of the Western powers could do little to prevent these measures. Even after they arrived in Berlin, they were unable to wrest control of the police from the Soviets, who appointed the trusted Communist Paul Markgraf as chief of police. In autumn 1945, the Soviets set up police administrations and units of so-called Kasernierte Volkspolizei in each of the five *Länder* belonging to their occupation zone (SMAD). On 31 October 1945, the SMAD ordered these units armed with carbines and pistols. Ten months later, in August 1946, the SMAD created an Interior Ministry and placed the Volkspolizei, which now numbered about forty-five thousand men, under its direction. In November Moscow established two more security forces, the Border Police (ten thousand men) and the Transport Police (seventy-five hundred men). By 1948, the Volkspolizei alone counted some sixty thousand men—more than double the size of the Western-zone police forces.[55] The Soviets insisted that none of this violated joint demilitarization policy, but their native security forces had a strong paramilitary quality from the beginning. In this regard, it is worth mentioning that in 1959 East Berlin would describe the creation of the Volkspolizei as the "hour of birth" of the armed forces of the German Democratic Republic.[56]

If the flood of refugees and displaced persons presented the Allied military governments with problems they could not handle by themselves, the destruction of Germany's material infrastructure also brought challenges that threatened to overtax Allied capacities. To help them remove mines and ruins, rebuild roads and bridges, clear waterways and railbeds, the Allies formed Dienstgruppen (Labor Service Groups) consisting largely of former German soldiers. These groups too soon became a focus of suspicion between East and West.[57]

The British built some of their Dienstgruppen from Wehrmacht and Waffen-SS units that were not yet fully demobilized. The Americans, though also relying on veterans, especially from tank units, did not absorb German outfits en bloc.[58] In both cases, many of the volunteers were refugees from central or eastern Germany and bitterly anti-Soviet. The French did not create Dienstgruppen until mid-1950 but compensated by zealously recruiting Wehrmacht veterans for their famous Foreign Legion. It has been estimated that in 1946 Germans made up about 60 percent of the Legion.[59]

Whether any of these measures constituted a form of protoremilitarization has been much debated, but at the time they certainly aroused the suspicions of the Soviets, who accused the Western powers of using the Dienstgruppen to preserve the Wehrmacht. While denying that their Labor Service Groups had a protomilitary character, the Western Allies accused the Soviets of giving military training to some three hundred thousand of the two million Germans who served in forced-labor organizations in the SMAD.[60]

By late 1945, indeed, the Truman administration had become so suspicious of the Soviets' disarmament policies that Secretary of State James Byrnes decided to "call their bluff" by proposing a "twenty-five year treaty between the four principal powers for the demilitarization of Germany."[61] The plan provided for a four-power inspection force, staffed by skilled engineers who would ensure that no German industries were being converted to military production. The beauty of this scheme, in Byrnes's eyes, was that it would "eliminate the need to maintain large armed forces in Germany." He quickly secured Truman's support for this plan, though the British were at best lukewarm and the French hostile, the latter because they wanted to secure peace through decentralization and territorial annexation rather than economic controls.[62]

If the French were not impressed with Byrnes's proposal, the Soviets were even less so. In late April 1946, V. M. Molotov began to raise objections, and at the Foreign Ministers conference in Paris in June he rejected it entirely. Byrnes's plan, said the Russian, was inadequate; it would need to run for at least forty years; in the meantime, the Americans should stop trying to obstruct the implementation of the Potsdam directives.

Byrnes was indignant over this rebuff of his pet project. Now convinced that the Soviets "did not want the U.S. involved in the maintenance of European security for the next twenty-five or forty years," he began planning his famous Stuttgart speech (6 September 1946), which, among other things, promised a continuation of the American military presence in Germany for as long as the other powers stayed.

Though Byrnes offered his disarmament plan once again at the Moscow Foreign Ministers Conference in March 1947, he did so in full expectation that it would be rejected, which it promptly was. Indeed, the Soviet delegation spent much of its time denouncing the West for "failing to demilitarize" its zones of occupation. "We must admit," they said, "that the elimination of the war industry potential in the Western Zones of Germany has hardly begun, aside from individual haphazard measures which have practically no effect on the state of the war-industry potential of the Western Zones." The Soviets also renewed their charges that the Western zonal commanders were keeping German military units intact under the control of German officers. And in addition to these German units, complained Moscow, the Western powers were harboring various anti-Soviet ethnic forces in their zones. In response to these charges, the British and American representatives insisted that "on the whole" they had carried out the demilitarization of their zones in a "satisfactory manner." But the American delegation also reaffirmed the "First Charge" principle, stating that industries such as synthetic fertilizers, synthetic gasoline, and synthetic rubber would "only be removed when German exports [were] sufficient to pay for the necessary amounts of these products to be imported from abroad."[63]

Even before the foreign ministers had held their abortive meeting in Moscow, General Clay had been given the go-ahead to begin fusing the American and British zones into "Bizonia," a step that foreshadowed the creation of the West German state in 1949. At the same time, Clay also ordered a stop to most dismantling of war industry in the American zone until progress could be made toward treating Germany as a single economic unit, as had been agreed at Potsdam. Clay welcomed this development because remaining war industry plants could now be converted to production for export, thus enabling the Germans to pay for some of their American imports. "So long as the American taxpayer is spending some 200 million dollars a year for support and assistance of the American zone," declared Clay, "we don't feel like we should leave him at the mercy of what may happen."[64]

General Clay could be sanguine about ending plant dismantling because he believed that in the short time since the war, Germany had been rendered about as "defenseless as a nation could be."[65] And indeed, for all the vicissitudes and nuances in Allied disarmament policy, Germany *was* thoroughly disarmed. Its vaunted army, navy, and air force were no more; its war industries were smashed or under Allied control; its industrial patents and technical processes had been plundered by the conquerors; most of its best scientists and engineers were in the employ of the victors; and its major cities were reduced to piles of rubble picked over by *Trümmerfrauen* (scavenger women). Assessing the German people's state of mind at this juncture, Clay was not sure that the majority of the population needed to be "demilitarized" because the horrors of war and defeat seemed to have significantly "dimmed the military flame in German hearts."[66]

As we shall see, Clay was perhaps even more correct than he knew in this assessment, but the Germans' altered consciousness was soon to become a source of consternation rather than comfort among those in the victors' camp who hoped to relight the military flame in German hearts.

CHAPTER

THE

QUESTION

IS RAISED   In the years following World War II, the Western powers repeatedly confirmed their determination to keep Germany "permanently disarmed." Nonetheless, sharpening Cold War tensions not only stimulated disagreements over demilitarization policy but also sparked unofficial calls for rearmament of the defeated enemy. These appeals occurred within the context of a major strategic reevaluation on the part of the Western Allies, especially the Americans, whose military planning in the period 1945 to 1949 underwent a series of reassessments that nearly amounted to a strategic revolution.

But if, within the framework of that reassessment, some Western military figures and politicians began to think seriously about rearming the Germans in their zones of occupation, most natives in the region were happy to leave external security to the self-appointed "protectors" of the postwar order. There was even a certain satisfaction in not having to carry the burdens of power and in looking to others for security in a dangerous world. It was only when the wartime Allies began to fall out among themselves that some Germans started to wonder who would protect what against whom. More specifically, a growing number of Germans questioned whether the Allies could be counted on to defend western Germany against possible Soviet expansionism.

Such considerations inspired a few of these doubters to ask if they might contribute in some way to the defense of their own common interests. Yet there was no consensus on what these interests were, how they might be defended, or even if postwar Germans, heirs of the Third Reich, had the moral right to take up arms. Thus the earliest ruminations on matters of military defense sparked an internal debate that addressed fundamental questions of national identity and purpose. Though the Germans' difficulties were especially acute in this domain, their struggle was emblematic of a larger problem that all postwar democracies faced: that of defining strategy in a contentious and relatively open political environment.

STRATEGIC REASSESSMENT AND THE REARMAMENT CALCULUS

When American military strategists began to think about ways to defend the Western European region against possible expansionism by their erstwhile partner, the Soviet Union, they were confronted by several painful realities. Western troop levels in the region were very low following rapid demobilization and the pullback of forces. Budgetary constraints placed severe limits on strategic choices, and interservice rivalries and battles between the military and civilian sectors made it difficult to articulate a coherent policy. Cooperation among the Western Allies was as urgent as ever, but the Americans and their European partners held disparate notions about how the West's defense should be managed.[1]

At the time of the German surrender in May 1945, Western Europe had been occupied by the largest coalition army the world had ever seen; the American force alone stationed in Germany counted some 1.6 million men. But as early as the end of 1945, the American forces in the region were down to three armored divisions and seven infantry divisions, plus a few independent regiments and formations. As one historian of the occupation observed: "Within three months of V-J Day, the army that had defeated Nazi Germany was no more." As Allied forces settled into their occupation chores during the next two years, they remained woefully understaffed and underequipped. Efforts to improve combat readiness of the remaining American forces in Germany made little progress until the end of 1947.[2]

Allied strategic plans in the early postwar years necessarily reflected the availability and operational status of forces on the ground, as well as financial constraints. Working under a $15 million budget ceiling imposed by President Truman in 1948, American military planners evolved a concept calling for "holding a line containing the Western European complex preferably no farther to the West than the Rhine. The logical extension of this line involves the United Kingdom on the left flank and the Cairo-Suez [area] on the right flank."[3] Yet General Eisenhower was doubtful that this ambition could be achieved because of the inadequacies of the American strategic arsenal, lack of sufficient bases in Europe, and the gaping disparity between West and East in conventional forces stationed on the Continent. This last issue was especially worrisome. According to American intelligence estimates in 1948 (now known to have been exaggerated), the Soviet land army totaled 2.5 million men organized in 175 divisions.[4] Eighty-four were said to be stationed in the Soviet Occupation Zone and in other "satellite" countries. Against this force the West could muster only sixteen divisions stationed in Germany, Austria, the Benelux countries, and France. Moreover, American analysts regarded the Dutch and Belgian forces as practically useless and were also unsure of France, which had a strong Communist Party and extensive colonial commitments.[5] The Russian superiority, it was believed, might allow their armies to cross the Rhine in five days and to reach the Channel in two weeks.[6] "All the Russians need to reach the Rhine is shoes," said Under Secretary of State Robert Lovett.[7]

If a defense on the Rhine indeed proved impossible, Eisenhower hoped at least for the retention of a "substantial bridgehead" in Western Europe. Should even this turn out to be unachievable, Ike wanted an early reconquest of the Continent so that the Soviets could not take over or plunder the entire region. An early reconquest required holding Great Britain, developing American bases in such places as the Azores and Ireland, and controlling the western Mediterranean. Eisenhower ordered the service chiefs to come up with a plan that would accommodate these strategic objectives and establish which forces would accomplish each specific task.

The American military services had been quarreling for some time over strategic planning and shares of the meager budgetary pie. Ike's order prompted a new round of interservice strife. The air force was the prime backer of a "peripheral" approach, code-named HALFMOON, which emphasized attacks by long-range strategic bombers. The navy was highly critical of this strategy, disliking its denigration of carrier groups in favor of bombers. But the navy was also critical of what it saw as conceptual weaknesses in the peripheral warfare doctrine. Its planners questioned whether air force bombers could penetrate Soviet defenses, or, even if they could, whether they would be able to do sufficient damage to force Russia to abandon its aggression. By the time American bombing began to have a significant impact on Soviet industry, said the navy, the Red Army would have overrun and thoroughly plundered all of Europe. Through its control of Western Europe and the Middle East, the Soviet Union would become the "dominant power in the world." Even though the Soviets might eventually be pushed back, the political damage would have been done. If the purpose of war was "to gain political objectives," huffed Admiral D. V. Gallery, a plan that resulted in ultimate "military success and political defeat [was] worse than useless."[8]

Instead of an emphasis on strategic bombing of Soviet cities, the navy proposed developing a capacity for tactical air attacks on Soviet forces as they tried to overrun Europe. Carrier-based aircraft and air force tactical wings based in Great Britain could strafe railroads and highways and blow up bridges. Atomic weapons might be deployed against Soviet troop concentrations, lines of communication, and supply depots. Such efforts should *precede* an all-out strategic bombardment of the Soviet motherland, which might not be needed if the tactical attacks were successful. Wrote Gallery: "When the Russian armies are stopped short of the Rhine, their leaders and people may see that they had better negotiate a peace or else they will be in for a large-scale atomic blitz. In this case, with their armies halted east of the Rhine, the threat of the blitz might have more effect than the actual blitz itself if their armies were overrunning Europe."[9]

In its critique of the air force's peripheral doctrine, the navy found a natural ally in the army, which also had a big stake in shifting away from an exclusive reliance on strategic bombing. In March 1949 Army Chief of Staff Omar Bradley argued vigorously that Washington's strategic planning ought to be more concerned with defending European land space. Various army studies were showing that a concentrated destruction of Soviet lines of communication could significantly slow a Red Army attack and perhaps allow a larger "bridgehead" to be retained for purposes of rapid counterattack. "Certain strategic areas such as Spain and Sicily can probably be held permanently and a successful defense of the Rhine may be possible if Western strength increases," argued a study by the Army Transportation Corps.[10]

From these and other internal calculations a new American emergency war plan code-named OFFTACKLE emerged in July 1949. For the first time, focus was placed on using strategic forces to impede a Soviet advance across Western Europe, though it was conceded that most of the region, with the possible exception of a bridgehead in Spain, might have to be abandoned pending the outcome of the bombing campaign.

The new plan would have caught the Europeans off guard had it been divulged to them because it conflicted sharply with the declared ambition of NATO, formed in April 1949, "to restore and to hold" the territory of the signatory nations in the event of an attack. Not only the Continental Europeans but also the British argued for the defense of Western Europe "as far to the East as possible." A plan of the British Chiefs of Staff called DOUBLEQUICK rejected an evacuation of Western occupation troops in Germany without a stiff fight. But the British could not be too independent in their thinking, for they hoped for extensive financial support from Washington and were unwilling to commit the military resources to the Continent that most planners considered necessary for a successful defense against a large-scale Soviet attack.[11]

All Western planners who wanted a direct and "eastern" defense agreed that more ground forces would be necessary. The American Joint Chiefs of Staff thought that fifty-four divisions would be required even to prevent the Soviets from crossing the Rhine.[12] No one, however, including Washington, was anxious to maintain large armies in Germany and Western Europe. Budgetary considerations and domestic political realities spoke against sending vast new armies to Central Europe so soon after large numbers of troops had been repatriated or reassigned to other parts of the world.

In this complicated context a few Western military planners—and a handful of politicians and publicists—began to argue that there was no alternative but to undertake what everyone had been saying was unthinkable: rearm the

Germans. More specifically, the Western powers should put as many of "their" Germans in uniform as necessary to make a defense of Western Europe viable. The uniforms might not be German, and the men who wore them would certainly have no military independence, but the plan was nonetheless a bold one, considered risky even by its advocates.

The notion of exploiting German manpower for the defense of the West was first floated by American military commanders in Germany, who proposed as early as 1947 that some of their Labor Service Groups be turned into military outfits.[13] Also in 1947, the army's Operations and Plans Division began considering how to integrate both Germany and Japan into America's strategic posture. These speculations were carried out at the lower levels of the army bureaucracy and did not envisage an immediate change in official disarmament policy.[14]

Higher-level officials joined this discussion in March 1948, when the British, French, and Benelux powers created the Western Union, a defensive alliance to which Washington had to define its relationship. The main question was whether, in contrast to its policy after World War I, America would maintain close security ties with Europe buttressed by a military commitment. The Truman administration was prepared to commit economic assistance and extend America's nuclear umbrella to Western Europe. The Pentagon was not opposed to this idea, but it did not want to formalize it, much less add to it, without assurance that consideration would be given to including troops from Germany and Spain in the Continental defense. Thus, at a meeting of the National Security Council (NSC) on 20 May 1948, Secretary of the Army Kenneth Royall argued that America should withhold a formal commitment to the defense of Europe until the Europeans promised that they would "leave open" the possibility of a German and Spanish contribution. Before making this suggestion, Royall had asked General Clay whether he thought that the rearmament of these powers would "alarm Russia to such an extent that they might precipitate a war." Clay believed it would not.[15]

But the Pentagon constituted just one voice in American policy making, and its broaching of the German rearmament question opened another, more serious, rift in the American camp. The State Department representatives at the May National Security Council meeting opposed linking American support for European defense with a German contribution to the Western Union. State feared that even the most tentative commitment to German rearmament would sow discord within the blossoming Western alliance, as well as advance the Soviet cause in Eastern Europe, where anxieties over possible German revanchism ran high.

President Truman, who believed that the Allies had been wrong to let Germany rearm after World War I and who continued to harbor deep fears of German "militarism," supported State's position.[16] Washington therefore informed the Western Union in June 1948 that it was still too early to raise the question of German participation in the European alliance.[17]

No sooner had this declaration been made, however, than it was called into question by the Soviet blockade of Berlin, which dramatically illustrated the West's vulnerability in Central Europe. Western sectors of the city had to be supplied by a massive American airlift aptly dubbed "Operation Vittles." Though the airlift kept Berlin from starving, only the addition of German troops, the Pentagon now insisted, could make the West's determination to defend its rights and interests in this region truly credible.[18]

American military men were undoubtedly the most important early partisans of this "German solution," but they were not the only Western strategists who were thinking along these lines. In July 1948 the prominent British military expert Basil Liddell Hart insisted that the West could build a viable conventional defense only with German participation; he added that enhanced conventional defenses were needed because America's atomic bomb would probably not prevent the Soviets from trying to expand their empire in Europe.[19] Field Marshal Montgomery and the British Chiefs of Staff expressed similar views.[20] By contrast, British Foreign Secretary Bevin declared in a cabinet meeting on 22 December 1948 that it was still "premature" to define a defense relationship between Western Germany and the Allied occupiers. He had ample company. On the whole, the cabinet's view at this point was that the Western zones of Germany ought to be anchored to the West but only in a nonmilitary way. London saw this integration, moreover, not just as a means of deterring possible Communist aggression but also as a safeguard against any independent inclinations on the part of a new West German state.[21]

In France, awareness of a Soviet threat was gradually spreading through the general populace by 1947–48, but it had done so earlier among that country's military leadership. General De Gaulle, who had originally hoped for extensive cooperation between Paris and Moscow, began to perceive a Soviet danger at the end of 1945, when it became clear that the Red Army was not demobilizing. Increasing fears of Soviet ambitions in Eastern and Central Europe led to some early speculation among French military men about a possible German rearmament within some broader alliance structure. An internal memorandum prepared by the General Staff on 25 October 1945 recommended a defense organization in Europe of some fifty divisions, including 450,000 Americans, and possible participation of an unspecified number of Germans under strict alliance control.[22]

A somewhat broader discussion of French security needs, including a possible German role in European defense, evolved in the wake of the failed Moscow Conference of March–April 1947. At a meeting of Western military leaders in New York in January 1948, General Pierre Billotte agreed with American general Matthew Ridgway and British general Sir William Morgan on the need for German rearmament within the context of a global security arrangement jointly orchestrated by America, Britain, and France. In November of that year, Vice-Admiral André Lemonnier, chief of the French navy, suggested that arming the Germans in the Western zones was necessary because the Eastern zone was already remilitarized through the Kasernierte Volkspolizei.[23]

The Western Union, of which France was a member, certainly contained no provision for German rearmament. Nevertheless, some members of the French General Staff, most notably General Jean-Marie de Lattre de Tassigny, thought that the union's call for a defensive line east of the Rhine would be feasible only if the Germans were included. Generals Paul Ely and Paul Stehlin added colorfully that it would be "unjust" if the Germans did not help "pay for their own defense with their own blood."[24] Finally, General De Gaulle himself came out openly for a German defense commitment, though he favored organizing it on a *Land* basis to prevent the revival of centralized German power.[25]

Whatever their trepidations and caveats, it is significant that it was primarily military men who first considered German rearmament. They did so not only because they considered "military necessity" preeminent but also because they admired the fighting qualities of the German soldiers they had just defeated. Thus General Ridgway could defend his advocacy of German rearmament on the grounds that it would be impossible to stop a Russian attack without "the best infantry in Europe."[26] Pentagon analysts concurred that the martial skills of the "German male" were "among the highest in the world."[27] British and French officers, who had had more experience with German military prowess than their American counterparts, could hardly disagree. Montgomery based his appeal for German rearmament partly on his experiences fighting General Erwin Rommel in Africa, and Admiral Lemonnier spoke enthusiastically of drawing on the martial skills of a "warlike, fiercely anti-communistic people."[28] Despite the enthusiasm among some Allied military men about German fighting prowess, their ruminations about a possible German partnership did not alter official policy, which remained firmly opposed to putting armed Germans on the Cold War front.

In spring 1949 the Berlin Airlift ended the Soviet blockade and briefly quieted Allied discussions about German rearmament. This lull was deceptive, however, because Pentagon planners continued secretly to ponder deploying German forces in the defense of Europe. On 2 April Assistant Secretary of Defense Tracy Voorhees informed General Clay that his planners assumed "it may become reasonable for the West Germans to contribute to the armed security of Western Europe," but only if the other powers considered this "necessary and desirable." Though supporting this proposition, Clay urged that it not be made public, for it conflicted "both in spirit and in fact" with "our present emphasis on demilitarization" and would certainly have a "sensational" public effect. Voorhees agreed that the German rearmament option was "not appropriate for present publication."[29]

Clay retired from his post in autumn 1949 and returned to the United States, where Senator Joseph McCarthy was exploiting anti-Communist hysteria fed by alarm over the "loss" of China and the successful test of a Russian atomic bomb. Sharing this alarm, Clay held a press conference at Harvard University in November in which he called for the creation of a European army that would include small contingents of West German troops. Such a force, he suggested, would serve "as a means of building a united Europe free from fear of Russian aggression." Because many Europeans still feared the Germans more than the Russians, however, Clay proposed that all German units be composed exclusively of foot soldiers and be integrated within existing Western armies. This arrangement, he said, "would be strong enough to contain the Russians, while leaving the participating nations incapable of waging aggressive war individually."[30] The Germans, in other words, would be held in check by the very alliance that their presence was supposed to augment.

THE DISCUSSION WIDENS

Although Allied military figures were the first to conclude that some form of West German rearmament was necessary, they were soon supported by influential politicians and civilian officials. This broadening of the rearmament debate subjected the prevailing doctrine of "military necessity" to a more systematic discussion than it had heretofore received. For the time being, however, it too did not lead to any changes in official policy.

Congress joined the debate in summer 1949 during discussions over American aid to Europe's military buildup, which some congressmen believed was not being pursued with sufficient vigor. Senator H. M. Griffith of New York criticized the government appropriations bill because it made no mention of drawing on German military support, without which a defense of Europe was "illusory." Griffith cautioned, however, against allowing the development of a "powerful reunified Germany," which might misuse its power and turn against the West.[31]

The congressional debate over German policy heated up following the creation of the new West German state in September 1949. It was now time, some congressmen believed, that the Germans started pulling their "fair share" of the West's security load. Representative William Poage (D.-Texas), demanded that the Germans field twenty-five divisions (under American generalship) as repayment for their Marshall Plan aid. Comments like this adumbrated an issue that was to remain central to much of the German rearmament discussion and eventually to the German-American security partnership: that of "burden sharing." Increasingly, German rearmament was seen not just as a matter of military necessity but as a means of lightening the security load of the other Western powers. It would also be viewed as a way of removing the "unfair economic advantage" that West Germany gained as a result of its "free ride" in the security arena.

A few congressmen also advanced the notion that rearmament would help anchor West Germany in the Western security system and assist her reentry into the community of civilized nations. Thus a study mission from the House Foreign Affairs Committee announced in Berlin that it would recommend including the Federal Republic in the newly created Western Union. One member of the group justified this idea on the grounds that Bonn was now "part of the family." On the other side of the Capitol, the chairman of the Senate's Subcommittee on Appropriations, Elmer Thomas, urged the "gradual rearmament of West Germany starting immediately" to help tie the young republic to the West. He did not, however, favor allowing Bonn to manufacture its own weapons for the time being. Five of Thomas's colleagues took issue with his recommendation, arguing that no rearmament should commence until the FRG was economically stable and democratic "in the western sense of the word." Senator Jacob Javits, a Jewish-American who apparently did not consider Germany part of *his* family, declared that Bonn should not be armed "under any circumstances."[32] With such a wide disparity of views, it was apparent that Congress could not yet offer the administration any clear signals on this immensely sensitive question.

Nor could the combined resources of American diplomacy and strategic planning. Disagreement over German policy between the Pentagon and State Department became embarrassingly apparent at a congressional appropriations hearing on 5 June 1950. Secretary of State Acheson, at this time still full of diplomatic scruples regarding German rearmament, told the House Foreign Relations Committee that no thought had been given to rearming West Germany even though existing NATO forces were "totally inadequate." Yet General Bradley testified: "From a strictly military point of view, I do believe the defense of Western Europe would be strengthened by the inclusion of Germany because we do know that they have great production facilities that we could use and we know that they are very capable soldiers and airmen and sailors." In response to questions from the committee, Bradley admitted that "political considerations" were involved, but he said he was not qualified to say how much they augmented "the purely military picture."[33]

But they certainly did augment the picture. On one hand, Washington had to worry that pushing German rearmament would alienate its NATO partners, especially France. On the other hand, there was the nagging worry, most cogently expressed by Henry Byroade (the State Department's German expert), that the West must not "lose" the new Bonn Republic the way it had "lost" the Weimar Republic; arrangements must be made to ensure Bonn's timely integration into the Western system. Wrote Byroade: "If we fail to inspire the Germans with a sense of confidence and faith in the Western democracies and with a genuine conviction that they are on the road to full restoration of their legitimate prerogatives as a nation, they will almost certainly turn to the East. In that event we would lose Germany by default and Russia would make a great stride toward the battle for Europe."[34]

Yet several key questions remained. Should Bonn's integration in the West entail military integration? Was the creation of armed forces one of the FRG's "legitimate prerogatives as a nation"? And if the answer was yes on both counts, what about the timing and the order of events? Should, as many Western politicians believed, economic and political stabilization come before any troops were recruited?

In addition to Byroade, a key figure in the emerging American debate on West German rearmament was Washington's new high commissioner for Germany, John McCloy.[35] While serving as assistant secretary of war under Stimson, McCloy had shared his boss's strong reservations about Morgenthau's approach to containing the Germans, but he was just as dedicated as the treasury secretary to crushing German Nazism and militarism. He believed that rearmament was a "problem that one day we shall have to face," but not now.[36] Thus he stated categorically in February 1950 that there "will be no German army or airforce."[37] Nor did McCloy favor a large centralized police apparatus; rather, he preferred small local forces backed up by the Allied armies. He also opposed Clay's idea of enlisting Germans individually in the Allied forces, believing this would give Bonn officials the idea that the Allies were "dependent" on them. Furthermore, he thought that any steps toward rearmament might destabilize Bonn's fragile young democracy and alienate its largely antimilitary citizenry. As to the problem of "military necessity," McCloy believed that German rearmament could be avoided as long as sufficient Allied forces remained in Central Europe to serve as a "trip wire" that the Soviets would not dare cross. No doubt he was also aware that American intelligence agents now dismissed the possibility of an imminent Soviet invasion of Western Europe. Only at some later time, after West Germany had been thoroughly integrated into a "united Europe," could a German military contribution to Western defense be safely contemplated. McCloy held to this position until about a month after Communist troops had crossed a different Cold War trip wire—the thirty-eighth parallel in Korea.[38]

The British Labour government also remained committed to German disarmament. When, in January 1950, the Czech press alleged that Britain was secretly rearming the Germans in its occupation zone, Foreign Secretary Bevin assured the Czech ambassador that this was nonsense. German disarmament was "one of the few matters in which the three Western Powers and the Germans were of one mind," he said. The Foreign Office denied that proposals for German rearmament voiced by some Allied military figures accurately represented "professional military opinion in the Western countries."[39] Upon taking office, Britain's high commissioner for Germany, Sir Ivone Kirkpatrick, declared that London was "not arming the Germans and did not intend to, whatever the Russians and the East German government might allege." He added that the Germans were "a clumsy and stupid people and that from this point of view difficult to deal with, but so long as they remained disarmed they were without doubt the easiest nation in Europe to control."[40]

The Foreign Office hardened this position on 5 April 1950, declaring its opposition "to *any* kind of German rearmament" and insisting that there was "no likelihood of change [in this policy] in the foreseeable future." Informal suggestions to the effect that Germany might be rearmed through the creation of some "international force" made no sense because "few would be naive enough to believe that such a German force would not lead very soon to the establishment of a national army." Once in possession of such an agency, continued the Foreign Office, Germany would be "in a strong bargaining position between East and West, and *the possibility of [their striking] a bargain with the Soviet Union must never be excluded."[41]

Here, vividly restated, was the old fear of German *Schaukelpolitik* (literally, "seesaw politics"). The Foreign Office clearly worried that the new Germany might try to maneuver between East and West as had Otto von Bismarck in the late nineteenth century and the Weimar government in the early 1920s. Even worse, Bonn might elect to side with the East, as Hitler had temporarily but devastatingly done with his Stalin pact of August 1939.

On another front, and echoing the concerns of the American high commissioner, the Foreign Office also warned that the "young and inexperienced West German government" (an odd description of Adenauer) might be "too heavily influenced by an organized body of military opinion which the German High Command would represent."[42] Finally, Bevin and his colleagues argued that German rearmament might give the United States an excuse to withdraw its troops from the Continent, which they believed would be disastrous for the future of Europe.

Despite this strongly worded official stance, a few voices in the Tory opposition were already demanding significant modifications in the government's policy on Germany. In November 1949 Winston Churchill publicly called for a West German contribution to European defense, though he was careful to insist that it not take the form of a "national German army."[43] Viscount Hinchingbroke, an influential Tory member of Parliament, told an audience in Exeter on 4 December 1949 that Britain had no choice but to support an early rearmament of West Germany because America planned "soon to build up the German army to serve the needs of Europe"; if Britain did not go along with this, it would "lose out, be boycotted and left in the cold like a small Scandinavian state interested only in its own little social scheme."[44] Another Conservative, Lord Winster, urged allowing the Germans to rearm (like most Britons, he assumed that they were eager to do so) because West Germany could not be denied "the natural rights of a sovereign nation." He further insisted that Bonn's forces must have "full equality" within the European alliance, for anything less would impose upon them "a pariah status they would never accept."[45]

Lord Winster's assessment turned out to be prescient, but his insistence upon "full equality" for the new Germany was very much a cry in the wilderness at this early date. Making use of German manpower was one thing—some Britons could support that readily enough—but allowing Bonn complete military equality was quite another. In any event, these initial prorearmament comments from a few Conservatives were too tentative and scattered to provoke much discussion in Parliament or the press, let alone to change official policy.

In March 1950 Churchill provoked the first full debate in the House of Commons on this question. He was inspired to do so, he said, by a recent War Office publication containing alarming information on the growth of the Volkspolizei in East Germany. In Churchill's opinion, the government seemed not to be drawing the necessary conclusions from its own revelations. When not wallowing in "indecision," it was persisting in "petty annoyances" like the "belated dismantlement of a few remaining German factories and the still more belated trials of aged German generals." These policies, he argued, only played into the hands of Communists and neo-Nazis. Yet more troubling was the government's apparent unwillingness to face the "painful question of [German] rearmament" arising from the sad fact that the Continent "could not be successfully held without the active aid of West Germany." This evasion was wrongheaded for economic reasons as well, he said, for in allowing the Germans to avoid defense expenses it gave them an unfair advantage in the marketplace. While Britain was spending £800 million annually on defense, the Germans were engaging in a "commercial competition" that was "growing and spreading with every month."[46] Churchill, in other words, fully shared the Americans' reservations about giving the Germans a free military ride, but in Britain's case this concern was soon to loom even larger because of that country's economic weaknesses and emerging commercial battle with a revived West Germany.

Responding to Churchill, Prime Minister Attlee argued that such "matters of high policy" could not be "decided offhand" in a parliamentary debate. Britain could not act unilaterally, but "only in concert with her Western Allies." By this he meant that London had to work not only with the Americans but also with the French, whose hostility toward German rearmament was known to all. Indeed, Labour MP Richard Crossman predicted that an Anglo-American initiative on German rearmament would yield a Communist-led government in France, surely a greater threat to European security than the absence of a few thousand German troops.[47]

Although Crossman's argument was hypothetical and Attlee's weak, Churchill did not prevail. At this point, only a handful of politicians—all Conservatives—were willing to risk putting weapons back in the hands of their recent enemy. The British government's reluctance to countenance such a move found ample support among the public at large, where bitter anti-German feelings and stereotypes about the "beastly Hun" were well entrenched.

While remaining officially opposed to German rearmament, however, London was at this very moment—early spring of 1950—undertaking a reexamination of its strategic posture that implicitly, if not explicitly, raised the possibility of bringing in the Germans. The Soviet Union's successful atomic bomb test and the rise of Communist China had begun to undermine Britain's faith in the deterrent effects of the American nuclear arsenal. Many believed that Britain would have to do more to defend Western Europe, which seemed so vulnerable in light of America's preoccupation with the Far East and France's commitments in North Africa and Indochina. Thus, in March 1950, the Chiefs of Staff proposed a shift in strategic priorities from the Middle East to Western Europe. They now said that it was "vital" to Britain's "first pillar, the defense of the United Kingdom," to "hold the enemy East of the Rhine." The cabinet subsequently agreed that two additional infantry divisions might be added to the British army on the Rhine in the event of a Soviet attack. But Montgomery, now chairman of the Commander in Chief Committee of the Brussels pact (NATO), debunked this plan as mere tokenism, insisting that it was "utterly futile to pretend that we can delay the Russians east of the Rhine for longer than a period of two or three days."[48]

He did not need to add that the notion of defending Europe "east of the Rhine" represented a significant change from existing NATO doctrine of a defense *on* the Rhine. Thus the ambitious (but inadequately supported) new

Eastern approach was, in the words of one recent student of British security policy, "bound to raise the question of what to do about West Germany: should she be abandoned by the West in the event of war, or should she be encouraged to fight for the West against the Soviet Union? In the latter case, this would mean that the West would have to confront the question of her rearmament."[49]

In France, meanwhile, few politicians of note shared the French General Staff's willingness to rearm the Germans even under conditions of strict control. Opposition was especially strong among the Communists and right-wing nationalists—another example of the French adage that "les extrêmes se touchent." In a debate over ratification of the new NATO alliance in July 1949, the government came under attack from both the far Left and far Right for advocating a pact that (it was claimed) could only lead to German rearmament. The Communists charged that NATO's principal backers, the United States and Britain, were so anxious to rearm Germany that they had returned Ruhr industries to Nazi bosses, acquitted or pardoned "war criminals and torturers of the death camps," and eschewed reparations. The rightists, for their part, saw the Germans as more dangerous to French security than the Russians; and one of their spokesmen (General Adolphe Aumeran of the Parti Républicain de la Liberté) insisted that "the only possible solution [to the problem of perennial German aggression] is to return to particularist, autonomous, and independent Germanies." In defense of NATO, Foreign Minister Robert Schuman argued that by participating in the alliance, France could ensure that a possible German membership was never even discussed.[50]

By November 1949, when the National Assembly returned to the German problem in a major debate on foreign policy, recent events had hardened France's attitude toward its eastern neighbor. In campaigning during the first Bundestag elections, the influential Social Democratic leader Kurt Schumacher had demanded that the Saar be returned to Germany and that Bonn not do the bidding of the Quai d'Orsay. Approval of the Petersberg Protocol, in which the occupation powers had agreed to reduce factory dismantling in exchange for German participation in the International Ruhr Agency, provoked even greater unease. The Left venomously attacked the measure as an act of collusion between American high finance and West German neo-Nazism: "The American imperialists order, the neo-Nazis in Bonn propose, and the French government acts!" they shouted.[51] Again, Schuman was forced on the defensive, citing his Lorraine origins as proof that he ought to know what "the German problem" was. Because "militarism" was certainly part of this problem, he said, there could be no question of "envisaging or even contemplating any rearmament of Germany whatever."[52]

Yet even in France there were exceptions, politicians who were ready to accept German rearmament as a "necessary evil" in light of the Soviet threat. Former prime minister Paul Reynaud, for example, pointedly asked if the government really believed that the five Anglo-Saxon divisions currently stationed in West Germany could stop an invasion of "the five-hundred Soviet divisions" that would pour across the border in the event of war. Personally convinced that they could not, he proposed German participation in a new "European army" under French, American, or British control. Eugène Monteil, a representative of the Radical Party, argued that German participation in European defense was in France's interest for three reasons: it would push Europe's first line of defense farther to the east, it would help secure the Ruhr, and it would enhance West German ties to Western Europe. But Monteil wanted West Germany's defense contribution to be in the form of money, not soldiers: it would be much safer, he said, if the Germans *paid* the Western powers to build up their own forces on German territory.[53]

"COUNT US OUT"

Tentative and hedged as the earliest Allied speculations regarding German rearmament tended to be, they went far beyond what the majority of Germans were prepared to contemplate in the first half decade following World War II. Many of them, after all, were still digging out from the rubble of their shattered cities and scrounging for food and coal on the black market. The vaunted *Wirtschaftswunder* had not yet begun; factories were still being dismantled in some places and foreign trade was stagnant because of an overvalued mark. Seeking to explain their plight, most Germans blamed the war in general rather than the specific Nazi policies that had produced it. They also tended to see war as an inevitable by-product of maintaining an army— perhaps not an entirely unwarranted assumption given their recent history. As Erik Reger, editor of Berlin's *Tagesspiegel*, put it: "As soon as Germany has soldiers, there will be war."[54] This perspective was reflected in the immense popularity of such antimilitary works as Hans Hellmut Kirst's novel *08/15*, and Carl Zuckmayer's play *The Devil's General*. Moreover, many Germans welcomed their country's demilitarization as an opportunity to found a new nation without having to contend with the demands and pressures traditionally imposed by the military class. Allied policy, wrote the journalist Eugen Kogon, could become "an instrument of freedom," facilitating "the only true revolution Germany has ever had."[55]

Not surprisingly, then, rumors that the Allies were considering putting Germans back in uniform elicited outraged cries of "Nie Wieder Krieg!" (No more war) and "Ohne Mich!" A British journalist visiting the Ruhr in 1949 recorded the following conversation between two workers, which he said was typical of attitudes he encountered throughout the area: "They want to call us up again. I'm not going to play, neither is my son. They've hanged our generals; they've brought our army into contempt." The other man responded: "You're right, and I couldn't care less if the Russians come."[56] In some circles the Allies' apparent confusion about how to handle the German defense issue generated a certain *Schadenfreude*, as evidenced in a popular joke involving two Americans conversing on their way to assignments with the occupation government: "What's your job?" one asks. "Demilitarization," the other answers. "That's funny," says the first, "mine's remilitarization."[57]

Jokes aside, protests against any steps toward rearmament came from all parts of the political spectrum. The journalist Winfried Martini, whose views may be taken as representative of the conservative Right, argued that the Western Allies' punitive occupation policies ruled out rearmament for the time being. No "honorable" German, he declared, would make sacrifices for a political order that treated the entire German nation as a "criminal state."[58] General Heinz Guderian, who enjoyed tremendous prestige among veterans, wrote that the Allied policies of dismantling, territorial division, and de-Nazification had so undermined the morale of the German population that they lacked the will to defend themselves.[59] Meanwhile, from the liberal Left, *Der Spiegel* publisher Rudolf Augstein (writing under the pseudonym Jens Daniel) insisted that the Germans were psychologically unprepared for rearmament and would be unable to overcome this "block" until war was imminent, when it would undoubtedly be too late. "Hang yourself or not," he concluded, "you'll regret either."[60] Claiming in November 1948 that the Anglo-Americans were already secretly setting up German military forces, Eugen Kogon warned that this might sabotage efforts to create a new democracy. The tragic history of Weimar might "repeat itself even more rapidly than before," he declared.[61]

Kogon's accusations, though unsubstantiated, generated considerable hand-wringing in the German press. The idea of putting young Germans back in uniform, editorialized the *Westfalen Zeitung*, could not help but produce "a feeling of deepest depression." The paper added that though it might be Germany's "heavy, bitter fate to become once again a political and military factor in world affairs," this decision could be made only by the Germans themselves. In the meantime, there must be "no secret rearmament of German men."[62] The *Rheinische Post* agreed that it was far too early to consider German rearmament, for without a well-established democratic order any new army would likely become "a dangerous plaything" in the hands of political adventurers.[63] Taking the Western Allies to task for reversing their own policies, the *Wiesbadener Kurier* insisted that the German people, having had their military zeal "thoroughly beaten out of them," would no longer jump to the command "Germans to the Front!" The world must take note, it warned, that "the Prussians don't shoot so quickly anymore."[64]

Hostility to things military was also evident in the drafting of the *Grundgesetz* (Basic Law). The delegates to the Preliminary Constitutional Convention in Herrenchiemsee in August 1948 and the Frankfurt Parliamentary Council in the fall were reluctant to take up this issue, but they realized that matters of defense needed some consideration given the increasingly polarized international situation. As Theo Kordt put it at Herrenchiemsee: "We need protection. We cannot remain pariahs forever, vulnerable to every aggressor."[65] Aware that the Americans were thinking of attaching native units to their own forces, German politicians feared becoming the passive objects of a rearmament process over which they had no control. Some, including Konrad Adenauer, the future chancellor, insisted that a capacity for self-defense was an inherent right of statehood.

Nevertheless, when the conservative Union parties proposed adding a clause to the Basic Law making the future federal government responsible for questions of "external security," the majority rejected the motion. This was a historic decision. In the German tradition military matters had often preceded political decisions; now, for the first time, a German state would begin its existence not only without an army but without the legal basis for one. Inevitably, this would be a source of legal and constitutional disputation for years to come. From the initial decision to rearm, through the controversy over joining the European Defense Community and NATO, to quarrels over where Bundeswehr soldiers might serve, wrenching constitutional questions were to play a fundamental role in the evolution of West German security policy.

Having taken their momentous decision to eschew military institutions, the constitutional planners still faced the problem of their new nation's geostrategic vulnerability on the main fault line of the Cold War. They therefore concluded that the future Federal Republic must be included in some international security system, albeit not as a military participant. Article 24 of the Basic Law accordingly allowed the federal government to transfer powers of sovereignty to international agencies for purposes of collective security and to join in the settlement of disputes through international arbitration.[66]

The discussions in the Parliamentary Council touched on matters of security in another respect. The framers wanted to record their aversion to "militarism" by including a programmatic denunciation of war and the manufacture of war materials. A debate ensued about whether *all* war should be denounced or only "aggressive war." Thomas Dehler, a former Nazi and now member of the Freie Demokratische Partei (FDP), declared that no people had the "right to renounce the duty to defend themselves." This formulation eventually prevailed: Article 26 of the Basic Law duly condemned "aggressive war"—the kind, of course, that no one ever admitted to waging.[67]

Rather more significant was the framers' decision to enshrine the principle of conscientious objection in the Basic Law. Because the future state was not meant to have an army, let alone a conscript force, this provision was instituted mainly to protect young West Germans from possible enforced enlistment in the military forces of the Western powers. This clause, however, would later be used by the government to buttress its case for rearming without amending the constitution.

While the framers of the *Grundgesetz* were engaged in their historic project of creating a German state without an army, some influential political and former military figures were quietly discussing ways the new nation might create a defense force without it becoming the "dangerous plaything" either of its own generals or of the Western powers. This group, which called itself the Lampheimer Circle, included such prominent personalities as Gebhard Müller of the Christian Democratic Union (CDU), justice minister in Württemberg-Hohenzollern; Carlo Schmid of the Sozialdemokratische Partei Deutschlands (SPD), a leading Socialist parliamentarian; Theodor Heuss (FDP), future federal president; and Hans Speidel, a former general and prominent military intellectual.[68] The political and professional diversity of this gathering is significant: it anticipated the later collaboration among former officers and key politicians from all the major parties in laying the groundwork for the Bundeswehr. These men hailed from southwest Germany, a region that combined illustrious military traditions with a history of liberal parliamentarianism. The former inheritance would prove useful in dealing with former military men, and the latter helped make these intellectual Swabians less threatening to the Bundestag and the populace as a whole. The southwestern heritage would also be important in building bridges to West Germany's most prominent Prussophobe, Konrad Adenauer.

In 1948 this group commissioned Speidel to prepare a memo on security. In it, as in two previous memos, Speidel insisted that Germany was threatened by Russia's huge armies and that the Germans could not count on the Western powers to protect them.[69] Adequate security was possible, he said, only through the creation of a "European force" to which the future West German state should contribute. Yet the contribution must be contingent upon Germany's full participation in a European political framework and its equal representation in the prospective European "High Command." With these proposals, Speidel introduced the issue of *Gleichberechtigung* (equal treatment), another theme that was to bedevil the debate on German rearmament for years to come.

Speidel might have remained nothing more than a former general with provocative ideas had he not come to the attention of the man who was to shape West Germany's political destiny for the next fifteen years: Konrad Adenauer. The future chancellor was the first key German politician to conclude that the new Federal Republic needed some defensive capacity beyond that which the Allies seemed willing to provide. Just as significantly, he linked security questions with a drive for full sovereignty, insisting that a state which lacked a means to defend itself could hardly call itself a state. As chancellor he would never see security policy as an end in itself but as a means to secure Bonn's integration in the Western community as a sovereign state.

In December 1948 Adenauer asked Speidel to discuss with him his conception of European security. Their meeting hardly began on an auspicious note. Adenauer had little use for the military world and dropped derogatory remarks about professional soldiers. Miffed, Speidel observed that Adenauer had not been involved in the anti-Nazi resistance, as some top professional soldiers had been.[70] Nevertheless, Speidel managed to convey the essence of his political and strategic conception, and Adenauer asked him to prepare another security memorandum for his own use.

The document that Speidel duly produced summarized his earlier arguments regarding Western vulnerability and the need for a German defense contribution. He said that the weakness of Britain, France, and the Benelux countries made a defense on the Rhine—let alone on the Elbe—questionable. To hold the Rhine, America would have to commit at least twenty more tank divisions to the Continent. Should the Western Allies contemplate anything more ambitious, said Speidel, they would need German help. This support must take the form of "unified units organized within the framework of a European army." Supplied with "the most modern weaponry, including tanks," the German units would be roughly equivalent to French or British mechanized divisions. Speidel carefully added that the European army framework, while allowing the Germans military equality, would militate against a revival of nationalist militarism.[71]

Adenauer did not acknowledge having read Speidel's memo, but very likely he did, for he asked for further commentaries. In his next effort Speidel joined forces with another former Wehrmacht general, Adolf Heusinger, who was also to become instrumental in the creation of the Bundeswehr.[72] Their joint memo began by rejecting a defense on the Rhine because that would mean an "abandonment" of Western Germany, Austria, and Switzerland to the Soviets. Indeed, they insisted that a relocation to the east of the "defensive line of the Atlantic world" had already been accepted as necessary by "influential political and military personalities of the Atlantic Powers." Following an assessment of Soviet operational alternatives, the memo went on to argue that the only viable Allied strategy was one employing highly mobile units rather than a rigid defense line. In advancing this view, the generals were drawing on established practices of German forces in the East. The Reichswehr, lacking the larger numbers of the imperial armies, had evolved a mobile defense vis-à-vis Poland in the 1920s, and of course the Wehrmacht had perfected mobile tactics both in its eastern offensives between 1939 and 1941 and in its defensive struggles on the Eastern front after 1942. But whatever its impressive pedigree and apparent current logistical advantages, these generals believed that a mobile defense required a dramatic expansion of Western forces and the addition of German personnel, who were seasoned veterans of the war against the Soviet Union.

It was crucial, however, that the Germans' participation be made dependent on certain political and military "conditions." The future West German state must enjoy immediate and full "political equality"; the state of war still existing between Germany and the Allied powers must be ended; and the German units, "homogeneous" [*reinrassig*] in composition, must be no smaller than divisions and possess the latest weaponry, including tanks and aircraft. "We cannot be expected to contribute cannon-fodder," declared the generals.[73]

In June 1949 Adenauer broadened his informal circle of advisers to include yet another former general, Hasso von Manteuffel, from whom he also solicited a security paper.[74] This document, which its author called a "Confession of a Freedom-loving German," argued that Germans could be safe from the "world evil" of expansive Communism only by siding with the Atlantic powers.[75] But if the Germans needed to cooperate with the West to remain free, said Manteuffel, the West also needed Germany to keep the Soviets at bay in Europe. The Allied powers' troops in Central Europe were "weak in numbers and in spirit," whereas the Germans had substantially retained their "unmatched fighting capacity." Like Speidel and Heusinger, Manteuffel said that the West's defense must begin "in the East," not on the Rhine, which he likened to the medieval practice of releasing galley slaves to fight only when the ship was sinking. Once rearmed, Germany would have to find military men of proven ability to take charge of the new army. Here it was crucial, said Manteuffel, to employ only men who had "kept their oath [to Hitler]"—not the "so-called resistance fighters who out of cowardice or personal ambition" had "tried to stab their leader in the back." Such oath-breakers would be unable to command the respect of "decent Germans." This was a damning reference, of course, to the Twentieth of July assassination attempt against Hitler; and in insisting that future German officers not be "tainted" by this heritage, Manteuffel was anticipating one of the more bitter struggles that flared up over the definition of a "usable past" for the new German armed forces.[76]

ADENAUER'S TRIAL BALLOON

Konrad Adenauer had been careful to keep his dealings with these former generals confidential, for he was well aware of the German public's hostility toward a military revival. Following his election to the chancellorship of the Federal Republic in September 1949, he also faced diplomatic reasons for discretion. In December the Allied High Commission (AHC) announced a new law confirming earlier Allied bans on activities "which directly or indirectly further the techniques of war or promote the revival of militarism."[77] This law was imposed to reassure the world that the Western powers were not—contrary to widespread allegations and the unofficial commentary of some politicians and military men—intending to remilitarize the Germans. Unquestionably, however, the decree was also meant as a warning to the new West German leadership not to become too bold in its own handling of the security issue: Bonn must not get the idea that in the military realm it could start behaving as if it were fully sovereign.

Adenauer got the message. Though determined eventually to gain full sovereignty for the FRG, he was happy to use such restrictions to justify keeping security planning under his personal control. Like Otto von Bismarck, whose dictum was *"Vox Populi = Vox Rindvieh"* (Voice of the People = Voice of Cattle), Adenauer regarded foreign policy his personal fiefdom, a domain whose complexity and importance ruled out "interference" from parliamentarians, not to mention the press and public.

Personal proclivities aside, Adenauer found himself in a situation that demanded the greatest dexterity. On the international plane, he was hemmed in by the AHC, whose headquarters high on the Petersberg overlooking the "provisional" capital of Bonn was symbolic of the Germans' inferior status and limited sovereignty. The limitations on sovereignty were spelled out in the Allied Occupation Statute, which gave the Allies final control over German foreign affairs, the Ruhr, external trade, reparations, and security. To complicate matters, Adenauer's relationship with the three high commissioners was none too smooth. While he sought to expand German authority, they expected deference and gratitude for what powers they had deigned to restore. This clash of perspectives was symbolized by a famous incident during the ceremony marking the official transfer of the Occupation Statute on 21 September 1949. Adenauer had been informed in advance by the High Commission that Allied guards would not salute him when he arrived at the Petersberg; he replied that this made no difference to him—*he* was no "militarist." But he was determined not to appear inferior to his hosts; and when ushered before the commissioners to receive the statute, he strode quickly across the carpet on which they were standing, thereby positing his "equality" with them. Somehow he even managed to avoid formally accepting the occupation document, which, encased in brown wrapping like a piece of pornography, was furtively thrust into the hands of an aide at the end of the ceremony.[78]

The domestic political scene added further limitations to Adenauer's freedom of action. Aware as we now are of his later semimonarchical status, we may be inclined to forget that he was elected chancellor by just one vote (his own) in the first Bundestag; that his government was a somewhat shaky coalition including such potentially independent spirits as Jakob Kaiser, Franz Blücher, and Gustav Heinemann; and that, like so many chancellors before and after, he had trouble getting along with the Bavarians.

Adenauer's security policy was conditioned also by his broader vision of Germany's role in the postwar world. There was little place in this world for the state that had long dominated German affairs—Prussia. Of course, Adenauer's native Rhineland had been part of Prussia since 1815, but the Rhinelanders regarded themselves as *Beutepreussen* ("booty-Prussians") and had never wholly identified with the kingdom that had swallowed them up. It has often been remarked that Adenauer himself had something of the "Prussian" about him—he was known for his stern rectitude, stiff bearing, and firm sense of duty—but to him Prussia and Berlin embodied all that was deficient and even dangerous in the German experience: extreme nationalism, statism, militarism, Protestantism, and, more recently, socialism and Nazism. (Adenauer tended to overlook Nazism's South German and Austrian origins.) Prussia to Adenauer also meant the inscrutable East, for, as far as he was concerned, "the steppes began at Magdeburg." Referring to his own "almost mongoloid" physiognomy, he once said that it was no wonder that he looked like a "Hun"—he had a grandmother from eastern Germany![79]

Adenauer's antipathy for Prussia was nothing new. At the end of World War I, as mayor of Cologne, he had urged the separation of the Rhineland from Prussia and the end of Prussia's domination over Germany. The curtailment of Prussian power, he said, would also facilitate a reconciliation between western Germany and Latin Europe, especially France. It is striking how much this program of 1919 anticipated his policy as chancellor thirty-odd years later. Though he paid lip service to the ideal of German reunification—he could not have become chancellor had he not done so—he was more than content to rule it out for the time being.[80] His priority in the early 1950s, as it had been in the early 1920s, was to reestablish the historic ties between western Germany and Western Europe.

Following the creation of the Bonn Republic, Adenauer turned his attention to the delicate task of consolidating this precarious creation. His task was difficult because this new entity generated little enthusiasm among its own citizens, many of whom hoped that it would be no more than a way station on the route to German reunification, which indeed was what it was formally meant to be. Moreover, another, albeit much smaller, segment of the population believed that reunification could be expedited if Bonn eschewed its West orientation in favor of some kind of neutralist gambit.

Neutralism, however, was anathema to Adenauer. He resolutely opposed any notion of making the FRG a "free-floating" arbiter between East and West, let alone a power that made secret deals with the Soviet Union, as the Weimar Republic had done. Much like the American Cold Warriors with whom he was soon to work so closely, Adenauer saw Russia as an insatiable expansionist power whose traditional imperialism had been compounded since 1917 by a Communist commitment to "world domination."[81] Although the sincerity of this conviction should not be doubted, it is equally true that Adenauer, like Gustav Stresemann and Hitler before him, was prepared to exploit the Red bogey for his own political purposes. The new West German state, after all, was a creature of the Cold War, and if the Cold War were to ebb, so might Adenauer's importance and diplomatic leverage.

Despite the precariousness of his political position at home and abroad, the seventy-three-year-old Adenauer was determined to employ what he (and his doctor) believed would be a very brief chancellorship to anchor the young Federal Republic solidly in the European and Atlantic West. Thus he applauded when Secretary Acheson announced at a NATO meeting in November 1949 that Washington saw in West Germany and Japan "future allies" against the Soviet Union. Directly after the NATO meeting, Acheson visited Bonn—he was the first Allied foreign minister to do so—thereby giving Adenauer the opportunity to impress upon him personally his commitment to integration in the West and reconciliation with France. Acheson came away convinced that Adenauer deserved full support from the Western powers.[82]

Adenauer hoped that this support might extend to his plan to create an indigenous self-defense force in the FRG. Frustrated because his new government had no security forces at its disposal, Adenauer approached the High Commission with a "minimal demand": permission to establish a federal police organization (Bundespolizei). He thought this was not asking a great deal because the newly created East German state possessed such a force, and the GDR was not recognized by the West as a legitimate state.[83] Nonetheless, the AHC brusquely rejected his request as a contravention of the postwar demilitarization agreements. Exasperated, Adenauer renewed his demand for a "Security Guarantee" from the Western powers. If the Allies were so intent on maintaining exclusive responsibility for defending Europe, he argued, they must make this credible by guaranteeing a viable defense of the "Free World's" new eastern frontier.[84]

This was to be a persistent demand of Adenauer's over the next two years, but it was never meant to cancel out the need for additional security measures involving some form of German participation. Indeed, Adenauer's demand was undoubtedly designed to make the Allies ask why *they* should be expected to expand their forces to protect Germany if the Germans themselves made no contribution to this effort. Then Adenauer could reply that the Germans *were* prepared to make a contribution—provided, of course, that they were treated as "partners."

As it happened, however, the Western powers were agonizingly slow to ask this question. Adenauer therefore found it necessary to ask it himself in a pair of highly publicized interviews in the Western press. He chose this method partly because the FRG lacked a foreign ministry through which it might have carried on negotiations in the conventional manner and partly because if his media "trial balloon" floated off course, he could always insist that he had been misquoted or misinterpreted.

Adenauer's first interlocutor was Paul Baar of *L'Est Républicain* (Nancy). On 11 November 1949, he told Baar that the "disappearance" of the Wehrmacht had "lamed" the West in its standoff with the Soviet Union. The reestablishment of a German army would do much to redress the balance, he said, but West Germany could think of rearming only within the framework of the Western Union.[85]

Less than a month later, Adenauer granted an interview to John Leacacos of the *Cleveland Plain Dealer*. Here he repeated his "offer" of a defense contribution within the context of a European army. He explicitly rejected a "national" army or Germans' service in Allied forces. Off the record, he was even more categorical about the urgent need for German troops, telling Leacacos that the Germans were the "only people who [could] stop the Russians"— though if they were not given military training soon, they might lose their "martial skills."[86]

Adenauer's interviews, especially the second one, provoked a hostile response from the Western powers. The high commissioners were indignant over his circumvention of the established channels of negotiation and his apparent determination to force a confrontation on the rearmament question. McCloy was so angry that he suggested a public rebuke but ultimately agreed to give the offender a private slap on the wrist. The commissioners quietly told Adenauer that his rearmament "offer" was unappreciated and that in the future he should clear any public statements on this question with them.[87]

Realizing that his trial balloon had sailed off course, Adenauer quickly sought to rein it in. He ordered his press secretary to declare that he was "in principle opposed to any German rearmament" and had merely said Bonn *might* be prepared to make a defense contribution if the Western powers insisted on it.[88]

If Adenauer found himself backpedaling before the high commissioners, he faced even greater indignation from his own Bundestag. In its early years this body was not known for the high standards of its debate—Kirkpatrick complained that it was composed exclusively of "crazies and bores" who discussed everything in a state of "irresponsible euphoria"[89]—but it had enough amour propre to resent Adenauer's habit of conducting foreign policy with hardly a glance in its direction.

In the Bundestag's first debate on security affairs (16 December 1949), Erich Ollenhauer (SPD) protested that the chancellor had aired vital security questions in the press before raising them in the Bundestag. He demanded that the government "inform the parliament before making important policy declarations of this sort." As for the substance of Adenauer's remarks, Ollenhauer condemned even the idea of a West German defense contribution. The responsibility for defending the territory of the Federal Republic, he reminded the house, lay "entirely with the Occupation Powers." Adenauer's interview diplomacy had sowed "confusion" among the German people because it gave them the "illusion" that it was in their power to make decisions on security matters. Moreover, it had promoted "an increased activity on the part of nationalist and militarist elements in Germany, who now scented new possibilities." Finally, and most damning of all, Adenauer's "irresponsible initiative" threatened to prolong German disunity by widening the gulf between East and West. "The goal of any political action," Ollenhauer concluded, "must be to heal this division, not to intensify it."[90]

Ollenhauer's barrage had hardly lifted before Franz Etzel of the Bavaria Party leveled his guns on the chancellor. The Bavaria Party was an especially contentious lot, having opted to pursue an extreme particularist line as a challenge to the somewhat more moderate federalism of the Christian Social Union (CSU). Thus Etzel attacked Adenauer's rearmament initiative as an attempt to revive the tradition of centralized "Prussian militarism" to which the Bavarian people had "always been opposed." Bavaria had no intention of becoming "a pawn in an international power game," cried Etzel, and it would oppose any attempts to "employ German citizens as mercenaries under foreign command."[91]

If Etzel was determined to protect Bavaria from Prussian militarism, Max Reimann of the Kommunistische Partei Deutschlands (KPD) assumed a similar role on behalf of Germany's workers. Recalling that Hitler had "yoked the working classes to his monopoly-capitalist fascism," Reimann fumed that Adenauer now wanted to exploit Germany's manpower on behalf of "American imperialism's aggressive designs against the peace-loving peoples of the East." He warned that a "fighting front of workers" would eliminate Bonn's "puppet government" within forty-eight hours of a decision to rearm. This ludicrous threat produced such an uproar that debate had to be suspended. When it resumed, Helene Wessel (Center Party), a noted pacifist, took the floor to denounce "the idea of remilitarization in any form." She reminded her colleagues that there were still some five hundred thousand German prisoners in Russian custody, that people faced the sight of endless rubble in their cities, that millions had lost "Haus, Hof and Heimat." Germans could no longer be concerned with destroying, only with rebuilding. Moreover, Germany's democratic development was predicated on the absence of any new "military caste."[92]

The delegate from the Nationalen Rechten (National Rightists), Franz Richter, did not share Wessel's worries about a military caste, but he was equally opposed to rearmament. For him and his party the primary sticking point was the "dishonor" inherent in cooperating with foreign powers who still subjected former German officers to "humiliating" war-crimes trials. "At no time in previous history," cried Richter, "has a defeated nation been so defamed, so dragged through the mud, as we Germans since 1945." Until united Germany had regained "absolute sovereignty" and her "lost territories," the very suggestion of a military alliance with the West was an "impertinence."[93]

COUNT VON SCHWERIN AND THE ZENTRALE FÜR HEIMATDIENST

The Bundestag's choleric response to Adenauer's trial balloon, combined with the high commissioners' stern rebuke, convinced the chancellor that the time was not ripe to speak openly of rearmament. But he did not waver in his commitment to this goal, which he still saw as key to both Bonn's security and its political integration in the West. Thus he continued to lecture the commissioners on the need for a West German defense contribution, which he claimed was all the more urgent given the appearance of an "Eastern Army" in the GDR composed of "militaristic Prussians." He warned that this army, backed by the Russians, might attack the Federal Republic at any moment. By the time the West got around to striking back, the Soviets would have "decimated all of Western Europe." Did the Allies want to "liberate a dead continent"?[94]

Despite Adenauer's apocalyptic warnings, the Western foreign ministers again refused to approve a federal police force for Bonn at a meeting in mid-May 1950. At the same time, however, they unofficially agreed that Bonn might start *planning* ways to bolster security within its borders. These were confusing signals, typical of the ambiguity that marked the powers' entire policy toward Germany. But the Allies' apparent willingness to tolerate internal security planning prompted Adenauer to take a step he had long been considering: appointing a full-time "security adviser."

On 24 May, Adenauer offered this key post to Count Gerhard von Schwerin, a former Wehrmacht tank commander. The count came highly recommended by Britain's first high commissioner, Brian Robertson, who had become concerned that Adenauer was listening to "wild and irresponsible people like Manteuffel." In his search for the "right kind of German" to counsel Adenauer, Robertson had turned for advice to the liberal publisher of *Die Zeit*, Countess Marion Dönhoff, who gave him Schwerin's name. The count also had a good report card from the British Foreign Office, which described him as a "well known anti-Nazi" and "follower of the Pan-European ideals of Count Coudenhove-Kalergi."[95]

Adenauer was open to advice from the British on this matter because he did not want to accept the man the Americans were trying to foist upon him: General Gehlen, chief of the embryonic West German intelligence service. Understandably, Adenauer feared that advice delivered by Gehlen would have been shaped by American interests. By appointing Schwerin, he could send a signal to Washington that he intended to preserve a measure of independence in defining Bonn's security policy.[96]

Important as these considerations were, however, they would not have determined the issue had not Schwerin possessed the right background and personal qualities. During the war he had defied Hitler's orders to stage a last-ditch defense of Aachen, a gesture that helped to make him more politically acceptable in the postwar era. The same was true for his connections to the anti-Hitler resistance in the army: Schwerin was one of several officers whose wartime ties to the Twentieth of July conspiracy enhanced their attractiveness to a republican government searching for moral credibility in a still highly suspicious world. Finally, and perhaps most important, Schwerin did not give the appearance of being a professional soldier. Shy, soft-spoken, and unbemonocled, he might have been a businessman or teacher. When Adenauer met him, he was pleasantly surprised to discover that Schwerin "did not seem at all like a general, but rather like a completely rational man with whom one could talk!"[97]

In their opening meeting Adenauer told Schwerin that two problems worried him deeply: first, the East's campaign of "intellectual infiltration," which sought to "destabilize public life" in the FRG by fostering "pacifism and a rejection of West-integration," and second, West Germany's external vulnerability, which would leave it open to "catastrophic consequences" in the event of a military conflict between East and West. As far as he could tell, confided Adenauer, NATO's strategic plans were totally inadequate for a defense of the German population. Thus Bonn would soon have to adopt measures of self-protection, including possibly creating a "mobile federal police force." Schwerin's first job was to find ways to manage "the unobtrusive buildup" of such an organization.[98]

But the chancellor clearly saw this as a temporary expedient, a small but necessary step toward his broader project of making a full-fledged "defense contribution" to the Atlantic alliance. That Adenauer was thinking in these

terms during his initial interview with Schwerin is evident from his request
to be given a list of *unbelastet* (politically untainted) former officers whom
he might officially receive. He thought that this gesture would allow him to
build personal rapport with the veterans' community and win its support for
rearmament. These men might then form the beginnings of a new officer
corps.

Schwerin began his tenure as security adviser by preparing a lengthy memorandum that addressed Adenauer's principal concerns. Entitled "An Outline
of Practical Measures for the Development of German Cadres within the
Framework of a United European Defense Force," it evaluated three options
for the chancellor's consideration. The first, a "mobile federal police," had
the advantage of reflecting "most closely German national sensitivities" and
operating within a "purely German framework." But it would unfortunately
require permission from the Western foreign ministers, which Schwerin saw
as unlikely, and the acquiescence of the Bundestag, which he (rightly) feared
would generate acrimonious debate. The second alternative involved trans-
forming the existing Grenzschutz (Border Guard) into a centralized police
force. On the international level, this option would require permission only
from the AHC, but on the domestic front it would need the consent of the
Länder, which were extremely jealous of their prerogatives. Moreover, most
of the Border Guard personnel were "not suited for military tasks," in his
opinion, and new cadres would have to be recruited. Finally, as a third possibility, Schwerin mooted a military "coordination" of the Labor Service
Groups. Though this could be carried out without involving the Bundestag,
he considered the men in "no way suitable" for military duties because they
had low morale and enjoyed little public esteem. Moreover, the Allies depended on them to perform support duties and would be unlikely to give
them up. In the end, therefore, Schwerin proposed that only the first and second options deserved Adenauer's close scrutiny; both offered possibilities
"for quick and effective action in the event of a national emergency."[99]

As for Adenauer's other charge—his request for names of former
Wehrmacht officers whom he could officially receive—Schwerin duly produced a dozen or so suitable candidates. Atop the list was a veterans' activist
named Kurt Linde, who was slated to lead a delegation of deserving former
soldiers, "preferably including some cripples," to meet the chancellor.[100] This
would allow Adenauer to show solidarity with the organized veterans, who
continued to complain of ill-treatment by Bonn and the Allies.

After submitting his memos to Adenauer, Schwerin set about building a
small staff. Because part of his work—military planning—technically violated
Allied disarmament regulations, his operation was shrouded in secrecy. The
Zentrale für Heimatdienst, as it was code-named, operated under the nomi-
nal supervision of Adenauer's foreign policy expert, Herbert Blankenhorn,

and was squirreled away in the attic of the Palais Schaumburg.[101] The camouflage was so successful that few people working in the building knew what the count was up to.

Despite this preoccupation with secrecy, Schwerin convinced the chancellor to make one important concession to the principle of open government: the SPD leader, Kurt Schumacher, would be kept apprised of what the Zentrale was doing. Schwerin insisted on this because he believed that the SPD, unlike the "radical opposition" (Communists and neo-Nazis) needed to be consulted if the FRG were to develop a defense strategy that enjoyed the support of the Bundestag and the majority of the population.[102]

Another of Schwerin's activities involved setting up an intelligence-gathering operation. The chancellor had expressed his concern over "intellectual infiltration from the East." To counter such activity, the government had proposed to establish an "Office for Constitutional Protection" under the aegis of the Interior Ministry. But the head of that ministry, Gustav Heinemann, had shown little enthusiasm for this project, and it appeared that the agency could not begin operations until January 1951.[103] In the meantime, Schwerin's office seemed the perfect place to hide away a security service that would not be beholden to the Americans, as was the CIA-funded "Organization Gehlen."

Schwerin entrusted this task to Joachim Oster, son of the Abwehr officer and Twentieth of July conspirator Hans Oster. Oster, in turn, delegated day-to-day operations to Friedrich Wilhelm Heinz, a former Stahlhelm leader who had become the German correspondent for *Time-Life* publications. Heinz was chosen largely because he was a confidant of Blankenhorn's, who touted him as an expert on East Germany, where he had lived for a time after the war.[104]

As Oster described it, Heinz's purpose was not simply to constitute "another doubtful intelligence agency" but to be a "reliable" service that would keep the chancellor informed about "what [went] on under the table both at home and abroad."[105] Unlike Gehlen's organization, the Friedrich-Wilhelm-Heinz-Dienst would represent "a piece of sovereignty for the Federal Republic."[106] Oster urged that its members "behave like gentlemen" and restrict themselves to "Christian methods." Yet however Heinz may have interpreted this quaint injunction, it did not prevent him from taking up contact with a potpourri of doubtful characters from his nationalist past, including Walther Stennes, the former Berlin SA-chief, and Waldemar Pabst, a former Free Corps leader who had ordered the murders of Rosa Luxemburg and Karl Liebknecht in 1919.

The Zentrale's primary task was military planning, not intelligence, and it spent much of its time trying to identify candidates for a future military contingent. It focused on the veterans' community, from which it expected to recruit the bulk of the new officer corps. Lacking access to surviving Wehrmacht files, which the Allies kept under lock and key in Berlin-Tegel, the Zentrale set up its own office to identify former officers "who would be suitable for reemployment in active [military] service."[107] This Prüfstelle Godesberg employed many former members of the Wehrmacht's *Heeres-Personalamt* on the grounds that it would be "impractical" to forgo "proven organizational forms and expertise simply to create something new."[108]

As word got out about the Prüfstelle's activities, the agency was deluged with employment applications from former soldiers. The applicants invariably chronicled their sorry plight in a demilitarized land that seemed to want only to forget them. Typically, they based their appeals for reemployment on claims that they had been dutiful patriots reduced to destitution by their sacrifices for the fatherland. One applicant insisted that he had been connected to the Twentieth of July conspiracy; another claimed to have saved Adenauer's life. Sometimes the supplicants threatened to "go Communist" if their demands were not met. "If I continue to be treated like a second-class citizen," wrote one veteran, "I will make a 180 degree turn and place myself at the disposal of the [GDR]." Another fumed: "We old soldiers realize that these are difficult times, but we demand to be treated at least as well as the former civil servants, who were considerably more pro-Nazi than we."[109]

Fearing that the veterans were becoming "increasingly radicalized," Schwerin organized meetings with the Economics Ministry designed to facilitate the former soldiers' integration into the civilian economy. His office also assured the veterans that Bonn was determined to end the postwar "potshot campaign" against them.[110] To reinforce this pledge, Adenauer himself announced that his government "energetically opposes all attempts to defame the former members of the Wehrmacht."[111]

In addition to collecting the names of potential candidates for a new security force, the Zentrale took rudimentary steps toward arms procurement. The Germans expected the Allies to provide most of the arms and supplies that they would need in the early phases of rearmament. The Federal Republic, after all, had been banned from producing major weapons. Moreover, most German industrial firms were reluctant to get into the arms business even if allowed to do so, for they sensed better opportunities in the civilian economy, where there were fewer government controls and political dangers.[112] (Some German businessmen, like German officers, had been held accountable after the war for aiding and abetting the Nazis.) Adenauer's government also believed that producing some light weapons and technical equipment would be a good way to prop up the weaker segments of the economy.[113] The Zentrale, moreover, felt that Bonn should avoid total dependence on foreign suppliers. It therefore established a small subdivision to deal with "questions of procurement."[114]

Perhaps Schwerin's most challenging task was not organizational but political—to convince the SPD, particularly its prickly leader, Kurt Schumacher—of the wisdom of Adenauer's foreign and security policy. Schumacher, a refugee from West Prussia who had opposed the Communists in East Germany as steadfastly as he had previously resisted the Nazis, was passionately committed to German reunification.[115] Convinced, not without justice, that Adenauer cared more about integration with the West than reunification, he had publicly branded him "chancellor of the Allies." When informed by Schwerin that Adenauer hoped to arm the FRG within the context of a Western European army, he exploded that this aspiration amounted to a "national suicide" and sellout to the West.[116] Yet Schumacher was by no means antimilitary. He had been a reserve officer in World War I and later emerged as a severe critic of the SPD's alienation of the military during Weimar. His objections to the rearmament plan as advanced by Adenauer were strategic and political. Were the Allies to shift their first line of defense to the Niemen and Vistula rivers, he would have been more than happy to send Germans to the front. Here was the West Prussian patriot speaking, as well as a politician eager to win the sympathy of West Germany's large refugee community.

What Schumacher was proposing, however, was not only strategically unrealistic but anathema to Konrad Adenauer, for whom the reconquest of West Prussia was not worth the bones of a single Rhenish grenadier. Although Schumacher was careful not to close the door to further negotiations with the government on this issue, he had drawn the lines for an internal political confrontation that would dominate West German politics for many years to come.

3

A

SECOND

KOREA?

The Korean War has often been identified as the crucial moment in the history of West German rearmament, the catalytic event that galvanized the Western world to mobilize the Germans. Yet, as we have seen, initiatives to put the Germans back on the front, albeit of an informal nature, had been launched well before the Korean War began. The strategic reassessment of which German rearmament was a part was well advanced by the time the North Koreans attacked. Moreover, the Korean conflict did not convince everyone that this step was now unavoidable. Still, Korea *was* crucial, for that conflict's frightening evolution, if not necessarily its outbreak, finally generated a consensus among the Americans that Bonn had to be rearmed as soon as possible. Thereafter, Washington relentlessly employed its considerable political and economic leverage to bring the other Western allies around to its way of thinking.[1]

Korea also had a profound effect on the objects of Allied attention, the West Germans. Initially, much of the populace feared that Communist aggression in Korea presaged a similar fate for Germany, which of course was also divided into pro-Soviet and pro-Western spheres. For a time, West Germans wallowed more masochistically than ever in feelings of apocalyptic doom. Moreover, most Germans continued to feel vulnerable even after the fear of an imminent invasion had receded. But—and this was a key development—they gradually shed their conviction that they were so dependent upon their Allied protectors that they could do nothing whatsoever for their own defense. In the wake of the Korean War, stronger domestic support slowly crystallized behind Adenauer's security policies.

The chancellor, for his part, fully understood that Korea could help him not only to mobilize domestic support for his security policy but also to pressure the Allies to grant Bonn added sovereign powers. He now added new items to the package of conditions that he claimed were necessary to make rearmament palatable to the German people. Paradoxically, however, Bonn's determination to extract maximum advantage from its cooperation helped significantly to delay the moment when the first German troops made their appearance on the Cold War front.

PAX AMERICANA UNDER FIRE

In the early spring of 1950 an atmosphere of quiet desperation settled over Foggy Bottom. At the beginning of the year, Joseph McCarthy had attacked Acheson for harboring 205 Communists in the State Department, which he said was just the tip of the iceberg. A little later, the former State Department official Alger Hiss had been found guilty of perjury and, by implication, espionage on behalf of the Soviet Union. Now the Wisconsin senator was in full blood against the "stripe-pants boys" at State who were allegedly doing their best to make America lose the Cold War.[2]

And indeed, the situation *was* worrisome. China was "lost," Southeast Asia was in turmoil, the Arabs and Israelis were at each other's throats, labor unrest was disrupting the French economy, and the Communists were on the rise in Italy. In West Germany the economy had stagnated following a brief burst prompted by the currency reform of 1948; unemployment was climbing dramatically; the trade deficit remained huge; and Adenauer was under relentless attack from Schumacher and the SPD. The Germans, reported High Commissioner McCloy, were "nervous, hysterical, and uncertain."[3]

In the international realm, the most dangerous development was the Soviets' acquisition of an atomic-weapons capability. Washington experts did not think that this presaged an early attack against the West, but they feared that it would give Moscow the confidence to pursue more aggressively its disruptive political agenda around the world. At some point Russia might even undertake local or regional military adventures in the belief that the United States would not risk a nuclear war to protect its friends or allies. Thus it seemed imperative to reexamine American strategic doctrine with an eye to finding new ways to buttress the shaky Pax Americana.[4]

Some American strategists and military scientists, most notably those connected with the Atomic Energy Commission, proposed that America might still stay atop the nuclear mountain by developing vastly improved atomic weapons. Edward Teller urged the production of "super" (hydrogen) bombs that would be a thousand times more powerful than the original atomic weapons. Alas, there was no reason to assume that the Russians could not, perhaps sooner rather than later, create similar weapons themselves. Thus, in addition to embarking on the superbomb program, America also began evolving strategies to mix its enhanced nuclear capacity with beefed-up conventional forces. In April 1950 the Pentagon established a committee of top scientists and generals to study how Europe might be defended through the joint deployment of conventional and tactical atomic weapons. Among other conclusions, the committee proposed that new mobile antitank guns could neutralize the Russian threat in the European theater. Truman's science adviser, Vannevar Bush, argued that 280 mm artillery pieces could be built to deliver small atomic shells against enemy troop concentrations. These capabilities, along with tactical air strikes by the air force and close defense of shipping lanes by the navy, might allow for a very effective "forward defense" on the European continent.[5]

While the Pentagon was studying this option, Paul Nitze, who had succeeded George Kennan as head of State's Policy Planning Staff, produced a massive new report, entitled NSC/68, which reexamined American defense strategy on a global scale. Like the Pentagon's study, NSC/68 saw hopeful possibilities for mixing conventional, tactical atomic, and strategic nuclear capabilities in the European theater. Its major recommendation, however, was for a rapid and across-the-board buildup of "political, economic, and military strength in the free world." Insisting that America was "in greater jeopardy than ever before in our history," the report called for increases in defense spending totaling some $40 billion, three times more than the Truman administration's projections. The money should go not just to build more and better weapons but also to help America's allies develop the capacity to "defeat local Soviet moves with local action." Yet NSC/68, for all its apocalyptic tone, did not come down clearly for German rearmament. Instead, the paper simply speculated that it might be "desirable for the free nations . . . to conclude separate arrangements with Japan, Western Germany and Austria, which would enlist the energies and resources of these countries in support of the free world."[6]

NSC/68 had the backing of many eminent bankers, lawyers, university presidents, and military men, but it had one large drawback: it conflicted sharply with Truman's determination to save money. The president refused to endorse it when he found out how much it would cost. Instead, he referred it to Treasury and the Bureau of the Budget, which shared his reservations. At the same time, in early June 1950, he announced that the military budget for 1951 would actually be lower than the already tight outlays for 1950.[7]

Then, on 25 June 1950, North Korean troops invaded South Korea across the thirty-eighth parallel. Although no Soviet troops were involved, most Western policy makers believed that Stalin was using the Koreans to fight a "war by proxy" in this bitterly disputed region. It seemed that the Cold War had suddenly entered a dangerous new phase in which one of the contenders was willing to employ force even at the risk of starting a nuclear war. In the words of General Bradley, it was now clear "that communism is willing to use arms to gain its ends. This is a fundamental change and it has forced a change in our estimate of the military needs of the United States."[8]

Jolted by this new day of infamy, Truman tried to dam the North Korean flood with American troops rushed in from Japan; he also quickly endorsed NSC/68 and ordered yet another sweeping survey of military preparedness. Some Pentagon officials began to talk of launching a "preventative war" against the Soviet Union.[9] At the very least, army planners saw in the Korean attack additional justification for their plea to rearm the Germans, to which they now wanted to add the Japanese. Writing to the Joint Chiefs of Staff, Secretary of Defense Louis Johnson declared: "Recent developments in the international situation have caused me to reach the conclusion that the rearming of West Germany, in an appropriate manner, is required in order to increase the defensive capabilities of Western Europe."[10]

The State Department, however, was still reluctant to urge German rearmament for fear that it would compromise Western unity at the moment it was needed most. Acheson was not convinced that Korea offered an ominous "analogy" to the situation in Germany.[11] Nor, indeed, was John McCloy. He believed that the Korean attack actually lessened the danger of Soviet action in Central Europe because the Russians would now be focusing on the Far East.[12] Moreover, he and Acheson thought that European integration was not yet sufficiently advanced to restrain a rearmed Germany. Neither statesman would change his mind on this score until mid-July, when severe American losses in Korea generated a new, and stronger, sense of alarm.

THE WEST GERMAN RESPONSE TO THE KOREAN WAR

The outbreak of war in the Far East generated something close to panic in the FRG. McCloy's office was besieged by requests for air tickets to America. Thinking they saw red handwriting already on the wall, a number of Ruhr industrialists placed advertisements in Communist newspapers. Police in North Rhine–Westphalia stopped arresting Communists for fear of being subjected to later retribution.[13]

Other Germans, however, loudly declared their determination to fight to the death against a Communist attack. Charles Thayer, McCloy's aide, recalled that a dozen bureaucrats stormed into his office demanding weapons to shoot invading Communists or, if worst came to worst, themselves. A member of parliament complained that he could not obtain a single grain of cyanide because his colleagues had bought it all up. Kurt Georg Kiesinger, the future chancellor, wanted to establish a "defensive wall" in France, to store weapons and food for a final heroic stand. Adenauer himself requested two hundred automatic pistols to defend the Palais Schaumburg in the event of a "Communist uprising."[14]

The West German press fanned the fires of alarm. Leading newspapers spoke of a "case-study for Germany," "exemplary lesson," and "test run." According to the *Kölnische Rundschau*, Korea represented a "stage in Russian expansionism." The *Münchner Merkur* worried that a Korea-style invasion by the East German Volkspolizei might not elicit a military response from the Western powers because it could be perceived as a "civil war." "We have no desire," said the paper, "to be bolshevized through the back door." It demanded a "security guarantee" from the West that might save Bonn from "a Korean fate."[15]

Only occasionally, however, did German fears about Western resolve lead to calls for the creation of an indigenous security force. The *Münchner Merkur* suggested that the Korean War made it imperative to obtain, in addition to a security guarantee, a "new Wehrmacht." *Die Zeit* linked America's failure adequately to arm the South Koreans with Allied unwillingness to sanction a West German federal police force, adding that it readily understood why "the people in Seoul speak so bitterly about U.S. policy."[16] Yet however bitter they felt, most German publicists preferred stationing additional Allied troops on German soil to putting their own boys on the Cold War front.

Public opinion polls taken in the summer of 1950 showed that the West German people were also making anxious comparisons between Korea and the situation in Central Europe. As late as August, 54 percent believed that if the Soviets attacked, the Western powers would simply abandon the FRG. Another 65 percent thought that the imminence of an invasion meant that there would not be enough time to build up German forces, let alone to wage an effective defense.[17] Thus the Germans' fatalism regarding their destiny was not simply a product of the immediate postwar environment but lasted well into the Cold War era.

The West Germans' angst was hardly eased by pronouncements by their potential "liberators" on the other side of the Elbe. On 20 July, Wilhelm Pieck, president of the GDR, announced that it was time to extend the Communist Party's influence to the Federal Republic, and Otto Grotewohl, GDR minister-president, called for the outright incorporation of West Germany into the GDR. Party Chairman Walter Ulbricht declared on 3 August that Korea proved that "puppet governments" could not expect to maintain themselves; it was now "high time to liquidate the nest of warmongers [in Bonn], just as [was] happening in Korea."[18] Ulbricht added that he hoped to see Bonn's leaders tried by the "People's Court" in Germany before they could be "spirited away to South America" by their protectors.

Well before Ulbricht issued this blustering threat, Adenauer had recovered his equilibrium and begun to assess the implications of the Korean conflict. Unquestionably, it heightened his sense of alarm, for it seemed to confirm his darkest fears regarding Soviet intentions. America's initial retreat and the rapid progress of Communist troops down the Korean peninsula also added substance to his forebodings regarding the "spiritual" deficiencies of the United States Army. Yet he had nowhere to turn but to the Americans and their European allies. Thus his first major action in the wake of the Korean crisis was to demand again that the Western powers state they would regard *any* attack on the FRG as an attack on themselves.[19]

Having delivered this démarche, Adenauer left for his annual vacation in Switzerland. He did so not out of fear that he might face the People's Court but because his various intelligence sources indicated that the Russians and their East German clients were *not* planning an imminent *"Fall-Korea"* in Central Europe. One of these sources was John McCloy. Although McCloy believed that the Volkspolizei represented a "real danger," he assured Adenauer that American military intelligence indicated that there was little likelihood of a Korean-style attack in Europe in the immediate future.[20] Another source was Bonn's own intelligence service, the Friedrich-Wilhelm-Heinz-Dienst. In reports dated 5 and 10 July, Heinz reported that the Volkspolizei was not yet capable of launching an attack. On 23 July, he added that "The [East German] goal of creating an effective military force cannot be achieved before the middle of 1952." Moreover, though the East German forces were being indoctrinated in an "offensive ideology," their personnel, all Wehrmacht veterans, would be hard to "corrupt" with Communism. Indeed, Heinz believed they were "increasingly anti-Communist" and might even be tempted to engage in anti-Soviet "partisan activity."[21]

In early August Adenauer received a more sobering report from his security adviser, Count Schwerin. He reported that Soviet troops in East Germany had recently been supplied with tank and aircraft fuel in quantities that exceeded that needed for normal maneuvers and that "fresh young replacement troops" were arriving. All this suggested that the Soviet army was "in a high state of deployment readiness." His conclusion, nevertheless, was that though these developments should be "taken seriously," they did not give cause for "alarm."[22]

Adenauer seems to have agreed. He did not shorten his vacation or show any other signs of panic. But he certainly understood that the Korean crisis could be exploited to promote rearmament. Thus he ordered Schwerin to carry on exploratory meetings with the American High Commission aimed at gleaning its thinking on security and persuading Washington of the urgent need for action.

In late July and early August, Schwerin and Blankenhorn met several times with McCloy's deputy, General George P. Hays, at his private residence in Bonn-Mehlem. To keep the encounters secret, the Germans entered through the servants' entrance in the rear. This procedure underscored one of the more ludicrous dimensions of rearmament diplomacy: though these meetings had the blessing of their respective governments, they technically violated Allied demilitarization regulations and could have landed the German participants in jail.

Twenty-five years later, Schwerin insisted that Hays entered the negotiations convinced that World War III was about to break out.[23] Minutes kept by Blankenhorn and Schwerin do not bear out this assumption. On 22 July, Hays estimated that it would be twelve to eighteen months before the Soviets could mount an offensive in Europe. But this was no time to rest easily, he said, because the Korean War had created the right "psychological" climate in America and Europe for anti-Communist measures.[24] The rest of the talks focused on what measures might be necessary and politically acceptable in the immediate future. The discussions were more amiable and pragmatic than the often strained negotiations among the diplomats. They reflected a growing bury-the-hatchet mentality among former enemy soldiers, and they presaged the later wide-ranging intermilitary cooperation between American and West German officers in NATO.

Opening the talks, Schwerin said he was most concerned about what steps might be taken to contain the internal chaos attending a Soviet invasion, if it came. Something would surely have to be done about the pro-Communist "fifth column," which would inevitably try to paralyze the government and disrupt communications. Schwerin proposed that Allied intelligence put these groups under close surveillance. Germany's state police forces also needed strengthening, perhaps by organizing "paramilitary reserves" and Einwohnerwehren (Home Guards). Bonn's leaders would be prime targets for assassination so the government might have to move to France or Spain. Finally, it was imperative to have a plan for dealing with one of the key problems always attending "forward defense": the masses of refugees who would clog roads and transport systems. Estimating that there might be eight to ten million of them, Schwerin proposed setting aside certain routes for their use.[25]

Hays did not dispute any of Schwerin's projections, but he offered some refinements. Addressing the refugee problem, he suggested that men capable of fighting should be armed and conveyed to "secure areas." He added that the Americans were planning to train some of their Labor Service Groups for military duty. To Schwerin's objection that these groups had no military value, Hays responded that Washington was willing to replace up to 80 percent of their personnel.

As these meetings progressed, the Germans were emboldened to pursue other aspects of Adenauer's agenda. Blankenhorn relayed the chancellor's concern that the Germans would "lose faith" in the "defensive will" of the Western powers if rearmament did not begin soon. Further procrastination might even "encourage opportunistic tendencies" toward a rapprochement with the Soviets.[26] Here again, the Germans were conjuring up a bogey that they had used after World War I: the danger of "going Communist" if treated too harshly by the West. It was an effective ploy because many Western policy makers were very worried that an unstable or deeply malcontented Germany might indeed "drift to the East."

Of special concern were the Wehrmacht veterans, many of whom were severely alienated from Bonn and the Western powers. Schwerin noted that Adenauer hoped to cultivate better relations with the "Comrades' Associations" that had recently sprung up among the former soldiers. But for Adenauer's effort to be effective, he said, the Allies would have to curtail the war-crimes trials that represented a continuing "defamation" of the Wehrmacht.

These discussions were kept secret not only from the press but also from much of Bonn's political establishment. The only politician outside Adenauer's immediate circle to be kept informed was Kurt Schumacher. He was given regular briefings by Schwerin, who had insisted upon consulting the SPD leadership on national defense. Both Schwerin and Adenauer apparently expected that they could count on Schumacher's support once the urgency of the situation was brought home to him.

As he learned of the meetings' details, however, the Socialist leader reacted much more critically than had been hoped. The notion of establishing "reassembly centers" after a Russian attack appalled him because this would encourage "partisan" warfare and the destruction of Germany. The idea of using the veterans' organizations as the basis for a new army also aroused his "serious misgivings." He argued that many of these groups had fallen under the influence of rightist radicals, which was all the more threatening in light of the Anglo-Americans' apparent willingness to draw on "SS and similar formations" for the new army. As for the plan to create Einwohnerwehren, Schumacher recalled that such groups in the early Weimar era had been "protective organizations of the middle-class parties directed against the Marxists." Did Schwerin want to reintroduce a "Socialist-free police"? That would, he warned, inspire the "strongest resistance from the Social Democratic Party."[27] All in all, Schumacher's comments made it painfully evident that it was not going to be easy to bring the SPD around to German rearmament—at least in the form being unofficially contemplated by Bonn and Washington.

ADENAUER RESUMES THE OFFENSIVE: AUGUST 1950

Returning from the Swiss mountains to resume his rearmament campaign, Adenauer gathered more data on the threat from the East. The information he received, like the earlier situation reports, was somewhat ambiguous, but he chose to present the danger as massive and immediate. This was a case of

"*Zweckpessimismus*"—strategic pessimism calculated to elicit quick political results.[28]

This strategy was evident in the public relations and diplomatic initiatives Adenauer launched in mid-August 1950. On 17 August he granted another key interview to an American newspaper—the *New York Times*—followed by a meeting at the Petersberg with the high commissioners. It was characteristic of Adenauer to hold the interview before the diplomatic meeting; his intention was clearly to reach the American public with a grim critique of Western weakness in the face of the Red menace. He believed that this was a message which McCarthyite America was more than ready to appreciate.

Adenauer told *Times* reporter Jack Raymond that he had information that the Russians were preparing to attack and that only an immediate and convincing "demonstration of Western power and preparedness could forestall Soviet aggression." Moreover, Washington must now "set aside all diplomatic qualms and intervene in the political affairs of Western Europe to bring about the political and social unification [that] the non-Communist countries had been too slow to achieve by themselves." To underscore the urgency of the situation, Adenauer claimed that the German people were rapidly losing their "spirit" because their American protector seemed hopelessly bogged down in Korea. He warned that many Germans fatalistically believed that the Russians would soon take over. This sentiment was strengthened by the "obviously aggressive" intentions of the East German People's Police and by the activities of "Communist rioters" in West Germany, who were "already thumbing their noses at the helpless police." America must respond not only by enlarging its own forces in Germany—Adenauer recommended sending two or three divisions in the next three months—but also by approving "a strong German defense force" capable of warding off "any possible aggression by the Soviet Zone People's Police in the Korean manner." This force would "obviously" have to be armed by the United States, and the timing of its deployment would depend on delivery of necessary weapons from America. Further to justify such an extensive commitment, Adenauer proposed that a timely display of Western resolve might achieve "a complete reorientation of large segments of the peoples of Eastern Germany, Czechoslovakia, Hungary, and other Russian satellites."[29] Here, then, was another statement of Adenauer's *Politik der Stärke* ("Policy of Strength"), the doctrine that a strong, confident, and prosperous FRG would undermine the Soviets' Eastern European empire by making the free West an irresistible magnet to the peoples of the East. Some forty years later, with German reunification and the collapse of Communism, many commentators argued that Adenauer's policy had found its vindication.[30]

In his meeting with the high commissioners, Adenauer emphasized these same points but was somewhat more precise in defining what was needed by way of a "strong German defense force." He asked for permission to start assembling a 150,000-man "volunteer force" that would be armed by the Americans and capable of putting up effective resistance to an attack by the Volkspolizei. To a question from André François-Poncet regarding Germany's long-term security needs, Adenauer replied that he hoped this volunteer force, "with the understanding of France and the assistance of the U.S.," might become the nucleus "for something else"—a military contingent fully integrated into the Western alliance. To start recruiting volunteers immediately, Adenauer asked for access to the Wehrmacht personnel files held by the Allies; these data would allow Bonn to "bring together a significant number of competent people within a few months." He also promised to clear all this with Kurt Schumacher, for whom he claimed to have "the greatest respect."[31]

Content to entertain such requests in private, the high commissioners resented Adenauer's broaching them simultaneously in a prominent newspaper. McCloy in particular was angered by this new attempt to pressure the commission with the weight of American public opinion. Again he instructed the chancellor to show more "restraint," adding that his public comments would hardly make it easier for Washington to bring Paris around to a more positive position on German rearmament.[32]

Adenauer's response was to beat a strategic retreat. In a press conference on 23 August, he displayed an intriguing mixture of self-justification, backpedaling, and continued tenacity of purpose. Referring to his difficulties with the high commissioners, he reminded the reporters that he was obliged to air his concerns about security through the world press because Bonn still had no regular diplomatic representation. The FRG's lack of adequate defenses required urgent attention because the continued imbalance of military forces on the Continent invited aggression from the East. True, the prime responsibility for remedying this situation lay with the Western powers, particularly with the Americans, who had now assumed "a role similar to that of the Romans in ancient times." But the West Germans could not just sit back and say, "Please, dear Americans, pour out your blood and treasure on our behalf!" (The truth was, of course, that many West Germans had no problem whatsoever with this concept.) The specific role the West Germans might play in contributing to the Pax Americana would have to be decided by the Western powers. Adenauer could only say that "under certain conditions" the Germans would be "ready to fulfill [their] assigned tasks." Regarding those "conditions," he cagily suggested that it would be "inappropriate" to present the Allies with a list of quid-pro-quos such as a modification of the Ruhr Agreement or elimination of the Occupation Statute. These, he added, "would come of their own accord." What was required in the immediate context was a strong federal police force, but so far the commission had agreed only to allow expansion of the provincial police by 10,000 men. This meant that an area like South Baden would get a grand total of 250 more police. Meanwhile, the Communists were engaging in a "systematic undermining of the state," and the populace was rapidly losing respect for its impotent government.[33]

Although the commission had identified "internal security" as a domain in which Bonn might become more active, it had not meant to include defense against the "Soviet Zone" in this category. That was an "external security problem" and therefore the responsibility of the Allies. Unofficially, however, McCloy now encouraged the chancellor to refine his federal police concept as a possible counterweight to the Volkspolizei.[34]

Adenauer therefore believed he had a "green light" to proceed with planning a federal police force as a stopgap solution until Bonn could participate fully in NATO. Thus he instructed Blankenhorn and Herbert Dittmann to draw up a new security memo that could be presented to the NATO foreign ministers' meeting in September. He shrouded this initiative in secrecy, informing his own cabinet about it only two days after he had delivered the memo to McCloy, who was just departing for the foreign ministers' meeting in New York.[35]

This document contained little that was fundamentally new, but if offered some intriguing refinements of previous arguments, as well as a revised and even more alarming analysis of the Soviet threat. Moreover, it was submitted in tandem with another memo which for the first time officially linked the security issue with a revision of the Occupation Statute.[36]

The security memo opened by emphasizing the debilitating effects of the Korean War on West German morale. As in his public relations campaign, Adenauer related only the most worrisome information he had received, carefully excluding all caveats that might have allowed for a less alarmist view. When he spoke of Soviet troops being "assembled in their summer maneuver areas," he neglected to add that Heinz expected them to move back to their regular garrisons. He described the Volkspolizei as a "police-army" being trained in military tactics, equipped with heavy tanks, and rapidly building toward a target strength of 300,000 men. Heinz had actually reported that it had about 70,000 men, but *might* reach 250,000 if conscription was introduced.[37] All the indicators, Adenauer insisted, pointed toward "another Korea" in Central Europe in the very near future.

Because the Western powers might not respond militarily to an attack from the Volkspolizei, Adenauer reasserted his demand for a federal police force. Because time was of the essence, he proposed to start recruiting his police *before* taking the matter to the Bundestag. Aware that this might raise some eyebrows, he quickly added that "democratic control" could be assured by a parliamentary watchdog committee, while "international control" could be effected through the Military Security Office of the High Commission.

But he concluded, once again, that these measures were at best stopgap: in the long run the situation could be saved only through a Western European/Atlantic army in which Bonn played an integral part. His memo thus contained the pointed reminder that he "had repeatedly expressed his readiness to contribute a West German contingent to an international West European army," while explicitly rejecting "a national military force."[38]

The full significance of this latest "offer" becomes evident only when connected with the second memo Adenauer sent along to America. This document clarified the conditions under which Bonn might make good on the chancellor's offer of a defense contribution. Adenauer pointed out that the Occupation Statute had been conceived in circumstances that no longer obtained. Since its promulgation, the FRG had "come of age politically and economically" and emerged as a valued "partner" of the Americans and Western Europeans. But if Bonn were to fulfill the weighty "responsibilities" arising from its new status, it must be given the "freedom of action" to justify any "sacrifices" demanded of it. More precisely, the Allies must formally end the state of war between them and Germany; declare that the purpose of the Allied forces stationed in the Federal Republic was "security against external threats"; and replace the existing Occupation Statute with a set of "contractual agreements."[39]

Formal reply from the Western powers would have to await the New York Foreign Ministers' Conference. In the meantime, the High Commission (minus McCloy) met with Adenauer to discuss how the chancellor planned to muster domestic support for his security policy when all the signs pointed to widespread opposition. Adenauer assured the commissioners that he had gotten commitments of support for his federal police proposal from the coalition parties and the SPD.[40]

This was patently untrue, for Schumacher had made clear that he opposed a national police organization. The SPD had also repeatedly rejected a defense contribution under existing political and strategic circumstances. Apparently Adenauer hoped that a stunning success on the diplomatic level would allow him to win acceptance of his policy in the domestic arena. To secure the first goal he needed to convince the Allies that the second posed no problem. This was either political sleight of hand or wishful thinking; perhaps it was a bit of both.

In any case, Adenauer's cards were now on the table: he had established the conditions that would shape the diplomatic debate on rearmament for the next four years. But this debate had never been a purely diplomatic one, confined to Adenauer's men and the Western allies, nor was it likely to become so in the near future. Even as the chancellor was boldly showing his hand in the diplomatic poker game, his critics at home were hotly contesting his assumed right to be the sole German player.

Above all, Kurt Schumacher, who had been briefed on Adenauer's security memos by Schwerin, was not prepared to let this latest initiative go unanswered. On 23 August, the day of Adenauer's press conference, he called a rival conference to denounce Adenauer's policies and to publicize the SPD's alternative reading of Germany's predicament. The chancellor, Schumacher noted, had sought to justify his demand for a federal police force by citing the threat posed by the Volkspolizei. But all this hand-wringing about the Volkspolizei was nothing but "propagandistic twaddle." The East German police were not about to emulate the North Koreans, he insisted. Indeed, the whole "Korean Analogy" made no sense, because the FRG—unlike South Korea— was occupied by three of the most powerful countries in the world. If the Volkspolizei ever invaded, it could do so only with the backing of the Red Army, an eventuality that could hardly be averted by a piddling West German police force.

Schumacher also lambasted the chancellor for playing Germany's "trump card"—rearmament—before securing the necessary concessions from the West. Full sovereignty must not be seen as a reward for rearmament but as its "obvious precondition." Furthermore, if the Western powers eventually requested a defense contribution, they must guarantee that the German forces would not be used to do the alliance's dirty work. The Germans, after all, had lost more of their "national substance" in the recent war than any other Western European people, and they could not be expected to "to bleed away the remainder of their resources for others." Moreover, because the German "Fatherland" included "Middle Germany" (the GDR) and the territories ceded to Poland, sacrifices could be justified only if the West's defense began "east of Germany." In the meantime, any "offer" of forces was unwise because it would give the Western powers an excuse for not sending more troops to Central Europe, where they were needed to push back Communism. "We dare not offer any partial resolutions," he concluded. "We must steer resolutely toward a final solution [of the German problem]."[41] Again, when it came to setting conditions for Bonn's participation in Western defense, the leader of West German socialism was every bit as ambitious as the country's right-wing nationalists.

THE HEINEMANN AFFAIR

Adenauer could hardly have been surprised by Schumacher's attack, but it was otherwise with a bitter challenge from within his own camp: the impassioned and highly publicized protest of Interior Minister Gustav Heinemann, who offered his resignation upon learning that the chancellor had delivered a new security memo to the West.[42] Angrily, Heinemann declared that he could not accept a fait accompli in the policy area for which he was directly responsible. It seemed, then, that the chancellor's penchant for going it alone had again gotten him into trouble.

But there was much more behind Heinemann's gesture than injured amour propre. He had long harbored doubts about Adenauer's foreign policy, especially regarding reunification. Though not a refugee from eastern Germany like Schumacher—he had been mayor of Essen in the Ruhr—Heinemann firmly believed that Bonn's primary goal must be German unity. Indeed, he was the first West German minister to visit the GDR. He had opposed Bonn's joining the Council of Europe because he saw this as a step toward membership in NATO, which he thought would jeopardize chances for reunification. Finally, Heinemann regarded German rearmament in the immediate aftermath of the Third Reich as morally unacceptable. Germans must undergo a long period of spiritual reflection before taking up weapons again for any cause. He did not hold these convictions lightly. A veteran of the anti-Nazi "Confessing Church," he was as prone as Adenauer to cloak his pronouncements in divine authority, but the divinity he invoked was the unbending Lutheran "Word of the Bible," not the more flexible authority of Catholic Realpolitik.

The cabinet session at which Heinemann announced his intention to resign degenerated into a name-calling contest, with the interior minister referring to the chancellor as a dictator and the latter berating Heinemann as a turncoat. And yet Adenauer was not anxious to see his interior minister quit. As president of the Synod of the Evangelical Church of Germany (EKD), Heinemann was an influential figure among Protestants, and his exit would make it all the harder for Adenauer to win this constituency's support for his security policy. Moreover, his protest would hardly help Adenauer persuade the Western powers he had his domestic critics firmly in hand. Finally, the chancellor feared that, once outside the government, Heinemann might expose details of Bonn's security memo, parts of which Adenauer had belatedly read to the cabinet. He therefore swallowed his anger and tried to pacify Heinemann, at the same time pleading with him to remain silent until the conflict could be resolved.[43]

But news of the cabinet crisis quickly reached German newspapers, and Heinemann went out of his way to tell his side of the story. He protested against Adenauer's decision to place the prospective federal police under the Bundeskanzleramt, rather than under his own ministry, as had been originally intended. He also made it known that others in the cabinet, in particular Jakob Kaiser, minister for all-German affairs, were disinclined to yield to the chancellor's "Salaam-principle." Such revelations allowed one newspaper to speak enthusiastically of a "Fronde against Adenauer" that might bring his "authoritarian governmental practices" to an early end.[44]

Such speculation proved premature, to say the least. Adenauer managed to isolate Heinemann within the cabinet, and even Jakob Kaiser soon sided with the chancellor. This pushed Heinemann toward a more radical posture. In a long exposé of his differences with Adenauer, he lambasted the chancellor for pursuing rapid rearmament when what was really needed was the patient development of policies that would unite Germany. Seizing the moral high ground, he declared that he and Adenauer, as "Christian politicians," were duty-bound to ask if it could really be "God's will for Germans to take up arms again so soon after He had struck them from their hands." Remilitarization, he added hyperbolically, was tantamount to "re-Nazification." He informed Adenauer that he would remain in the cabinet only on the condition that he be allowed to take his "own path" on crucial foreign policy issues.[45]

Heinemann's path soon took him into the camp of Martin Niemöller, a noted Protestant theologian and bitter critic of Adenauer. Niemöller was a key contact because he was no ordinary cleric. He had been a decorated submarine captain in World War I and still enjoyed considerable standing among German veterans. In the Third Reich, having become a pastor, Niemöller used his pulpit in Berlin-Dahlem to denounce the Nazis, and he became a charter member of the "Confessing Church," which resulted in his incarceration in a concentration camp. After the war he emerged as a vocal champion of German neutralism, which he saw as the only viable route to reunification. His followers celebrated him as a prophet, while his critics condemned him as the most dangerous Protestant divine since Court Preacher Adolf Stoecker, who had roused the masses with *völkisch* sermons in the 1880s. In short, Niemöller was a compelling but highly problematical ally for the deeply malcontented Heinemann.

In early October, Heinemann promised to share the platform with Niemöller at a Protestant rally protesting the chancellor's policies. Adenauer, who regarded Niemöller as a traitor because of his neutralist stance, ordered Heinemann to cancel his appearance. This he would not do. Exasperated, Adenauer accepted Heinemann's resignation on 10 October. The following day, in a radio address, "The International Situation and Germany," the chancellor declared that Heinemann's policies would jeopardize West Germany's freedom and perpetuate "slavery" in the GDR. "Only those peoples deserve freedom who conquer it anew every day," he intoned, quoting Goethe.[46]

Heinemann's resignation by no means ended the "Heinemann affair." Two days after his departure, the former minister published a lengthy justification that recapitulated all his previous arguments, some of which he had heretofore made only in private. To his religious and political arguments he added the contention that Germany was economically unable to rearm because it was having enough trouble financing the reconstruction of its cities and the settlement of thousands of refugees. He reinforced his call for patience in foreign policy with a line from the Bible: "If thou turn about and remain still, thou will be helped."[47] Apparently God helped only those who did not help themselves.

Heinemann hoped that his open rebellion would find support within the government, but this proved illusory. None of the other cabinet ministers followed his lead, though some of them had their doubts about the speed with which the chancellor was pursuing rearmament. Heinemann's own party, the CDU, quickly closed ranks around Adenauer in the face of this first internal challenge to his rule. The FDP, which certainly harbored plenty of critics of Adenauer's foreign policy, might have been expected to be more sympathetic, but it distrusted Heinemann because he had refused to support its efforts to suspend Allied de-Nazification proceedings.[48] Among the major parties, only the SPD supported his stand, stating that the reasons for his resignation "coincided with the views" of the Social Democrats.[49] In fact, however, they did not coincide exactly, for Heinemann did not share Schumacher's belief in a "forward defense" in Poland. He would eventually join the SPD (after helping found the short-lived Gesamtdeutsche Volkspartei in 1952), but for the time being he stayed in the CDU, hoping to turn the party against the chancellor. His tenacity won him the quiet respect of some of his conservative colleagues, but it also exacerbated his political isolation. It would take him years to climb out of the political wilderness and reach the point where he could be elected federal president in 1969.

If Heinemann found himself politically isolated, he did not fade from the front pages. His resignation became a cause célèbre and brought his heretical views more prominently before the public. Every major newspaper carried accounts of his feud with the chancellor, and many sympathized with his rejection of Adenauer's "dictatorial practices." Others applauded his pro-reunification stance and his determination to build bridges to the GDR. The conservative press, in contrast, generally took Heinemann's resignation as an opportunity to to denounce all hints of neutralism and to reaffirm its faith in Adenauer's foreign policy.[50] Thus the Heinemann affair helped dramatically to polarize the debate over Bonn's political course in the early 1950s.

INTERVENTION OF THE CHURCHES

The Heinemann affair made abundantly clear that rearmament was an agonizing question of conscience for many Germans so it is not surprising that the nation's churches jumped passionately into the debate. In fact, German Catholics and Protestants had not waited for Heinemann's protest to add their voices to the growing chorus of Babel, but his dramatic gesture ultimately made their contribution more urgent and impassioned. In the end, their intervention helped ensure that this seminal debate would not turn simply on questions of military strategy and national security but also on fundamentals of political morality in the post-Hitler era.

Various Catholic spokesmen took an interest in rearmament as soon as it was first mooted—well before Korea. They were then almost unanimous in opposing *any* form of remilitarization. Walter Dirks, a prominent Catholic journalist, condemned Adenauer's *Cleveland Plain Dealer* interview as dangerously premature and irresponsible. "There is a growing sense within the Christian community," Dirks wrote, "that this matter is a serious and heavy question of conscience. It concerns a decision that our people, and perhaps even every individual, can answer only after a thorough investigation of all the ramifications."[51]

The outbreak of the Korean War did not immediately alter Catholic views on rearmament. Although some periodicals saw ominous parallels between Korea and Germany, most urged a greater security commitment from the Western powers rather than a German defense contingent. The Germans, it was argued, should confine themselves to "spiritual rearmament."[52]

By late summer 1950, however, several Catholic publications were swinging around to the chancellor's brand of muscular Christianity. This was partly a response to the deteriorating situation in Korea, partly a result of the intervention of Cardinal Josef Frings, chairman of the Fulda Bishop's Conference. Frings delivered a sermon in July admonishing Christians to be more vigilant in defense of the Christian Commonwealth. Citing a recent papal encyclical, he declared that pacifism in the face of godlessness was nothing but "sentimentality and false humanitarianism," and he urged support for a military defense against the spread of Communism.[53] His call was answered in August by the influential *Bonifatiusbote*, which lamented that the German people had become "all too used to the idea that the Occupation Powers carried the exclusive responsibility for West German security."[54] According to the *Kettler-Wacht*, another influential Catholic paper, war might be terrible, but the fashionable doctrine of "peace at any price" was worse.[55] Even Eugen Kogon, heretofore a bitter opponent of rearmament, now concluded that "peace with freedom" presupposed possession of "armed might." In September, *Mann in der Zeit*, a voice of the hierarchy, dropped its previous antirearmament stance, thus signaling the Catholic establishment's decision to follow Cardinal Frings in what became a highly vocal campaign of support for Adenauer's security policies.[56]

This journalistic volte-face was not simply a function of anti-Communism and hierarchical discipline; it also reflected widespread enthusiasm among German Catholics for the ideal of Western European unity that Adenauer's policies claimed to advance. This was not a sentiment that any leader needed to invent, for it was a direct outgrowth of the postwar revulsion against extreme nationalism.[57] At first, most Catholic publications preferred to see this ideal as a spiritual enterprise that could best be defended by moral and social accomplishments. But ongoing talk of a "European army" forced them to to decide whether military strength might not be a necessary supplement to idealism in securing Western European unity. Most concluded that it was.

As they confronted the rearmament question, Germany's Catholics also faced the threat posed by Heinemann's challenge to the confessional unity of the CDU. Most Catholic spokesmen were appalled by Heinemann's attack on the chancellor, but they knew that a full-fledged Catholic denunciation of the wayward interior minister would alienate Protestants who saw him as their leader in the cabinet. This in turn would exacerbate tensions within the CDU, where Protestants had long felt deprived of adequate influence. Because the catholic hierarchy was dedicated to maintaining the viability of this interconfessional party, most Catholic papers did not revel in Heinemann's departure; instead, they focused their criticism on Niemöller, who stood safely outside the political establishment.[58]

If German Catholics understandably remained aloof from Heinemann, Protestants might have been expected to make his cause their own. He was an important lay official of the EKD, and his views derived from an agonized soul-searching that had preoccupied the German Protestant community as a whole since 1945. Many Protestants (rather more than the Catholics) had emerged from the catastrophe of 1933–45 determined to undertake a "reckoning with the past" and to assess their responsibility for the crimes their country had committed. In the *Stuttgarter Schuldbekenntnis* (Stuttgart Confession) of October 1945, the Provisional Council of the EKD acknowledged the "endless pain" that Germany had caused. Though recognizing that many Protestants had fought in Christ's name against the Nazi regime, the EKD leadership flagellated itself for not "declaring itself more courageously, praying more fervently, believing more strongly, and loving more passionately."[59] Pastor Niemöller's own commentary on this confession was a characteristic mix of defensiveness and anguish over sins of omission: "The crimes of Hitler and his helpers are now being blamed on our nation as a whole, and, in fact, we are all to blame, but not in the sense that we are all murderers, robbers, or sadists, but in the sense that we let these things happen, without doing our utmost for the victims and against the crimes, as we should have done."[60]

The guilt reflected in this self-assessment contributed significantly to the passionate engagement that German Protestants brought to the question of rearmament. Immediately following the war, many Protestants were prepared to accept Germany's defeat and demilitarization as a "verdict of God." At its formal consolidation in July 1948, the EKD admonished Germans to stay clear of any military confrontations spawned by the growing "spirit of hatred" in world politics. "Violence enjoys no blessing, wars lead peoples deeper into bitter degradation, hatred and hopelessness," declared the church leaders. "The world needs love, not violence; it needs peace, not war."[61]

The Protestants' perspective stemmed not only from their agony over the Nazi past but also from their hope of achieving reunification through easing Cold War tensions. No Protestant faction was more committed to this goal than the group of radical neutralists around Niemöller. Following his spiritual mentor, the Swiss theologian Karl Barth, Niemöller denounced Adenauer's rearmament plans as a dangerous intensification of the Cold War. In response to the chancellor's *Cleveland Plain Dealer* interview, Niemöller granted an interview to the *New York Herald Tribune*, stating that he would prefer a Communist Germany to a perpetually divided one, though he hoped a "third way" might be found to bring the country back together. The present West German state, he added, did not reflect the wishes of the German people; it was "a child conceived in the Vatican" and "born in Washington."[62]

Niemöller's comments generated a fierce campaign to discredit him as a Communist sympathizer. He responded by claiming that he had really meant only that Germany would be better off accepting Communism than joining in a superpower conflict that would pit Germans against Germans.[63] Germany's chances of avoiding this fate would be much enhanced if it achieved reunification *before* the Cold War perchance escalated into a hot one. The essence of Niemöller's challenge to his fellow Germans, then, was to place reunification before all other political concerns.

Niemöller gave added substance to this challenge when he held a much publicized meeting in Darmstadt on 30 October 1950 with the SPD leaders Kurt Schumacher, Carlo Schmid, and Adolf Arndt.[64] This meeting was of considerable historical significance, for it signaled an attempt to replace the traditional animosity between Protestants and Socialists with a "revolutionary alliance" pitted against the "restorative" policies of Konrad Adenauer. The chief topic of the gathering was rearmament. The conferees agreed that they must work together to prevent the chancellor from "forcing" the nation to take up arms against its will. To this end they demanded that the government submit its security policies to the people's judgment in new Bundestag elections. Only a newly elected parliament would have the authority to decide whether West Germany should rearm, they argued. New elections could also determine whether Bonn continued its drift into the Western camp or perhaps struck out in new directions toward German unity.[65]

This call for new elections was a challenge not just to Adenauer but also to the more conservative factions in the EKD, who were very uncomfortable with Niemöller's talk of a "third way" in the German question. Although the EKD was committed to reunification, most of its members were also dedicated anti-Communists who did not believe that neutralism was a feasible route to this goal. In this respect they were no different from their Catholic counterparts, with whom they also shared a commitment to maintaining the viability of the CDU.

These reservations alone were enough to prevent the EKD Council from joining in the Niemöller challenge, but their reluctance was reinforced by another factor that was deeply rooted in the Protestant tradition: their embrace of Lutheranism's "Two Kingdom Doctrine," which distinguishes between the kingdom of God and the kingdom of man, demanding in the latter strict obedience to legitimate secular authority. Following this tradition, the conservative Lutheran faction in the EKD chastised Niemöller for "overstepping the limits imposed upon him by his churchly office." Bishop Hanns Lilje, a leader of this faction, made clear that Niemöller's line was only his "private opinion," adding that the church must avoid taking "political" positions and remain true to its "spiritual" vocation.[66] That such a stance was itself political was apparently lost on these church leaders, but this was nothing new. In the Lutheran tradition, as in the German conservative tradition as a whole, only liberal or leftist positions were defined as "political," while rightist or pro-establishment views were typically seen as "unpolitical."

Be that as it may, a modicum of unity was established in the EKD when Heinemann decided to accept an official church resolution declaring rearmament a "personal question" for believers.[67] Yet this attempt to defuse the divisive potential of rearmament by taking it out of the realm of the categorical imperative could not succeed for long: too many Protestants (and indeed too many Catholics) chose to see this issue as *the* fundamental political and moral question facing the German nation. Adenauer might ultimately win over the majority of West Germany's practicing Christians for his security policy, but he would fail to establish a clear "moral consensus" for his decision to rearm the Federal Republic. This failure was one of the most important underlying realities of the entire rearmament debate, and it would haunt the early history of the West German armed forces once they were finally created in the mid-1950s.

A KIND

OF

DECISION   Toward the end of 1950, that annus mirabilis in
postwar diplomacy, the Western Allies decided formally to foster the rearmament of West Germany.
Washington, the prime mover behind this historic
decision, predicted that it would mean an early appearance of Germans on
the Cold War front. But America's optimistic prognosis overlooked the continuing opposition of France, as well as heightened German demands for military equality and full sovereignty. The more America—reluctantly backed
by Britain—sought to appease the Germans, the more France became disen-
chanted with the entire operation. Thus the formal decision to rearm the
FRG did not produce German troops; it merely shifted the terms of the debate from "if" to "how" West Germany might make a military contribution
to the Western alliance. Attempts to answer this question brought the inter-
Allied quarrel over German policy to new levels of acrimony. This should not
be surprising. Details of German rearmament, after all, were not the only
matters at stake here: at issue too were huge questions of Cold War defense
strategy, financial reconstruction, sovereign power (of victors as well as vanquished), and relative place in the postwar pecking order.

THE NEW YORK FOREIGN MINISTERS' CONFERENCE

While the Germans wrestled with the moral and political implications of
rearmament, the Americans, though increasingly accepting the necessity of
this step, continued to argue among themselves over the timing and modalities of putting their erstwhile enemies back into uniform. Essentially, the
Pentagon demanded German rearmament as a price for American reinforcements to Europe, while the State Department still counseled delay on the
grounds that pressure and haste could only weaken NATO. As the Korean
situation deteriorated, however, State's Bureau of German Affairs moved

closer to the Pentagon's position, concluding in July that some steps toward German rearmament were now warranted.[1]

At the same time, State agreed with the Pentagon that NATO's plan for a defense on the Rhine had to be revised toward a more "eastern" posture. As Acheson explained in a Senate hearing, in the existing plan NATO would be "turning over to the Soviet government a tremendous asset, the whole Ruhr, the whole German industrial population; all of German military skill would be immediately in the Soviet camp. That would produce a transfer of power too great to be manageable. We just wouldn't know what to do in that case."[2] Yet even as he adopted this new stance, Acheson continued to fret about what German remilitarization would mean for the European power structure and America's role on the Continent. He wrote Truman on 31 July: "The question was not whether Germany could be brought into the great defensive plan but rather how this could be done without disrupting anything else that we are doing and without putting Germany into a position to act as the balance of power in Europe."[3] He understood that this delicate maneuver would not be easy, but he could hardly have known that the tortuous negotiations would go on for another four years and that the problem of balancing German power would persist long after Bonn was brought safely into the Western fold.

John McCloy's office was also shifting toward German rearmament. When the commissioner arrived in New York for the Foreign Ministers' conference, he told reporters that the Germans "should be allowed to defend themselves, if they wanted to."[4] The last part of this statement was as significant as the first: McCloy and his staff had become keenly aware of German popular resistance to rearmament and were searching for ways to overcome it. The commissioner's legal adviser, Robert Bowie, began advocating a "European army" in the belief that this might make rearmament more palatable to the Germans, as well as to the French.[5] Everyone would feel a lot safer, he reasoned, if German soldiers operated within the strict confines of a supranational force.

The Joint Chiefs of Staff (JCS), however, had little use for the "European army" concept. For them, traditional nationalism remained the heart of national defense, and they believed that the new "European enthusiasm" was not a viable fundament for security policy. Moreover, they were convinced that the European army scheme posed such formidable problems of military organization that it could only delay getting the Germans to the front. Their recommendation was "the immediate entry of German ground forces into NATO on a national basis."[6]

The question of timing, in fact, was becoming crucial in the American discussion, as more and more politicians were insisting that the Germans do something for their own defense. In August Senator Kenneth Wherry, a Mc-Carthyite zealot, lambasted Acheson for "obstructing" a German defense contribution that alone might "save Europe from Communism."[7] Feeling the political heat, Truman demanded that State and the Pentagon resolve their differences on American reinforcements and German rearmament. He made clear that he wanted some means to use West German forces because without them there could be no "defense in depth" in Europe.[8]

By early September an agreement was hammered out that represented a clear victory for the military. It involved a "single package" that tied together American reinforcements, a unified command under an American supreme commander, financial aid to Europe, and German rearmament. Though employing the term "European Defense Force," the package actually envisaged a more traditional alliance because integration of the national contingents would occur only at the top levels of command. The national contingents would be organized in divisions, of which the Germans would be asked to provide from ten to twelve.[9] Even while accepting this package, State worried that America's NATO allies would be up in arms over the American position.

This fear was certainly justified. Though conceding that *some* German security contribution was necessary, Britain preferred to see it in the form of a centralized police force, along with a militarization of the Labor Service Groups.[10] Full-scale German rearmament, insisted Attlee, should be contemplated only within the context of the entire defensive structure of Europe. He meant that the existing NATO powers should be strengthened *before* Germany was allowed to field an army. Meanwhile, in a House of Commons debate on the eve of the New York meeting, various Labour Party MPs expressed fears of a revival of German militarism. Bevin fully shared these fears, as well as the conviction that neither France nor the German people would tolerate German rearmament per se. Upon his arrival in New York, he declared that "a revived German military" was not the best way "for Germany to come back as a great power."[11]

If the British worried about the technicalities of German rearmament, the French remained determined to block it, or at least to postpone it for as long as possible. Thus on 1 August the French High Commission declared that West German rearmament was "unthinkable" before the "victims of Germany's aggression" could themselves adequately rearm—an achievement, it was quick to add, that would probably make it unnecessary to rearm Germany at all. If, in the meantime, the Germans insisted upon playing a role in European defense, they should do so with their economy, rather than with soldiers. With respect to Germany's internal security, France was prepared to see the *Länder* police strengthened but insisted they remain decentralized so that "no German general of the old school like Seeckt could use them for aggressive purposes."[12]

Aware that the Europeans were not going to like what Washington would propose in New York, Acheson wanted to give them advance warning but was unable to do so until four days before the conference was to begin. When notice of the American plan reached Paris and London, Bevin was already at sea and Schuman was on the point of departure. Hearing the news, neither was entirely surprised, for rumors of Washington's intentions had been circulating for days. The French, nevertheless, were particularly distraught. Defense Minister Jules Moch, a bitter opponent of German rearmament, later insisted that Acheson's announcement hit Paris "like a bomb."[13]

Once the New York conference got under way on 12 September, Acheson did his best to reduce the bomb to a firecracker. Arguing that no "really valid plan for the defense of Western Europe" could leave out West Germany, he quickly added that including Bonn would present "various difficulties," such as "how we should handle" the new allies. The American solution, he explained, involved drawing on German manpower while denying Bonn any possibility of using these forces independently. "It was envisaged," he said revealingly, "that the German Government should recruit, pay, promote, etc., its units, but that these units would be dependent upon ordnance supplies from sources external to Germany and would not be organized with a German commander nor high ranking officers. These German contingents would have no existence apart from the forces for freedom." Aware that such reassurances might not be enough to secure European approval of the American initiative, Acheson reluctantly combined them with the coercive part of the Pentagon "package"—the threat that Europe would get no more American troops unless it accepted German ones as well. Noting that America was willing to take the unprecedented step of "putting troops in Europe [in peacetime] and joining in a collective force," he warned that this historic venture could not be realized "unless the other powers were prepared to take sufficient steps to make the defense of Europe a success."[14]

Acheson's European colleagues, however, were not prepared to toe the American line. Bevin doggedly pursued London's federal police option, which he insisted was preferable because it was a measure that the Germans themselves had asked for, rather than something the Western powers were asking Bonn to produce. Asking the Germans for anything was ill-advised, he added, because that would "put them in a bargaining position, which would make the situation very difficult."[15] Schuman, for his part, refused to budge from France's categorical rejection of *any* German rearmament. Reinforcing François-Poncet's earlier declaration, he insisted that NATO's limited resources be distributed among the existing Atlantic Pact powers. Only when a "minimum level" of rearmament had been reached, and only *after* a combined NATO Staff and Supreme Command had been established, might France be induced "to consider the German matter on a different basis."[16] As for Bevin's federal police option, Schuman and François-Poncet reiterated Paris's objection that this would give Bonn "a strong instrument of authority over the local governments, which could lead to tyranny." At most, France might accept an arrangement allowing Bonn "supervisory" powers over the *Länder* police in times of emergency.[17]

The American delegation also opposed a centralized police force, which McCloy argued would be "dangerous" because the record of the German police "had been so bad in the past." Acheson proposed instead that a percentage of the *Länder* police should be "available" to the federal government at all times so they could be quickly mobilized to meet an emergency. He hoped this compromise would satisfy the British and French and "go a long way toward meeting the request made by Chancellor Adenauer."[18] The ministers agreed to Acheson's suggestion, turning it over to the high commissioners for refinement.

This was, however, the only progress the conference could claim after its initial sessions. Because of the impasse on German rearmament, Acheson demanded a private meeting at which he could "talk about this question with the gloves off." Describing this session to Truman the next day, he claimed to have "blown out of the water" all the French and British objections to the American plan.[19] Yet if this were so, the conference's first communiqué did not reflect it: it said only that negotiations were "continuing" on the rearmament question. Nevertheless, Acheson was confident that in the NATO Council meetings he would be able to put additional pressure on the British and French by mobilizing the smaller European powers. He was sure, he told the president, that Bevin and Schuman would "become increasingly uncomfortable in their seats."[20]

When the Big Three foreign ministers joined the NATO Council meetings on 15 September, the American secretary found that the Benelux nations were willing to sanction the principle of German rearmament in the interest of shifting NATO's defensive line to the east. Yet, like the British, they wanted this step delayed until after *they* had been effectively rearmed. Recalling the horrors of the German invasion and occupation, they also insisted that the German contingent, once created, must be no larger than their own forces.[21] Their manifold anxieties yielded a strange proposition: creation of a German defense force potent enough to frighten the Soviets but not strong enough to threaten Luxemburg, Belgium, or Holland. (The phrase "deter the Russians but not scare the Belgians" later tripped off the agile tongue of German defense minister Franz Josef Strauss and became a kind of motto for the Bundeswehr.)

Bevin, too, gradually gave way to Acheson's pressure, but when he asked London for permission to change Britain's position, the cabinet dithered. Defense Minister Emanuel Shinwell apparently felt "terrorized" by Acheson's tactics, which he regarded as "plain blackmail."[22] The cabinet as a whole resented the linkage between American aid to Britain and London's stance on German rearmament. Some of Bevin's Foreign Office colleagues also resisted following Washington's line, insisting that America's volte-face was another sign that this was a nation upon which power had been "prematurely thrust."[23]

Yet fume as it might about Washington's tactics, the cabinet soon concluded that it had to support Bevin's request because Britain could not adequately build up its own defenses without American financial help. Thus Attlee instructed Bevin to back the American position "in principle," though also to press for a thorough strengthening of existing allied forces before adding any German troops. In the meantime, to avert "adverse public reaction," the Western powers should avoid generating any "premature publicity" about their intentions.[24]

Of course, the government's change of policy could not long be disguised, and it shocked many Englishmen because it so starkly pointed up Britain's dependence on America. Washington, it seemed, was determined to rub Britain's nose in the subordinate status it occupied in the postwar "special relationship" with America. Even Churchill, though a backer of German rearmament, criticized the government's action as a blow to British national pride.[25]

The Labour Left and the trade unions were indignant over what they regarded as the government's repudiation of the bitter "lessons of the past." The National Union of Furniture Trade Operatives expressed "deep disgust" over this decision, which seemed to overlook "the recent treachery of the Germans and the orgy of destruction and mass murder for which they bear guilt." The Amalgamated Engineering Union condemned the policy as an "outrageous violation of Yalta and Potsdam and a betrayal of the heroic sacrifices made in the last great war."[26] Predictably, Britain's Jewish community was especially outraged. The Union of Jewish Ex-Service Men and Women protested: "It is our view, that the rearming of western Germany, under any pretext, will be a betrayal of those millions of Jews who were destroyed by the Nazis, and that Jewish Ex-Servicemen cannot be a party to the building up once again of those forces which destroyed our brethren."[27]

If, as Acheson feared, some British officials were secretly hoping that the French would prove more resistant to American pressure than they could be, they must have been relieved by Schuman's continuing intransigence. At the NATO Council meeting on 16 September, he insisted that by raising the prospect of rearmament, the powers had made Bonn "difficult to deal with." The best way to handle Germans, he said, was to be "tough" because it was in their nature to bow meekly before strict authority.[28]

Acheson's patience was quickly evaporating. He was struck by the contradictory nature of the French position: Paris wanted an "eastern" defense but was unwilling to accept the German divisions that would make it possible; France did not want to commit more of its own industrial production to defense but also refused to allow the Germans to produce arms of their own. Convinced that Moch was behind all this, Acheson decided to try his "gloves-off" approach on the French defense minister. He asked Ambassador David Bruce to invite Moch to New York, suggesting that he "soften him up" in advance by impressing upon him "the extreme gravity with which continued French unwillingness to concur in a decision of the other eleven NATO members will be viewed in official, congressional, and public opinion here." Though suspicious of Acheson's invitation, Moch decided to come to New York to "clarify to our friends the moral, psychological, and political reasons for our fidelity to the wartime accords guaranteeing the total disarmament of Germany."[29]

On the day before Moch's arrival, Acheson told Truman that he planned to "press the French very hard in private and . . . be as moderate as possible in public." Above all, Paris had to realize that America "could not accept any French position which puts us back to the position of the twenties, when we were adamant in not making any concessions to the Germans who were on our side, and then yielding under pressure to the Germans who were against us." David Bruce offered a different line of attack. Should Schuman and Moch continue to resist reason, they should be flattered into submission. More specifically, Washington should propose to Schuman that he do in the field of European defense what he had so brilliantly done in the area of coal and steel cooperation, where his plan for pooling the productive resources of France and Germany under supranational authority was making good progress. (In 1952, as revised by Jean Monnet, the Schuman Plan would result in the European Coal and Steel Community, which was the cradle of the Common Market and the European Community.) Schuman should be told that "leadership" in Continental security matters ought properly to come from France, the nation with "the greatest European army." If Paris—despite its great army—worried about its security vis-à-vis Germany, it "might advance a proposition as to how German troops could best be bracketed into defense dispositions" without endangering France and other Western European nations. Moch, said Bruce, might be "difficult and dogmatic," but he was also vulnerable to appeals to national pride and "personal vanity." Properly handled, he too might be induced to follow "a course of conduct inspired by us but giving the French government the opportunity to assert Continental leadership."[30]

Acheson must have been impressed with Bruce's appreciation of the French character, for he used this subtle tactic in his subsequent discussions with Schuman and Moch. At least as far as the former was concerned, the strategy seemed to bear fruit. On 26 September, Schuman told Acheson in confidence that he was now considering a personal initiative on German rearmament because France "must not be drug on the end of a chain in this matter." More precisely, he was considering German-French talks on security and a "common Defense Budget between the two nations, with the idea that the other six Ministers in Europe would eventually join him." At the New York conference, however, Schuman pleaded for more time to discuss the problem in the French cabinet and parliament. And he added pointedly that his proposal must not be taken to imply "acceptance of the principle [of rearmament] by the French government."[31]

Upon his arrival in New York, Moch immediately took an obstructionist position, but his hard-line stance began to soften when George Marshall promised that France could expect expanded American support of its own military buildup if it became more cooperative on the German question. Now Moch suggested that there might indeed be a chance of getting a "package agreement from Parliament, including German participation"—but this depended on what else was in the package. It must, he said, "include precise information on what the French can expect from the United States under the aid program and how many and at what date U.S. divisions would arrive in Europe." Later he was more specific as to what was needed to sell German rearmament to the National Assembly. If Washington could help resolve France's financial crisis through subsidies, production assistance, and $100 million worth of raw materials, "then the German problem [would] be much easier to handle." This was to say, in effect, that France could not simply be flattered into accepting the American line; it also had to be bribed.[32]

Despite its apparent vulnerability to financial inducements, Paris still refused to bind itself to the principle of German rearmament. Nonetheless, Washington believed sufficient progress had been made to warrant the reinforcement of American troops on the Continent and the establishment of an integrated command in Europe. The final communiqué from New York included a statement to this effect, along with assurances that Allied forces stationed in Germany were there to "defend the Free World, including the Federal Republic and Berlin." The Allies would regard any attack on West Germany or Berlin as "an attack against themselves." With respect to West Germany's internal security, the foreign ministers agreed to allow the creation of "mobile police forces" based in the *Länder* but available in whole or in part to the Federal Government "as required by the situation." On the political front, Bonn would be entitled to establish a foreign ministry and to "enter into diplomatic relations with foreign countries in all suitable cases." Finally, the powers also agreed to begin the legal process aimed at ending the state of war with Germany.[33]

The section of the communiqué dealing with rearmament stated only that the matter was "now under discussion by the three Occupying Powers [and] the German Federal Government." The NATO Defense Committee had been charged to "make specific recommendations regarding the method by which, from the technical point of view, Germany could make its most useful contribution to the successful implementation of the plan, bearing in mind the unanimous conclusion of the Council that it would not serve the best interests of Europe or of Germany to bring into being a German national army or a German general staff." [34]

On 23 September the high commissioners met with Adenauer to explain the decisions reached in New York. They told him that the Western powers had made every effort to accommodate his requests, insisting that the results constituted a "significant step forward" in the relationship between Germany and the West. McCloy added that the concessions offered by the Allies were designed not simply to protect the Federal Republic from foreign aggression but also to promote German unity. Nevertheless, none of the plans to modify the Occupation Statute could come into effect until Bonn had agreed to assume responsibility for the foreign debts of prewar Germany and to take over part of the costs of the postwar occupation. Moreover, the FRG would have to supply a fair share of the raw materials and industrial products necessary for the security of Europe, and it would have to agree formally to contribute troops to the common defense. At a later meeting McCloy cautioned Adenauer not to place any "political conditions" on military cooperation with the West. The American public, McCloy warned, would be indignant if Bonn "criticized" the raising of troops when the Americans had just committed themselves to defending the Federal Republic and Berlin. [35] The unspoken subtext of McCloy's admonition was that the Germans must know their place and be cooperative, lest their benefactors abandon them to their fate.

Adenauer, like the high commissioners, tried valiantly to put the New York resolutions in the best light. Agreeing that they signaled the beginning of a "new era," he chose to interpret the security guarantee as a pledge to defend the Federal Republic not just against a Soviet invasion but also against aggression from the GDR. But he registered certain misgivings about the powers' apparent expectation that the Germans would happily produce soldiers at the drop of an Allied command. He told McCloy that if countries like France needed to "get used to" the idea of German rearmament, so did Germany because the whole business had come a little too "suddenly." [36] In taking this line, Adenauer was being disingenuous, for of course he himself had done much to bring the rearmament question to the fore. But he was also aware of the profound distress that this issue was producing among his countrymen. Clearly the SPD was not lining up smartly behind his policy, and the Heinemann affair had highlighted the bitter opposition of vocal segments of the EKD. The New York meeting had done nothing to alter these realities. After

Adenauer met with the high commissioners, Niemöller published an open letter accusing him of making "secret deals" to deliver German divisions.[37]

Infuriated, Adenauer went on the radio to warn that such "absurd" accusations could only damage Germany's image abroad. At the same time, however, he admitted that the German people were "very sensitive" about comments by foreign politicians regarding the exploitation of German resources. He wished in particular to caution France, which was apparently ready to ignore Bonn's "goodwill" and to continue viewing its eastern neighbor with an unseemly "distrust." He also insisted that he had told the powers that no steps toward rearmament could be undertaken without approval from the Bundestag, which in turn could act only after a request for troops had been "precisely and officially" issued from the Allies.[38]

By deftly throwing the ball back in the Allied court, Adenauer had turned rearmament diplomacy into a game of "Catch-22": the Allies were hesitant to "ask" Germany for troops for fear of giving Bonn too much leverage; Adenauer, for domestic reasons, needed to receive a formal request from the Allies before making any further "offers" of cooperation. The stage was thus set for a prolonged stalemate.

THE PLEVEN PLAN

In the weeks following the New York conference, the NATO Defense Committee worked diligently on recommendations for Bonn's integration into the defense of Europe. Washington interpreted this integration primarily as military, and its strategic planners accordingly drew up a scheme for the rapid establishment of German divisions. Yet the American plan also sought simultaneously to control the projected German forces by proposing such "safeguards" as Allied supervision of German officer training, restrictions on armaments, and limits on the size of the German contingent. It also forbade Bonn from creating a defense ministry; the Germans would be allowed only a "Federal Agency" to coordinate defense planning under Allied supervision. These controls, the Americans hoped, would be extensive enough to placate the French.[39]

But they were not. Moch, who came to Washington to conduct negotiations on American financial support for France's military, insisted that the Assembly would reject a German rearmament plan based on the American proposals. Before leaving for Washington, he had told Britain's ambassador to France that a German contingent would actually *weaken* Western defenses because two Allied units would be required to watch over each German unit to ensure that it did not "go over to the East Germans." Somewhat contradictorily, Moch added that he "was not prepared to support a crusade for the recovery of Königsberg," which he was sure was every German's fondest wish. But even as he protested, he knew that Schuman and French premier René Pleven did not expect to hold out against American pressure and were searching for a formula that would allow German rearmament without endangering French security.[40]

Pleven and Schuman indeed realized that it was high time for Paris to launch its own plan, but they did so cautiously, knowing that domestic resistance to any German rearmament remained fierce. In early October, two Foreign Ministry officials told Bruce that Schuman was considering "a possible French initiative" that he hoped to present to the cabinet on 18 October. The plan involved creating a "European continental army within the North Atlantic framework," which would include some (unspecified) German components. The program would not be implemented until after the Schuman Coal and Steel Community had been adopted and existing NATO forces were adequately rearmed. The French officials indicated that a "private" American endorsement would greatly facilitate the plan's acceptance by the cabinet.[41]

Washington did not bite. Bruce warned that France's plan would take vital decisions on European defense out of American hands and allow Paris to pursue "purely delaying actions" that would put off German rearmament for many months. Acheson agreed, suggesting that the purpose of Schuman's proposal was to "postpone any resolution of the German problem for many months." He instructed Bruce to tell Schuman that his proposal did not constitute significant "progress." If the French could not accept the American program, they should immediately come up with a "workable" alternative of their own.[42] The subtext here, of course, was that France also had to know its place in the postwar order, or Washington might abandon it as well.

Indeed, Paris now had to follow Washington's marching orders or risk an open break with the United States. The latter option was unacceptable, for France was broke, its government unstable, its foreign and colonial policy in disarray. Pleven and Schuman, moreover, feared that Washington was so intent upon rearming the Germans that it would do so even without French approval. Then Paris would have no control whatsoever over the shape of Bonn's army. Among the most vocal proponents of an activist role for France was Jean Monnet, the leading spirit behind Schuman's Coal and Steel Community project. Using this plan as a model, Monnet and his staff put together a new security package—dubbed the Pleven Plan—that the government hoped would placate the Americans, satisfy the Germans, and win over the Assembly.

In unveiling this plan on 24 October, Pleven promised his anxious countrymen that it would protect French security while allowing Bonn's participation in the defense of Europe. Paris's scheme, indeed, included safeguards for containing the Germans that went well beyond what the Americans had proposed. The national contingents in an envisaged "European army" were to be organized in the "smallest possible units" (battalions) and fully integrated under a "common political and military authority." There was to be a common defense budget and a European defense minister responsible to a European parliament. Most important, these political institutions were to be in place *before* the troops were assembled.[43]

The plan was patently discriminatory against the FRG because it allowed the other European powers to retain their defense ministries and to keep some of their forces outside the European army, while Bonn would have no defense ministry or general staff and would have to place all its troops under European command. Moreover, during an undefined "transition period," West Germany could deploy no air or naval forces. Finally, Bonn would not be a direct partner in NATO because the European army was to be a separate entity linked by treaty to the Atlantic Pact.[44]

In historical perspective, the Pleven Plan recalled the Versailles Treaty's hobbling of the Weimar-era Reichswehr, which had been limited to one hundred thousand men, deprived of offensive weapons, and denied a general staff, war academy, or cadet schools. Upon learning the terms of the Versailles Treaty, General Wilhelm Groener, first quartermaster general of the army, had observed in his diary: "The proposals will be contested all the easier because they are so laughable."[45] Yet onerous as these limits had been, the new restrictions contained in the Pleven Plan went much farther, for they allowed no independent German army or arms production at all, and they wrapped Bonn's prospective military in a tight supranational cocoon. In light of Groener's comment, one had to wonder whether the Pleven Plan might also become the target of mocking derision, and not just from the Germans.

In the meantime, the safeguards proposed in Pleven's plan allowed the premier to win a vote of confidence in the Assembly in October. Yet this was not so much a vote *for* a European army as a vote *against* German rearmament.[46] The victory, moreover, did not come easily. The Communists and Gaullists remained firmly opposed to German rearmament under any terms, as did significant elements of the Socialist Party, who hoped that a last-minute agreement with Russia would make this dreaded step unnecessary. To secure parliamentary endorsement, the government had had to argue that its plan did not envisage German rearmament in the strict sense. As Schuman jesuitically explained: "To arm a country means to make fully available to it—to its government—a national armed force capable of becoming the instrument of its policy. If Germany is prepared to authorize or compel her people to enlist in a European army, that does not mean that she is rearming herself." France, as one commentator aptly noted, had embarked upon a "long, futile attempt to rearm the Germans without rearming Germany."[47]

French officials admitted privately that the Pleven Plan had its problems. An official of the French embassy in London told a British colleague that the plan's "real purpose" was to meet a parliamentary emergency and to throw a wrench in the machinery of German rearmament. He added that it was probably not workable and amounted to "military nonsense."[48]

Secretary of State Acheson was inclined to share this view. Publicly, he called the Pleven Plan a "positive step" toward the integration of Europe, but privately he condemned it as "hopeless."[49] He believed that the new plan, like Schuman's earlier trial balloon, "would raise problems necessitating almost endless delay." He added that since Pleven's proposal seemed "to give Germany permanently second-class status," it "would never be accepted by the German people."[50]

The British responded no more favorably. Having seen an advance draft of Pleven's speech, London's ambassador to Paris cabled that the French plan would undoubtedly cause delays in German rearmament because no units could be raised until the proposed European political institutions were in place. Britain's ambassador to Washington agreed that the project's main purpose was to put off the day when Bonn got an army. Attlee's government announced that it opposed the Pleven Plan on structural grounds as well: the European army would only weaken NATO's coherence and shift its center of gravity away from the Atlantic powers. Moreover, it involved "a substantial relinquishment of national sovereignty," something the British could never accept.[51]

American diplomatic officials in France and Germany reacted more positively to Pleven's initiative. Bruce claimed to see in it "an approach which would do much toward bringing about a closer association among the free nations of Europe."[52] McCloy, though concerned that the scheme might yield unacceptable delays, considered France's proposal to be sincere. He came away from a meeting with French officials prepared to defend the principle of military integration, but he remained skeptical about the plan's details and was unwilling to endorse it without revisions.

NATO's military leaders showed no such ambiguities, condemning the Pleven Plan roundly. Secretary of Defense Marshall confessed that he could not penetrate the "miasma" of the thing, and Chief of Staff Bradley said that he "couldn't believe [his] ears" when told about it.[53] British defense minister Emanuel Shinwell insisted that the plan "would only excite laughter and ridicule" in the Soviet Union.[54] Even some French generals privately agreed that the Pleven Plan was militarily dubious because its integration of national contingents below the divisional level would engender inefficiency if not chaos.[55]

Given the defense experts' reception, it is not surprising that Moch had little success when he pressed for the plan's acceptance at the NATO Defense

Ministers' meeting in late October. Most of the smaller NATO powers joined Washington and London in criticizing the French plan and pushing for the American alternative. Faced with strong opposition to a proposal that he believed already went too far, Moch dug in his heels once again. Although he disputed the contention that Pleven's plan sought a "permanent discrimination against Germany," he said that Paris "would be amply justified" in demanding just that. He went on to insist that for political, psychological, and military reasons, France was obliged to "oppose totally" the creation of German divisions and a German "Federal Agency," which would "inevitably lead to a camouflaged German general staff and [national] German army." He also insisted that France "must say no" to the participation of Germans "in a NATO army." Addressing his American counterpart, Marshall, he expressed his confidence that Washington would not seek to "impose its will" on European countries that were not, after all, "U.S. satellites."[56]

Such talk infuriated Acheson. He instructed Bruce to discuss the "Moch situation" with Pleven to see if he could not be silenced or neutralized. Bruce could report on 4 November that Pleven was willing to "manage" Moch and did not himself "intend to be stubborn on details of the French point of view if he were convinced that any of them were unreasonable or impracticable." A few days later, Bruce reported that the Socialist leader, Guy Mollet, was also anxious for a compromise. Mollet could not help adding, however, that America would be acting inconsistently with its own principles if it rejected Paris's proposal "without careful examination." Washington, after all, had consistently supported the ideal of closer association between the European nations, which was "precisely the goal" of Pleven's plan.[57]

THE SPOFFORD COMPROMISE

Although most American policy makers remained skeptical of the Pleven Plan, they also, like the French, wanted to find a compromise solution to the German problem. Acheson was eager to begin integrating European forces under an American commander and did not want this project to founder because of French resistance to German rearmament. In mid-October he suggested to Marshall that they "leave open the possibility of a reexamination of their position" because any further delay would "not be in the best interests of the United States."[58]

As if to underscore the urgency of a cooperative defense buildup in Europe, on 25 November China poured thousands of its own troops into the Korean War. The subsequent rout of UN forces produced new scenes of panic in Western capitals; President Truman even seemed to be considering using atomic weapons against the Chinese, though this rumor was quickly denied. The upshot was that both the Europeans and the Americans pushed for a quick resolution of their debilitating split over German rearmament.

In an effort to break the deadlock, American negotiators came up with a new proposition that foresaw making brigades the basic units of military integration. German brigades might be put under the Supreme Headquarters Allied Powers Europe (SHAPE) to avoid creating "a purely German agency unpalatable to the French." The political aspects of integration would be put off for later resolution. In mid-November, Charles Spofford, Washington's representative on the North Atlantic Council, refined this idea by suggesting that German units be integrated in the European army at the level of "nationally homogeneous regimental combat teams" (five to six thousand men).[59]

As further elaborated in a NATO White Paper, Spofford's "compromise" provided that if a European defense force could *not* be created, Germany would contribute its troops directly to NATO. Because the JCS favored nationally homogeneous divisions over the smaller "combat teams," the working paper stipulated that these teams could be reorganized on a divisional basis "as soon as SHAPE determines that this is necessary." Under this arrangement, Germany would be allowed a "defensive air force of limited size and a naval force of light craft." Other provisions included limiting German land formations to one-fifth the total of the Allied ground forces allocated to SHAPE. German industrial production would be exploited "to the greatest extent possible," but Bonn would not be allowed to produce heavy military equipment or aircraft. Perhaps most important, German troops would be raised *before* common European political institutions might be created. This would speed the military buildup and also allow the eventual political unification to be accomplished "without the pressure of military urgency."[60]

Though endorsed by the NATO Council, this plan required approval from the various governments to become the basis for further negotiations. The British were willing to go along, though they had severe doubts about a European federal army. As an alternative, Bevin proposed an Atlantic Federal Force integrated into NATO and including the Americans, who could be counted upon both to contain the Germans and to prevent French domination of the Continent. The British Chiefs of Staff, however, had little use either for France's European defense force or Bevin's Atlantic army, which they dismissed as a bad idea designed primarily "to kill the French idea." They would accept the Spofford Compromise as a working arrangement because they felt the "French idea [was] bound in any case to die." The military, combined with most of the cabinet, elected to go with Spofford's plan, and Bevin too came around, though only because he believed it offered "the one hope of getting the integrated force established without delay."[61]

With the Anglo-Americans pushing for the Spofford Compromise, France had to decide how to respond to this new challenge. On 6 December the

French Council of Ministers held what one historian has called "the most dramatic foreign policy debate in the history of the Fourth Republic."[62] Stating that they were now confronted with the "gravest decision that a French government had faced since the war," Guy Mollet pleaded for a rejection of the plan. His Socialist colleague René Mayer countered that a French refusal to accept the Spofford Compromise would mean "the end of the Atlantic Pact" and leave France alone to face Russia and a resurgent Germany. Pleven himself weighed in with a report on his recent visit with Bevin and Attlee, who had strongly advised acceptance. After a full day of acrimonious debate, the council voted to approve the compromise. It did so knowing full well that this signaled France's weakness in the face of American pressure. At the same time, however, the decision brought an American commitment to keep the Germans in check. Acheson had helped to sell the idea through a last-minute letter to Schuman promising American support of a new European order that permanently ended "the threat of German domination."[63] Whether this generous extension of the Pax Americana would be sufficient to reassure the French Assembly and the French people, however, remained to be seen.

THE HIMMEROD MEMORANDUM

While the Western powers were struggling toward a decision on German rearmament, Bonn was beginning to lay the groundwork for its future army. October 1950 saw the drafting of the "Himmerod Memorandum," a document that has justly been called the "magna carta for the Bundeswehr."[64]

The Himmerod Memorandum was drafted by a "Committee of Experts" set up by Schwerin's Zentrale. The committee was dominated by former Wehrmacht officers whose names had been cleared with General Hays and the Bundeskanzleramt. Though supposedly guided by "the primacy of politics," the enterprise was kept highly confidential.[65] Indeed, secrecy was the main reason for holding the sessions in the Himmerod Cloister, a Benedictine abbey hidden away in the Eifel Mountains.

One of the participants later recalled that the conferees were full of doubts about the moral and political acceptability of planning a German defense contribution when some of their former comrades still languished in Western prisons.[66] Thus they argued that German "sacrifices" would be warranted "only when freedom and equality [were] returned to the German people."[67] Much of the memorandum was devoted to spelling out exactly what this implied and how it should be achieved.

In the military area, the Western powers would be expected to grant the German contingent "full equality within the European-Atlantic community." More specifically, Bonn must be allowed to create "nationally homogeneous" units up to corps level and to deploy "tactical air and naval units." Its officers must share fully in the alliance's command structure. "Psychological preconditions" included an Allied declaration that the Germans had acted "honorably" in the last war, along with the release of "alleged 'war criminals' who had acted under orders and in accordance with then-existing German law." Admirals Karl Dönitz and Erich Raeder, who had been found guilty of war crimes by the Nuremberg tribunal and were serving their sentences in Spandau Prison, were explicitly included in this category. Finally, the basis upon which Western troops were stationed in Germany could no longer be one of "control" because this would obviously put the German contingent in a subordinate status; the Western forces would have to be present as "allies."

Regarding the mechanics of raising a defense force, the memo said that German soldiers should swear allegiance to Bonn's president pending the establishment of a common European political entity. To ensure centralized control over the military, all matters relating to federal defense would be handled by Bonn. It urged the government to work with the Socialists and the unions so that "the entire German people" would stand behind the new army. It also called for a "campaign of enlightenment and a concerted attack against divisive elements that threatened the rearmament program."

As to the strategic framework in which the German contingent would operate, the memo demanded an "offensive defense, wherever possible." In addition to a "forward" posture, it advocated "mobile" tactics because the area between the Rhine and the Elbe could not be defended by "static" lines. A mobile approach would also facilitate a "rapid shift of military operations to East German territory." A full-fledged campaign against Russia itself, added the memo modestly, would have to wait until an invading Red Army had been brought to a standstill in eastern Europe, but Anglo-American air attacks on Soviet communications, as well as the use of atomic weapons against targets within the Soviet Union, might begin with the opening of hostilities.

The strategy outlined here presupposed a German military contingent considerably more ambitious in size, scope, and structure than even the Americans had envisaged. The German experts concluded that a minimum of twelve fully equipped tank divisions would be needed by autumn 1952, when the Soviet danger was expected to reach its peak. The tank divisions, grouped within six army corps, represented a manpower commitment of 250,000 men, exclusive of civilian support personnel. In addition to the ground troops, the memo foresaw a deployment of several Luftwaffe squadrons, whose ultimate operational scope would depend on the size of the Allied air forces committed to the defense of Germany. Whatever the extent of that commitment, however, adequate protection of the German tank divisions required the immediate deployment of German fighter squadrons. The Himmerod Memorandum proposed as a "minimum" for this purpose 831 aircraft, consisting of 180 reconnaissance planes, 279 fighter-bombers, and 372 pursuit fighters.

On the naval front, the memo foresaw control of the Baltic as the Western powers' prime strategic necessity. In the event of war, Western forces must be able to disrupt Soviet naval operations through coastal shelling, amphibious landings, and commando raids deep behind Russian lines. The difficulty here was that the Russians had built up an extensive Baltic fleet, but in this area the Western powers were very weak. The British had no ships in the western Baltic, the Swedish navy was "good" but lamentably neutral, the Danes "weak and without war experience." This left, of course, the Germans. "A German naval contingent appears necessary, since it would bring to bear extensive knowledge of the region and of the opponent." Final strength of this contingent would, like that of the air force, depend on the Atlantic powers' naval commitment and the operational role assigned the Germans. The naval experts in the group nonetheless demanded as "minimum" requirements such items as armored landing craft, minesweepers and minelayers, submarines, reconnaissance and fighter aircraft, and torpedo boats.

This ambitious vision of tank divisions, tactical air wings, and a new navy was a far cry from the humble centralized police force mooted by Schwerin a few months earlier. Indeed, Bonn's military consultants were now thinking precociously along the lines of the heavily mechanized "Air-Land" approach that would ultimately become the basis of NATO strategy on the Continent. That such a doctrine was pushed so vigorously by former Wehrmacht officers, however, should not be surprising for in many respects it recalled the highly mobile, coordinated air-land tactics of the German forces on the Eastern front in World War II.

The Himmerod experts knew that any military force, however well equipped, could not be effective without proper training. Realistically, they admitted that training had "not been adequate in the Wehrmacht during the last two years of the war." Moreover, times had changed since 1945; the Allied forces now had new weapons. Thus the German contingent would be extremely dependent on the Allies in the initial phases of its existence. The memo recommended, however, that the Germans try to restrict this dependence to *one* Allied power—the United States (the power with which indeed the later Bundeswehr was to be most intimately associated). Given proper training, said the Himmerod men, the German contingent ought to be able to make up in competence what it lacked in numbers.

"Just as important as technical training is the spiritual education of the soldier." With this unobjectionable phrase, the Himmerod Memorandum introduced a series of propositions involving the shaping of the new army's "inner structure."[68] This was very tricky terrain, for what the Germans called "inner structure" (*Inneres Gefüge*) amounted to nothing less than the dense fabric of customs, traditions, laws, regulations, command ideals, standards of loyalty, and sources of legitimacy that were essential in defining the morale and battle worthiness of a military organization. Not surprisingly, the Himmerod recommendations in this area, as modified over the next few years, became the most publicly controversial aspect of the military planning process. The "inner structure" debates were especially difficult because they involved an attempt to identify those values that might somehow accommodate Germany's changed social-political situation without categorically repudiating its still-prized military traditions. Himmerod's answer was to "strike a balance" between necessary new departures and the retention of earlier practices and forms. The reforms should also accommodate the "justifiable wish for the [reestablishment of] the soldier's traditional position of prestige in German society." Moreover, loyalty to the new "ideas of Europe" would have to be combined with cultivation of a "healthy love for the German Fatherland." Alluding to the Weimar era, the memo warned that the German contingent must not become a "state within the state." At the same time, however, the army must stay "above the parties" and refrain from engaging in day-to-day politics. As we shall see in more detail below, it was one thing to lay out the broad goals of "inner structure" reform, quite another to come up with the specific regulations necessary to make them practicable, and yet another to put the new rules into practice.

Some of the future difficulties were adumbrated in the Himmerod meeting itself. For example, the experts wrestled long and hard over the question of how the common soldier should respond to "unjust" orders. This had special meaning for Germans in light of the Nuremberg verdicts against military men who had claimed the sanctuary of "higher orders." Though some of the Himmerod officers recognized the principle of ethically motivated disobedience (as, in theory, the Nazis had also done), they naturally did not want this ideal to undermine military discipline. Eventually, after much discussion, the experts adopted the following statement as a recommendation: "The right and duty to disobey [unjust orders] can only apply to those cases where the subordinate clearly and decisively recognizes that the order in question represents a crime against humanity, international law, or other military and civilian legal principles." Obviously, this rule of thumb simply begged new questions. What did "clear and decisive" mean and how were these qualities to be recognized? Who defined injustice? Many Germans believed that the postwar trials showed that the only "justice" in war was "victors' justice."

Also with an eye to the recent past, the Himmerod Memorandum proposed introducing civilian judicial procedures for all crimes that did not not involve transgressions against military duty. Punishment of military derelictions must not involve "humiliating" measures that had been typical of the Reichswehr and Wehrmacht. To prevent a return to the old *Kommiss-System*—the unchecked dehumanization and brutalization of soldiers by their superiors—the Himmerod men suggested that the new military might experiment with *Vertrauensmänner* (ombudsmen), who could represent the interests of the common soldiers. Another departure would be to eschew the infamous "Honor Courts" that had played such an unsavory role in German military history, most recently in the Third Reich, where among other acts of political justice they had condemned to death the officers of the Twentieth of July conspiracy.[69]

Recognizing that the new army's success would depend on the quality of the men chosen to lead it during its crucial buildup phase, the Himmerod experts devoted considerable attention to the principles and mechanics of officer selection. Their most important proposal involved the creation of a committee to screen officer candidates on the basis of "their personal behavior in the past." Such a committee might help to reassure domestic critics of rearmament and to improve the "internal coherence" of the new military. But here too the memo added a caveat, warning against the revival of a *Spruchkammer* system that might subject officer candidates to a new "political inquisition." Alas, as we shall see, the approach that was eventually adopted in this domain by no means escaped the charge of political persecution.

One dimension of the future military education program that promised to present particular difficulties was the host of issues raised by a possible war of "Germans against Germans." The Himmerod Memorandum had little to say about how young West Germans might be made to overcome a potential resistance to killing young East Germans. Instead, it proposed that a Western campaign of "persuasion and propaganda" might win over the East without recourse to military measures. The memo's final admonition, therefore, stood in sharp contrast to the gloomy prognostications that had inspired it: "The danger of the East must not be underestimated, but also not emphasized to the point that people give up hope."

If the Himmerod conferees were initially hesitant about their task, they seem to have cast this hesitation aside as their meeting progressed.[70] The document they produced betrayed an unquenchable enthusiasm for the old military profession. These former officers had been asked to state what was necessary to get West Germany armed quickly and efficiently. They had replied by drawing on expertise that, though recently discredited, now seemed back in demand. They believed that their main asset was their knowledge of fighting the Soviets, whose tenacity and courage they respected but whose military skills they considered inferior to their own. Yet their returning pride and confidence made them all the less inclined to cooperate unconditionally with the West. Thus the Himmerod Memorandum constituted a challenge as well as a recommendation; it suggested that getting the Germans back to the front might indeed take more than a simple Allied command.

Count Schwerin, whose office had organized the conference, was somewhat troubled by the document it produced. In a confidential assessment, he accepted most of the conclusions but voiced doubts about the recommendations regarding the "internal reform" of a future German army.[71] He worried that if the new officer corps were to be selected by representatives of the old one—as the Himmerod Memorandum envisaged—the guiding spirit might be restorative rather than reformist. At this point, however, Schwerin's reservations did not count for much; he was not even able to present them to Adenauer in person because the latter was busy preparing for an upcoming CDU congress. In fact, Schwerin got the impression that he was being deliberately "kept away" from the chancellor.[72]

His suspicions were well founded. Adenauer, though originally praising Schwerin as more civilian than military, had concluded that the count was too closely associated with "the old Wehrmacht crowd." Schwerin further undermined his position by violating the confidentiality of his office. On 19 October he discussed recent developments in security policy with several journalists, giving vent to his private opinion that Bonn would eventually be forced to introduce conscription to meet its manpower needs.[73] Though this turned out to be true, it was something that very few Germans wanted to hear five years after the end of World War II.

Horrified by this impolitic act, Adenauer told a CDU gathering on 27 October that Schwerin was not "the appropriate person to deal with problems relating to [German] security."[74] Hans Globke, the chancellor's chief hatchet man, commanded Schwerin to approve a press release that stated: "The chancellor's adviser on security questions has in certain areas transcended his responsibilities. Though Count von Schwerin attributes this to misunderstandings, he has asked the chancellor to be relieved of his duties. The chancellor has accepted this request."[75]

Schwerin was the first, but hardly the last, German military planner to fall victim to the extremely delicate and demanding requirements of the rearmament project. In many ways, moreover, his experience anticipated the thankless lot of Bonn's future defense ministers, from Theodor Blank (the first one) on down to the most recent holders of that office. The defense job became the hottest seat in Bonn because, as Schwerin's story adumbrated, its field of operations embraced commitments and responsibilities about which few Germans were enthusiastic, even if they accepted their necessity. There was also the challenge of finding a modus vivendi between many different and sometimes mutually hostile constituencies. Schwerin had been pulled willy-nilly from the seclusion of his Palais Schaumburg attic into the uncomfortable world of partisan politics and public scrutiny, a condition in which his successors would forever live.

BONN'S RESPONSE TO THE PLEVEN PLAN AND SPOFFORD COMPROMISE

As Count Schwerin was taking his leave, his boss was facing one of the most difficult periods of his long chancellorship. In late 1950 and early 1951, public opinion polls registered only 24 percent approval of Adenauer's foreign policy and widespread dissatisfaction with his plan for a defense contribution.[76] Thus it was increasingly clear to Adenauer that rearmament might become palatable to the German public only if the Western powers made some "generous gestures" toward the FRG. More specifically, he hoped to convince the Allies to abolish the Occupation Statute, curtail industrial dismantling, discontinue war crimes trials and extradition procedures, and commute pending death sentences for Nazi crimes.[77]

Given his hope for Allied grand gestures, it is not surprising that Adenauer was disappointed with the Pleven Plan. When François-Poncet assured him that the French scheme "excluded any discrimination against Germany," Adenauer begged to differ. He criticized "the time-consuming methods proposed for organizing the European Army" and objected that the plan "in certain particulars expressed mistrust of the Federal Republic."[78] Such discrimination, he added, guaranteed that the German people would have "deep reservations" about the plan. He therefore informed the high commissioners privately that the scheme was unacceptable from the German point of view.

Adenauer's concern about public opinion was amply justified. In early November, Hesse, Württemberg-Baden, and Bavaria held Landtag elections resulting in severe losses for the government. Adenauer interpreted these results as a revolt against the discriminatory conditions set down by Paris and as a victory for the neutralist forces around Niemöller and Heinemann. He therefore began to criticize the Pleven Plan, stating in a Bundestag speech on 8 November that it offered only "a basis for further discussion." At the same time, he pointedly called for "equality" and an end to the "confusion" that characterized West Germany's position in the world.[79]

Adenauer's nemesis Kurt Schumacher could afford to be less circumspect in his response to the Pleven Plan. Denouncing it as "the murder of the European idea," Schumacher said it would make the German contingent little more than a "foreign legion." He argued that it made no sense militarily because the integration of units at battalion level was inefficient. Even worse, it would mean that the Germans were giving up their own national interests to serve the Allies. "Nothing could be more foolhardy," he revealingly declared, "than sacrificing the defense of one's own country to the interests of others."[80]

In the midst of its critical dissection of the Pleven Plan, Bonn was obliged to assess another diplomatic grand gesture—one from the USSR. In October, Moscow orchestrated the "Prague Resolution," which called for a United German Constituent Assembly composed equally of delegates from the FRG and GDR. The assembly's purpose should be to create a "sovereign, democratic, and peace-loving" provisional government for a reunited Germany. On 3 November the Soviets demanded the convocation of a Four-Power conference to discuss this initiative.[81]

To Adenauer the Prague Resolution was anathema because it provided representation to a government that was not "freely elected." Even more troubling was the prospect of a "new Potsdam"—another Four-Power conference at which the wartime Allies could decide Germany's fate with little concern about what the Germans themselves might think. Adenauer demanded that the Western powers consult him before replying to the Soviet démarche. He also made clear that he regarded this initiative as nothing more than an "attempt at obstruction" designed to frustrate the consolidation of the Western alliance.[82]

Although the Soviet action may indeed have had this purpose, its immediate effect was further to complicate Adenauer's position at home. Many West Germans, especially in the SPD and the EKD, believed that the Prague Resolution offered at least the basis for fruitful discussion. They saw Adenauer's automatic rejection of it as another indication of his obsession with West integration at the expense of reunification.

If the Russian intervention threatened Adenauer's foreign policy by holding out the tantalizing vision of unity through Great Power negotiation, the Americans did not substantially ease his discomfort with the Spofford Compromise. The proposal did little to reduce the Pleven Plan's discrimination against Germany: in Adenauer's view, it simply allowed for larger groups of German cannon fodder, for "second-class troops."[83] He was also bothered by the plan's restrictions on German weaponry and command positions, which in his mind made no sense. Did anyone really believe that Bonn's defense contingent would invade France? The envisaged limitations showed that the West still refused to trust the Germans. Adenauer therefore rejected the Spofford Compromise more decisively than he had the Pleven Plan, declaring that the Allies must not try to impose rearmament as a "backwards Diktat"—Versailles in reverse.[84]

THE BRUSSELS NATO CONFERENCE

For the French, Bonn's game of hard-to-get was not unwelcome, for it promised to obstruct Washington's efforts to rearm the FRG as rapidly as possible. France held fast to the essence of the Pleven Plan, which made European integration and the European army prerequisites for German rearmament. The French reiterated this position during a series of meetings linking the Spofford Compromise with the Brussels Atlantic Council Conference on 18–19 December. During this period NATO's Military Committee and Council of Deputies agreed on recommendations to present at Brussels that essentially recapitulated the Spofford plan, with the proviso that the new NATO supreme commander might eventually combine the German regimental combat teams into nationally homogeneous divisions.[85] As Washington argued, the priority in strategic planning "must be the production of effective and acceptable military units."[86] This was obviously a sore point for the French, and they made clear that they would have to be consulted before any German divisions appeared.

The American campaign to line up support for the Spofford Compromise was further complicated by the Russians' Prague initiative, which the Soviets followed up with notes warning against a "revival of the Wehrmacht." Acheson dismissed this as a transparent "scare campaign," but it had its effect on European opinion. Bruce noted that the French were now more jittery than ever about "provoking the Soviets." He added that some recent articles by the American columnist Walter Lippmann suggesting that the Russians might launch a "preventive war" to stop German rearmament had fallen on "fertile ground" in Paris. France was therefore "more anxious than ever" to convene a new Four-Power meeting on Germany.[87]

In Acheson's view, the British were not behaving much better than the French. When Attlee visited Washington in early December, the American secretary had difficulty getting him to talk about defense at all. Finally, he had to bring in Truman, Marshall, and Bradley to convince the Briton of the importance of maintaining a united Anglo-American front. Contemplating the upcoming Brussels conference, Acheson insisted that "the only way to make progress with NATO was for our two countries to go ahead and through a judicious combination of bullying and cajolery get the others to follow."[88]

When the NATO foreign ministers met on 18 December, the recent Russian warning was very much on their minds. Acheson described the meetings as "tinged with fear," the delegates constantly asking each other if they thought there would be war. Bevin reverted to his "go slow" stance, and Schuman "kept finding difficulties in the four-power agreements." Acheson, again losing patience, insisted that the NATO powers had to get on with their program and "not be tied up by Yalta or Potsdam—documents outmoded and dead." But they also had to avoid making more concessions to the Germans until the latter had "carried out the New York decisions, acknowledged their debts, and shouldered their proper burdens."[89]

The result of Acheson's cajolery—sweetened by Truman's final approval of the plan to create an integrated force under the command of Eisen-hower—was a two-track agreement on European security. In the first track, the NATO powers would pursue negotiations in Paris designed to produce a European army to which the Germans would contribute their "regimental combat teams"; in the second, the occupation powers would carry on parallel talks with the Germans in Bonn on the political and military details of their contribution.

Even as they were made, the Brussels decisions came under sharp criticism. The decision to restrict the German contingent to regimental combat teams struck many defense experts as a sacrifice of military effectiveness to political expediency.[90] Even some of the diplomats thought it made little military sense. As Kirkpatrick put it: "We registered [at Brussels] a very meagre de-gree of progress in the sense that the French agreed to German rearmament provided the German units were kept so small as to have no military value." Two junior members of Kirkpatrick's staff were moved to compose the fol-lowing ditty, which they sang at diplomatic parties to the tune of *Hark! The Herald Angels Sing*:

Hark! the Foreign Ministers sing
A German Army in the Spring
Peace on earth and goosestep mild
Sturmbannführers reconciled.
Joyful all you Germans rise
Join the peace of your allies!

Hark! The Foreign Ministers say
The Statute's out of date today.
As equal partners we must sign
A contract on the dotted line.
Nur mit Gleichberechtigung
Can we have your Verteidigung.

But you can't have everything,
Every contract has its sting,
Just in case the Bundesmensch
Might turn round to fight the French
We will keep your units small
So they'll be no good at all.[91]

There were other inconsistencies as well. The Americans saw the Brussels agreements as the go-ahead for active German rearmament planning. The French, clinging to their Pleven Plan, regarded them as an opportunity for further delays. To Paris, the whole arrangement was something like a "hunting license" enabling the hunters to nose about in the woods without actually bagging any game.[92] For the Germans, too, the Brussels agreements provided a hunting permit—but in their case the "game" was those additional political concessions that all the Western powers were so anxious to avoid.

Indeed, the Brussels agreements pointed up more starkly than ever the essential contradiction in Allied policy toward Germany. Eisenhower had betrayed this contradiction on the eve of the conference when he said that the Germans were the "crux" of the NATO buildup but also that they should not be allowed to gain a "trading position." Acheson agreed, insisting that Washington "should ease up on saying how important the Germans were" and simply "forget about Adenauer for a while."[93] But the powers could hardly forget about Adenauer and simultaneously negotiate with the Germans about rearmament. They could not talk about the West's "vulnerability" without German troops and expect the Germans not to exploit this situation for their own purposes.

Acheson left Brussels full of hope that the agreements reached there would lead to rapid German rearmament. In fact, however, the dual-track arrangement proposed at this conference opened up a Pandora's box of confusion and multilateral recrimination: not a "step toward European unity," but a revival of traditional nationalist rivalries and suspicions.

2

THE

EUROPEAN

DEFENSE

COMMUNITY

THE ONLY

WAY OUT In the wake of the Brussels Conference, Bonn and
the occupation powers began an exhausting series
of negotiations aimed at rearming the skittish Germans. For Bonn, much of the negotiating was con-
ducted by Adenauer's new security adviser, Theodor Blank. A tough negotiator, Blank pursued the goal of equality particularly assiduously. Bonn also
formalized earlier appeals for a "rehabilitation of the German soldier," which
many officials considered essential to secure the cooperation of the World
War II veterans. Germany's escalating demands, combined with Allied determination to retain strict control, ensured that the Brussels formula did not
produce quick results.

Hopes for a breakthrough surfaced when America, after initially debunking France's plan for a European army, became a zealous advocate of what became known as the European Defense Community (EDC). For a time, the
EDC seemed the fastest way to get the Germans to the front and to solidify
the movement for a "United States of Europe." Although all this turned out
to be illusory, the EDC negotiations were instrumental in laying the groundwork for the later NATO solution.[1] Moreover, even though it was a failure,
the EDC merits close analysis as an intriguing case study in the politics of
European integration in the early 1950s.

THEODOR BLANK AND THE DIENSTSTELLE BLANK

Theodor Blank took up his duties on 25 October 1950. His official title was
deputy to the chancellor for questions relating to the increase of allied troops.
This cumbersome title was meant to reassure the world that Blank's job was
limited to facilitating the Allied buildup, but from the outset he was seen for
what he was: the successor to Schwerin in planning a West German military
contribution to the Atlantic alliance.

Adenauer selected Blank largely because he had concluded that this task
should be entrusted to a man with a civilian background. He also wanted

someone with organizational experience and solid democratic credentials. Blank seemed to fill this bill perfectly. Born into a working-class family in 1905, he learned the craft of cabinetmaking, joined the Christian labor movement, and became secretary of the Zentralverband der christlichen Fabrik- und Transportarbeiter at age twenty-five. During the Third Reich he turned down a position in the Nazi Labor Front. Unemployed, he used his free time to undertake the high school studies necessary for entry to the university. When war broke out, he enlisted in the Wehrmacht and worked his way up to command an antitank company, winning an Iron Cross. Following the war he worked as a carpenter before returning to the revived Christian trade union movement, in which he quickly rose to prominence. This earned him a place in the CDU's delegation to the Frankfurt Wirtschaftsrat, where he established himself as an expert on economic and social questions. He eventually won a seat in the first Bundestag from a district on the northern edge of the Ruhr.

Putting this information together, we can see why Blank was attractive to Adenauer. He was a self-made man with ties to the labor movement but not to the *Socialist* labor movement. He was a good Catholic who hailed from the western part of Germany. He had been a capable officer but not a career military man. He had sound political credentials and parliamentary skills. Most important, he was an Adenauer loyalist, a man the chancellor thought he could count on to take some of the heat in the extremely bitter and divisive debate on rearmament.

Characteristically, Blank understood his job in modest terms. He told a friend that he was setting up something like a "fire department," adding, "No person would think of entrusting control over a city to the fire chief. He is always subordinate to the mayor."[2] In employing this metaphor, however, Blank was perhaps being more accurate than he realized. He would end up fighting many political brush fires, and he would always have to take the blame when they caused damage.

If Blank did not see himself in traditional military terms, he was also convinced that the army he was expected to develop must diverge significantly from past models. It would, he promised, never become a "state within the state," as had the Reichswehr during Weimar. Nor would it become a bastion of the old caste-consciousness typical of the Prussian officer corps. To ensure the triumph of civilian values, he forbade the informal use of military ranks by his subordinates, most of whom were former officers. He also let it be known that as an old union leader he regarded "social progress" as the "best guarantee of peace." As to the "necessary evil" of building a new army, he said that he would have preferred to "wait fifty years before even speaking again about a military in Germany" because there were "many political ruins" to be cleared away before "the superiority of democracy could be firmly established." Lamentably, however, circumstances obliged the Germans to start thinking about preventing a new catastrophe "before they had had time to deal adequately with the one they had just experienced."[3]

Like Schwerin, Blank operated under the immediate supervision of the Bundeskanzleramt. The Bundestag had had no say in his appointment or in the delineation of his duties. Adenauer justified these procedures on the grounds that Allied restrictions prohibited appointing a conventional defense minister. Although technically correct, Adenauer was clearly exploiting this situation to guarantee his exclusive control over Blank's operation.[4] As always, he wanted to keep parliamentary "interference" to a minimum.

Blank's office, informally known as the Dienststelle Blank or Amt Blank, began modestly. Initially staffed by only twenty people (including messengers and stenographers), it set up shop in a Wilhelmine-era barracks in Bonn's Argelandstrasse. The yellow brick building was ringed with barbed wire, suggesting that Blank meant to operate in the tightest security. Indeed, he had few words for the press as he took up his duties.[5]

After demanding letters of resignation from Schwerin's co-workers, Blank retained three members of the former Zentrale—Graf Johann Adolf von Kielmansegg, Axel von dem Bussche-Streithorst, and Joachim Oster. Significantly, all had had ties to the Twentieth of July conspiracy. In retaining them, Blank was attempting to establish a connection with the anti-Hitler resistance legacy, which he saw as a brief moment of light in the dark history of Nazi tyranny. He also thought that Germany's new military could learn something positive from the Twentieth of July example.[6]

In the beginning, the Dienststelle divided its time about evenly between its official task as coordinator of the Allied troop buildup and its unofficial work of planning a German defense force. Over the next two years, however, the former declined in importance while the latter absorbed most of the agency's energies.[7] This was all to the good, for Blank had little influence over the Allied expansion. When the British decided to build a new airbase in North–Rhine Westphalia against protests from local citizens, they neglected to inform Blank, who was then unable to stop the project. It was frustrating, too, that some of the new quarters taken over by Allied troops had been occupied by refugees from the East, whom the powers summarily evicted. Ironically, the Refugee Office was located in the same building as Blank's Dienststelle.[8]

Eventually, Blank's office managed to establish a regular liaison with the High Commission. The initial embarrassments, however, left a residue of ill-will and contributed to the Germans' growing desire to gain a larger role for themselves in the shaping of security policy. Yet the early frustrations also illustrated how difficult this would be because the Allied impulse to make decisions over German heads remained as strong as Bonn's determination to carve out a place for itself.

THE "REHABILITATION" OF THE GERMAN SOLDIER

An important dimension of the Germans' struggle for a modicum of independence involved their campaign to end what they saw as Allied "defamation" of the Wehrmacht. There was nothing new in this: the various German security memos had demanded the release of former Wehrmacht officers convicted of war crimes and had urged Allied leaders to acknowledge the "good behavior" of the German soldier in World War II. Schwerin's Zentrale had gingerly taken up this cause, but Blank was determined to pursue it more assiduously, not least because his agency included veterans like Speidel and Heusinger, for whom this issue was of great importance.[9]

The German officers focused their revisionist efforts on NATO's new commander, Dwight Eisenhower. Ike had gone out of his way to display contempt for his Wehrmacht counterparts during the war. In defiance of traditional military courtesy, he had not received a single captured general, and he had refused to shake hands with General Jürgen von Arnim after the surrender in Tunisia or with General Alfred Jodl at the capitulation ceremony in Rheims. After the war he had defended such "impolite" behavior by categorizing the German officers as "a thoroughly evil bunch of conspirators with whom one couldn't compromise."[10]

Nevertheless, Ike was not a man to hold a grudge or to remain ideologically rigid in the face of changing political realities. Convinced by General Clay of the need to rehabilitate and rebuild Germany, he told reporters in January 1951 that he was ready to let "by-gones be by-gones" and to help the "great German people . . . line up with the rest of the free world."[11] When he met Speidel and Heusinger in the same month, he flashed his famous grin and immediately extended his hand. According to Thayer, "with that one gesture [Ike] liberated at least two of his former opponents from the burden of resentment they carried against him."[12] Ike told the Germans that in 1945 he had been under the impression that "the *Wehrmacht* and the Hitler gang were all the same." Since then, however, he had read a book about Rommel arguing that one "ought to draw a line between the army and the Nazis." Speidel pointed out that his own book, *Invasion 1944*, took the same line. Blank, joining the group, added that *he* had been a Wehrmacht officer, and no one could accuse *him* of being a "militarist." Declaring that he was glad to hear this, Ike added that he had never meant to "challenge the honor of the German soldier, even though some members of the armed forces had committed misdeeds." He then signed a statement in which he admitted that he had been in error about the Wehrmacht. It contained the key sentence: "The German soldier fought bravely and honorably for his homeland."[13]

Though initially pleased with Ike's gesture, the German former generals soon feared that they had gotten too much. This declaration might embolden radical rightists, who would revel in such a far-reaching mea culpa. Thus the version of Ike's statement that was published the following day omitted his admission of faulty judgment and simply said he realized there was a difference between the Wehrmacht and Hitler's henchmen: "I have come to know that there is a real difference between the regular German soldier and officer and Hitler and his criminal group. For my part, I do not believe that the German soldier as such has lost his honor. The fact that certain individuals committed in war dishonorable and despicable acts reflects on the individuals concerned and not on the great majority of German soldiers and officers."[14]

Though this last version was certainly more nuanced than the original declaration (which Speidel and Heusinger circulated privately among former officers), it nevertheless reflected a problematical temptation to which many American policy makers were succumbing: a willingness to substitute one simplistic judgment for another, to replace the old "collective guilt" accusation with a new Wehrmacht legend, according to which the German military was essentially blameless for the criminal deeds of National Socialism. According to such thinking, the brutalities that had occurred during the war were simply to be expected in any hard-fought conflict.[15]

This is not the place for a discussion of the Wehrmacht's role in the German catastrophe, but it should be clear that the story is more complicated than the competing mythologies would suggest. First, the Wehrmacht, as one of the "pillars" of the Third Reich, was absolutely crucial to the Nazi enterprise.[16] As early as the infamous "Blood Purge" of June 1934, the army's top officers had made themselves accomplices in Nazi criminality. Leading generals were quick to embrace the concentration camps as necessary for the "renewal" of Germany. They further compromised their "honor"—what was left of it—in the Blomberg and Fritsch affairs of 1938.[17] Though in World War II some Wehrmacht units may have behaved no more brutally than their adversaries, the army as a whole did not stay aloof from Nazi crimes, especially during the "war of annihilation" on the Eastern front. As extensive research has shown, Wehrmacht units cooperated with the SS and Order Police in murdering political prisoners and Jews. Across the Eastern front, Wehrmacht officials "solved" the logistical problem of holding masses of captured enemy soldiers by shooting, starving, or gassing them. Zyklon B, the poison gas made infamous through its use in the death camps, was first employed against Russian prisoners of war.[18]

Of course, many German veterans chose to ignore or repress these dimensions of their wartime experience, preferring to see the military either as a helpless "tool" of Hitler and his henchmen or even as a haven for "internal refugees" from National Socialism. Such perspectives became firmly established in the 1950s and 1960s and remain influential in some circles today. Certainly, they were evident in the notorious "Bitburg affair" of 1985, which depicted the Waffen-SS and Wehrmacht soldiers as "victims" of National Socialism.[19]

The rehabilitation campaign in the early 1950s did not solve the problem of Wehrmacht "defamation," though Eisenhower's whitewashing gesture pleased many German veterans. There remained the crucial matter of the former German officers still held in Allied prisons or yet to face trial. These alleged "injustices" could not be remedied through an exculpatory declaration by one American general, however influential. After all, German officers were held by *all* the Allies, and neither the British nor the French (not to mention the Soviets) believed that their original judgments needed review.

The Americans, nonetheless, had already begun reviewing the cases under their jurisdiction during the military occupation, and McCloy took over this arduous task when he became high commissioner. In March 1950 he appointed a panel headed by Judge David W. Peck to review roughly one hundred cases, including those of a handful of senior officers. The most agonizing decisions involved fifteen verdicts carrying the death sentence. McCloy's task was not rendered any easier by the extreme pressure placed on him by German leaders. Adenauer himself urged clemency, noting that the Basic Law had abolished the death penalty. Carlo Schmid led a delegation of parliamentarians urging commutation of the death sentences. This was especially urgent, the Germans said, because of the "political and psychological factors at a time when Western Germany was being called upon to make a military contribution to Western defense."[20] To add to the drama, McCloy and his family received death threats from all over Germany. And finally, on the night before he was scheduled to announce his verdicts, his assistant Charles Thayer was visited by "a German friend" from the Dienststelle Blank who insisted that if McCloy did not commute the death sentences, it would be impossible to get the Germans "ever again to bear arms for any cause." Generals Speidel and Heusinger showed up to reinforce this dire warning. To Thayer's protest that some of the prisoners had been found guilty of truly heinous crimes, the generals replied that "higher issues" were at stake. They also reminded the American that justice must be tempered by mercy, which wisdom they buttressed by quotations from Shakespeare, Milton, and the Bible.[21]

In the end, McCloy confirmed five of the fifteen death sentences and commuted the rest to prison terms varying from life to ten years. He reduced the sentences of sixty-four of the other seventy-four cases he reviewed. In many instances he opted for more lenient sentences than Peck's panel had recommended. Despite the Germans' threats regarding rearmament, however, he was not particularly soft on the military men. One prisoner, Speidel's brother Wilhelm, was given a reduced prison term, and the original sentences of

Field Marshal Wilhelm List and Generals Walter Kuntze, Hans Reinhardt, Hermann Reinecke, and Hermann Hoth were confirmed.[22]

Shortly after McCloy's decisions were announced, Thayer's German friend called to tell him that Speidel and Heusinger regarded the verdicts "as the best they could have hoped for under the circumstances." Another former general, however, insisted that McCloy's decisions would "quench the enthusiasm for rearmament among career officers."[23]

Reinforcing this view, Ernst Achenbach, an FDP politician, wrote to McCloy warning that the Landsberg officers whose sentences had not been revised might resort to "collective suicide." If this happened, continued Achenbach, "I imagine it would mean thousands of votes for extremist parties, which otherwise we could channel into a reasonable middle-of-the-road policy." He appealed to McCloy to reduce all the Landsberg sentences by one-half, adding that this would help those former officers "now dealing with the problems of the prospective European Army and German participation in Western defense."[24]

McCloy replied that such a ruling "would not be advantageous, to Germany or to the maintenance of good relations between Germany and the other countries. To apply a method of reduction which would indicate an indifference to the crimes or suggest their inconsequential nature would be the opposite of the effect it is desirable to create." In reply to a clemency appeal from Professor Karl Brandt of Stanford University, McCloy explained that the generals imprisoned in Landsberg were kept there "for a very definite reason"—their compliance with the "Führer order to kill all Jews, gypsies, etc." McCloy said that he looked upon such generals in the same way he did "lawyers and judges who collaborated with the Peoples' Court, and the doctors who carried out medical experiments in concentration camps." All these people, he said, had betrayed their professions; it would do "Germany no harm to know that their generals must be held to a standard of conduct as well as the other professionals."[25]

Yet not all American officials were prepared to enforce such standards against their erstwhile German adversaries. Not long after McCloy's review decisions, General Matthew Ridgway (SACEUR 1952–53) urged the high commissioners to pardon all German officers convicted of war crimes on the Eastern front. He himself, he noted, had recently given orders in Korea "of the kind for which the German generals are sitting in prison." His "honor as a soldier" forced him to insist upon the release of these officers before he could "issue a single command to a German soldier of the European army."[26] Ridgway's stance was emblematic of the growing tendency among Western military men to accept their former adversaries as peers rather than as pariahs.

McCloy himself did not stick to his tough line regarding imprisoned German professionals. He ultimately reduced the sentences or even freed most of the concentration camp doctors and Nazi judges who had been convicted under American jurisdiction. In these and other cases of leniency he was undoubtedly motivated by concern over the domestic political situation in Germany. He worried that a harsh policy would undermine Adenauer's position and benefit the SPD. At the same time, he also knew that blanket pardons would revolt opinion around the world. He hoped that his decisions would be perceived as a balanced compromise. Here he erred grievously. Many Germans felt he had been too draconian, while most in the West thought he had been shockingly soft. Telford Taylor, one of the American prosecutors at Nuremberg, was among his sharpest critics. "Wittingly or not," he wrote, "Mr. McCloy has dealt a blow to the principles of international law and concepts of humanity for which we fought the war."[27]

THE PETERSBERG NEGOTIATIONS

In addition to pursuing the rehabilitation of the German soldier, the Dienststelle Blank took an active role in the international negotiations surrounding West German rearmament. As agreed upon at Brussels, these negotiations took place on two levels. The first series, involving Dienststelle personnel and the deputy high commissioners, opened on 9 January 1951 at the Petersberg near Bonn; their subject was a West German contribution to NATO. The second round began in Paris on 15 February and concerned the creation of a European army based on the Pleven Plan, as modified by the Spofford Compromise.

The existence of two sets of discussions with different guiding principles was a major source of confusion, but it was not the only one. The Germans were not aware of the ground rules for the talks because the powers—in hopes of preventing Bonn from "bargaining"—had not divulged the details of the Brussels compromise. The Americans and British wanted a commitment from Bonn to begin rearmament immediately, followed by a concrete plan of action. Only after receiving this commitment would they reveal to the Germans the parameters within which they would be expected to operate. Yet the Germans were understandably loath to make such a commitment until they knew whether their central demand for political and military equality would be accommodated.[28]

Bonn's preoccupation with equality affected the composition of its delegation to the Petersberg talks. Because the occupation powers were represented by deputy high commissioners with no authority to make binding agreements, Adenauer sent Blank rather than attending the meetings himself.

Here was another indication of the mutual suspicion with which these former enemies faced each other, at least at the diplomatic level. Ostensibly prepared to lay the groundwork for a new military alliance—and a new political "partnership" of free world states—they in fact came together like wary dancers who feared that a close embrace might signal embarrassingly amorous intentions.

For a moment it appeared that they would not come together at all. When the German delegation, consisting of Blank, Speidel, Heusinger, and Kielmansegg, tried to enter the Petersberg complex through the main door, a British sergeant told them that they would have to use the servants' entrance in the rear. Confronted by this symbolic reminder of the very inequality they had come to remedy, Blank and his aides refused to cooperate until they were shown more respect.[29]

In the opening meetings, the deputy high commissioners (Hays for the Americans, John Ward for the British, and Armand Bérard for France) demanded to know how Bonn planned to proceed in establishing a military contingent. Blank and the generals tried to evade answering until they knew what the Allies wanted in terms of size and organizational structure. They were told that these matters were "secret." Eventually, however, the Germans put their cards on the table in the form of a mobilization plan derived from the Himmerod Memorandum—which *they* had kept secret from the Allies. Speidel and Heusinger outlined a timetable featuring three phases ending in the fall of 1952. By that time, given adequate Allied assistance, the Germans could have a 250,000-man force ready for combat. On the all-important question of military organization, they stressed the need for fully operational tank divisions supported by tactical air and coastal defenses. In making this argument, they drew on their unique experience fighting the Russians, as well as on the *U.S. Army Field Manual*, which stated that "the only unit that is organized to act independently is a division." When asked to comment on the notion of combining national "Regimental Combat Teams" in multinational divisions—the Brussels formulation—Speidel replied that this was ill-advised: coordination would be impaired, communication difficult, and there would even be quarrels over food because "the Bavarians would want sauerkraut and beer, the French troops white bread and red wine, the Italians spaghetti and chianti."[30]

Concern with equality and efficiency was also evident in military administration. Blank insisted that Bonn must have a ministry of defense, which was the only option compatible with the FRG's "democratic structure." Though unobjectionable, Blank's argument was disingenuous, for Adenauer had tried (and would continue to try) to circumvent parliament in shaping security policy. Clearly, the chancellor's men were capable of using domestic factors to try to wring concessions from the Allies, just as they used Allied constraints to avoid parliamentary involvement. Nonetheless, the Allies rejected the demands for a defense ministry and an "Inspectorate General" as steps toward a revival of the General Staff.[31]

One area in which the Germans did *not* want equality was in footing the bill for security.[32] Pressed to state how much they might contribute to the costs of their rearmament, they replied that their "social situation" (refugee problems, urban reconstruction, Berlin assistance, and others) "left no funds available for the financing of German contingents."[33] If the Western powers wanted German troops, Bonn's negotiators said, they would have to put up most of the money themselves.

Though the Allies had some sympathy for the FRG's economic difficulties and did not want to see the government destabilized because of financial overcommitments, they were not prepared to give Bonn a complete free ride in this domain. Indeed, the one point upon which the powers could completely agree was that Bonn should help carry the financial burden of European defense. The only question was how much each of the various partners, including Bonn, should ante up. That would have to be settled by financial experts in subsequent negotiations.

When it came to discussing arms and equipment, the Germans revealed another intriguing gambit. Asked what the FRG might contribute, Blank said Bonn could supply clothing and other nonlethal items, but the "production of arms was another matter" because this would undoubtedly alarm the French, with whom Germany wanted to mend fences. Only if France *asked* the Germans to produce arms would they consider doing so.[34] Here again, Blank was being disingenuous, for his agency had concluded that the other European army countries would be unable to equip the multinational force without German help.[35] In fact, General Hays had confided to Blank that Germany would be asked to produce some of its own arms because the current NATO states had exhausted their capacities.[36] Blank was playing coy in this matter so that the Germans could obtain maximum freedom to produce the kinds of arms they wanted.

The technical questions raised by the Germans presented a host of difficulties for the Allied negotiators, who could only take them up with their governments and the NATO Council. But these considerations were not nearly so problematical as Bonn's political demands. Blank listed five "preconditions" for German rearmament, key ones being the transformation of the occupation into an administration based on "contractual agreements" and replacement of the AHC by a "Conference of Ambassadors." The deputy high commissioners were not authorized to bargain on these issues. "As most of [Blank's] pre-conditions are of a political nature and beyond the competence of our committee," wrote Hays, "I am not in a position to comment on whether or not difficulties will be encountered in meeting these pre-conditions."[37]

Nor could Hays and his colleagues contend with the legal objections the Germans raised to waging war under existing political conditions. Blank brought in an expert on international law to argue that since Bonn was not fully sovereign, it did not have the legal "right" to go to war. If it did so, its soldiers could be classed as "guerrillas." Moreover, as violators of the Quadripartite Demilitarization Laws, they might be executed if captured by the Russians.[38] This was simply another way of saying that Bonn could not be expected to contribute troops to the alliance unless it were fully sovereign.

The deputy high commissioners could make no decisions on their own so they summarized their achievements in an interim report. They tried to do so without consulting the German delegation, fearing again that Blank would make trouble. But Blank managed to secure a draft of the report and to correct what he saw as "errors" in its wording. He also managed to include himself among the signers, thus giving the "Petersberg Interim Report" the quality of an agreement (albeit nonbinding) between sovereign states. As for content, the most significant point was an emphasis on the NATO framework for German rearmament. Bonn should contribute its troops directly to the Atlantic alliance. This became known as the "Petersberg Solution."

In evaluating Blank's performance, McCloy commented that the German negotiator "was not above sowing a little dissension between the Allies."[39] This was certainly true, but the Allies made it easy because they still disagreed fundamentally over how the Germans should be rearmed. Given French objections to a German role in NATO and Paris's apparent determination to hold up such an option, Washington and London felt obliged to consider the European army format advanced by Paris. The French, fearing that Washington might still find a way to bring the Germans into NATO, decided to put some life into the European army conference they had been desultorily hosting in Paris. Increasingly, it seemed that this might be the only way out.

THE PARIS EDC CONFERENCE

While the Petersberg talks were still in progress, diplomats and military experts assembled in Paris to discuss France's proposal for a European army. They came together with little enthusiasm, for most of them had serious reservations about the scheme. Many of the smaller European countries sent "observer" delegations, as did Canada, America, and Britain. Bonn dispatched a delegation that was less august than its Petersberg counterpart—a demonstration of Adenauer's preference for the NATO option.[40] It was led by State Secretary Walter Hallstein, but most of the work was done by his assistant, Lieutenant Colonel Ulrich de Maizière, a former General Staff officer who had fought on the Eastern front before serving as army liaison in Hitler's *Führerbunker*. De Maizière was an ideal choice for this post because, as he put it, he had "never lifted a finger against the French." It also helped that he had a French name and a relatively low rank, though Adenauer would have wished it even lower: "Couldn't you have found a major?" he asked Blank.[41] De Maizière was later joined by Kielmansegg and Speidel, who as a former member of Germany's occupation army in Paris was not welcome in the French capital; only by threatening to withdraw Germany's entire delegation could Blank get him accredited. France's reluctant acceptance of Speidel meant that the Germans—under the principle "Haust Du meinen Juden, hause ich deinen Juden"—had to tolerate as a member of the French delegation General Guillaume Widmer, former commander of the occupation of Baden-Baden.[42]

The Germans came to Paris with instructions to pursue the same tough line they had taken at the Petersberg but to avoid being blamed for any breakdowns. They fully expected them, for, as Speidel put it, the French scheme seemed little more than an effort to "torpedo" German rearmament.[43] In the opening phases of the talks, therefore, they vigorously reasserted their demands for full equality and nationally homogeneous divisions.

As the initiator of the European army plan, France might have been expected to stand solidly behind it, but this was not the case. The "Europeans" in the delegation—men such as Robert Schuman and Hervé Alphand—certainly hoped to bring the plan to reality, but many officials at the Quai d'Orsay opposed it as a dangerous dilution of national sovereignty.[44] The leadership of the French army also had its doubts. Though the French General Staff remained committed to German rearmament, it wanted this accomplished in a way that would not undermine the French army's cohesion or dominant position on the Continent. They believed that the European army threatened to do both. The top French generals therefore preferred the NATO solution.[45]

Of course, no solution was possible without consent of the Assembly, which, to say the least, also had its skeptics. The Gaullists and the Communists uniformly opposed the European army; the Socialists were divided. With elections impending, all politicians had their eye on popular opinion, and polls showed that the public was increasingly hostile to the project.[46]

France's neighbor, Italy, harbored more enthusiasm for the plan; Prime Minister Alcide De Gasperi, after all, was one of the great "Europeans" of the era. At the Brussels NATO meeting in December, Italy's chief delegate, Count Carlo Sforza, had advocated a unified Europe as the best means of containing Germany's "tremendous productive capacity and powers of initiative."[47] Italy, however, was financially dependent on America and inclined to support Washington's demand that a European army be firmly integrated into NATO. Above all, Rome wanted to prevent an Anglo-Saxon exodus that would leave Italy and the smaller NATO nations to contend with a Franco-German struggle for Continental hegemony.

Holland, which (until October) confined itself to observer status at Paris, shared Italy's fears that a Continental army, unless closely tied to NATO, might alienate the Anglo-Saxons and entangle Holland "in the French net."[48] Moreover, the Dutch, despite their loss of Indonesia, retained interests overseas that might be undermined by a strictly European focus. Holland's leaders had come to accept German rearmament as a means of enhancing Dutch security, but they regarded the Pleven Plan as a poor way to achieve this because it was unlikely to win Bonn's approval and might even "promote German neutralism."[49] Moreover, the Dutch General Staff saw the European army as a threat to Holland's own rearmament, which was heavily dependent on American assistance. Thus, instead of the Pleven Plan, the Dutch delegation pushed for the Petersberg/NATO solution. Interestingly, it added to this option some homegrown military wisdom: if attacked, Germany should follow the Dutch example and flood its lands. When General Speidel expressed astonishment at this idea, a Dutch officer assured him that Holland could supply the "experts" to do it and that northern Germany's canal system offered ideal opportunities for mass inundation.[50]

While Holland had its doubts regarding the European army, Britain treated this scheme with as much respect as it usually mustered for French innovations. When he first heard of it, Bevin dismissed the plan as "a manoeuvre in French domestic politics," and the cabinet condemned it as "unworkable and unsound."[51] Part of the problem was that European unity was not an ideal that generated much enthusiasm in Britain. Or, more precisely, unity was fine for Continentals, but Britain, distrusting any dilution of national sovereignty, was loath to become part of a "new Europe" with supranational institutions. Beyond its inveterate distrust of "Frogs and Wogs," London feared that submerging Britain's interests in Europeanism might undercut her imperial commitments and further compromise her status as a world power. Tories shared these concerns with right-wingers in the Labour Party. Left-wing Labourites, for their part, believed that the postwar European unity movement had fallen into the hands of reactionaries bent on using it as a cover for their crusade against socioeconomic reform.[52] (Conversely, thirty-five years later, Margaret Thatcher would reject far-reaching European unity as a cover for an alleged left-wing plot to reverse her dismantling of the welfare state.) Thus it is hardly surprising that Britain adopted a stance of "benevolent neutrality" at Paris. Its delegation made clear that Britain would not oppose the Europeans' efforts to achieve unity in military matters but would refuse to be part of a European army. On the narrower question of West German rearmament, Attlee's government indicated its clear preference for the Americans' NATO solution as the fastest way to get the Germans into uniform and the surest guarantee of a continued (and expanded) American presence on the Continent.[53]

THE AMERICAN REALIGNMENT

As the Paris conference got under way, Washington adopted a wait-and-see posture toward France's plan. In a letter to Schuman, Acheson said that if the Europeans could "work [it] out in a practical manner," it might constitute "a sound basis" for future military and economic strength. But in another letter he made clear that by "practical manner" he did not mean the original Pleven scheme, an "unrealistic and undesirable plan" that had been "hastily conceived without serious military advice." Washington would, he added, judge the Paris conference on the basis of "whether or not it serves to strengthen the North Atlantic community"—in other words, whether it could rapidly generate a German defense contribution.[54]

Acheson had good political reasons to push for rapid German rearmament: the congressional Right, especially Senator Joseph McCarthy, was accusing him of abetting international Communism by delaying the rearming of West Germany and Franco Spain. On 14 March 1951 McCarthy declared in the Senate that Acheson's "periodic discussions" about measures to counter "the powerful army built up by the Russians in East Germany" were "nothing but talk designed to lull the American people into a false sense of security." "It is absolutely clear," continued the senator, "that there is no way on God's earth to defend the richest prize for which Communist Russia is aiming— the industrial heart of Europe—unless we use the two great wells of anti-communist manpower, West Germany and Spain. The talk of doing otherwise is either the talk of those who know not what they say or the talk of traitors planning a phony defense." And speaking of phony defense, concluded McCarthy, the Pleven Plan was just that: "The Germans are not going to put their platoons and battalions under a communist-infiltrated ground army in France," he cried.[55]

Given these pressures, it is understandable that Washington soon grew impatient with the negotiations, which had become bogged down on several fronts. One of the main problems was that Paris was unprepared to resolve anything until after the Assembly elections, scheduled for 17 June. Another complicating factor was the sheer complexity of the questions requiring resolution. Acheson complained that among the Americans only Bruce and one of

Bruce's aides understood the negotiations, and neither was able to explain them to anyone else.[56]

By late June, after roughly four months of meetings, Acheson cabled Bruce that the time had come for "energetic" American leadership to remove the "deadlock." He had in mind pressure on the French to accept an immediate commencement of German rearmament within the NATO context pending solution of the military, political, and economic issues surrounding the European army plan. Acheson reminded Bruce that Washington had backed the French plan *only* as a "long term approach to the problem of European defense"; in the short run it would be best to proceed on the basis of the Petersberg option.[57]

David Bruce did not agree, and his disagreement inaugurated the most important development in the Paris negotiations: Washington's switch toward solid, even fervent, support for a European army. Bruce strongly warned against any interim German rearmament outside the European army context. Such a move, he insisted, would be a "serious blow to our objectives in Europe," for it would amount to the "recreation of a German national army, something opposed by just about everyone, including the Germans." Moreover, the European army option would actually produce German troops faster than the Petersberg/NATO alternative because it offered the only framework in which France "and perhaps other nations" would accept the necessary concessions to Bonn.[58]

At the time he made this proposal, Bruce could not have known how quickly his advice would be heeded. The key figure in the American realignment was not Bruce's immediate superior, Acheson, but the new Allied supreme commander, Eisenhower. Ike began his tenure as SACEUR in January 1951 with strong doubts about the European army idea. He said that the Pleven Plan would be "more divisive than unifying in its effect" because it included "every kind of obstacle, difficulty and fantastic notion that misguided humans could put together in one package."[59] In early March he told Cyrus Sulzberger of the *New York Times* that the European army was like "putting the cart before the horse" because it represented a political entity that did not yet exist.[60]

Then, however, Eisenhower began discussing European military integration with several European army partisans, including Bruce, Jean Monnet, and McCloy (who had been converted to the idea by Monnet). Of these, McCloy was the most important, for he was an old and trusted friend who had the ability "to make the people he dealt with feel each idea [he advanced] was their own."[61] Under the influence of McCloy and the other men, Ike not only dropped his objections to the European army (which diplomats now began calling the European Defense Community—EDC), but very quickly emerged as a veritable missionary for the concept of European unity.

Eisenhower's passionate conversion to the ideals of Europeanism was evident in a speech he delivered in London on 3 July 1951. Here he declared that unity would bring the Europeans "miracles for the common good," as well as military security. Given these advantages, he said, the goal of a European federation should not be pursued "by slow infiltration" but "by direct and decisive assault, with all available means." Elsewhere he explained that a quick, total assault made sense because Europe was like a sick person, and when one went to the hospital for surgery the doctor "didn't operate ten per cent each time."[62] As a timetable for the completion of European unification, Ike suggested six months, or perhaps a year.

It has been suggested that these astonishing declarations were typical of Eisenhower's lack of sophistication regarding the complexities of European affairs.[63] There may be some truth to this, but Ike's conversion to the EDC was also rooted in considerations that were not idealistic or naive. His own extensive experience as commander of a coalition army in World War II led Ike to believe that a multinational force was feasible. His conversations with Monnet and McCloy convinced him that the EDC would provide the fastest route to German rearmament.[64] Finally, and most important, his conversion sprang from a conviction that had deep roots in the American political tradition: the belief that it was not in America's best interest to become "permanently entangled" in the affairs of Europe or to serve as the world's policeman. Ike came to see the EDC as the most effective means through which the Europeans could become secure enough to allow America to bring its troops home. He hoped that this would not take too long. "If in ten years, all American troops stationed in Europe for national defense purposes have not been returned to the United States, then this whole project will have failed," he declared.[65]

What is notable about this perspective, aside from its optimism, is its irony. While Eisenhower saw the EDC as a means to facilitate a rapid American military exodus from Europe, the Europeans who favored the scheme saw it as a way of guaranteeing a long-term American presence by demonstrating Europe's shared commitment to the defense of the West. Actually, this was on Ike's mind too, but only as a short-term weapon against the isolationist tendencies in the Republican Party. Thus he spent much of his brief tenure as SACEUR trying to promote the Europeans' own defense buildup and their flagging interest in the EDC. Indeed, he told George Marshall that he had shifted his position on the European army because NATO needed "some spectacular accomplishment" to convince the American public that the alliance warranted continued American support.[66]

Eisenhower's promotion of the European army included support for German rearmament on the basis of military equality. But on the political dimensions of the German question, he was considerably more patient and also rather inconsistent. In a somewhat puzzling statement issued on 1 February 1951, he declared that German political equality would have to *precede* the appearance of German soldiers yet also be "eventual and earned."[67] Bonn still had to prove that it deserved to be treated as a political equal. No doubt this insistence derived from Ike's resentment over Bonn's growing determination to exact a "price" for its willingness to contribute to its own defense. At one point, he suggested that all the bickering and bargaining over rearmament had given the Germans the impression that "they can sit there and blackmail us." But *he*, the commander of the armies that had defeated the Reich, was not about to go "on [his] hands and knees" to the Germans. If they, a "conquered nation," did not see that their welfare lay with the free West, he was not going to "beg" them to do so.[68]

Here again, Eisenhower's frustrated protestations pointed up the lingering ambiguities in Western, especially American, policy toward a gradually resurgent Bonn. At one moment, Germany's conquerors were (whatever Ike might claim) almost pleading with their former enemy to help them defend the postwar order; in the next moment, they were complaining that the Germans were getting uppity and proposing that they be taken down a notch or two.

Eisenhower, indeed, was not the only American policy maker to worry that the Germans were becoming arrogant in response to calls for their assistance in European defense. Acheson had become frustrated by Adenauer's punctiliousness about equality. He found it galling that the Germans were setting extensive conditions on their readmission to the community of civilized nations. They should be happy that they were being rehabilitated so soon, he thought. But no one expressed this conviction more forcefully than Assistant High Commissioner Benjamin J. Buttenweiser, an American Jew: "It is obvious," he declared in March 1951, "that after the diabolic occurrences of Germany's Nazi regime, equality in the society of nations is not a status to be automatically accorded to her. It is a standing which she must win in the forum of nations. . . . This can only be achieved if there has been a real and sincere inner purging of the convictions of the German people themselves." To Buttenweiser the fact that no German leader had publicly accepted or supported McCloy's decision not to commute the death sentences of five "mass murderers" raised questions regarding the sincerity of Germany's repentance for the past and the genuineness of its conversion to principles of humanity and justice. He concluded: "This ominous silence of key figures, when they had this opportunity to disavow this black spot on German history, is causing wonder and disappointment abroad, especially in the United States."[69]

Also causing wonder and disappointment was the appearance of unreconstructed nationalists and neo-Nazis in West Germany who not only refused to disavow the "black spot" on German history but did their best to paint it white. At this critical juncture in the rearmament discussion, three prominent former Wehrmacht officers went on record with views that made many people around the world wonder just how "reformed" the postwar Germans really were.

In February 1951, General Hermann (Papa) Ramcke, who had been serving time in a French prison for war crimes, took advantage of a provisional release to flee to West Germany, where he quickly became a celebrity among rightist veterans. (Ramcke's celebrity was buttressed by his association with the glamorous paratroopers, the elite of the Luftwaffe.) He told his former comrades that he had fled France to focus world attention on the "persecution" of German prisoners "at a time when [the West] was trying to harness the military skills of former German soldiers."[70] In another statement, Ramcke said that the veterans' "natural desire to participate in Europe's revival" was being impeded by an "awareness of all the injustices committed against them since 1945." Only when the Wehrmacht was fully rehabilitated and "our brave comrades in Spandau" released would former German soldiers be prepared to "forgive" the Western powers and be ready "to take up once again the cause of European civilization against Asiatic barbarism."[71]

Two months after Ramcke's return to Germany, the highly decorated former officer Otto Ernst Remer led the neo-Nazi Sozialistische Reichspartei (SRP) to a credible showing (11 percent) in the state parliament elections in Lower Saxony. Remer had been one of those zealous young officers who owed his entire career to the Nazis and who had precious little respect for the older officers of the Prussian aristocratic tradition. At the time of the 20 July 1944 assassination attempt against Hitler, Remer, then a major, happened to be commander of the Berlin Guard Battalion. After talking on the telephone to Hitler following the abortive putsch, Remer assisted in the arrest of the conspirators in Berlin. In reward for his services in foiling the coup, he was promoted to colonel and ended the war as a major-general. Now, in his speeches for the SRP, he ritually denounced the resisters as "traitors" whose efforts to "stab their commander in the back" had been one of the blackest moments in German military history.[72] Remer's comments caused understandable anxiety among all those who worried about a possible neo-Nazi revival, but what was especially troubling to many foreign observers was the youthfulness of his party's membership and its popularity among former soldiers.[73]

The third popular former officer to scandalize the world's Germany-watchers at this troubled time was the famous tank general Heinz Guderian. In his widely circulated tract, *Kann Westeuropa verteidigt werden?*, published in late 1950, he lambasted the Western democracies for "falling on Hitler's rear" when he was doing his best to protect Western European civilization from Soviet barbarism. He complained that the Western powers had foolishly chosen to believe that the Soviet regime was "just another democracy," rather than "a tyranny compared to which Hitler's dictatorship had been but a pale reflection." The Western victors had then compounded their error by approving the "robbery" of Germany's eastern territories and the crippling division of what remained. Certainly they should expect no cooperation from Germany, least of all in security matters, until the Reich was reunified and the German territories now in Polish and Russian possession were returned and resettled with Germans. "We are not willing to perpetuate the horrible policies of Yalta and Potsdam," he declared. "Give us our rights and our freedom if you want to see Europe defended!"[74]

No wonder John McCloy, upon returning to Washington briefly in June 1951, encountered a host of uneasy questions from the press about the "new Germany" America seemed so anxious to rearm. How "realistic" in its political thinking was the Federal Republic? he was asked. Could America really expect it "to take a respectable and helpful part in the maintenance of Western Civilization and the preservation of its liberties"? Was it true that nationalism was on the rise? What was the significance of the "recent expression of neo-Nazism in Lower Saxony"? And above all, would there eventually emerge in Germany "a liberal, democratic, tolerant nation," or might the world "have to endure once more from Germany some new political aberration that [would] mark her fundamental unreliability as a world power"?[75] McCloy was relatively optimistic about Bonn's political future, though he proposed that the Western powers would have to watch their prospective new partner very closely.

The cautiousness about Germany expressed by McCloy, Eisenhower, Buttenweiser, and others should serve to remind us that America's conversion to the EDC was a function *both* of a desire to get Germany rearmed *and* of a continuing determination to keep it under firm control until the Germans could prove their "worthiness" for full and unrestricted membership in the community of free nations. America's allies in NATO, especially the French, were determined to emphasize the control side of the rearmament equation. But given Bonn's insistence that the FRG was already reformed and democratized, fully worthy of equal treatment, an Allied decision to rearm West Germany through the EDC would mean that much more bargaining would have to take place before any German soldiers actually appeared on the Cold War front.

THE

POLITICS

OF

EQUALITY

The American reversal on the EDC caused consternation in the FRG. Adenauer saw in the American volte-face a potential derailment of his entire foreign policy. So did Theodor Blank. When McCloy told him that French resistance to the Petersberg option required reorientation in favor of the EDC, he countered that the Pleven Plan was simply "not discussable," and if it were up to him, the Germans would provide no military contingent at all.[1] Of course, this was just bluster. Once the Germans had recovered from their shock, they realized that they had to work within the EDC or risk diplomatic isolation and perhaps abandonment by Washington. Nevertheless, if Bonn had to rearm within the context of a European army, it was determined to help shape that army's design and to stick to its demands for military and political equality. Indeed, it soon discovered ways to turn the proposed EDC solution to its own advantage—to profit from the pressure to which it was being subjected. Such assertiveness was becoming a hallmark of Adenauer's foreign policy and a leitmotiv in Bonn's relations with the West as it slowly emerged from the diplomatic doghouse built by defeat and occupation.

FRANCO-GERMAN STANDOFF

To signal his greater commitment to the European army negotiations, Adenauer sent Blank to Paris to take charge of Bonn's delegation. Blank arrived on 8 July and immediately launched an attack on the discriminatory parts of the Pleven Plan. With American support, he achieved a significant victory: the elimination of a provision forbidding German responsibility for its own troop recruitment. To assuage French fears regarding the possible creation of a "national" German army, Blank suggested that German troops be placed under SHAPE. Although the French reeled from the impact of what they called *La Bombe Blank*, Alphand did not summarily reject the proposal. Instead, he said France would have to "study" the matter.[2] An agreement was eventually reached whereby all EDC members would be responsible for their own recruiting.

This agreement formed part of an "Interim Report" issued on 24 July. Significantly, the report did not contain compromises on other major issues of disagreement between Paris and Bonn, such as the size and organizational structure of the national contingents or the relationship of the EDC to NATO. On the contrary, the report stated—as Blank insisted it must—that these questions "required further discussion." The Paris Conference then stopped holding formal meetings for about three months. During this period small delegations remained to work on various technical details of the EDC treaty, while the NATO governments tried to resolve the political, economic, and organizational conflicts left hanging in the Interim Report.

Prospects for progress seemed to be enhanced by a cabinet shuffle in Paris following the Assembly elections in June. Losses by the Section Française de l'Internationale ouvrière (SFIO) allowed Pleven to jettison the nettlesome Moch. At the EDC talks, the atmosphere improved when military experts took over the negotiations. These officers prided themselves on their ability to work together as soldiers across international boundaries. They were not given to haggling over fine points of language, and they were less anxious than their civilian counterparts over questions of domestic politics and public relations. Reflecting this military self-image, France's General Stehlin spoke of the "close cooperation of the soldiers," which he contrasted to the "sterile finessing and diplomatic games" of the professional politicians.[3]

The German and French military experts agreed to "depoliticize" the troublesome level-of-integration dispute by turning it over to SACEUR for adjudication. After some discussion, this agency proposed *groupments de combat* as the basic national building blocks in the European army. Though slightly smaller than the standard division, these units would be operationally self-sufficient and more or less capable of doing everything a division could do. The Germans readily accepted this compromise; so—rather less readily—did the French. No doubt it helped that France had been invaded in 1940 by German *divisions*, not by *groupments de combat*.[4] (Later on, the preoccupation with divisional organization became less acute because with the shift to strategies involving tactical atomic weapons, NATO increasingly made brigades the principal building blocks of its field armies.)

Having given in on the knotty level-of-integration issue, Paris felt justified in asking Bonn for a formal commitment to the EDC, which the Germans had as yet evaded. As recently as early August, Adenauer had proposed beginning rearmament before the EDC was in place. But later that month, the chancellor decided to embrace the European army, telling McCloy that he accepted the plan's principle, though adding that many details needed to be clarified.[5]

By early fall the chancellor was warming to the European army concept. In September he said in an interview that the EDC made more sense than traditional alliances because defending Europe was a "common concern of all the European peoples."[6] He was careful to add, however, that this also required the participation of the United States. Speaking to the Junge Union, Adenauer again praised the EDC but insisted that the FRG could join it "only if we have exactly the same rights and privileges as the other [members]." He also claimed that Bonn's participation would help bring about German reunification because the Soviets would be "ready to talk" once they saw that they could not forcefully expand their empire.[7]

It is hard to know whether he actually believed this last claim, which of course amounted to another version of his *Politik der Stärke*. In all likelihood, he did not really expect the Soviets simply to hand the GDR over to the West because they had no ready prospects of colonizing the FRG. Reunification was not a priority of his foreign policy, but it was necessary to keep *saying* that this was the grail for which German diplomacy was ever searching; and it made good political sense to offer it as an eventual reward to the German people for accepting the burdens of rearmament.

Whatever effect it might have had on the East, Adenauer's embrace of the EDC did little to dampen opposition to German rearmament in France. Indeed, the more concessions to the FRG that French negotiators were forced to make, the less most Frenchmen liked the plan. Increasingly, the architects of France's policy began to believe that they were being hoisted by their own petard, drawn by their very efforts to hold Germany down into an arrangement that might at once liberate their former enemy while shackling France in the bonds of supranationalism. Thus when Bonn demanded in August 1951 that the occupation regime be terminated before Bonn fielded any soldiers, Paris replied that no modifications of the Occupation Statute could come into effect until the EDC was established and West Germany was safely integrated within it.[8]

The Western foreign ministers acknowledged the conjunction between German rearmament and the end of the occupation regime at a conference in Washington in mid-September. Accepting the recommendations of a three-power working group, the ministers proposed formal talks between West Germany and the high commissioners on a new "Contractual Agreement" to replace the Occupation Statute. While the ministers stated clearly that Bonn was to be treated as an "equal" partner, they also reaffirmed their rights relating to the maintenance of Allied troops in Germany, the protection of Berlin, and the reunification question. A new relationship would also require the adjudication of various financial matters, including German debt repayment and "burden sharing" in the prospective alliance.[9]

In early fall, Theodor Blank returned to Paris to lead a beefed-up German delegation. His return reflected Adenauer's determination to have a treaty as quickly as possible. To this end, Blank also met informally with his French counterpart, Alphand. In one of their first meetings, Alphand warned (as if this were necessary) that Bonn must not be "taken in by seductive blandishments from the East" aimed at reunification. Blank revealingly replied that Adenauer had to deal cagily with "offers" from the East. He would avoid any agreements that might lead to reunification under conditions of neutrality, but "for psychological reasons" he could not simply refuse to negotiate. Rather, he needed "*to feign flexibility* in order to be free to go with the West." When East Berlin tried to court neutralist sentiment in the FRG, said Blank, Adenauer would make a counteroffer designed to be "too much for Grotewohl [to accept]." At the same time, Bonn would establish "concrete realities," that is, membership in the EDC, that "could not be overturned." But all this needed to be done expeditiously, Blank warned, because domestic support for Adenauer's security policy was precarious. Indeed, he speculated that if national elections were held at the present time, they would probably turn into a plebiscite against the chancellor's *Europapolitik* and bring the government down. Germany's dam against "neutralist" Socialism and militant neo-nationalism would be broken.[10]

Here, then, was a blunt warning to the French: either deal with Adenauer or face a considerably less cooperative chancellor in the future. It was the old Red bogey again, and it had some credibility because West Germany still seemed a shaky place, one that if treated badly by its Western friends might "tip to the East" or perhaps toward some virulent nationalist revival. An American visitor in late 1951 could report hearing widespread dissatisfaction for "that dull fellow Adenauer and the follies of his government," a "government of the Americans and the rich." The observer heard people terrifying themselves with horror visions of the next war, in which Germans would have to fight Germans at the behest of the superpowers; but he also heard hopes that the "Russians and the Americans would kill each other off and leave Germany free to rise again."[11]

Though domestic and international politics argued for expedition in the EDC negotiations, Blank insisted upon raising points requiring resolution before a treaty could be completed. One was Bonn's insistence on a clause obligating member states to come to each other's defense if they were attacked by *any* aggressor—by which Bonn meant to include the Volkspolizei. Blank hastened to add that this contract could be understood as "strictly defensive" so France would be spared "the ugly thought that a French soldier might have to die for Königsberg." When Alphand raised the sensitive question of arms production, Blank replied that a complete exclusion of German arms would make the EDC dangerously dependent on American largesse. He noted that at a recent NATO maneuver he had observed American weapons that "would have been out-of-date in Germany in 1923." (This was a complaint the Germans would make even more forcefully once they started receiving American weapons in the mid-1950s.) The French, in contrast, possessed "the world's greatest artillery." He therefore proposed a Franco-German weapons consortium that would take advantage of the expertise in both countries. Alphand accepted this proposal, suggesting that it offered the best guarantee against the revival of national (German) weapons programs.

If Alphand worried about independent German arms production, he also wished to prevent Bonn's exclusive control over the appointment of its top military officers. Because this was a sensitive "political" matter, he proposed that it be handled by the prospective EDC Commission, which could be counted upon to "act without discrimination against any member country." To illustrate the mutual advantages of this proposition, he noted that it would allow the exclusion not only of "the German general who had been a Nazi" but also of "the French general who had fought with the Spanish Reds." Understandably, Blank responded coolly to this idea. Realizing that Bonn would hardly allow its highest military officers to be selected by an outside agency, he insisted that the appointments be made at the national level, though the EDC Commission might make "suggestions." He added that there were some two thousand former Wehrmacht generals living in the FRG, of which the EDC could use at most thirty. Clearly, Bonn ought be able to find a couple of dozen former generals who had not been Nazis.[12]

While Blank was meeting with Alphand, Speidel, Bonn's representative in the Military Planning Group, was conferring with French generals. In late October he talked with General Clément Blanc, chief of the French General Staff, who (according to Speidel) "declared himself entirely in agreement with the principles of the EDC and ready to cooperate." General Charles Lecheres, chief of staff of the French air force, also indicated his support, adding that he found Bonn's proposals in the plenary sessions very "reasonable."[13]

Yet such sentiments were restricted to the highest levels of the French army. Most of the officer corps remained suspicious of the EDC idea because it sacrificed traditional military sovereignty. Supranationality, after all, would mean that most of the restrictions on Germany would also apply to France. The French were not eager for this kind of "equality." Nor could most officers accept having their army split between units posted to Europe and those that could be sent abroad. France's colonial obligations, moreover, might allow the Germans to become the most powerful contingent in the EDC. Thus, when General Blanc tried to explain "the necessity of the EDC" to some younger officers, he met "an iron silence."[14]

Moreover, although Speidel and Blank may have found some sympathy for the German cause among top French officials, precious little progress had been made on several points of disagreement. The most pressing of these remained Germany's relationship to NATO. Adenauer had long been pushing for immediate German membership in the Atlantic alliance. In the past, Bonn had had American support for this, but at the Paris foreign ministers' conference in November, Washington began to waffle. Fearing immediate German NATO membership might destroy chances for EDC ratification in the French Assembly, Acheson advised Adenauer to show "restraint."[15]

But this was very difficult for Adenauer to do if he wanted the EDC to be ratified at home. He was under considerable domestic pressure to stay firm on questions of equality. Aside from the SPD, the FDP had become especially vocal in pushing the nationalist line. After the turn of the year, the FDP members of Adenauer's cabinet explicitly demanded that West Germany be taken into NATO the moment it joined the EDC.

This demand came at an especially tense moment in the postwar relations between West Germany and France, for on 25 January 1952, Paris issued a new declaration on the Saar that one French general admitted was a victory for the "forever yesterdays" in the Quai d'Orsay who hoped to sabotage the EDC.[16] The declaration, which made the French high commissioner for the Saar an ambassador and established a Saarland diplomatic mission in Paris, was seen in West Germany as a deliberate provocation. Again, the sharpest response came from the FDP, which charged that France "was more preoccupied with its national interests than [was] compatible with the general European welfare."[17] The party demanded that a resolution of the Saar dispute be a precondition for Bonn's participation in the EDC. Even the CDU urged a hard line against Paris in a party meeting on 4 February. Chastened, the chancellor promised the CDU Bundestag delegation that he would not sign an EDC treaty until Germany's positions on the Saar and NATO membership were accommodated.[18]

PARLIAMENTARY DEBATES

As if to underscore these mutual concerns and animosities, the Bundestag and the French Assembly now held major debates on the EDC and contractual agreements. The debates proved a great disappointment to those on both sides of the Rhine who hoped that the wounds of war and occupation had healed sufficiently to allow Franco-German harmony on the pressing questions of European security. Indeed, the very process of discussing these questions in such a public forum inflamed hostilities in both countries.

The Bundestag's *Wehrdebatte* of 7–8 February 1952 was widely recognized as a historic occasion, the most significant debate this body had held since its inception. It was broadcast to the nation, an innovation that encouraged the speakers to display their best oratorical skills and to fight for favorable speaking times. The debate's importance was also underscored by "warning strikes" and public demonstrations. The KPD sent busloads of workers from Hamburg and the Ruhr to protest Bonn's rearmament plans. The police responded by dousing the demonstrators with water cannons. The rearmament question, it seems, launched another trend in West German politics: the tendency to accompany crucial political debates with "extraparliamentary actions."

Adenauer opened the debate with a two-hour disquisition on the status of the EDC and contractual agreements (or "General Treaty") negotiations. After recalling the fate of the "poor defenseless men and women" in eastern Germany during the Soviet advance in 1945, he held up the EDC as the best defense against a repetition of such horrors. He then touched on the two issues that most directly threatened Germany's participation in the proposed security system: the Saar dispute and France's unwillingness to accept Bonn's membership in NATO. French policy in the Saar, he said, was "highly dangerous" and led one to wonder whether Paris was "truly serious" about international cooperation. But he offered no solution here, only the insistence that "true democratic freedoms come some day to the Saar." He was hardly more precise on the NATO question: "For my part, I have no doubt that [West Germany], once it enters the EDC, will one day become a member of the Atlantic Pact; this will come about automatically." Moving to the "General Treaty," he argued that it promised "equality" along with "the peaceful creation of a completely free and reunified Germany." Unlike Versailles, it was "no Diktat." True, the Western powers would retain certain rights, but "only those . . . whose preservation was necessary in light of the peculiarities of the international situation." He did not say what those rights were or under what conditions they might be abandoned. He concluded by urging his colleagues to keep the "distant goal of European unity firmly in sight" and to tolerate the "painful moments" that must accompany "the birth of anything new." Above all, they must not endanger that birth by untimely interventions or uninformed criticism.[19] Adenauer did not exactly repeat the old German dictum that the citizen's first duty was to keep his mouth shut, but he came close.

The chancellor's speech, which even his aide Otto Lenz admitted was "not very good,"[20] was followed by a lengthy rebuttal from Erich Ollenhauer, who had taken over leadership of the SPD from the gravely ill Kurt Schumacher. A colorless but capable communicator, Ollenhauer proceeded in calm and deliberate fashion to attack the government's position at its most vulnerable points. He began by noting that the Bundestag was expected to "debate" these treaties without having been given full information on them, a situation that "directly violated the principle of cooperation between government and parliament." As to Adenauer's claim that the Russian threat was increasing, Ollenhauer argued that, if anything, world tensions had abated in recent months and that if the danger of Soviet aggression really *had* risen, German rearmament, which would require several months even to begin, could hardly avert catastrophe. But the real "subterfuge" in the government's position, he argued, was its assumption that the fundamental issue had already been decided. In fact, he insisted, the German people had "not accepted rearmament under existing political circumstances," which meant that Bonn had no popular mandate for participation in the EDC. As to the alleged security benefits of cooperation with the West, especially with the Americans, Ollenhauer proposed that Washington wanted to get the Germans to the front so it could bring its own boys home, which would hardly make Germany safer. Furthermore, the occupation powers' offer of "sovereignty" in exchange for rearmament was little short of "blackmail" because it made the former contingent upon the latter. In any case, "full sovereignty" was not being offered because the powers would retain a number of rights that institutionalized the existing Occupation Statute. At the very least, the timing should be reversed: Bonn must not join the EDC *before* the General Treaty went into effect.[21]

Ollenhauer's speech left many observers with the impression that Adenauer had been outmaneuvered. The question now was whether other government speakers could present a more forceful and coherent defense of Bonn's policy. The prognosis was not good because the Union parties were ill prepared for their confrontation with the SPD. Although the CDU *Fraktion* had been briefed on the Paris and Petersberg negotiations, it had only a rough sense of the treaties' contents, which provoked considerable resentment toward the chancellor and his immediate entourage. Other concerns included the fear that Adenauer was not demanding enough from the occupation powers in exchange for rearmament; that the Dienststelle Blank lacked the capacity to prevent the new army from becoming a state within the state; and that the EDC initiative, especially if it required conscription, could cost the government parties the next election.[22]

One of the most vocal critics of Adenauer's tactics was Franz Josef Strauss, a young Bavarian firebrand who was chairman of the Union parties' Defense Policy Working Group and who was rumored to be behind a plan to create a "Bundestag Defense Committee" that might challenge the Bundeskanzleramt's monopoly over security policy.[23] At a CSU *Fraktion* meeting on 22 January, Strauss had urged his colleagues to prevent Adenauer from "rolling over" parliament and signing an EDC treaty without adequate debate. Bonn's negotiators, he warned, seemed all too ready to accept something less than full equality. They were apparently even willing to allow occupation forces to remain in requisitioned housing without compensating their owners—a major issue in Bavaria, where there were many American troops. He hinted that he would oppose the the EDC unless this situation was changed.[24]

Strauss nevertheless led the Union's counterattack against the SPD in the Bundestag. He began by accusing the SPD leader of playing to the emotions of the radio audience while affecting distaste for the "politics of feeling." Ollenhauer, said Strauss, had asked loaded questions without offering any answers or "genuine alternatives." He went on to blame the "unhappy necessity" of rearmament on the Western powers, who, after all, had made the "tragic error" of allowing the Soviets to expand their empire after the war. Yet he also argued that by rearming, Bonn would not simply be responding to Western pressure; rather, it would be recognizing Germany's geographical vulnerability on the Cold War frontier and articulating its own national interests. "The Americans," he added pointedly, "cannot tell us what to do."[25]

If Strauss showed signs of making trouble for Adenauer, so did the chancellor's FDP partners. The relationship between Adenauer and the Liberals had never been cordial, and it had grown more strained when the FDP began to criticize the chancellor for deemphasizing reunification. The FDP made itself difficult, too, by cozying up to the nationalist veterans' organizations, whose strident rhetoric the government hoped to dampen.[26] Party leaders such as Erich Mende and Hasso von Manteuffel echoed the veterans' demands for restoration of the German soldier's "honor" as a prerequisite for rearmament. Mende insisted that the Allies' resistance to an immediate release of all Germans convicted of war crimes was simply an extension of the "Morgenthau psychosis."[27] Such demands went well beyond what Adenauer considered feasible or prudent in this sensitive domain.

The Liberals' intransigence was very much in evidence in the *Wehrdebatte* of 7–8 February. While agreeing in essence to the need for rearmament, August Martin Euler, a key party spokesman, set out several "preconditions" for German participation in the EDC. These included not just a release of German prisoners but a general recognition on the part of the Allies that "the past was a closed matter, that there were no longer any victors or vanquished, but only comrades in a common enterprise." On the question of sovereignty, Euler echoed Ollenhauer's concern that the General Treaty would "institutionalize" parts of the Occupation Statute, something the FDP would "never tolerate." He also insisted that Bonn's rearmament effort not "overburden" the country's economy and undermine its material recovery.[28] In advancing these points, he was highlighting some of the key trouble spots in Bonn's emerging "partnership" with the West.

The first day's proceedings closed with short speeches from three rising CDU politicians: Ernst Majonica, Robert Tillmanns, and Kurt Georg

Kiesinger. Among these, Kiesinger was the most important, not only because of his illustrious future—he was to become chancellor in 1966—but also because of his problematic past—he had been a member of the Nazi Party. Paul Sethe of the *Frankfurter Allgemeine Zeitung*, one of the FRG's leading journalists, saw the presence of a reformed ex-Nazi in the CDU lineup as a hopeful sign that capable and repentant men with a "Brown Past" might henceforth be allowed to play a prominent role in the affairs of the new republic.[29] As if to prove he had changed his spots, Kiesinger cloaked his argument for rearmament in the fashionable rhetoric of internationalism. West Germany was not embarking upon "remilitarization," he claimed, but upon the creation of a new kind of defensive force that reflected the postwar triumph of international cooperation over the discredited nation-state. "The time of the nation-state is over," he said. "We are in a new era. Our new army will not be a national force [and] certainly not an imperialist one, but simply a force for the defense of freedom."[30]

Alas, Kiesinger's dismissal of the national state had little basis in political reality, even that of the early 1950s, when so many Europeans waxed enthusiastic about the dawn of a new supranationalist order. The internationalist enthusiasm, after all, ran head-on into entrenched nationalist sentiments and institutions. Moreover, supranationalism and Europeanism could also serve nationalist interests, and no more so than in the case of West Germany, which assiduously pursued its own sovereignty—as it was later to pursue its vaunted *Ostpolitik*—"in the name of Europe."[31]

The second day of the *Wehrdebatte* brought a series of speeches which in large measure reiterated the opening arguments and therefore need not be treated in detail. But one of the speeches bears discussion, for it was arguably the most impressive of the entire debate. It was delivered by Carlo Schmid, who turned out to be one of the most important figures in the politics of rearmament. The SPD's resident intellectual, Schmid was an academic from Tübingen who combined elements of the German romantic tradition (he had been a member of the Wandervögel) with a commitment to the rough and tumble of practical politics. Since the opening of the rearmament debate, he had been one of the most articulate opponents of Adenauer's policy. Later, however, he would find common ground on aspects of rearmament with members of the government parties and thereby help signal a move by the SPD away from its historic opposition to all things military. But in the initial parliamentary debate, he combined attacks on the principle of rearmament with technical and political objections to the design of the treaties.

Beginning with the General Treaty, Schmid focused on apparent discrepancies between the preamble and various provisions contained in the text (a draft of which he had been shown, on condition that he not betray its contents). It seemed that the preamble offered vague promises regarding "equality" and "unity" that the text either contradicted or failed to address. In the preamble, the occupation powers declared themselves duty-bound to restore German unity, but the treaty itself said nothing about how this might be accomplished. The reason, suggested Schmid, was that the powers could do nothing without agreement from Russia, a prospect unlikely to be enhanced by rearming the western half of Germany. The preamble also spoke glowingly about "equality," but it was evident that the Allies were prepared to allow only a "symbolic" renunciation of the occupation regime. This became especially clear when one examined the "Emergency Clause," which allowed the Allies to reclaim full control in case of foreign attack or "domestic disorders." Obviously, said Schmid, this opened the way for many "abuses"; the Allies might act simply because "changes of power took a direction unwelcome to [them]." The same held for the regulations on stationing non-German troops in the FRG: these forces would now be called "allies," but they would retain privileges that hardly qualified them as "equal partners." Not only was the equality here "illusory," but so was the "security" supposedly guaranteed by the EDC. Echoing a previous SPD speaker, Adolf Arndt, as well as Schumacher, Schmid questioned the meaningfulness of adding twelve German divisions to the Western alliance. This would do nothing to enhance security because the Soviets would hardly be deterred from aggression by a "plastic pistol." At best, the German troops could fight a rear-guard retreat while the Russians destroyed their land. But no politician had "the right to ask a people to watch their country reduced to ashes for symbolic effect," he shouted, in what became a famous phrase.[32]

Schmid's incisive attack severely unnerved and wounded Adenauer. He rose and demanded a copy of Schmid's speech, noting that it was based on information given "in strict confidence." He threatened to "take appropriate measures" if it turned out that Schmid had compromised national security. But this attempt to muzzle the opposition only strengthened the SPD's determination to challenge the chancellor and caused some of Adenauer's defenders to worry that the old man was losing his grip.[33]

At the conclusion of the long debate, Heinrich von Brentano asked for an endorsement of Bonn's participation in the EDC "as an equal partner."[34] Though this motion passed 204 to 156, with 6 abstentions, Adenauer had little reason for satisfaction. Not only had the SPD frustrated his hope for consensus, but elements within his own coalition had demanded preconditions for rearmament that went further than Adenauer thought prudent. It seemed indeed that the Bundestag did not intend to be "rolled over" by the government. As one commentator put it: "The voice we heard most distinctly [in the debate] was not that of our Lord [Adenauer], but that of our elected representatives."[35] It was a voice that would grow in volume, if not necessarily in clarity, as the rearmament debate progressed.

France's equivalent of the Bundestag's *Wehrdebatte* took place in mid-February and bore remarkable similarities to what had just transpired in Bonn. In Paris, too, the debate was widely seen as an "existential question"—the most important issue France had faced since the war. Indeed, Raymond Aron went so far as to insist that this was the "greatest ideological-political quarrel that France [had] known, probably, since the Dreyfus Affair . . . a quarrel whose most apparent issue was German rearmament, but whose deepest significance affected the very principle of French existence, the national state."[36]

As might have been expected in such a quarrel, the conflict of opinion was profound. Schuman (very much like Adenauer) would have preferred to avoid or postpone a parliamentary showdown, but when he could not, he sought to win a vote of confidence for the EDC by presenting it as a step toward European unity. In essence, he insisted that the modifications proposed for the Pleven Plan did not weaken France's position but actually improved it. France would not suffer as a result of greater European unity but would prosper. Indeed, she could find true security only in a united Europe.[37] This, too, sounded distinctly Adenauerian, but the argument had less resonance in France than in Germany, where traditional nationalism was more suspect (though by no means dead) and where the prospects for profiting from partial absorption in Europe seemed more convincing. In any event, the intellectual ground upon which Schuman stood was considerably shakier than Adenauer's.

The foreign minister faced a formidable phalanx of EDC opponents dominated by the Communists and Gaullists. The Communists were quick to denounce the entire enterprise as an extension of "American imperialism." The Gaullists' opposition was motivated primarily by an unwillingness to abandon the French national army, whose potency would allegedly be lost in the mongrel EDC. Recalling Free French successes in World War II, a Gaullist general (Pierre Billotte) passionately declared: "The breakthrough on the Garigliano and the victory of Rome would not have been possible if . . . there had been no purely French divisions to take the Majo and to cross the mountains of Petrella." Particularly galling to proud defenders of French military tradition was the fact that—as Jacques Soustelle put it—"Only France among the great powers is expected to sacrifice its national army on the altar of the European army." Echoing concerns expressed by some junior officers, the Gaullists also worried that Germany might regain its military clout under the convenient cover of the EDC. Said General Billotte: "There will [again] be fine and good German divisions [and they will be the source] from which a new German military supremacy could one day spring." This view was shared by many members of the Conservative Party, who worried as well that a rearmed Germany might either side with the Soviets as in 1939 or pull its new allies into a disastrous war for reunification. "I ask you to think of the fate of the Roman Empire when it formed legions composed of Germans to defend itself!" pleaded Louis Marin, a Conservative deputy from Briey.[38] (Marin might also have borne in mind, however, that the contemporary French Foreign Legion was heavily German, and hardly the weaker for it.)

Jules Moch, the former defense minister, led the attack for the SFIO. He complained that the EDC treaty contained so many concessions to Germany that it amounted to little more than a blind behind which a new Wehrmacht could be created. Moch and the right wing of the Socialist Party made it clear that they would not give the government a vote of confidence unless it managed to amend the treaty with provisions banning Bonn from entering NATO, recruiting any soldiers before the treaty was ratified, or *ever* fielding more troops than France. The Socialists also demanded British participation in the pact to "counterbalance" the Germans and an Anglo-American promise that Germany would not be allowed to leave the EDC.[39]

The left wing of the SFIO was unwilling to endorse the EDC even with these added guarantees. Claude Bourdet and Daniel Mayer were convinced that *any* German army would be dominated by old Nazis and revanchist eastern expellees anxious to liberate their former homelands with the help of French blood. They thought that Germany's "contribution" to Western defense should therefore be limited to digging antitank traps, installing (and no doubt testing) minefields, housing Allied troops, and joining the common financial effort. It was a vision of an eternal German Labor Service, armed with checkbooks as well as shovels.

Opposition to the EDC surfaced even among the government-coalition parties, in which anti-German feeling led to some notable defections. One was the old Radical Party warhorse, Edouard Herriot, who insisted that the EDC's "paper guarantees" of German good behavior were useless because history showed that the "Germans [did] not have an undue respect for signatures." Edouard Daladier, a Radical politician who knew something about paper guarantees (he had represented France at the Munich Conference in 1938), argued that Bonn would surely go the way of Weimar as soon as the German military caste was allowed to reestablish itself.[40] André-François Monteil of the Mouvement Républicain Populaire (MRP), a former minister of the navy, declared that the European army would be nothing more than an incoherent amalgam "in the service of the strongest state in the Atlantic Alliance." By this he obviously meant America, implying that France and the other EDC nations would be little more than vassals of Washington. Like his colleagues, Monteil also questioned the wisdom of encouraging the revival of

"German militarism," and he was disinclined to see such a fateful decision made by a weak French government backed by a fragile majority.[41]

The government of Edgar Faure was indeed weak, and Schuman's vote-of-confidence motion on the EDC had to be modified three times before it passed by a vote of 327 to 287. This close result offered little comfort to the EDC's backers because the far-reaching concessions with which it was purchased would probably not be acceptable to the Anglo-Americans, let alone to the Germans. Moreover, the Faure government, never popular, slipped even further in public esteem as a result of its German policy. No wonder Hervé Alphand, one of the French architects of the EDC, spoke of a "horrible debate," which showed how "bitter" his countrymen remained toward their former adversary.[42]

"GRAND SLAM"

As France's Assembly debate was concluding, a meeting of the foreign ministers of the prospective EDC states was taking place in London. Attending for the FRG, in his self-appointed capacity as Bonn's first foreign minister, was Konrad Adenauer. Adenauer had been in London once before, in December 1951, when he met with the recently reelected Churchill. On that occasion, demonstrators had greeted the chancellor with cries of "No arms for the Nazis!" and "Down with Prussian Militarism!" Wounded, Adenauer had reminded Churchill that he was "no Prussian," though his rival Schumacher was. Now, aware that continuing fears of German militarism were delaying the FRG's acquisition of armed sovereignty, Adenauer pressed for rapid resolution of the knotty questions still separating West Germany from its would-be partners. One of these involved a pledge of good behavior that Paris was asking Bonn to make in three separate places in the treaty package. Adenauer complained that it was a "strange partnership" that required a prospective member to promise repeatedly that he would be a "good fellow who harbored nothing but the best intentions." He added that such a pledge would cause him insurmountable difficulties at home.[43]

Adenauer also reintroduced the question of German arms production. He had earlier agreed that certain kinds of weapons manufacture might be banned in the FRG on the grounds that it was a "Strategic Zone," but it remained unclear which weapons would be outlawed. Despite his insistence that German industrialists had no desire to produce weapons, he knew that some forms of arms manufacture might bolster the civilian economy. He therefore protested the EDC treaty's "vagueness and imprecision" in this area. What about gunpowder, for example? It was needed for many innocent purposes, including mining. In exchange for a pledge to refine the list of prohibited items, he agreed to forgo production of warships and aircraft, as well as atomic, biological, and chemical (ABC) weapons.[44] At the time, this was an easy enough concession to make, for German firms were generally disinclined to get back into the business of heavy arms production and (as yet) had no interest in ABC weapons.[45]

At the conclusion of the London meeting, the participants drew up an uninformative communiqué and agreed to continue their negotiations in Bonn and Paris. Adenauer flew home and announced that he had achieved a "great victory" in the British capital. Bonn's demand for "full equality," he said, had been met.[46] This of course was hyperbole, but the chancellor undoubtedly felt that the difficult times called for a little poetic license.

In any event, the treaty system was not yet ready to be initialed, and negotiations aimed at resolving the final sticking points seemed to go on endlessly. In addition to the formal discussions, there were more meetings among the military planners. In March, Speidel and Blank met repeatedly with their French counterparts. Despite the conviviality that attended these sessions, there were occasional painful confrontations. One occurred when General René de Larminat reported France's intention to include black African troops in the contingent it stationed in Germany. Knowing that this would awaken bitter memories of the *Schwarze Schmach am Rhein*—France's use of black troops in its occupation of the Rhineland in 1923—Blank objected strenuously.[47] The irony is that Germany would eventually have far more blacks stationed on its territory through the military presence of its closest ally, the United States.

The diplomats made significant progress during the NATO Council meetings in Lisbon in late February. Two issues dominated these proceedings: the French demand for a guarantee against Bonn's withdrawal from the EDC and the financial arrangements for the European army. The first issue was partially resolved through the intervention of Anthony Eden, Churchill's foreign secretary, who agreed to declare that Britain would not tolerate any action that "threatened the integrity of the EDC."[48] The financial question proved more difficult. The Benelux countries opposed a common budget, fearing that the larger nations would control it. Bonn insisted that its contribution to the maintenance of British and American troops on German soil should count toward its EDC obligation. The French declared that the mounting costs of their Indochina war would necessarily limit their contribution. So complicated and intractable was the financial imbroglio that the question was turned over to an independent consulting group popularly known as "The Three Wise Men."[49]

The Wise Men soon came up with recommendations that led both France and Germany to question their wisdom. They proposed that Bonn contribute DM 11.2 billion in the fiscal year 1952–53. The Germans complained that this assessment overestimated their capabilities but agreed to pay providing they could scale down their obligation if they ran into financial difficulties. The French objected that this might allow Bonn to reduce its payments below France's, adding that without extensive financial assistance from America, Paris might have to reduce the size of its EDC contingent below that of Germany, which would be intolerable. On the final day of regular meetings at Lisbon, America agreed to grant France $600 million toward meeting its EDC obligation.[50]

Additional unscheduled discussions were required to harmonize the French and German budget figures with America's aid proposals. In the end, after an exhausting session lasting long into the evening of 25 February, Acheson, Schuman, and Eden thought they had reached an agreement that needed only to be polished by their technical assistants. Schuman went to bed. The assistants, however, ran into difficulties, and rather than awaken Schuman they proposed that the meetings be suspended. This was too much for Eden. He exploded in what the somewhat Francophobic Acheson called a "satisfying pyrotechnical display," replete with complaints that every time a crisis occurred "some damn Frenchman went to bed." Schuman was awakened, and the negotiators were able to complete their arduous task by 4:00 A.M.

Acheson was now convinced that the "pieces in the puzzle" had all come together. Resorting to the sports metaphors that were the bane of American diplomacy, he cabled Truman that he and his colleagues had hit a "grand slam," and he told a press conference the next morning that the EDC was now "clinched."[51]

THE STALIN NOTE: A "MISSED OPPORTUNITY"?

But it was not clinched at all. The exhausted negotiators were obliged to continue their seemingly Sisyphean labors for almost three more months, their goal constantly receding just as it appeared attainable. In their struggle they had to contend not only with continuing domestic pressures but also with a new diplomatic onslaught from Moscow, which chose this moment to launch yet another "peace offensive."

On 10 March 1952, Moscow delivered identical notes to its wartime allies urging a reunification of Germany (west of the Oder-Neisse line) and the completion of a peace treaty. The initiative included proposals for the withdrawal of all foreign troops from German soil within one year of the treaty's inception; a guarantee of "free activity for democratic parties" and a ban on groups "inimical to democracy"; equal civil and political rights for former soldiers and rehabilitated former Nazis; and a prohibition on German membership in an alliance directed against any of the wartime powers. Finally,

Germany would be allowed to field a national army and to produce its own arms, subject to limits set by the treaty powers.[52]

The Stalin Note's most striking feature was its provision for a German national army. This, along with the offer of full political rights for former Nazis and soldiers, was probably designed to impress West Germany's embittered veterans and rightist groups, who—despite occasional threats to "go the East"—had so far kept their distance from the Communists. With this appeal, Moscow could draw upon earlier traditions of Soviet-German military partnership, most notably the secret cooperation between the Reichswehr and the Red Army in the 1920s. More recently, Moscow had courted Nazi officers through its wartime Committee for a Free Germany. More than the Western allies, Moscow had tried to distinguish demilitarization from wholesale attacks on the Prusso-German military tradition. The paramilitary police forces it had built up in its occupation zone and the proto-army it then sanctioned in the GDR were animated by slogans of "antifascism" and "anti-imperialism," but not so much by antinationalism.[53] This was important because of East Berlin's claims that the GDR represented the true German "nation," while the FRG was said to stand only for the heritage of monopoly capitalism and class exploitation. Not surprisingly, therefore, the Soviets' March initiative was accompanied by an East German propaganda campaign glorifying the older military traditions of Germany and Prussia. The GDR's Volkspolizei was also beginning to take on the Prussian look that was later to characterize the Nationale Volksarmee and from which the Wehrmacht had also extensively borrowed. Very possibly, Moscow hoped that the allure of building a national army for a unified Germany in this traditional style would be irresistible to Germans on both sides of the Elbe.

But speculation along these lines raises the question of whether the Soviets, given their great fear of German arms, were truly serious with their March note, along with an additional démarche dated 9 April proposing free elections for a united Germany. Since the mid-1950s scholars have debated this question. One faction has argued that the Soviets were so intent upon preventing Bonn's adherence to the Western alliance that they were genuinely prepared to see a reunified and rearmed (albeit neutral) Germany. Others have suggested that the Soviets may not have been willing to go this far but that their offer nonetheless provided a basis for further discussion. Still another faction has insisted that the initiative was little more than a propaganda ploy designed to obstruct Bonn's rearmament in the Western bloc.[54]

Pending an assessment of possible new sources from the former Soviet archives, it is difficult to know exactly what Moscow intended. Perhaps it was pursuing several strategies at once: trying to discourage Bonn's militarized integration with the West, which Russia undoubtedly feared; exploring the chances for German reunification on terms favorable to the USSR; and, if both these efforts failed, allowing the GDR government to expand the military clout of its Kasernierte Volkspolizei.[55]

Whatever Moscow's motivation, Washington's response was clear enough.[56] Since the Korean War, America had not been anxious to hold a four-power conference on Germany, much less to reach a peace settlement entailing the Allies' withdrawal from Central Europe.[57] With the impending completion of the EDC treaty, the Truman administration, according to George Kennan, "did not want any agreement with the Soviet government about Germany."[58] Although Acheson conceded privately that the Stalin Note marked a "considerable advance upon previous proposals," he publicly denounced it as another "spoiling operation intended to check and dissipate the momentum toward solutions in the West brought about by the years of colossal effort."[59] The American general Alfred Gruenther, meanwhile, worried about the effects the Soviet initiative might have on German veterans. After querying General Speidel about his colleagues' views on the overture from "*Väterchen* Stalin," Gruenther assured him that once Bonn was safely ensconced in the Western alliance, it would have no difficulty resisting such dangerous enticements.[60]

French and British officials, too, found the Russian initiative troubling; as much as some of them may have wanted to negotiate with the Russians, they had no brief for a reunified Germany free to "float" between East and West. Thus the Quai d'Orsay described the Stalin Note as a "serious but very dangerous attempt to settle the German question," and Eden opined that the Soviets were "serious in these proposals because, though there is danger in them, they would, on balance, suit them well."[61] Eden's position reflected the fear—strongly articulated by his secretary, Evelyn Shuckburgh—that a neutral Germany simply could not be trusted, for it might well "slide to the East."[62]

Determined to put off any negotiations on Germany with the Russians until after the EDC treaty was safely signed, the Western powers quickly countered the Soviet initiative with their own barrage of notes that zeroed in on what Allied diplomats saw as the most vulnerable point in the Soviets' plan: its vagueness regarding the formation and nature of the new German government that was to negotiate a peace treaty. The Western notes demanded that the proposed all-German elections be supervised by the United Nations, which the Russians had never found acceptable. They also insisted that the new German government be "free before and after the conclusion of a treaty to enter into associations compatible with the United Nations Charter."[63] This, of course, amounted to a demand that united Germany be free to join the Western alliance if it so chose, a prospect Moscow could hardly be expected to welcome. Indeed, it seems likely that the West was—in the spirit of Adenauer—deliberately making the Soviets a counteroffer they could not accept.

The German chancellor did what he could to undermine Moscow's initiative, while at the same time trying not to appear a saboteur of German unity. On 11 March he privately told the high commissioners that Bonn would not change its foreign policy in light of Stalin's note, which he hoped would not lead to a four-power conference. As for the Soviets' motives, he said he saw a delaying operation at work, suggesting scornfully that the Russians were now trying to become the spokesmen for the Nazis and the nationalist veterans.[64] In public, meanwhile, Adenauer sang a slightly different tune, not rejecting Moscow's call for talks but objecting to various details in the Russian plan. At a CDU meeting on 16 March, he warned about the dangers of "neutralization," insisting that a neutral Germany would be a "no-man's land," highly vulnerable to pressures from its eastern neighbors. He said also that the Soviets' proposal for an independent national army was really only a "paper concession" because under existing economic conditions Germany would be unable to field a creditable national defense force. Most revealingly, he objected strongly to the Russian note's insistence on maintaining the Potsdam boundaries after reunification, demanding instead that Germany's "lost territories" be included in the restored state.[65] Here again he was undoubtedly being disingenuous for in reality he cared little for the recovery of these territories, but by demanding their return he could effectively undermine the Soviet initiative without appearing to be un-German.

The chancellor had good reason to fear the effects of the Soviets' initiative on West German opinion. Since the beginning of the decade, influential politicians inside and outside the government coalition had been calling for a more "flexible" policy toward the East, one that would take heed of Bismarck's famous admonition to keep a line open to Russia. To such politicians, the Soviet initiative seemed worthy at least of careful consideration, if not serious negotiation. Thus the minister for inter-German affairs, Jakob Kaiser, warned against "hasty statements" that would prejudice a potential accommodation with the Russians. "Germany and the Western powers," he said, "will have to determine if [this note] really constitutes a turning point in East-West relations."[66] Paul Sethe suggested that a "turning point" had in fact occurred, demanding that its implications be pursued by the Western powers.[67] The ailing Schumacher took a similar line, as did voices within the EKD.[68] Some of Adenauer's CDU colleagues, meanwhile, expressed consternation that his demand for a return of Germany's "lost territories" would make serious negotiation with the Soviets impossible. Thus Heinrich von Brentano and Kurt Georg Kiesinger complained to the chancellor that his aggressive "Ostpolitik" went too far and added unwonted complications to the already complex German question.[69] This was, no doubt, precisely what Adenauer had in mind.

HOME STRETCH

If Brentano and company worried that Adenauer's sudden embrace of the lost territories jeopardized reunification, they also believed that his acceptance of a provision in the General Treaty known as the "Binding Clause" might have the same effect. The Binding Clause stipulated that the "rights and obligations" assumed by the FRG would automatically apply to a reunified Germany. Thus if Bonn joined the Western alliance, a reunified nation would have to join it too, which of course would hardly endear Moscow to reunification. Vice-chancellor Franz Blücher (FDP) complained that acceptance of this clause would destroy chances for "normal relations with the Soviets, without whose approval there could be no reunification."[70]

Since Adenauer refused to demand changes in the clause, claiming that this would cause "chaos," a delegation of dissident ministers (Blücher, Brentano, and Dehler) went over his head to Acheson. The result was a modification whereby commitments undertaken by the FRG would not automatically be taken over by reunified Germany but become subject to "further negotiation."[71] (This is in effect what happened when Germany became unified in 1990.) Another part of the revised clause, however, stipulated that Bonn could not undertake any agreements that limited the rights enjoyed by the three Western powers under the General Treaty without their approval. Obviously, the powers were loath to give up control over that dimension of German foreign policy which concerned them most: the reunification question.

The Western powers employed yet another clause to protect their interests in Germany—the *Notstandsklausel* (Emergency Clause). This provision had already come under fire in the Bundestag's *Wehrdebatte*, and it was subjected to renewed criticism in the last weeks of the negotiations. As originally conceived, it gave the Allies the right to resume full powers in Germany during an international crisis or domestic emergency, but the terms were not clearly defined. Responding to criticism from the Bundestag, German negotiators insisted that the clause was dangerously vague and far-reaching. Again, Blücher's committee took the lead in demanding revisions. After considerable bargaining, the Germans were able to secure two important changes: "emergency" was defined as a "situation that could not be contained by the *Länder* police or by Germany's EDC contingent," and Bonn was guaranteed a voice in determining that an emergency indeed existed. This would presumably prevent indiscriminate Allied intervention, but it did not go far enough to satisfy some German critics, who opposed the retention of any Allied right to intervene.[72] Disputes over relative powers in times of emergency remained a troubling dimension of Allied-German relations until Bonn's passage of the Emergency Law of 1968, when the Allies gave up their right to intervene.

Similar dissatisfaction attended the resolution of the emotion-laden "war crimes" issue. Article six of the Treaty on Questions Relating to the War and Occupation Era, a supplement to the General Treaty, provided for a joint German-Allied Review Board to examine the sentences of all remaining war prisoners in Allied hands. But the treaty stipulated that the review process would not begin until the EDC was ratified by all members. This provision infuriated some of the German veterans' organizations, who declared once again that there should be no rearmament while Wehrmacht officers were still imprisoned by the Allies.[73]

A host of other questions could not be settled until the eve of the treaties' signing by the foreign ministers. For example, Paris suddenly demanded that America join Britain in issuing a formal prohibition against a member state's withdrawal from the EDC. The Truman administration balked at this, noting that Congress would hardly make such a commitment to an organization of which the United States was not even a member. Finally, a compromise stipulated that Britain, America, and France would jointly declare their "abiding interest" in the integrity of the EDC and their determination to consult with each other if the "integrity or unity" of the European Community was threatened.[74]

Once this dispute was resolved, it was Adenauer's turn to raise difficulties. He had been informed by observers in France that Paris would sign the treaties only to enhance Eisenhower's presidential election prospects and, having done so, would delay EDC ratification for as long as possible.[75] The General Treaty could come into force only after the EDC had been ratified so Bonn might have to wait a long time for full sovereignty. Adenauer therefore demanded that the main provisions of the General Treaty should take effect even if EDC ratification were delayed. France at first objected, but Adenauer persisted until he received written assurance that in case of delay the powers would consider actualizing the General Treaty independent of the European army initiative.

As the moment for signing the treaties approached, Adenauer cranked up a public relations campaign designed to portray the diplomatic package as a victory for German national interests. He repeatedly sounded his *Politik der Stärke* theme, insisting that "once the free world had strengthened itself, it would be able to negotiate with the East with good prospects of success."[76] His point, again, was that the only realistic hope for German unification "in

peace and freedom" was for the FRG and the rest of Western Europe to become so strong and prosperous that the Soviets would abandon the GDR and
perhaps the rest of their Eastern European empire in favor of better relations
with the West. Reasserting an oft-claimed personal commitment to the goal
of national union, he insisted that he would much prefer a "free unified Germany with the SPD as the strongest party to a separate West German state
with the CDU as dominant."[77] To critics who (with justice) doubted this and
who complained that his German policy had never amounted to much more
than anchoring the FRG in the West, he testily replied: "I'm just as good
a German as you are!"[78] He insisted time and again that Bonn's adherence
to the EDC would be good for *all* Germans, West and East. As if to prove
his nationalistic commitment, he appealed to President Theodor Heuss formally to recognize the old "Deutschlandlied" as the national hymn, which
he believed would add an important symbolic dimension to Bonn's claim to
represent all Germany. In mid-May, he appealed to the high commissioners
to change the name of the General Treaty to "Germany Treaty." The commissioners said no, but Adenauer began using the term *Deutschlandvertrag*
anyway.[79]

The chancellor hoped to celebrate the signing of the General Treaty as a
national holiday. He made plans for a torchlight parade, hanging flags on
public buildings, and closing schools. Alas, one of his critics (Adolf Arndt) had
the ill grace to point out that the last time Germany had held torchlight parades, the whole country had gone up in flames.[80] The parade idea was quietly
dropped. The state governments, complaining that most Germans had no
idea what was in the General Treaty, rejected the school holiday proposal.[81]

On 26 May 1952, delegates from the Western nations descended upon un-
prepossessing little Bonn for the signing of the General Treaty. They met in
the sterile Bundesrat room where the Basic Law had been signed. That document had provided the legal foundation for what was supposed to be a "provisorium" (they should have known that nothing lasts like a provisorium), but
this new treaty seemed to point toward the FRG's permanence. No wonder
Adenauer felt obliged to insist, once again: "At this hour we Germans remember especially our brothers in the East. We send them our greetings, and
we give them the assurance of our deepest conviction that what we are doing
here is the first step toward unification in freedom and peace."[82] Acheson,
however, chose to see this moment only as a time of Bonn's integration into
the free West. "On behalf of the President of the United States and the
American people," he pompously intoned, "I welcome the Federal Republic
on its return to the community of nations." Meanwhile, seeing this moment
as the seal on Germany's division, a bedridden Schumacher declared: "Whoever approves the General Treaty ceases to be a true German."[83]

On the following day, German and Allied diplomats gathered in Paris for the signing of the EDC treaty. No one, least of all the hosts, tried to make this a day of national celebration. The ceremony took place in the gilded precincts of the French Foreign Ministry, whose officials had opposed the treaty. Eden and Acheson, the EDC's self-proclaimed "godparents," signed the various security guarantees that were designed to protect this fledgling enterprise not only from a hostile outside world but also from one of its own members, the newest addition to the Western "family." Acheson, trying to get into the spirit of things, grandiloquently declared that this moment was "the beginning of the realization of an ancient dream—the unity of the free peoples of Western Europe." Adenauer, characteristically, felt obliged to go further: "The [EDC]," he declared, "will pull toward it other European lands and thereby serve as a tool . . . for the establishment of European unity."[84]

The fact of the matter, however, was that the EDC treaty was in many ways more a triumph for Bonn than for "Europe," however the latter was defined. Blank was not far off the mark when he boasted that "the German delegation [had] succeeded in overcoming the initial [anti-German] tendencies of the Pleven Plan [to produce] a treaty based almost exclusively on German ideas." The Germans, added Blank, had "caught the French in the logic of their own scheme" and made them pursue it farther than they had ever intended.[85] Through the mechanism of Europe, West Germany had taken a significant step toward full sovereignty and military revival.

It was precisely this aspect of the EDC treaty that worried some of the more thoughtful commentators on the European scene. Adelbert Weinstein of the *Frankfurter Allgemeine Zeitung* noted rightfully that the Germans' apparent commitment to a new form of supranational defense was not shared by the French, who remained "conservative to the bones" regarding their army. The French were also, added Weinstein, conservative in their political affiliations; they had fought Germany and been allied with Russia in two world wars. Was it surprising that they tended to "see Bonn as a greater danger to their security than Moscow"?[86] Actually, by May 1952 this was no longer the case, but Paris *did* see Bonn as a dangerous rival to its supremacy on the Continent, and many Frenchmen were disinclined to enhance the power of that rival in the name of some vague ideal of "Europe."[87]

Some Germans continued to condemn the EDC as a loss for Europe and for Germany, both of which, it was argued, would be kept divided by this widening of the Cold War schism. Less than a month after the EDC signing, a prominent FDP Bundestag delegate, Karl-Georg Pfleiderer, forcefully articulated what he called the "negative conjunction" between militarized West integration and reunification. In a well-publicized speech in Waibling on 6 June, he proposed, as an alternative to the EDC, the withdrawal of all foreign troops from German soil in preparation for eventual reunification and the adoption of a nonaligned stance by the new Germany. His contention was that a peaceful solution to the German problem could come only by mending fences with the Russians, whose "legitimate security interests" had to be taken into account.[88] By improving relations with the East—with Soviet Russia as well as the other Eastern European states—Bonn could gradually dissolve the anxieties that made German reunification so difficult. This argument was, in essence, the opposite of Adenauer's "Politics of Strength," and in some ways it anticipated Willy Brandt's *Ostpolitik*—though certainly not in its suggestions of neutralism and an independent role for Germany between East and West.

Pfleiderer's plan was roundly denounced as neutralist, and it found little resonance even in his own party.[89] Nevertheless, it struck a sympathetic chord among the many Germans who feared that the treaties might be the final nail in the coffin of reunification.[90] It also appealed to those who wanted all foreign troops out of Central Europe and who still believed that Germany's true mission was to travel a "third way" between East and West, a mission rendered impossible by Bonn's alleged "subservience" to the West. This notion of general military disengagement and a German path between the superpowers was a siren call that would beckon many West Germans over the next quarter century, especially in the heyday of the "peace movement" of the late 1960s and 1970s.[91]

With the signing of the EDC and General treaties in May 1952, Adenauer had undoubtedly moved the FRG closer to his goal of armed sovereignty within the Western alliance. The chancellor was now confident that he could push the treaty package through both houses of parliament before the approaching summer holidays. He did not achieve this ambition, however, because the SPD saw fit to take the government to court on rearmament, a tactic that did not succeed in scuttling Adenauer's security policy but substantially delayed the ratification process.

While the court was deliberating, the rearmament debate was joined by the new Bundestag Security Committee and by a surprisingly obstreperous Bundesrat, further complicating the issue. Their discussions pointed up abiding concerns among the German political elite regarding Bonn's status in the Western community. The judicial and political struggles over rearmament also brought into the open a complicated jockeying for power among various government agencies—the Federal Constitutional Court in Karlsruhe, the Bundeskanzleramt, the Bundestag and Bundesrat, and the president's office—thereby subjecting the young democracy to its most demanding test yet. It was a test that Adenauer's Bonn passed, though not without falling back on some problematical habits of the past and launching some troubling trends for the future. The chancellor himself often behaved like an *Ersatz-Kaiser* or latter-day Bismarck, while the parliamentary and judicial agencies showed that they still had a way to go to realize their full potential in a democratic society.

BONN VS. KARLSRUHE: THE ROLE OF THE
FEDERAL CONSTITUTIONAL COURT

In January 1952 the SPD lodged a brief with the Federal Constitutional Court, which argued that since the Basic Law did not explicitly provide for an army or conscription, a German contribution to the EDC would require a constitutional amendment. (In fact, the Basic Law neither specifically allowed nor disallowed rearmament.) In essence, the party asked the court to prohibit any steps toward rearmament pending a constitutional amendment. Because such amendments required a two-thirds majority in the Bundestag—a hurdle that in the first legislative period (1949–53) the government coalition could not clear—the SPD hoped to achieve through the court what it had not been able to manage through the ballot box. After the EDC treaty had been signed, the SPD added to its "preventive injunction" a petition to enjoin the EDC treaty's ratification until the constitutional question was settled.

The Federal Constitutional Court was barely five months old when the SPD submitted its petition. It was a novelty in German legal history; previous high courts had never had the authority to annul existing laws on constitutional grounds. In its new powers and duties, it borrowed extensively from the model of the United States Supreme Court. Bonn's high court, however, was organized quite differently. The Karlsruhe agency consisted of two sections, or "senates," each with twelve members jointly elected by the Bundestag and Bundesrat. The election procedure resulted in an informal division between the two senates. The first was regarded as "Red" because its members reputedly voted SPD; the second was "Black," for it had upheld the constitutionality of earlier compacts such as the Petersberg Protocol, which the Bundestag had never ratified. The chairmen of both senates—Hermann Höpker-Aschoff (Red) and Rudolf Katz (Black)—were members of the FDP, whose battle color was yellow (thus making the high court a mirror of the West German flag, symbolically fitting given its importance to the new state). There was also a division of labor between the two bodies. The first had exclusive jurisdiction over disputes involving the compatibility of federal and state laws with the Basic Law (*Normenkontrolle*), while the second handled quarrels between organs of the federal government and complaints affecting a specific government agency (*Organklagen*). The two senates met together when they wished to render "advisory" opinions on important constitutional issues.[1]

The SPD framed its petition as a *Normenkontrolle* so that it would be heard by the supposedly Red senate. At the same time, the SPD warned that if the government tried to force ratification before the court had rendered its verdict, the party would mobilize the unions to shut down the country. This threat carried a faint echo of the party's old revolutionary rhetoric (itself never entirely convincing) and anticipated later halfhearted efforts at "extra-parliamentary agitation" against Adenauer's security policy.

Although the government would have preferred to amend the Basic Law before trying to build an army, its lack of a two-thirds majority induced it to claim that such amendments were unnecessary. Adenauer himself declared (falsely) that "all members of the Parliamentary Council—with the possible exception of the Communists—had understood that the introduction of a Wehrmacht and conscription was the natural right of every state, including the Federal Republic."[2] The justice ministry now argued that the absence of specific provisions for defense in the Basic Law had stemmed not from a desire by the framers to rule out rearmament but only from a determination to prevent the revival of "militarism"—a concern adequately addressed in the proposed EDC.[3] Moreover, it said, certain provisions in the existing constitutional structure *implied* a right to rearm. Article 24, for example, permitted Bonn to join "international organizations." Article 4 codified the right of conscientious objection—a right, it was argued, that made sense only if the framers had expected there to be conscription. Article 26 outlawed preparations for "aggressive war," implying that measures for peaceful defense were fully acceptable. Article 25 stated that "international law" was part of federal law and created "rights and duties for the inhabitants of the federal territory." Because international law, specifically Article 5 of the United Nations Charter, acknowledged the "right of all states to wage defensive war," West Germany too had this right. Indeed, it was argued that this was particularly true for Bonn because the Basic Law, unlike the Japanese constitution, did not explicitly renounce national military sovereignty.[4]

In response to these arguments, the SPD insisted that the government had no right to divine implications in the Basic Law that the framers may or may not have intended. Adolf Arndt, the party's chief legal expert, recalled that the Parliamentary Council had defeated a number of attempts to include a defense clause in the constitution. He argued that Bonn's right to join international organizations, including ones aimed at promoting collective security, allowed only nonmilitary participation. The constitutional provision for conscientious objection, said Carlo Schmid, had been inserted to protect German citizens from enforced conscription in Allied armies, not to break legal ground for a domestic draft. He and his colleagues added that there were other important issues relating to *Wehrgewalt* (military powers) that the framers had left unclarified. For example, would the federal government have sole jurisdiction over the military, or would the states play a role? What powers of control would the parliament have, and how would these be enforced? Would there be a defense ministry, a commander in chief, a general staff? Where would the powers of *Oberbefehl* (supreme command) reside? Would the soldiers have the same constitutional rights as other citizens? If these rights were restricted, exactly how far would the restrictions go, and what form would they take? The Socialists argued that a failure to resolve these questions before rearmament began would be to risk creating a military capable of "going its own way," as German armies had so often done in the past.[5]

Though the Adenauer government certainly did not welcome the SPD's legal challenge, it tried at first to dismiss it as a propagandistic stunt without genuine prospects for success. When it became evident that the Socialists would succeed in having their case heard by the Red senate, however, the justice ministry admitted its trepidation. Worry turned into alarm when, in early summer 1952, Höpker-Aschoff leaked word to Adenauer that the first senate would likely rule in the Socialists' favor and grant their "preventive injunction" against rearmament.

Now it was Adenauer's turn to act and in a way that showed that he too understood how to manipulate the legal process. His administration requested President Heuss immediately to petition the court for an "advisory opinion" on the constitutionality of rearmament under the EDC framework.[6] Because such advisory rulings could be rendered only by the plenum of the court sitting en banc, this maneuver would take the decision out of the exclusive hands of the Red senate.

It is unclear whether the chancellor's office pressured a reluctant president into taking this step or simply reinforced Heuss's determination to seek advice from the court. Unlike Adenauer, Heuss was a consensus politician who favored policies that united contending parties; perhaps he thought that the court would provide such a solution. Moreover, though he opposed the legalization of political disputes and did not believe that rearmament or conscription required a constitutional amendment, he would not have wanted to sign a treaty into law had there been any doubts about its constitutionality.[7] Therefore, on 10 June he asked Karlsruhe for an advisory opinion on whether the EDC treaty and conscription were "compatible with the *Grundgesetz*." Left unclear was whether the court's opinion would be legally binding on the government.

Though the president's action was legally unimpeachable, the SPD immediately objected that it showed political partiality, thereby undermining the ideal of *überparteilichkeit* (nonpartisanship) on which the president's office was based, at least in principle. Adolf Arndt was so incensed that he declared that for him, Heuss was "no longer president."[8]

The court, however, was pleased by this turn of events, for by accepting Heuss's request it could render its decision through a procedure that seemed more appropriate to the weightiness of the case. The first senate therefore agreed on 13 June to defer judgment on the SPD's petition until the president's request could be heard by the plenum. At the same time, the supposedly Red jurists proposed that the plenum's advisory opinion be considered binding for any further adjudication by either senate.[9] So much, then, for the reliability of the Red and Black labels.

The joy with which this announcement was greeted in the Bundeskanzler-amt reinforced suspicions in the SPD that Adenauer was the wire-puller be-hind the president's action. Crying foul once again, Arndt demanded that the Socialists' original petition be heard first, and he also contested the constitu-tionality of turning an advisory opinion into a binding judicial verdict.

The court was apparently convinced by the first of Arndt's arguments, for the first senate now changed its mind and agreed to finish its deliberations on the Socialists' petition before responding to Heuss's request. On 30 July 1952, it rejected the SPD petition on the grounds that judicial review could be applied only to statutes that had been formally ratified by the parliament.[10]

Of course, the court's work was not yet over, for it still had before it Heuss's request for a judgment on the constitutionality of rearmament and conscription. Because this involved only an advisory ruling, the court could act before the parliament had passed judgment on the treaties. The next few months witnessed an escalation in the "battle of the bulging briefs," with lawyers and bevies of experts on both sides weighing in with learned opin-ions.[11] In the early phase of the proceedings, the Adenauer administration was so confident of securing an opinion in its favor that Walter Strauss, state secretary in the justice ministry, demanded that this ruling be binding on all arms of government, including both houses of parliament. Arndt responded that this contradicted the court's rationale for rejecting the Socialists' peti-tion: if an advisory opinion were to be treated as binding, then it had the same weight as a definitive legal ruling and could not be rendered before the par-liament had acted.[12]

Before this matter could be satisfactorily resolved, the government had reason to regret its boldness: rumors leaking out of Karlsruhe now intimated that the court might *not* decide in favor of the government. Again this pro-duced consternation in the government ranks. Justice Minister Thomas Dehler (FDP), suddenly recalling the sanctity of judicial procedure, warned that the "spirit of socialism" was rearing its ugly head in Karlsruhe. "I hope," he added, "that in our highest German court only *legal*, not *political*, decisions are rendered."[13] Heinrich von Brentano, in contrast, observed candidly that the court was faced with an eminently *political* decision, which it ought to treat as such: "A constitutional court," he said, "has not only the right, but the duty, to assess a political matter in a political light. Any judge whose intellec-tual talents surpass those of an ordinary mediocrity should see that [this case] has to be understood politically, not simply juridically." But he added: "Ac-cording to my most recent information on the climate in Karlsruhe, there is considerable cause for worry."[14]

Hoping that a vote favoring rearmament in parliament would persuade the jurists not to decide against the government, Adenauer tried to secure a more rapid ratification of the EDC treaty in the Bundestag by forcing the pace of its debates. His colleagues should not be so wordy, he said; they should stop their infernal talking and make a decision. This effort failed, however, because twenty government-coalition delegates voted with the SPD against an acceleration of parliamentary proceedings. These rebels were animated by a growing conviction that Adenauer's foreign policy was not securing what the chancellor had promised: full equality for the FRG in the international arena. After all, just before this vote, the French had refused to allow the pro-German parties in the Saar to participate in impending elections there. The delegates had also observed that on 10 November the CDU had suffered a defeat in the North Rhine–Westphalia Landtag elections, a result that many pundits attributed to disenchantment with the chancellor's foreign and security policies.[15]

Despite these domestic and international setbacks, Adenauer was able to pull together enough support to secure a second reading on the EDC in the Bundestag on 3 December. Opening the debate, the chancellor delivered an impassioned speech in defense of the treaty system. A vote against ratification, he declared, implied a willingness "to deliver up the peoples of Western Europe, and especially the German people, to the bondage of Bolshevism." He urged the delegates to "examine the treaties as closely as they liked" (something that he had long prevented them from doing), but to remember that what was at stake was "their freedom, their lives, the future of their children and of generations yet unborn."[16] The clear implication was that antirearmament politicians were willing to condemn their young nation to a future of indefinite servitude to the powers of darkness.

This bombastic speech, which ominously recalled Bismarck's penchant for calling his opponents "enemies of the state," provoked lively applause from the coalition parties and outrage from the SPD. Shouts of "shame" and "infamy" rang through the hall. Nonetheless, the government had the votes to pass the treaties by a simple majority, and it was expected that Adenauer would now press for the third and final reading in the Bundestag. But two days later, on 5 December, word filtered through the house that Adenauer had decided to postpone the third reading. The coalition parties were thrown into disarray, not knowing that the chancellor had just received notice from Karlsruhe that the court—whatever the Bundestag's action—would not confirm the view held by the government. Adenauer's entire security system seemed on the verge of collapse.

The chancellor now tried to head off a possible negative ruling through another legal maneuver—one his authorized biographer calls "masterly"[17]—but that more objective observers might describe in less flattering terms. At his instigation, the delegations of the coalition parties (acting as "the majority of the Bundestag") filed a complaint with the Constitutional Court against the SPD, asking Karlsruhe to declare that the Socialists were in violation of the Basic Law by contesting the right of the Bundestag to ratify the treaties by a simple majority vote. The point of this maneuver can be understood when we recall that petitions of this type—*Organklagen*—had to be adjudicated in the Black senate. Adenauer's plan, then, was to get the case into the hands of the supposedly friendly jurists in the second chamber. Fearing defeat on the fundamental issue of constitutionality, he hoped to win his case on technical grounds. In an effort to protect the envisaged victory, the coalition then petitioned the court to obligate the president to sign treaties passed by a simple majority without further inquiry into their constitutionality.[18]

These moves raised eyebrows even among the chancellor's closest supporters, some of whom had advised him against them. One of his aides, the ever-resourceful Otto Lenz, tried to dampen the criticism by claiming that Adenauer had taken this tack on the advice of the Americans. But this argument was unconvincing, for no one could have expected the Americans to understand the complexities of the German legal system, let alone appreciate Adenauer's byzantine maneuvers.

The jurists in Karlsruhe, however, understood very well what the government was trying to do, and they would have none of it. On 8 December the court announced two important decisions: first, it refused to hear the latest government petition before deciding on Heuss's request for an advisory opinion; and second, it stated that though this advisory opinion could not be interpreted as binding on the government, it would bind the court in its consideration of the original petition from the SPD.[19] (Since this second verdict *would* bind the government, the first judgment would be decisive.) The court's reasoning was obvious: a determination of the plenum should not be overturned by either senate acting alone.

Adenauer's response to this display of independence by one branch of government was to renew his assault on another: the president's office. On 9 December, accompanied by several of his advisers, he visited Heuss, asking him to withdraw his request for an advisory opinion. In this instance Adenauer apparently did not need to apply pressure, for Heuss was genuinely distressed that an *advisory* opinion could become a binding resolution and decide the fate of the EDC. Like Dehler, he believed that the court had no business making foreign or security policy. Germany had had enough "political justice" during the Third Reich, he argued.[20] (This was an odd reading of the legal inheritance from the Third Reich, where "political justice" had not involved the courts' acting in place of the political authorities, but acting at their behest—something Adenauer was trying to make them do once again.)

In any event, however pure his own motives, Heuss had difficulty convincing the nation that he had acted solely according to the dictates of his conscience. The press speculated that he had caved in to pressure from Adenauer.[21] Smarting from these aspersions on his integrity, Heuss (unbeknownst to Adenauer) promised Ollenhauer that he would not sign the EDC treaty until the court had ruled on its constitutionality. Nonetheless, the withdrawal of his petition again embroiled his office in partisan struggle, further undermining his status as a representative of the entire nation.[22]

While controversy swirled around Heuss, the Black senate handed down a ruling on the government parties' complaint against the SPD, rejecting the suit on the technical grounds that the Bundestag majority, a strictly political constellation, lacked the legal capacity to submit an *Organklage*. It also rejected the parties' contention that the SPD minority had prevented the majority from exercising its parliamentary mandate. Shaking its constitutional finger at the government, it wrote:

> It is not only the right of the opposition to make known, in addition to their political, also their constitutional objections, but this is, in the parliamentary-democratic state, its duty. . . . There exists neither the legal right of the parliamentary majority to impose its legal viewpoint within the parliament, nor does an obligation exist of the minority to submit to the legal viewpoint of the majority.[23]

Yet the constitutional question remained unresolved because the judgment against the parties' *Organklage* did not address the legality of rearmament under the Basic Law. It was also increasingly evident that the Karlsruhe jurists were not anxious to render a verdict on this politically explosive question. Doing so might pull the court apart, while subjecting it to attacks by the losing party. The court's reticence, combined with Heuss's retraction of his petition, suggested that Adenauer, despite having lost some legal battles, was winning the political war over rearmament. Indeed, most observers expected that the Bundestag and Bundesrat would now promptly pass the treaties and that President Heuss would duly add his imprimatur.

THE BUNDESTAG SECURITY COMMITTEE

Parliamentary ratification of the treaties, however, would not occur until late spring 1953 and presidential approval a year after that. In the interval, the treaties were subjected to intense scrutiny by a new and extremely important parliamentary committee, the Bundestag's Sonderausschuss zur Mitberatung des EVG-Vertrages und der damit zusammenhängenden Abmachungen (Special Committee for Consultation on the EDC Treaty and Auxiliary

Agreements, hereafter referred to as the Bundestag Security Committee).[24] Founded in September 1952, the Security Committee held dozens of closed meetings involving members of the Dienststelle Blank and other government agencies. As its cumbersome title suggests, the committee expected to help shape the agreements defining Bonn's place in the Atlantic community. Its ability to do so was considerably enhanced by its direct access (denied most parliamentarians) to the treaty drafts and various ancillary agreements. Though party differences inhibited unanimity on many points, the principle of secrecy encouraged committee members to trim their rhetorical sails and to reach agreements that would have been elusive in open debate. As a result, its sessions signaled not just a more insistent claim to parliamentary participation in foreign affairs but also the beginnings of an informal interparty alliance that would, by early 1955, effectively challenge the chancellor's near monopoly in security policy. Just as important, the Security Committee's deliberations and accomplishments revealed once again the extensive cooperation between former soldiers and politicians in shaping defense policy. A remarkable departure from the generally acrimonious civil-military relations of the Weimar era, this cooperation augured well for the political stability of the Bonn Republic.

Among its first items of business, the committee explored the organizational structure of the EDC, its ties to NATO, and Bonn's place in the new security framework. Possession of extensive information on these issues did not make committee members less doubtful about the treaties as a whole. Observing that the EDC structure outlined in the draft was "provisional," August Euler (FDP) proposed to investigate ways to turn this "highly problematical provisorium" into a more viable enterprise. Fritz Erler (SPD) noted a "gap" in the EDC-NATO relationship that might hurt Germany: because joint meetings could be called only if a majority of EDC members demanded them, questions affecting Bonn could be decided in NATO without any German input. Most grievously, Germany would have no role in NATO strategic planning. This meant, suggested Wilhelm Mellies (SPD), that America, which had recently called for a "roll-back of Communism" in Eastern Europe, might launch a "preventive war" into which Germany could be pulled. It was equally possible, however, that NATO would simply abandon West Germany in the event of a Soviet attack. When Theodor Blank assured the committee that NATO would neither abandon Germany nor drag it into a war without its consent, Erler replied: "Your faith in NATO makes sense only if [Bonn] is represented in its planning; otherwise [such faith] is built on sand." As matters stood, he added, Bonn was being asked to supply troops without even knowing how they would be used. "We have to be assured," he declared, "that our 400,000 troops will be used to defend our homeland."[25]

Erler and other committee members were also concerned that the tie between NATO and the EDC might mean that contingents of the latter could
be sent anywhere NATO chose, even outside of Europe. Would the German
troops, Erler asked, be obliged to intervene if Russia attacked Alaska? And
what about colonial conflicts? France had extensive colonial commitments,
which raised the question whether EDC contingents might be pressed into
service to protect France's holdings in northern Africa or Indochina. To ensure that German troops would not be exploited under the old rubric "Germans to the Front," committee members from the coalition parties as well as
the SPD insisted the parliament pass laws defining precisely how Germany's
contingent might be used.[26]

To some committee members, the proposed treaty complex left Bonn vulnerable on another front as well. The Emergency Clause in the General
Treaty, noted Erler, might be exploited by the occupation powers to take
over Germany's vote in the EDC Ministerial Council, thus denying Bonn
any control over its own contingent, which the powers might deploy for domestic purposes such as strikebreaking. This was another reason, said Erler,
why parliament must pass laws governing the use of German troops.[27]

The committee also worried about what other EDC states would do with
their own units and with the forces they controlled that stood outside the
EDC framework. France, for example, might wish to remove troops from its
EDC contingent to fight in Indochina or northern Africa, thereby compro-
mising the viability of the European army. Alternatively, Paris might rotate
into its EDC contingent troops from its colonial forces who were not, as
Carlo Schmid delicately suggested, noted for their "European mentality."
When Paul Bausch (CDU) countered that EDC-trained troops rotated into
territorial or colonial units might "infect" the latter with the "European
spirit," Schmid replied: "When one speaks of 'infection,' the bacillus of the
tricolor is considerably more virulent than that of the white-green [flag] of
the European Union." This assertion echoed an observation by Erler that
Paris was not serious about European unity, only about its own national and
imperial interests. If French egotism were not checked, he huffed, Europe
"would remain perpetually divided and weak, just an object in the Great
Power rivalry between the United States and Soviet Russia."[28]

Of course, the EDC and General treaties affected German as well as European unity. The EDC treaty, noted Erler, was meant to last for fifty years: did
this mean that Germany would have to remain divided for at least half a century? And if reunification could be achieved earlier, how would this affect the
EDC? More specifically, asked Franz Josef Strauss, would Germany's contingent continue to be drawn only from the western part of the country, allowing a "national German Wehrmacht" in the former Soviet Zone? Not know-

ing the answers to such questions, Blank could only respond that in the event of reunification, the powers would have to call a conference to decide how to proceed.

Another topic to which the Security Committee devoted considerable attention was weaponry—a question that had also exercised the military planners. What kind and how many arms would the German contingent receive? Who would produce them? And how they would be paid for? Early in the discussions, Erich Mende asked Blank and his aide Kurt Fett how Bonn could be sure that the Americans would deliver suitable weapons to the German contingent. Might the West German force, having been hastened into existence, become a dumping ground for outmoded American army surplus? he wondered. And when could the Germans start producing their own arms? Fett replied that Bonn would use German-made equipment "wherever we can." Blank observed that there were some classes of arms that the Germans were not allowed to manufacture: ABC weapons, rockets, bombers, fighters, and submarines. But he added that Bonn's promise not to *manufacture* such arms did not mean that it could not *possess* them. On the contrary, the government had insisted that the German forces must not be "less adequately armed than the other contingents."[29] Here Blank was opening the door to an issue that would become highly contentious in the coming years—the question of whether, in the name of equality and efficiency, West Germany's armed forces should be equipped with the most "modern" weapons, including tactical nuclear arms.[30]

Such reassurances did not mollify those on the committee who felt that the restrictions on weaponry represented intolerable discrimination against the FRG. Arthur Stegner (FDP) said that Bonn's vow not to produce strategic weapons might undermine Germany's economic recovery because many valuable products and processes were "spin-offs" from research in arms production. He mentioned, for example, America's gains in synthetic fibers resulting from its chemical weapons research. "We must ensure," he said, "that the future development of our *Volkswirtschaft* is in no way impeded." This view was seconded by Mellies, who added that the ban on strategic arms production was incompatible with equality. He also objected to the so-called *Pulverlinie* (Powder Line), which stipulated that no weapons could be produced east of a line running through the FRG because this area was too vulnerable to attack. Finally, like Stegner (and indeed like Adenauer earlier), Mellies argued that military production could not be easily separated from production for the civilian economy and that Bonn would "cripple" itself by accepting far-reaching restrictions.[31] It is significant that German Socialists were taking this line, showing again that when it came to issues of military equality and national prosperity, they were as vigilant as their conservative colleagues.

Turning to the costs of the military buildup, committee members expressed their concern, as had their colleagues in the plenum debates, that the demands of rearmament might bankrupt the young Federal Republic. Bonn's economic recovery was still in its infancy and based on the export of civilian products, they said; it must not be undercut by overly ambitious outlays for defense. In response, an official from the Ministry of Economics offered assurances that the EDC procurement system would make effective use of member states' relative strengths, take account of respective weaknesses, and guarantee that no country would suffer "severe disruption" of its economy. Blank added that there would be no repetition of the Third Reich's practice of subordinating general economic policy to military needs; nor would there be anything like a "Speer Ministry"—a reference to Albert Speer's Ministry of Arms and War Production, which (at least toward the end of the war) channeled much of Nazi Germany's economic and industrial resources into the war effort. Other committee members, Strauss in particular, worried that German industrial resources could be unfairly exploited by Germany's partners. A "corrupt" EDC procurement system, Strauss warned, might allow other countries to make use of Germany's technical advances for their own gains, as the Allies had done after the war when they had plundered German patents and secured the services of the Reich's best scientists. Just as Bonn had to protect its future soldiers from exploitation, the committee believed, so too did it have to protect its reemerging industry from co-optation in the name of cooperation.

The committee noted that West Germany's economy would be seriously affected by the proposed conscription system, which would take tens of thousands of young men out of the civilian market for long stretches of time. Noting that agriculture was especially dependent on able young males, Strauss wondered whether the policy would take account of this sector's "special needs." He added that many Bavarian farmers had expressed concern to him on this point. Blank responded tartly that every profession claimed to be indispensable, and his office was not planning to allow wholesale deferments on this basis. He hoped, however, that any losses of income incurred because of the draft would be compensated by the state or by the EDC as a whole.[32]

Conscription, however, raised other, more fundamental problems for the young Federal Republic. Above all, there was the question of which "Germans" would be subject to it. As Erler pointed out, Bonn informally considered all sorts of people "German citizens" who were not technically *Bundesbürger*: these included native Berliners, Saarländers, and "Soviet Occupation Zone" citizens temporarily residing in the Federal Republic. Were the young men belonging to these groups all fodder for the West German draft? And what about West German men of draft age who moved to Berlin? Was Berlin *militärtechnisch* part of the FRG, or was it a "foreign country"? Blank replied that Berlin was clearly off-limits for the West German draft, and a good thing too, for otherwise the Russians would undoubtedly claim "certain rights" in the western part of that city. But he speculated that many young men would move from Berlin to West Germany "in order to be able to serve."[33] (The reality, of course, was just the opposite. West Berlin became a haven for draft dodgers, which was one of the reasons for the city's pronounced counter-cultural flair in the 1960s and 1970s.)

Throughout its early discussions, the Bundestag Security Committee registered misgivings not only about specific details of the treaty drafts but about a general paucity of parliamentary control in the proposed arrangements. Delegates from all the major parties told Blank and his aides that the system as then conceived must not be regarded as final, that new laws would have to be passed governing such issues as troop deployment, soldiers' rights, procurement, expenditures, and staffing of officer corps. The committee, in other words, was joining parliament as a whole in insisting that *this time*, as opposed to past experience, Germany's army must be largely shaped by civilian legislators.

This was a message that the government seemed to have received clearly enough, for it was quick to offer assurances that parliament would indeed be intimately involved in shaping the legal groundwork for rearmament. Having gotten these assurances, and despite some continuing reservations about the treaties, most of the Bundestag delegates from the government parties voted to approve the package when it came up for its third and final reading on 19 March 1953. The treaties were passed by a simple majority, all the SPD delegates voting against. But the struggle for parliamentary ratification was by no means over, for the Bundesrat still had to vote on those parts of the treaties affecting the states, and the president had to be persuaded that the entire complex was constitutionally acceptable. As ever, the situation was exhaustingly complicated.

FINAL HURDLES: THE BUNDESRAT AND CONSTITUTIONAL AMENDMENTS

Konrad Adenauer had been no more anxious to include the Bundesrat than the Bundestag in the making of foreign and security policy. But like their counterparts in the lower house, the Bundesrat delegates had come to resent their exclusion from the diplomatic process, as well as the chancellor's tendency to treat them like toadies. As Lower Saxony's minister president, Heinrich Wilhelm Kopf (SPD), archly put it: "Our function is not to sing the Horst Wessel Song and say yes."[34]

The Bundesrat's rebellious mood ensured that the upper house would subject the treaties to unusually careful scrutiny. Though Adenauer could hardly have welcomed this development, it need not have been more than a nuisance had that body remained under the domination of the coalition parties, which it had been until early 1952. But in March of that year the consolidation of Baden, Württemberg-Baden, and Württemberg-Hohenzollern into the new state of Baden-Württemberg altered the political balance in the upper house because the new regime in Stuttgart was a coalition of the FDP, Deutsche Volkspartei (DVP), and the SPD. Now, instead of controlling twenty-four of forty-three available votes, the Union had only eighteen of thirty-eight, while the SPD had fifteen and the new coalition in Stuttgart five.

Even more significant, Baden-Württemberg's newly elected minister president, Reinhold Maier, was an articulate and resourceful critic of the chancellor's security policy. He did not oppose rearmament per se, but he believed it premature in light of Germany's recent demilitarization and continuing division. People who had just witnessed the "destruction of everything that had the slightest military connotations," he said, could hardly be expected "to jump with both feet into the new situation." Like many Germans, he worried that Bonn's rearmament might provoke the Russians to a "preventive war." Maier objected that "foreign generals" would control the German contingent in the EDC. Nor was he impressed by Adenauer's *Politik der Stärke*, dismissing as "absurd" his contention that EDC membership would promote reunification. Germany's quid pro quo for rearmament, the General Treaty, struck Maier as equally flawed. Like many of his colleagues, he objected to its provision for continued Allied privileges through which future German foreign policy would be unduly "corseted."[35]

Given these reservations, Maier was determined to subject the treaties to critical examination in the Bundesrat and, if possible, to delay their ratification until the Constitutional Court had rendered its verdict regarding their legality. He believed that the longer Bonn waited to rearm, the more diplomatic pressure it could exert.[36] His shaky position within his own party, however, did not allow him to engage in an uninhibited assault on the chancellor's policies. Although the Vorstand (Executive Committee) of the FDP shared some of Maier's reservations regarding the treaties, it was committed in principle to ratification. Most of the Vorstand, moreover, believed that his views were all too close to those of the SPD. At a national FDP congress at Bad Ems (1952), August Martin Euler denounced Maier for echoing the SPD's condemnation of the veterans' associations as neo-Nazi. Maier's mistake, said Euler, was to "forget our duty to win over the ex-soldiers and former Nazis for the democratic *Rechtsstaat*."[37] Attacks like Euler's meant that Maier had to proceed somewhat cautiously if he was not to find himself driven out of his own party. His coalition with the SPD in Baden-Württemberg also limited his freedom of movement because the Socialists could bring down the *Land* government should Maier decide to throw his weight behind the chancellor's policies. Thoroughly understanding his difficulties, Maier soon proved that he was just as much a political "fox" as Adenauer.

The chancellor, for his part, quickly became aware of the danger that Maier and the Bundesrat posed to the rapid ratification of the treaty package. Characteristically, Adenauer's strategy in the face of this new threat was to try to exclude the upper house from its constitutional right to pass judgment on those dimensions of the treaties affecting the states. In late April, shortly after the formation of the new government in Stuttgart, he asked the High Commission to countenance a "simplification" of the treaty system that would cut out the sections touching on states' rights. The commissioners seem to have been genuinely shocked by the audacity of this proposal. John McCloy spoke for his colleagues when he insisted that the clauses Adenauer wished to exclude were fundamental to the treaties; one must not, he declared, try to sidestep the constitutional process through "clever maneuvers."[38]

Unable simply to evade the Bundesrat, Adenauer now tried a different tack. Shortly after the treaties were signed, he submitted them to the upper house in two sections, one containing provisions requiring Bundesrat ratification, the other containing material that needed only to be *considered*, but not actually *ratified*, by that body. The latter embraced the most significant components of the treaty legislation, while the former were restricted to technical issues involving taxation and finance. Because the Bundesrat's procedural rules allowed only three weeks for initial consideration of any measure, the upper house's role would be restricted in both time and scope.

The Bundesrat's response to this maneuver was to dig in its heels: on 20 June it announced that it would vote on all parts of the treaty complex relevant to the states. Moreover, because a thorough consideration would take longer than the three-week period allotted for the first round of discussions, no vote would be taken until after a second reading, by which time Karlsruhe might have rendered its constitutional verdict. The upper house pointedly added that the ratification process might have been expedited had the government taken the trouble to keep the Bundesrat apprised of the negotiations from the outset.[39] Once again, it appeared that Adenauer's high-handedness had come back to haunt him.

Reinhold Maier welcomed this standoff between Adenauer and the Bundesrat. Given his delicate political balancing act, he was not in a position to vote directly for or against the treaties. In late 1952 he happily embraced the argument that nothing ought to be done until the Constitutional Court had pronounced on President Heuss's request for an advisory opinion. Heuss's withdrawal of his petition in December therefore greatly distressed him.[40] Nevertheless, he continued to insist that the Bundesrat could take no final action until the treaties' legal status had been clarified.

A decision became harder to evade, however, after the Bundestag ratified the treaties on 19 March. Now the ball was definitely in the upper house's court, the government having sent the treaty legislation to that body on 13 April.

Shortly thereafter, Adenauer returned from a long trip to the United States, the first time a sitting German chancellor had ever visited America. During his stay he had assured his hosts that he would have no trouble pushing the treaties through the upper house. News of this boasting reached the minister presidents and confirmed some of them in their determination to thwart the chancellor's will. Yet Adenauer's prestige in Germany was greatly enhanced by press reports about his lionization in America—in those days, it was still an advantage to be lionized in America—where he had been hailed as a great anti-Communist statesman by Vice-President Richard Nixon and Secretary of State John Foster Dulles and made an honorary chief of the Iroquois tribe, an honor for which his physiognomy certainly fitted him.[41]

Basking in his status as international statesman, Adenauer told a CDU gathering upon his return that West Germany faced a "decision of the greatest magnitude for its future and that of the entire free world."[42] Should the Germans fail to ratify the EDC, he warned, they would be abandoned by the West, particularly by the Americans, who would remove their troops from Germany and stop investing in the Federal Republic. "Could anyone believe," he asked rhetorically, "that [America] would continue to help the German people if they were guilty of wrecking the entire policy of [West integration]?"[43]

Adenauer did not, however, attempt to rely solely on his enhanced prestige and apocalyptic warnings to maneuver the treaty package through the Bundesrat. Upon his return from America, he passed word to Maier that if he were to support the government's position, the CDU in Baden-Württemberg would be willing to form a new coalition with the FDP and retain Maier as minister president. Of course, this was a transparent attempt at bribery, and Maier claims in his memoirs to have been "insulted" by it.[44] Thus he stuck to his demand for a postponement of a final decision on rearmament until Karlsruhe had rendered its judgment. The Bundesrat was split evenly on rearmament so this proposal, which Maier put into a formal motion, seemed to have an excellent chance of prevailing.

Before a vote could be taken on Maier's resolution, however, Adenauer again intervened in the parliamentary process, this time hinting that Washington might be willing to replace its high commissioner with an ambassador if Bonn quickly ratified the treaties. Maier, suspicious, asked to see written confirmation of this promise. None was forthcoming, for the simple reason that it had never been made. America, after all, could not take such a step until all the prospective EDC member states (especially France, which also had a high commissioner) had ratified the treaties. Maier did not hesitate to accuse the chancellor of trying to pull the wool over parliamentary eyes.[45]

When the Bundesrat finally voted on Maier's motion, the result was as he had predicted: a narrow passage, twenty to eighteen. Some delegates voted for the motion out of fear that if they did not, Maier might swing the votes he controlled against the treaties and thereby effect their defeat. The result was to hand this hot potato back to President Heuss because, two weeks after the Bundesrat's vote, the government could legally ask for the president's signature on the treaty bills not requiring Bundesrat sanction. The upper house had had its chance to render a clear verdict on the substance of the treaties and had chosen not to do so. Maier fully understood the implications of this action; above all, he understood that the *schwarze Peter* would now rest with the president, not with him.[46]

But when Adenauer approached Heuss with the request that he sign the treaties, the president demurred. He had, he now informed Adenauer, promised Ollenhauer that he would not approve the bills until the Constitutional Court had certified their constitutionality. Despite considerable pressure from the chancellor, he refused to be dissuaded.[47] Like parliament, he would not be "rolled over."

Heuss's independence threatened to destroy the chancellor's entire laboriously constructed foreign policy. Determined that this should not be, Adenauer now tried to topple the SPD-dominated government of Lower Saxony in an effort to alter the political composition of the Bundesrat. A politically realigned upper house might be prevailed upon to pass the treaty bills before Heuss acted, thereby putting added pressure on the president to go along. But this dubious campaign also failed.[48]

Following this reverse, Adenauer turned his attention to those politicians most vulnerable to pressure from the Bundeskanzleramt: the government coalition delegates in the Bundesrat. Returning to his scheme to divide the treaties, he announced that he intended to resubmit the treaty package in two parts and expected a definitive vote of approval. He again warned darkly that further delays would endanger West Germany's integration into the free world community. At the same time, he convinced the FDP leadership to put pressure on Maier, who was threatened with political exile if he did not come around.[49]

This pressure was effective. Bundesrat federalists were in the end unwilling to take responsibility for the failure of the EDC and with it Bonn's bid to gain full sovereignty. This would be carrying states' rights too far, they thought. Maier, too, was not anxious to be banished to the wilderness further to delay an initiative about which he had serious reservations but whose ultimate acceptance he believed inevitable.[50] Thus when the treaty package, now di-

vided, again came before the Bundesrat on 15 May, that body gave up its resistance. It voted not to contest the two main treaty bills, which passed
twenty-three to fifteen. Thus Adenauer finally had the parliamentary endorsement he needed to give his foreign policy credibility, though he had had
to employ all his political wiles to get it.

Even so, the treaty bills were still in limbo, for the fundamental constitutional questions had not been answered or the president's signature secured.
To remind the nation (and the government) that such matters still required
resolution, the SPD and some of the smaller parties petitioned Karlsruhe
anew to decide on the legality of rearmament. In their petition, the plaintiffs
also contended that the Bundesrat had acted improperly in accepting the
treaties.[51]

Though the first senate agreed to consider this petition, it again showed no
inclination to act expeditiously, patiently sorting through an avalanche of
briefs and counterbriefs, which, in their lack of originality or substance,
confirmed Goethe's bon mot that "Getretener Quark wird breit, nicht stark"
(Yoghurt when mashed becomes flatter, not stiffer). Clearly the court did not
want to make a crucial political decision on the eve of a new Bundestag election, which, if sufficiently favorable to the government, might relieve the
jurists of the unwelcome duty of making a decision at all.[52]

As it happened, the court's caution paid off (as least for the jurists), for, after an election fought mainly over security policy issues, the pro-EDC parties
emerged the big winners. The CDU/CSU garnered 45.2 percent, the FDP
9.5, and the Deutsche Partei/Bund der Heimatvertriebenen und Entrechte-
ten (DP/BHE) 5.9. With the latter group joining his coalition, Adenauer
now controlled 69.4 percent of the Bundestag votes. In the Bundesrat, he advanced the government's position from eighteen to twenty-six mandates by
gaining control of Baden-Württemberg and Hamburg. The big losers, in
addition to the SPD, which received only 28.8 percent in the Bundestag,
were the smaller antirearmament parties like Heinemann's Gesamtdeutsche
Volkspartei (GVP), the KPD, and the far-rightist Deutsche Rechtspartei
(DRP). None of them managed to clear the 5 percent hurdle that had recently been instituted to inhibit the proliferation of splinter parties—the
curse of Weimar.[53]

With his convincing victory—the size of which surprised almost everyone—Adenauer was in a position to secure changes in the Basic Law that
would make rearmament unquestionably constitutional and therefore acceptable to the president. Blankenhorn could write confidently in his diary that
the coalition would now "easily achieve the two-thirds majority required for
constitutional amendments. Thus final approval of the treaties is assured."[54]

Not surprisingly, then, the government lost little time in drafting the req-
uisite constitutional revisions, though it was careful not to admit their neces-

sity, which would have buttressed the SPD's still pending (albeit soon to be moot) case. The first of the amendments called for a revision of Article 73, which would now read: "The federal government has exclusive power to legislate on foreign affairs and defense, including conscription for men over 18 years of age." Article 79, governing the rules for amendments, now said that a simple "clarification" in the Basic Law would be enough to allow Bonn to conclude "international treaties designed to protect the Federal Republic or abolish an Occupation Regime." The relevant "clarification" was contained in a new Article 142(a), which stated: "The Basic Law's provisions do not conflict with the completion and implementation of the treaties signed in Bonn and Paris on 26–27 May 1952, nor with the Related Conventions, especially the Protocol of 26 July 1952."[55]

Armed with its two-thirds majority, the coalition had no trouble securing Bundestag approval of the amendments on 26 February 1954 and that of the Bundesrat on 19 March. Because the new laws directly affected Bonn's relations with the occupation powers, the high commissioners also had to approve them. At first, the French refused approval pending ratification of the treaties by all the EDC member states. Under pressure from America and Britain, however, France accepted the amendments. Now that rearmament was explicitly provided for in the constitution, President Heuss signed the treaty bills, though he noted in a codicil to the EDC treaty that Bonn would not achieve military sovereignty until the European army came into being.[56]

Even now, however, the long legal battle over rearmament was not entirely over, for the SPD launched one last petition to Karlsruhe, asking the court to decide whether the treaties had been constitutional at the time they were ratified in 1953; if not, they would need to be debated anew, for constitutional amendments could not be retroactive. But the court was less than ever inclined to pass judgment on this petition, which it relegated to a back burner of its docket. Like courts the world over, it had learned to turn strategic foot-dragging into an exquisitely refined dance. Karlsruhe did not have to be dilatory for long, however, for the French Assembly's rejection of the EDC in August 1954 made the issue irrelevant and necessitated new treaties and a whole new debate.

PYRRHIC VICTORY

In his memoirs, Konrad Adenauer insisted that Bonn's protracted battle over treaty ratification spelled doom for the EDC because every passing month worsened the prospects for ratification in France.[57] Though the French environment indeed became increasingly inhospitable to the EDC, it is very possible that the Assembly would have rejected the pact whenever it came up for a vote. In retrospect, one might argue that the ratification process was significant less for its effect on the EDC than as a window of observation on Bonn's young political and legal system. Through his mastery of this system, Adenauer ultimately prevailed, but his victory can be regarded as Pyrrhic: not only did it fail to secure final success of the EDC, it also crowned a bitter domestic struggle that (in the words of one commentator) "left injured on the battlefield practically all the protagonists."[58] A brief recapitulation of how the main contestants behaved in the long confrontation can bring out the full truth of this assessment and clarify the meaning of this episode for the political culture of the young Federal Republic.

In adjudicating—and failing to adjudicate—the complicated rearmament issue, the Constitutional Court showed the strain of having to deal with a politically explosive question in the first half decade of its existence. To its credit, the court asserted its right to judicial review and showed itself independent of political labels. Throughout its deliberations it practiced what conservative American jurists would approvingly call "judicial restraint." While maintaining its right to pronounce on the constitutionality of rearmament, it deliberately avoided doing so, thereby relegating a divisive political decision to the political arena, where many thought it belonged. For other observers, however, both lay and expert, this was less an act of admirable restraint than an evasion of responsibility. The eminent legal scholar Karl Loewenstein summed up this criticism when he wrote, damningly: "In the first major test of its usefulness the Court has been found wanting. A great opportunity to live up to the expectations of the Basic Law was sacrificed to extra-judicial considerations."[59]

The two main contestants in the ratification struggle, Adenauer's government and the SPD, also revealed less auspicious sides of their political character. Adenauer himself acted in a way that recalled, at least for some, Bismarck's disregard of constitutional norms in his conflict with the Prussian Landtag in the early 1860s.[60] Although such a comparison perhaps overshoots the mark, Adenauer was indeed willing to attempt end runs around the Basic Law when it complicated his political aspirations. This was evident in his efforts to prevent the Bundesrat from exercising its constitutional duties and in his struggle to stop the Constitutional Court from intervening in foreign policy. When it proved impossible to circumvent the court, Adenauer tried to manipulate its proceedings, showing little respect for the principle of judicial independence.

The SPD, for its part, appeared hardly more respectful of constitutional principles than the government. The party launched its "preventive injunction" and subsequent petitions to stop rearmament, not (as it often claimed) simply to achieve constitutional clarification or to guarantee the rule of law. The SPD's flight to the court revealed a lack of confidence in parliamentary institutions and a willingness to supplant ballots with judicial fiat. And, once having turned to the court, the Socialists, like Adenauer, sought to manipulate it. When they then failed to get the judgment they wanted, they accused the jurists of practicing political justice. Much of this sounded like SPD rhetoric of the past, as did the occasional relapses into knee-jerk antimilitary dogma. Soon, some of the Socialists would resort to other extraparliamentary measures to stop rearmament—plebiscites and pressure from the streets. There was a streak of desperation and hysteria in these actions that confirmed in many Germans' eyes Adenauer's contention that the SPD could not be relied on to govern.

To their credit, however, key SPD politicians were already working behind the scenes to find compromises in some of the most difficult security issues. The party's bark in the plenum was clearly worse than its bite in committee. In the end, Socialists like Erler, Carlo Schmid, Wilhelm Mellies, and (later) Helmut Schmidt ensured that the new West German army would not be established without a major contribution from the SPD—traditionally a source of little more than ideological objections from the sidelines. For the Social Democrats, Bonn's rearmament battle turned out to be a key phase in their postwar political education.

That sometime target of the Socialists' ire, President Heuss, was not, strictly speaking, a contestant in this case, but he proved unable to preserve an image of impartiality, and he came out of the imbroglio with his reputation tarnished. Acutely aware that his appeal to the court for an advisory opinion on rearmament had been counterproductive, he fully concurred when the power to lodge such appeals was later removed from presidential purview. It took the presidency some time to recover from this early blow to its prestige, and the recovery was hardly aided by the unfortunate tenure of Heuss's successor, Heinrich Lübke, one of most embarrassing figures in modern German politics.[61]

Bonn's two parliamentary bodies, the Bundestag and Bundesrat, showed signs of political maturation in the ratification debate: it seemed that they were acting somewhat less like collections of "crazies and bores" (in Sir Ivone Kirkpatrick's terminology) and rather more like serious players in the government process. In the realm of security policy, where they had heretofore played a purely negative role, they were beginning to demand their say, putting the chancellor on notice that he could no longer proceed as if they did not exist. As we have seen, this was especially true of the Bundestag Security Committee, in which coalition and opposition politicians worked profitably together.

And yet many German parliamentarians, including most Socialists, were not yet ready to take full responsibility for the momentous decisions involved in rearmament. They preferred that the onus of these difficult choices rest anywhere but with themselves. Their evasiveness was reminiscent of past German parliaments' tendency to defer to the executive on issues of seminal importance. The result of this "political meandering"[62] was a somewhat ambiguous and incomplete challenge to Adenauer's "democratic dictatorship." Considerably more experience would be required before parliament could replace its "practice run at rebellion"[63] with a more sustained and convincing challenge.

SCHARNHORST

REVISITED:

THE POLITICS

OF MILITARY

REFORM   While Chancellor Adenauer was struggling to has-
ten the EDC and General treaties through Bonn's
legal and parliamentary system, his security planning agency, the Dienststelle Blank, was busily de-
signing the structural and organizational features of the new military. At the
heart of this enterprise was an effort to create another novelty in German history: an army that would be responsive to and reflective of the democratic society it would serve. But what did "democratic" mean in the military realm?
To what extent could (or should) a "democratic army" be created? What connections would the new army have to martial legacies from the past, and how
much of Germany's military heritage would have to be jettisoned in the name
of reform? How should the relationship between the military leadership and
civilian authority be defined? What role would the soldiers have in the political life of the nation? All these questions were as vulnerable to political pressure as the original decision to rearm and therefore resisted easy answers. By
their very nature, moreover, they demanded a complex wrestling with the
layered legacies of the past—a baggage collection containing a jumble of embarrassing souvenirs, unwanted ballast, as well as some genuinely useful items
for the trip ahead.

The internecine battles that the reform project ignited among Bonn's military planners, parties, and interest groups not only complicated efforts to
find a consensus on military structure but pointed up larger fractures in the
body politic. Here again, rearmament revealed itself as the crucible in which
the young republic's political culture was tested and shaped.

But the problem did not end here, for the politics of military reform could
no more be confined to a purely domestic context than could the basic question of creating an army in the first place. Given the imperative to integrate

West German forces in a common European army, Bonn's military planners had to work with one eye firmly cocked toward their future partners, who of course had their own ideas about how armies should be organized. It quickly became evident that Allied conceptions differed fundamentally from those of the Germans. Put simply, Bonn's eagerness to break new ground in matters military was not shared by the Western powers, who even began to feel a little nostalgic for the "militaristic" Germans of old.

Though the eventual failure of the EDC obviated the need to iron out all the interalliance disagreements over military design, some of the differences continued to be at issue as the new Bundeswehr groped its way into NATO. Aside from their practical consequences, moreover, the disagreements over military reform were telling indicators of Bonn's special status in the postwar West; they were emblematic of its position as a not-quite-nation with a very problematic past working to cooperate with fully sovereign entities possessed of healthy national traditions and well-entrenched national interests.

COUNT WOLF VON BAUDISSIN AND *INNERE FÜHRUNG*

No figure connected with West German rearmament gained greater notoriety than Count Wolf von Baudissin.[1] Often held up (not least, by himself) as the "father" of the ambitious military reform program known as *Innere Führung*,* he was both celebrated as a courageous innovator and disparaged as a meddlesome "dreamer." Early on, he gained prominence largely because he was the figure in the Dienststelle primarily responsible for presenting the reform plans to a skeptical public. He did this well, for he combined eloquent passion with a certain aristocratic reserve that made him seem trustworthy. Moreover, perhaps more than any of his colleagues, he had a fine sense for the anxieties that so many of his countrymen harbored about rearmament. It soon became evident, however, that he was not so well suited for harmonious collaboration with his fellow former officers and that he would have trouble winning over Germany's fractious veterans' groups to the reform project. His difficulties in this realm derived partly from his personality, which was prickly and aloof, and partly from his own military career, which raised questions about his qualifications among his critics. Because of his prominent status, the controversy that grew up around him eventually complicated the new army's struggle to establish itself as a viable and respected institution on the West German scene.

Baudissin's contributions to and place in the reform process are incompre-

*Innere Führung has been variously translated as "internal guidance," "inner leadership," "moral leadership," "independent leadership," and "moral education." In fact, it means all these and more. To avoid confusing the issue, I will use the original German term.

hensible without some appreciation of his background and training. Though born into an aristocratic family in Trier in 1907, he grew up in West Prussia and identified strongly with that region. He loved the rural landscape and always retained something of the eastern squire in his demeanor. Yet he did not value the traditional Prussian stereotypes—militarism, worship of authority, exaggerated sense of hierarchy. He liked to say that his models were the great reformers of Prussia during the Napoleonic era, particularly the military innovators Gerhard von Scharnhorst and August von Gneisenau, who had struggled to recast the antiquated Prussian army according to the political and technical demands posed by Prussia's French conquerors. In his own career as self-proclaimed military "radical," Baudissin sometimes cloaked himself in Scharnhorst's mantle, even claiming on one occasion that he had decided to participate in the military planning process so as to "carry on the reforming impulse that had foundered in 1819."[2]

Of course, he meant this loosely, for Baudissin was aware that the challenges and conditions of the mid-twentieth century differed substantially from those of the early nineteenth. Unlike the reformers of that earlier era, he and his colleagues had to convince their nation that an army was necessary at all. In contrast to the Prussian military of Scharnhorst's day, West Germany's army could not be founded in the cause of nationalism but had to be grounded in the new spirit of European integration and cooperation. At least in theory, the new German army would be not so much a "school of the nation" as a "school of Europe." Rather than fighting a war of revenge and liberation, its primary role would be to deter wars by making aggression too costly.

Aside from his reverence for the great military reformers, Baudissin was guided by his own experiences as a soldier. In 1926, at age nineteen, he had joined the Reichswehr's famous Potsdam-based Infantry Regiment Number 9, which was at once the inner sanctum of Prussian military tradition and the regiment that spawned the greatest number of opponents to Hitler in World War II.[3] Later, during his career as a reformer, Baudissin claimed that he had been put off by his regiment's continuing reverence for the old monarchy and its traditions. On one occasion, he recalled, he had stalked out of a banquet when his colleagues toasted the memory of Emperor Wilhelm I. He also claimed to have been disgusted by the Reichswehr's aloofness from the Weimar state, a posture he considered both dangerous and "un-Prussian."[4]

It is possible that these claims owed something to the benefits of hindsight. Some of Baudissin's military critics and rivals in the 1950s and 1960s insisted that he had been a model of aristocratic *Corpsgeist* during his Reichswehr career.[5] Records of his unit do show, however, that for a time he used his position as regimental adjutant to advance technical innovations that anticipated in some ways his later work as a reformer. He promoted training programs keyed to specific missions and sought to open his colleagues to outside ideas by organizing meetings with civilian experts.[6] None of these efforts suggested a contempt for what had gone before, and all of them stayed within accepted traditions of technical modernization. Though his initiatives in the 1950s were often bolder, earning him a reputation for radicalism, they too were generally informed by a respect for the past, or at least for those aspects of the past that Baudissin considered positive and serviceable.

Whatever reservations Baudissin may have had about the Reichswehr's "extraterritoriality," he remained in military service while that agency was transformed into Hitler's Wehrmacht. He later insisted that he had opposed from the outset the aggressive purposes to which the Wehrmacht was ultimately put.[7] That may well have been so, but he was denied the opportunity to become part of the emerging military resistance, for he was captured by the British at Tobruk in 1941 and spent the next six years in prisoner of war camps in Egypt, Palestine, and Australia. (Of course, had he not "missed his chance" to become an active military resister, he might have also missed the chance to become a reformer, for most of the principal resisters were executed.) Because he had sat out most of the war, missing crucial battlefield experiences like the invasion of Russia and the defense of the Reich, some of the nationalist veterans later argued that he was unfit to help shape the new army.[8] But his prolonged captivity gave him ample opportunity to assess why the German officer class as a whole had proven itself such a willing accomplice to Hitler's crimes. He concluded that most of the soldiers, understanding little of democracy, had been "helpless in the face of the temptations presented by the Third Reich."[9]

Released from British captivity in 1947, Baudissin briefly earned his living as a potter, crafting garden ceramics with his wife, a professional sculptor. If this seems something of a comedown for a Prussian aristocrat and former major, it was not untypical of the postwar fate of the German officer class, many of whom found themselves selling soap, waiting tables, or even singing for their supper in cabarets filled with Allied soldiers. That Baudissin attempted an "artistic" career is revealing: though no bohemian, he liked to think of himself as imaginative and creative, even something of a "romantic."[10] For better or worse, this quality would also find its way into his reformist efforts of the 1950s.

Equally important for the future was Baudissin's volunteer work as a counselor in an EKD-sponsored industrial relations program in the mining industry. Here he began to develop the theories on personnel management that were to play a significant role in *Innere Führung*. His experience with lay Protestantism convinced him of the need to infuse all public institutions, including the military, with Christian ethical principles. It also prepared him to collaborate with the many theologians who were called upon to help formulate the ethical principles upon which the new army would be based. Unfortunately, however, Baudissin's religious zeal, while giving depth to his reforming mission, also made him somewhat intolerant of colleagues less high-minded than himself. Like Gustav Heinemann, he was a man whose strong moral convictions, combined with no small amount of personal vanity and amour propre, inhibited his ability to work smoothly with the Realpolitiker of the Adenauer era.

In September 1950 Baudissin was invited by a former colleague from Infantry Regiment Number 9, Major Axel von dem Bussche-Streithorst, to join the "Committee of Experts" that gathered at Himmerod. There the count was given the assignment, along with former general Hermann Foertsch, to prepare the "internal guidance" components of the Himmerod Memorandum. That Baudissin's co-worker had written a pro-Nazi tract for Wehrmacht officers and still thought largely in traditional military terms helps explain the ambiguities and inconsistencies in that first blueprint for military reform.[11]

In May 1951, on the initiative of Kielmansegg, Baudissin became a member of the new Dienststelle Blank, charged with further developing the ideas he had put forth at Himmerod. As head of the *Wehrwesen* section of the agency, he had the job of elaborating the military regulations that would define the "inner structure" of the new army. He remained in this capacity throughout the life of the Dienststelle, doggedly promoting the cause of *Innere Führung*.

Before analyzing the essentials of that concept as they evolved in the early planning process, we need to say something about other important figures concerned with these issues: though military reform might sometimes have seemed like a one-man show, in fact it was a cooperative effort.

Count von Kielmansegg, as one of the holdovers from Schwerin's Zentrale, was intimately involved in the Dienststelle's initial effort to define the parameters of military reform.[12] Though this first impulse, which preceded Baudissin's arrival in the agency, did not get very far, Kielmansegg continued to work on reform questions. He was particularly interested in the problem of officer selection, having discussed with Blank the possibility of some sort of "screening board" as early as 1950–51.[13] Officer selection was to become one of the most controversial aspects of the reform program.

Ulrich de Maizière, like Baudissin a Kielmansegg recruit (the two men had served together in the General Staff in 1942–43), took up reform questions as a Dienststelle functionary at the Paris EDC talks.[14] His central task was the unenviable one of trying to reconcile German approaches to military organization and discipline with those of Bonn's future allies. Fortunately for Germany, de Maizière proved to be an exceptionally skillful negotiator, often more skillful than many of the diplomats.

When it came to articulating the fundamentals of reform, perhaps the most important of Baudissin's colleagues was Heinz Karst, a former Wehrmacht captain who joined the Dienststelle in 1952. Karst, who later fell out with Baudissin and sharply criticized him,[15] was a South German Catholic of lower-middle-class origins who had worked his way into the officer corps from the enlisted grades. He had been one of those ambitious young men who was able to take advantage of the Wehrmacht's practice of rapidly promoting talented and aggressive soldiers. Ever after, as he rose in the Dienststelle and defense ministry (he ended his career as a brigadier general), he retained the quality of self-made man. If nothing else, his example showed that this was a condition as susceptible to vanity and self-importance as was privileged birth. In his early career in the Dienststelle, he clashed with Baudissin not over substantive issues—that came later—but because he rivaled the count in popularity outside the agency. In his case, however, the admirers tended to be Wehrmacht veterans rather than politicians and academics. Karst appealed to the former soldiers with his earthy humor and readiness to support their sense of grievance against allegedly uncomprehending political leaders.

Karst, Baudissin, Kielmansegg, and de Maizière all considered themselves military men, though technically, like all the Dienststelle's employees, they were civilians. There were, however, other functionaries of the agency involved in the reform process whose backgrounds were thoroughly civilian rather than military. This was true, for example, of Adenauer's confidant Ernst Wirmer and of Wolfgang Cartellieri, head of the agency's personnel department. Their collaboration was extremely important, for it guaranteed a certain civilian perspective even in technical questions of military organization—another sharp break from Germany's martial past.[16]

The Dienststelle section explicitly concerned with *Innere Führung* had a tiny staff and woefully inadequate material resources. These deficiencies, combined with a genuine desire to draw the public into the discussion of military reform, prompted the agency to farm out some of its planning work to outside experts. It also organized countless conferences with influential figures from academia, the churches, unions, industry, and parties. These occasions featured spirited discussion of virtually all the major issues associated with military reform. Whatever complaints might be leveled against the reformers, one could not legitimately claim that they had excluded the public.

Baudissin aired his reform ideas at a major conference held in the Evangelical Academy of Hermannsburg in December 1951. Here he argued that Germany's recent "catastrophe" represented both a crisis and an opportunity. The nation's sociopolitical institutions had been thoroughly discredited, but the "grace of the zero point" (*Stunde Null*) offered a chance to start fresh with new ideas that could be of especial appeal to dislocated young people search-ing for a sense of direction.[17]

At about the same time, an even more far-ranging symposium took place in Weinheim under the auspices of one of West Germany's new public interest groups, the Institut zur Föderung öffentlicher Angelegenheiten (Institute for the Advancement of Public Issues).[18] Here, Dienststelle functionaries met with legal experts, union leaders, businessmen, youth group representatives, and Bundestag delegates from all the major parties. They discussed such cru-cial issues as parliamentary control over the military, location of the *Kom-mandogewalt* (power of command), relative jurisdiction of military and civil-ian officials, political rights of soldiers, and criteria for selection of officers. In essence, they came down squarely for civilian control, even in areas tradition-ally dominated by the military. They thus helped establish the framework in which the agency reformers would work for the next four years.

A closer look at the essentials of the reform program will indicate just how far Dienststelle planners hoped to depart from practices and principles of the past. I will feature the writings and speeches of Baudissin because they pro-vide a clear and convenient summary of the reform enterprise at this stage.[19]

Key to the reform project was the conviction that a new army would have to adapt itself to the radically altered political, social, and cultural realities of the postwar world. In this process, of course, the new military would also have to come to grips with the role the armed forces had played in Germany's recent catastrophe. This need not entail a wholesale rejection of the past, even the recent past. But overall, Germany's military would have to find ways of giving new meaning to the old business of soldiering because it seemed that many of the traditional sources of legitimization had lost their validity.

To Baudissin, rearmament could not be seen as an end in itself but only as "an act in the general context of an international civil war." It was required because the West was "threatened by an ideological principle [communism] that denied all personal values and demanded total submission of the individ-ual." But it was precisely the *ideological* nature of the threat that required countermeasures that went beyond merely recruiting troops and stockpiling weapons. The contemporary soldier was "already fighting in a jungle of ideas," and he needed more intensive mental and moral preparation than ever before. Soldiers of democracy had to defend a pluralistic value system that was "hard to comprehend" and "vulnerable to the down-draft of totalitarian-ism." This was especially true in the FRG, a country that was just beginning to institutionalize democratic values. Thus Bonn's prospective armed forces would need to "occupy and hold an important sector of the internal front," assisting the country in building up "a form of life and government that every citizen would consider worth defending."[20] This idea bore some similarities to the old "school of the nation," but now it had to be combined with the imperatives of integration in the larger value framework of the Western world. Indeed, Baudissin hoped that service in the army would make young Germans better Europeans and firm advocates of closer European unity. Hence he spoke not so much of "German soldiers" but of "European soldiers of German nationality."[21]

For Baudissin, *Wehrwille*—the will to fight—had to be based on an informed identification with the society to be defended. Traditional discipline and esprit de corps were not enough. Thus the new German soldier could not be "unpolitical," as had often been demanded in the past, especially in the Reichswehr. He had to be a *Burger in Uniform* (citizen in uniform)—a phrase that soon became the mantra of the reform program, invoked reverently by some, mockingly by others.

Because the members of Germany's new army would be "political soldiers" in an age of nuclear weapons and potential nuclear holocaust, noted Baudissin, their raison d'être must be to *deter* wars rather than actually to fight them. Indeed, the reformer argued that nuclear-era soldiers were faced with the paradox that they would have failed in their mission if forced to implement their deadly skills. In this emphasis on deterrence, Baudissin was articulating a view that would become central to the strategic thinking of the Western alliance. Yet it was a new and by no means uncomplicated challenge to learn skills that one hoped one would never use.

Because the traditional gap between military and civilian occupations had narrowed significantly in an age of advanced technology and organizational complexity, soldiers needed the same sophisticated technical and personal skills required of their civilian counterparts. Officers had to be able to "manage" complicated organizations, while enlisted men, once they had acquired their own complicated skills, needed to assume greater responsibility. There was, therefore, no place in modern military life for the old world of *Kommiss*—for barracks-room bullying and drill-pad dehumanization.

Baudissin recognized that Germany's armies had not been the only ones to employ dehumanizing drill. Virtually all militaries, and certainly those of Bonn's future allies, had their own histories of internal brutality and disciplinary excess. For Germany, however, the case could be made that dehumanization had abetted the Wehrmacht's complicity in Hitler's crimes. As Baudissin put it: "A secularized 'soldier's honor' that enshrines obedience, duty, hardihood, and readiness for action as unquestioned and absolute principles, leaves the soldier blind and helpless against the whims of criminals and charlatans." To him, the German army's moral and political failings during the Third Reich made it clear that "military pathos"—the cult of obedience perpetuated through unending drill and hazing, along with solemn oaths and sacred ceremonies—was not only anachronistic but dangerous.[22]

Among other departures, this conviction led Baudissin to propose that

Germany's most momentous example of ethically and politically based "disobedience," the Twentieth of July 1944 episode, should be regarded as a source of inspiration for its new soldiers. He even believed that a positive attitude toward this legacy should be a criterion for admission to the officer corps. Also with reference to the Twentieth of July, he advocated the elimination of the soldiers' traditional oath of obedience. Corrupted during the Third Reich into a personal pledge of fealty to Hitler, the oath had helped bind soldiers to a criminal regime. Instead of swearing an oath of allegiance, Baudissin proposed that soldiers participate in a "ceremonial obligation" that would signal their commitment without setting up potential conflicts of conscience.[23]

Though most of Baudissin's colleagues and consultants agreed with these ideas in principle, the task of refining them into practical laws and regulations generated heated debates within the Dienststelle and among the public at large. On the domestic level, as on the international scene, questions over how Bonn's new army should be constituted proved just as fractious as the question if it should exist at all.[24]

THE POLITICS OF *INNERE FÜHRUNG*

Adenauer and Blank

Many years after the foundation of the Bundeswehr, Baudissin complained that West Germany had not fully taken advantage of its unprecedented opportunity for a "new beginning" in military politics; it had failed to exploit the "grace of the zero point." Despite a plethora of laws and regulations that formalized parts of *Innere Führung*, he said, the new approach had not been adequately "internalized." Baudissin blamed this largely on a lack of support from Bonn's political leaders, particularly Adenauer and Blank. The chancellor, he said, was so determined to get Germany rearmed that he cared little about how it was done. And Blank was so concerned with *selling* rearmament that he used the reform program as a public relations smoke screen to hide less salutary realities. Baudissin also complained that, apart from Blank, some of the Dienststelle functionaries did their best to blunt the reform initiative. Though such charges undoubtedly reflected the count's bitterness over what he took to be the unsatisfactory evolution of his own military career—he was moved out of the Ministry of Defense to a field command in 1958, then stuck away in a NATO staff job—his criticisms offer a useful basis for assessing attitudes toward *Innere Führung* among the key decision makers in the FRG.

Taking the chancellor first, we should recall that Adenauer's major personnel decisions regarding military planning reflected a determination to avoid a revival of "militarism." He was undoubtedly serious when he said that he did not wish to restore "the old Wehrmacht crowd." In the same vein, the chancellor once proposed that the new army be organized on the militia principle because militias "don't putsch."[25] In a Bundestag speech in 1952 he insisted that "the future German soldier can be true to his national and European mission only when he is animated by the political principles upon which our state is based."[26] Such sentiments were not just window dressing: Adenauer *was* determined to secure civilian control over the army. But control by which civilian agencies? Baudissin and the reformers focused on parliament as the chief guarantor of the "primacy of politics." Though Adenauer admitted that the new military must be established through laws passed by the Bundestag, he had tried from the outset to minimize parliament's role in security policy.

On the advisability of creating an "army without pathos," Adenauer was at best lukewarm. Though certainly no admirer of things military (he insisted he felt a cold chill every time he heard the term *Panzerschrank*), he was a firm believer in the importance of tradition as a source of coherence and discipline. He was also convinced that a certain measure of pomp would improve morale and increase the army's popular appeal. He argued for bands and frequent parades because "the people like that sort of thing."[27] More significantly, he strongly urged that all future soldiers swear a religious oath of allegiance, as had been the German custom in the past.[28] He pressed this point despite opposition from Baudissin, who argued that such oaths had been discredited in the Third Reich. To anticipate a bit, Adenauer was in the end able to resurrect the traditional oath, though only for career officers; enlisted men would merely engage in the "ceremonial obligation."

The chancellor's chief defense planner, Blank, also professed solid commitment to military reform. Upon taking office he declared that he would do all he could to realize reformist conceptions "that guarantee a radical break with the militarism of the past."[29] He insisted that the new army would be safely integrated into Bonn's democratic structure. Some of Blank's colleagues in the CDU, however, doubted his ability "to stand up the generals," who allegedly wanted to restore the old ways.[30] The press also expressed worries on this score; one paper even suggested that Blank's willingness to staff his agency with former officers showed that he was a "secret militarist."[31]

This last charge was unfounded, for Blank remained a complete civilian throughout his career. Indeed, the problem with Blank was less that he could not "stand up to the generals" than that he could not stand up to Adenauer, who pushed the pace of rearmament with little regard for reform. Blank would have liked to have fully established the legal structure of the new army before recruiting any soldiers. He could not do so because the chancellor, who continued to see rearmament as a means of diplomatic leverage, insisted upon expedition. In attempting to accommodate Adenauer's ambitious timetable, Blank alienated the parliamentary backers of Baudissin's reform program.[32]

The Dienststelle Blank

Whatever Blank's own commitment to reform, some students of the planning process have accepted Baudissin's claim that the Dienststelle was weighted toward military traditionalists determined to sabotage fundamental change.[33] This is a distortion of reality, especially for the EDC period, when much of the reformist agenda became official policy. On the whole, members of the *Sektion Innere Führung* worked effectively enough with other departments in the Dienststelle. But there was indeed a faction in the agency, supported by elements in the media and veterans' community, that questioned some of Baudissin's ideas and tried to replace them with a more conventional approach.

The conservative criticism tended to take two somewhat contradictory directions. Some critics insisted that Baudissin unjustly denied the legacy of progressive command styles in the Wehrmacht. They argued that if Hitler's army had been as oppressive as Baudissin implied, it could never have fought so well.[34] The second line of criticism made much of the difficulties that would supposedly attend any attempt to apply a doctrine that departed so dramatically from the either/or quality of traditional military thinking. Baudissin's principles were dismissed as too "philosophical." Enlisted men, it was said, could not be expected to weigh the ethical implications of military orders, and officers could not be asked to explain why they had given them. Such fastidiousness would undermine discipline and render the army incapable of fighting efficiently. These criticisms were often combined with contemptuous commentary on Baudissin's intellectual style, which was said to involve a resolute "fuzzy-headedness" and inability to come down out of the clouds.[35]

Within the Dienststelle, resistance to Baudissin's ambitions was spearheaded by Colonel Bogislav von Bonin, the agency's chief of planning.[36] Von Bonin, who was eventually to become almost as controversial as Baudissin, hailed from a prominent military family and personified the traditional Prussian martial virtues. Courageous, resourceful, and confident, he had distinguished himself during World War II by his superior leadership, perhaps best exemplified in his decision in late 1944 to allow the troops under his command to evacuate Poland before they could be annihilated by the Red Army. This decision, which contravened Hitler's orders, led to his arrest and brief incarceration in Dachau. Von Bonin, however, was no military resister (indeed, he had succeeded Heusinger as chief of operations in the General Staff after the Twentieth of July debacle); and, despite a proclivity for independent thinking, he was a firm adherent of the old military forms and values, which he thought should provide the essential blueprint for a new army.

Apart from these personal predilections, von Bonin opposed the military reform program because he believed that the danger of an imminent Soviet attack did not allow the luxury of developing a large conscript army of "citizens in uniform." Instead, he argued, Bonn should create a small volunteer force made up largely of antitank units, which could be posted along the inner German border as an impenetrable *Sperriegel* (fortified barrier). To this strategic prescription he soon appended a political agenda calling for German reunification based on complete neutrality and the removal of all nuclear weapons from German soil—a right-wing harbinger of the leftist "nuclear-free zone" proposals of the late 1950s and 1960s.[37]

Von Bonin's strategic and political vision, so out of harmony with official policy, gradually alienated him from his superiors and ultimately caused his dismissal from the Dienststelle in March 1955. Yet in 1952, shortly after his appointment as planning chief, he felt strong enough to attempt an interagency coup involving the standardization of the Bonn and Paris staffs of the Dienststelle; this would have meant the absorption of Baudissin's department into his own.[38] Von Bonin's initiative was widely regarded as an attempt by the "traditionalist" wing in the agency to dismantle or substantially weaken the count's operation.[39]

Certainly this was the way the Dienststelle's two press secretaries, Axel von dem Bussche-Streithorst and Konrad Kraske, saw the matter. They confronted Blank with the choice of dismissing von Bonin or accepting their own resignations. Although Blank had no personal regard for von Bonin, he was advised by Heusinger that his technical skills were indispensable. Therefore, though he did not go along with von Bonin's reorganization plan, he refused to fire him. Bussche-Streithorst and Kraske thus made good on their threats to resign, causing the Dienststelle considerable public embarrassment.[40]

Though failing in its prime intent, von Bonin's attempted coup did lead to a restructuring of the reform program within the Dienststelle. In February 1953 Baudissin's Sektion Innere Führung was placed directly under Heusinger's supervision, and an interagency Ausschuss Innere Führung was established to coordinate all aspects of reform planning.[41] This change weakened Baudissin's influence because he did not become chairman of the new committee and was restricted in his duties to ensuring the compatibility of his own group's reform proposals with those put forth by other departments. The task of coordinating the Dienststelle's reform work with study groups and lobby organizations outside the agency was entrusted to a separate entity, the Studien-Büro Pfister, with which Baudissin's group carried on a fierce rivalry.[42]

Another figure in the Blank agency with whom Baudissin increasingly crossed swords was his co-worker and rival Heinz Karst. Baudissin later

charged that Blank had "thrust" this South German Catholic on him to counterbalance his own North German Protestantism. He also described Karst as
an "ambitious reactionary," whose appointment illustrated the Dienststelle's
"lack of commitment to *Innere Führung*."[43]

There is no evidence, however, that Karst was a critic of the reform program at the time of his appointment. Indeed, he participated actively in the
shaping and promotion of the ideals of *Innere Führung*, especially in the area
of officer training.[44] Yet by 1953–54 Karst had begun to worry that aspects of
the reform program were inflaming antimilitary attitudes in the body politic.
Although he did not yet question the reforms per se, he took issue with the
spirit of "Wehrmacht bashing" that seemed inherent in the demands for a
radical break with the past. This, he believed, was dangerous and self-defeat-
ing. Thus in a critical review of Hans Hellmut Kirst's popular antimilitary
novel *08/15*, Karst complained that the fashionable revulsion against Germany's martial past threatened to "ghettoize" former soldiers and to impede
their "inner conversion" to democracy.[45] As we shall see, Karst would considerably sharpen this line of attack on the eve of the Bundeswehr's establishment in 1955.

Veterans' Associations

Heinz Karst's tentative critique of the military reform program was mild
compared to the attacks mounted by West Germany's community of organized veterans. Since 1949, following a relaxation of the Allied ban on veterans' groups, a host of organizations had sprung up to lobby on behalf of the
former soldiers and their families.[46] With the implementation of Basic Law
Article 131 in 1951, which partially accommodated the veterans' demands for
a restoration of their pensions, some of the groups had shifted their focus to
other matters of concern, including rearmament. They were convinced that
they were highly qualified to speak out on this question by virtue of their military experience and sacrifices for the fatherland. Yet they did not speak with
one voice. Regarding the basic decision to rearm, some groups, like the Verband der Kriegsbeschädigten, argued that the victims of the last war ought to
be taken care of before scarce resources were expended on a new army.[47] The
majority of organizations, reflecting their members' careerist ambitions, expressed a willingness to assist the rearmament effort, but only if the "defamation" of the Wehrmacht ceased and the new German forces were given full
equality with their alliance partners.[48] Admiral Gottfried Hansen, head of
the Bund versorgunsberechtigter ehemaliger Wehrmachtsangehöriger und
deren Hinterbliebenen, argued that if the Western nations retained their "national armies," Bonn too must have a national army. He also repeated the old
refrain that the FRG must not rearm until all German officers had been released from Allied custody because "an honorable German soldier could not

be expected to take up weapons as long as any of his comrades, who had simply done their duty as soldiers, remained in prisons and camps."[49]

An even more provocative position was taken by former general Johannes Friessner, acting chairman of an umbrella organization called the Verband deutscher Soldaten (VdS), founded in September 1951. Friessner held a press conference in which he boldly stated the "conditions" that Germany's veterans would place on their cooperation in rearmament. Above all, he demanded that "the ethical and moral value of the military profession" be fully restored. Bonn's new partners, he added, must openly admit that Germany's invasion of Poland in 1939 had been a legitimate defense of national interests and its campaign against Soviet Russia a necessary "preventive war."[50]

Friessner's comments generated a storm of indignation at home and abroad. While the foreign press—especially the French—warned of a revival of German militarism, Bonn's political elite wrung their hands over "unspeakably stupid statements" that made Germans "look ridiculous to the entire world."[51] Some veterans' representatives agreed that Friessner's remarks were hopelessly unpolitic, while others applauded. Their varying responses were indicative of the political schisms in the German officer corps that dated back to the Reichswehr and Wehrmacht. On the whole, however, Friessner was perceived to be a political liability for the veterans' movement, and he was soon forced to give up his chairmanship of the VdS.[52]

Yet Friessner was by no means the most extreme of his ilk. He was quickly outdone by that other firebrand of the radical right, Otto Ernst Remer. Convinced that Bonn had forfeited all rights to support from the old Reich's defenders, Remer worked to sabotage any cooperation between veterans and the government. In one of his speeches he cried: "We will so defame any German general who offers German blood [to Adenauer and the Allies] that no dog will take a piece of bread from his hand."[53]

In addition to proposing conditions for rearmament, or in some cases trying to scuttle it altogether, prominent former soldiers offered advice concerning the shape and structure of the new German army. A few well-known veterans admitted the need for substantial reform. Major Karl Helfer, for example, told the journalist Adelbert Weinstein in 1951 that he believed Bonn should take advantage of the opportunity to create something "genuinely new" in military life. Helfer's colleague Helmut Heye, a future Bundeswehr ombudsman, insisted that the new German army should do without "military display" even if its allies did not. "We Germans should have the courage to step off decisively in a new direction," he said.[54]

Such views, however, did not set the tone among the veterans' groups, most of which tended to see the reform enterprise as a condemnation of the Wehrmacht. Thus, although some spokesmen might endorse the principle of reform, they almost always cautioned that the reforms must not go "too far."

Former sergeant Otto Mosbach (VdS) vented a widely held sentiment when he condemned "*überreformer*" in the Dienststelle who were "giving young people the idea that military service was just another job, complete with an eight-hour day." Mosbach also warned against allowing "civilians" to set the training goals and standards for the new army.[55] Former Waffen-SS colonel Ludwig Gumbel, head of the Bavarian branch of the VdS, complained that Baudissin and his colleagues were borrowing ideas from the Western powers, who had nothing to teach the Germans about military standards. "In the matter of soldierly ethics," he cried in 1953, "the powers that need to justify themselves are those who violated [humane standards] against Germany in World War II, then in Korea, and even now in their continued inhuman incarceration of our comrades in Spandau, Werl, and Landsberg." The Americans in particular could provide no model, said Gumbel, for they had "deliberately corrupted our young men with their cowboy films and hot jazz, rendering them unfit for genuine soldierly discipline."[56]

The hostility of the soldiers' associations toward the reform campaign also found expression in their attitude toward the Twentieth of July and its meaning for the new military.[57] In 1951 the VdS executive council attempted to defuse this explosive issue by formally recognizing that both anti-Nazi resisters and soldiers who had "remained true to their oath" had acted in "good conscience."[58] But for Friessner, who was then still chairman of the organization, this dubious and halfhearted statement went too far. He promptly called for an end to the "glorification" of the Twentieth of July legacy. "The soldier," he declared, "cannot condone clandestine attempts to murder his supreme warlord."[59] Friessner added that positive sources of inspiration could be found in "timeless" soldierly values that had nothing to do with changing political conditions. He recalled with pride that he had served three different political systems—the *Kaiserreich*, Weimar, and the Third Reich—without ever questioning his duty or altering his perspective.[60]

When it became known that the Blank agency was considering evaluating officer candidates' moral and political suitability partly on the basis of their attitudes toward the Twentieth of July, Friessner and his like-minded colleagues fumed that there was no place in the German army for men who accepted the principles of the military resistance, much less for those who actually had had some connection to the plot. As Ludwig Gumbel put it, former soldiers with Twentieth of July credentials should not contemplate returning to a military career because "their presence would undermine the soldierly spirit fundamental to any army."[61]

The attacks of the veterans' associations on the Twentieth of July legacy were generally accompanied by claims that the soldiers who had "loyally served the Führer to the bitter end" had nothing to be ashamed of. Like the former generals who had pushed hard for the German soldiers' rehabilitation when rearmament was first raised, the organized veterans' leaders insisted that the military had had little or no part in Hitler's crimes.[62] They saw no reason to follow the reformers in backing away from the practices and traditions of the Wehrmacht.

This was particularly evident in the highly sensitive realm of insignia and symbols. Many of the veterans urged a revival of the Stahlhelm and field-gray uniforms. They also demanded that World War II veterans be allowed to wear medals they had earned in battle. As for the swastikas that were often attached to the medals, one veterans' association suggested they presented no problem because they were a "state symbol" and not a party emblem.[63] Admiral Hansen, ever vigilant about equality, argued that the Germans should not change their campaign decorations because the Allies had not done so. The Allied decorations, he added, had been awarded "by men who were responsible for all the crimes committed against the Germans and Japanese— Dresden, Hamburg, and Hiroshima."[64]

Such views could not help but concern the Adenauer government, which was very mindful of former chancellor Heinrich Brüning's warning of 1950: "The Bonn government will suffer shipwreck like Weimar unless it succeeds in making the generation of the Second World War committed bearers of the state."[65] In hopes of countering radical nationalist and *ohne mich* sentiments, the Dienststelle Blank sought valiantly to unify the disparate veterans' movement around a moderate and "constructive" platform. To this end, members of the Dienststelle met repeatedly with leaders of the soldiers' groups, promising support for "legitimate" veterans' claims.[66] Leading Union party politicians joined in this effort. Franz Josef Strauss, for example, promised the Kyffhäuserbund that the government would support its demand for the return of its confiscated property if the group would "cooperate in forming a German military force based on the people."[67] To the same end, Bonn provided subsidies to the more moderate veterans' journals, especially the VdS's *Soldat im Volk*. Alas, this did not prevent that journal from dismissing the reform program as an exercise in starry-eyed idealism reminiscent of 1848.[68]

Yet the government could not go too far in its efforts to cultivate the veterans' groups, for it knew that these organizations generated fear in the German populace and Bonn's prospective EDC partners. General Schwerin spoke for many when he warned that the veterans' movement, especially the VdS, was filled with dangerous "radicals" who hoped to exploit the former soldiers' grievances for "nefarious purposes."[69] British high commissioner Kirkpatrick cautioned that "crypto-Nazi elements" were making headway in the veterans' movement. Though he saw no "immediate danger to democracy," he worried that "in a year or two," the radicals might have acquired enough influence to destabilize the state.[70]

But if the government had to keep its distance from the veterans' groups, many of the veterans were disinclined to cozy up too closely with Bonn. Recalling their *Gleichschaltung* in the Third Reich, the former soldiers were determined to maintain a measure of independence vis-à-vis the political authorities. Moreover, resentment and distrust toward the government remained strong among the rank and file despite partial accommodation of their material claims. Hasso von Manteuffel discovered this when he boldly announced that the veterans of his old outfit, the Grossdeutschland Division, had elected to stand behind Bonn and its democratic aspirations. Some of his colleagues responded indignantly that he should speak for himself because, as far as they could tell, the "Bonn democrats" had done nothing for the former German soldiers save "treat [them] as criminals."[71] Field Marshal Kesselring's suggestion that the Stahlhelm should show its loyalty to the Federal Republic by carrying the black-red-gold flag (in addition to the *Reichskriegflagge*) provoked protests against his "extreme pro-Bonn position."[72] Fearing that a too friendly attitude might lead to defections to more radical groups, even the more moderate veterans' associations tended to eye the government as warily as it eyed them.

A significant consequence of this mutual distrust was a generalized lack of useful cooperation between the veterans and the government in the area of rearmament. The various soldiers' associations, often quarreling among themselves and for the most part unable to commit individual members to any given policy, did not play a vital role in shaping the new military guidelines. To the extent that they did become involved in the debate, their contribution rarely went beyond kibitzing from the sidelines.[73] Precisely because the veterans tended to resist fundamental change, however, the reformers did not regret their lack of participation in the planning process. Moreover, the much delayed start-up of the Bundeswehr ultimately made support from the veterans' groups less crucial than it otherwise would have been. Nevertheless, the former soldiers' relentless criticism of the reforms ensured that the fledgling Bundeswehr would have to take as much flak from the unreconstructed Right as from the disappointed Left, which complained that the changes had not gone far enough.

The Parties and the Bundestag Security Committee

In the first phase of the security debate, the parties and parliament were concerned primarily with the question *if*, rather than *how*, Germany might be rearmed. But as remilitarization seemed imminent, all the parties, including the SPD, began insisting with increasing vehemence that parliament assume a more substantial role in shaping the design of the new army. All the major parties created internal experts' groups to work on questions of military organization. Justifying the SPD's intense involvement in these questions, Fritz

Erler commented: "A party like the SPD, which is fighting for power, has to realize that the army is a potent weapon. We should be sure that when weapons are distributed in the state, we get some ourselves."[74] The Socialists' *Wehrexperten* ensured that the SPD's role would indeed be crucial. Overall, this development was extremely important because it meant that, for the first time in German history, the army's shape and direction would be determined partly by the political opposition.

In their efforts to help shape the prospective army, legislators focused on the Dienststelle's reform program, which had received extensive coverage in the press. Most of the parliamentarians agreed with Baudissin that the new military must be fully integrated into society and reflect Bonn's democratic values. But while convinced of the need for parliamentary control and structural reforms, they differed on how extensive the changes should be and where their focus should lie.[75]

The FDP, for example, took a particularly conservative position on the question of how much the new army should break with the past. In the tradition of the old National Liberals of the *Kaiserreich*, the FDP appointed itself defender of national military legacies and aspirations.[76] Accordingly, some liberals echoed the veterans' associations' complaint that misguided *über-reformer* were attempting to build a new army without adequate reference to the past. "It is troubling," admonished a member of the party's security committee, "that we seem determined to denigrate and tear down our old Wehrmacht. We apparently want to get rid of everything that gave [this army] its backbone and discipline. This is stupid, for the German Wehrmacht was the best army in the world."[77]

Concerned that reformist zeal would alienate the *Ehemalige*, FDP spokesmen, again echoing the veterans, urged that former soldiers who enlisted in the new army be allowed to wear their World War II decorations. Prohibition of the medals, argued Mende, who was himself a holder of the Knights Cross, would signal a failure to recognize the sacrifices made by men who had fought for their fatherland "with the same good faith as the *Poilu* for France or the Tommy for his empire." As for the Twentieth of July legacy, the *Freideutsche Korrespondenz* insisted that any effort to make soldiers identify with it would be "divisive."[78]

The SPD, in contrast, favored an end to most traditions of military display and "pathos." The Socialists argued that rituals like the *Grosses Zapfenstreich* (an elaborate military review whose origins lay in the Prussian-Russian alliance against Napoleon) were now obsolete. The same was true, they said, of emotion-laden terms like "honor," "obedience," and "fatherland." There was, however, one significant voice of dissent here: Carlo Schmid, who had fought in World War I, warned that soldiers needed colorful parades and gut-grabbing concepts if their job was not to become sterile and monotonous.[79]

Another issue that proved very contentious was that of the *Oberbefehl* (supreme command). The FDP strongly opposed the Dienststelle's plan to lodge these powers in the chancellor's office rather than with the president, as had been the case in Weimar. Such a change, it argued, would give the chancellor too much power and endanger the "political neutrality" of the military.[80] The CDU, however, favored locating the *Oberbefehl* with the chancellor on the grounds that this crucial function required the firm political control that only that office could provide.[81] The CSU agreed, though unlike the CDU (and FDP), it urged that the "federal principle" play an important role in military organization so that the individual states (like Bavaria) would have more influence.[82] The SPD, for its part, wanted the supreme military powers to be vested with the defense ministry in both in peace and war; furthermore, it argued that the defense minister should be responsible directly to the parliament, not to the chancellor.[83] Clearly, differences of view were so extreme on this issue that considerable negotiating would be required before some mutually acceptable solution could be found.

Ironically, the parties' differing perspectives on military reform found prominent expression in that new forum created to give parliament a more coherent voice in shaping defense policy: the Bundestag Security Committee. Though it considered all aspects of the rearmament question, the Security Committee devoted more energy to *Innere Führung* than to any other issue. This emphasis reflected a growing fear that the central reform ideas might not be effectively institutionalized in the EDC. Indeed, even Union party delegates worried that the supranational European army might provide a "screen" behind which the German military could become a "state within the state."[84] By being enmeshed in an international bureaucracy with headquarters outside Germany, it was argued, the army might elude close military control from Bonn's parliamentary watchdogs.

Yet anxious as they were to promote the reform agenda, Security Committee members, like the parties as a whole, harbored differing versions of its scope and details. They also differed in their interpretations of the meaning and usefulness of Germany's military past. This is evident from the committee's discussions on three key aspects of military reform: the code of discipline, ideological motivation, and the value of military tradition.

Disciplinary matters were discussed extensively in the Paris EDC negotiations. Back in Bonn, the new Security Committee invited the Dienststelle's legal expert, Elmar Brandstetter, to brief the group on this issue. He duly outlined Bonn's position on obedience, one of the central areas of dispute. A firm commitment to military obedience, he noted, was a "fundamental virtue without which the prospective European Army would be unable to function." *Kadavergehorsam* (blind obedience), however, had no place in modern military organization. It had fostered inflexibility and had isolated the soldiers from the civilian world. This sounded very much like Baudissin. So did Brandstetter's insistence that soldiers *must* disobey orders that lacked military necessity or that contravened international law and human rights.[85]

This proposition sparked considerable dissension in the committee. Some members, including Fritz Erler, argued that an injunction to disobey "illegal" orders would place the common soldier before "agonizing and well-nigh unsolvable questions of judgment." Paul Bausch (CDU) added that a soldier could hardly be expected to disobey an order if he might be shot for doing so. Others, however, cited the Nuremberg Tribunal to remind their colleagues that "superior orders" did not absolve subordinates of responsibility for their actions. Blank, present at this session, agreed that German soldiers must understand that they were "fully accountable for their behavior." Had more of them appreciated this in the past war, he added, the Wehrmacht might not have participated in Nazi crimes like the *Nacht und Nebel* killings. As for the objection that a soldier might face summary execution for refusing to obey an unjust order, Blank insisted there was no dilemma here for the "Christian soldier": he must follow the "higher law," whatever the consequences.[86]

Related to problems of obedience and military discipline was the question of whether the European troops might be unionized, a possibility that Baudissin's section favored. When they learned of this, some members of the Security Committee (primarily CDU and FDP delegates) were shocked, while others (primarily SPD) applauded. Did not the Dienststelle realize, asked Mende, that an army was "hierarchical and not democratic" and therefore no place for unions? But Carlo Schmid insisted that unions *could* have a place in the military provided that they concerned themselves exclusively with social and economic questions. (Ultimately, Schmid's view won out, for the right of coalition enshrined in the Basic Law was extended to Bundeswehr soldiers, who formed their own association in 1956. After 1966, they could join the public service workers' union.)

The committee offered no clearer guidelines regarding an "ideological foundation" for the European army. Bausch wondered if the EDC was developing sound political and ethical principles that would be as compelling for its troops as communism seemed to be for those of the East. Convinced that the new military needed "a spiritual focus," he proposed that the troops be taught "fear of God, love of Fatherland, and moral responsibility." Mellies objected that the Germans had heard similar injunctions in the Third Reich. Echoing Baudissin, he said that the new army must avoid "high-sounding dogma," however well-meaning. Interestingly, Franz Josef Strauss agreed: he cautioned against repeating the Nazis' policy of enforcing rigid ideological conformity in the army, insisting that the new military should instead mirror the "pluralistic social and intellectual conditions" of contemporary society. He added, however, that since the German contingent would be part of a European army, it would have to be instructed in the "values of United Europe."[87]

This demand for "European values" found little sympathy among the Socialist delegates, who tended to see European integration as an impediment to German reunification. Noting that there was no common European flag or symbol, Erler said that the Germans had changed their own symbols so often that they could not take such matters seriously. Ernst Paul (SPD) insisted that "common European feeling" could not overcome enduring national stereotypes, such as German images of the French as *Lüstlinge* (pleasure-seekers) and Italians as *Katzenmacher* (impish troublemakers). Instead of the unrealizable goal of a common Europe, the new force should stress what it was united against: "tyranny, barbarism, oppression." Mellies added that young people "would only laugh at the concept of Europe," and it was "dangerous to offer as an ethical-political foundation something that was so nebulous, so unreal." Carlo Schmid agreed that it was necessary to deal in "realities." A recruit from Bavaria, he argued, might be prepared to risk his life for Hamburg but probably not for London. The "concept of Europe," he added dismissively, had currency "only among intellectuals." This comment struck Strauss as odd, coming from an intellectual. He replied that Europe's intellectuals really cared only about "Holy Germany, Holy France, or Holy Belgium." "Or Holy Bavaria?" countered the Württemberger, Schmid.[88]

The committee, no doubt exhausted by its trek through this conceptual bog, eventually decided that there were three ideals for which future German troops ought to be ready to die: "Freedom, Germany, and Europe." Yet it could not agree on what these concepts actually meant, how far they extended, and in what order they should be propagated. Their disagreements were a revealing index of the confusion over Germany's role in postwar Europe and indeed over the meaning of "Europe" itself in this era of division and ideological confrontation. As later debates over NATO and the European Community would show, these issues did not become easier as time went on.

The Security Committee did not do much better with the vexing problem of "military tradition."[89] Count Kielmansegg briefed the group on the Dienststelle's views regarding the importance of traditions and customs. "We must confront the problem of tradition because one can never start entirely from scratch," he said. "But we must draw only on those traditions that are sources of vitality and not dead weight or likely to lead in the wrong directions." He added that this would not be easy because Bonn's military planners confronted such "contradictory models" as Field Marshal Kesselring (former Luftwaffe officer and ardent Hitler supporter) and the Twentieth of July resisters. In response, Hans Merten (SPD) and Paul insisted that the Wehrmacht had been "too weighted with tradition"; the new army must not try to reclaim "useless and pernicious baggage of the past." By contrast, Anton Besold, chairman of the Bayern Partei, argued that Germany was "desperately in need of strong traditions" and should not pass over the Nazi era in its search for them because the Wehrmacht had much to teach the postwar generation about soldierly values. Merten disgustedly countered that "soldierly values" alone were never enough to make an army behave honorably or decently. Meanwhile, Maria Probst (CSU), the committee's sole woman, observed that although many of the old army's traditions had undoubtedly been useless or perverse, new values could not be found until the family and the kindergartens had been effectively reformed. "Morals begin at home and in childhood," Probst reminded her colleagues.

In the end, the committee could agree only on a few bromides to mix with Kielmansegg's platitudes. The new army should take over "timeless" verities and "practically useful methods"; it should scrutinize all traditions and customs for their inherent value; the military's intellectual and spiritual foundations should not differ from those of the civilians; and traditions that were merely formal, mechanical, or sentimental should be rejected.[90]

"WHERE ARE THE GERMANS OF YESTERYEAR?"

If Bonn's military reform program generated a measure of domestic confusion, skepticism, and even hostility, it also encountered opposition from the foreign powers with whom the new German forces would have to cooperate. Was it really the *Germans* who were putting forth such strange ideas? many asked. What had happened to the aggressive crusaders of yesteryear who had conquered most of Europe? How would the proposed European army function if it were shaped by the bizarre notions emanating from Bonn? No doubt it was a relief to see the old Huns so chastened, but now that they were finally on the right side, was it not a shame that they were so determined to turn over a new leaf?

Such sentiments, voiced here and there by Bonn's allies, emerged only gradually as the full scope of the German reform program became known abroad. In the early phases of the rearmament discussion, most Germans imagined that their effort to build a radically new kind of army would be welcomed by their foreign partners—especially by the Americans. Bonn's security planners assumed that the capital of Western democracy would have much to teach Germany about "democratic" military norms.[91]

Thus in April 1951 Blank asked General Hays for assistance in guaranteeing "that future German military contingents [were] created in a democratic atmosphere and on sound democratic lines." Hays sent Blank a series of reports on training, leadership ideals, grievance procedures, military justice, military schools, and off-duty education. But he cautioned that he "did not know how similar functions were handled in former German armies" or if "the adoption of the U.S. system would in all respects be sound from the German standpoint."[92] Later, Hays and Ernst Wirmer jointly proposed regular meetings between Dienststelle personnel and European Command (EUCOM) experts on the "democratization of military organization." An American colonel was detailed by EUCOM to discuss with Blank "problems connected with the establishment of a democratic base in the army."[93] These contacts, however, never came to anything, and they were not replaced with more fruitful ties.

Indeed, it soon became apparent to the German reformers that they would not find a helpful model for their ambitions in the United States Army. The Americans understood democracy in military organization to mean little more than guaranteeing soldiers' basic civil rights and promotion by merit. They did not countenance any dilution of traditional hierarchical structures or a blurring of fundamental distinctions between military and civilian life. The Korean War, moreover, suggested to German observers that there were fundamental deficiencies in the American military's training, discipline, and morale. Commenting to Heusinger on a very critical British appraisal of the American army in Korea, Baudissin concluded that the soldiers there had no firm idea of what they were fighting for.[94]

Many American officers, for their part, so admired German military traditions and accomplishments that they were loath to demand significant changes. Such admiration was an old story, reaching back to the late eighteenth century. General George Washington, when elected president, sent an American officer, Sylvanus Thayer (an ancestor of McCloy's aide Charles Thayer) to Prussia to study its military schools. Thayer returned to found West Point on the Prussian model. (The model held good for a long time: in 1937, young Charles Thayer was "astonished" by the similarity between West Point and some Wehrmacht cadet schools he visited.)[95] American military men had been impressed by Prussia's role in defeating Napoleon, then by the Prusso-German performances in the wars of unification. On his military fact-finding tour of Europe in 1876, General Emory Upton marveled over how efficiently Germany mobilized its troops and how "completely the nation [was] given over to warlike preparation."[96] Even when the Germans were opponents, as in the two world wars, they inspired respect among many of their American adversaries.[97] American civilian analysts and politicians might (simplistically) cite the Wehrmacht as the ugly culmination of an unbroken tradition of German militarism, but American officers looked for more positive lessons from the encounter in World War II. Especially commendable in their eyes was the Wehrmacht's ability to motivate its men to fight on even when all seemed lost. American officers were also impressed by the Germans' "very clever use of . . . honorary titles for units, medals and awards for individual achievements, and commemorative decorations for participation in outstanding combat engagements."[98] So extensive was the admiration, indeed, that by the mid-1950s American generals were busy remodeling their own forces according to lessons learned from the Germans in World War II.[99] Their main worry now, as General Gruenther put it in 1954, was that "the quality of the soldiers in the new German army would not be as high as those of the Second or Third Reich."[100]

No wonder Count von Baudissin discovered, on a study trip to America in 1955, that American officers had little use for *Innere Führung*. "They simply wanted German soldiers—as numerous, competent, and rapidly mobilized as possible," he complained. The last thing they wanted to hear was how radically "new" their German partners would look and behave.[101]

British military leaders reacted similarly to the German reform plans. Their postwar warnings about the dangers of German militarism soon gave way to pressure for quick and efficient rearmament. Thus when a group of German military planners visited England in December 1953, they were told by their British hosts that London expected "rapid development of a potent German army once mobilization [had] begun." The British officers added that they assumed future German soldiers would "display their well-known talents . . . their traditional superiority, especially in the attack." The Germans were shocked. "The British military authorities," they complained, "do not seem to have any appreciation for the altered moral and intellectual framework in which German rearmament must take place."[102]

Military authorities were not the only ones who expressed doubts about Bonn's reform plans. British deputy high commissioner F. R. Hoyer-Millar reported that the Germans were "as usual, taking themselves rather too seriously." Their ambitious plans were naive, he said, for the "German army will never be composed of Sir Galahads dedicated solely to the service of an ideal." This was a good thing, he added, for "the structure of an army must above all be designed to fulfill its primary task of fighting successfully."[103]

The Continental powers tended to agree. It gradually became evident during the Paris negotiations that the German conception was considerably more "liberal" or progressive than that favored by the other EDC nations, especially France. Bonn was also more inclined to sacrifice national prerogatives to the common European format because it had no existing military structure to protect. Thus, when the French presented a draft *Discipline générale* that looked much like the harsh code prevailing in their own army, Blank objected that it was "worse than anything the Nazis had tried to do." But German attempts to modify the code encountered stiff opposition from its authors. Highly frustrated, Hans Tänzler, a member of the German delegation, reported to the Ausschuss Innere Führung that the French were "very reluctant" to adopt new forms; they "always put the national before the European," he protested.[104] Speidel had great difficulty getting the French to accept the principle that a commander's powers over his troops should be subject to precise rules and laws.[105] Responding to such reports from Paris, the Ausschuss concluded that the German delegation must "sharpen [its] position relative to the French, so as to avoid false or poor solutions to the questions of *Innere Führung*." General Heusinger added that inadequate reforms could lead to "political problems" in Germany for the EDC treaty.[106]

Quarrels also developed over many details of the prospective European army's internal structure. Disagreement was especially pronounced on the right or duty of soldiers to disobey "illegal" orders. Noting that his countrymen had "learned through painful experience that high moral standards, as well as post-factum legal consequences, obliged the soldier to disobey orders under some circumstances," Blank pushed for a formal codification of this duty.[107] But the French opposed any significant modification of their time-honored code of "unconditional obedience," which indeed was more draconian than the old Wehrmacht practices, let alone what Baudissin and company hoped to achieve. Paris's hard-line position caused Baudissin to ask one of his French counterparts "who the real militarists were" in the postwar world. The Frenchman reportedly replied that French soldiers were not very good at following orders, and so France had to require strict regulations.[108]

Because the EDC states were expected to introduce conscription, rights of conscientious objection also needed clarification. The Dienststelle Blank had addressed this problem in a memo entitled "The Rights and Duties of the European Soldier." It proposed that political as well as religious factors should be weighed in assessing applications for conscientious objection. At Paris the Germans argued this cause with particular vehemence: as we know, the Basic Law enshrined conscientious objection as a fundamental right. They also hoped to make rearmament more palatable to public opinion by extending such rights to young Germans who objected to the conditions under which Germany was armed or to the prospect of serving in a "German civil war."[109] Again, however, the German proposal was too broad for the other EDC powers, who worried that it would produce more conscientious objectors than recruits.

As might have been expected, symbolic issues presented at least as much difficulty as questions of structure and law. The European army was supposed to have a common uniform. In line with the ideal of integrating the military into civilian society, the Germans proposed a highly functional uniform that resembled a factory worker's outfit. Here it was the Italians, with their long tradition of masculine high fashion, who called foul. No Italian, they insisted, would join an army dressed in olive-drab overalls. What was more, the air force, being the most "prestigious branch," would have to have more impressive uniforms than the army and navy.[110]

If the Germans generally favored bold new departures in martial structure and style, they sometimes strove to retain practices from their military past that they considered inherently useful and consistent with modern requirements. For example, they urged that merit carry more weight than seniority in securing promotions.[111] In the realm of officer training, they pressed for the incorporation of the traditional German *Dienst in der Truppe*, a system whereby prospective officers served for a time with line troops before they were commissioned.[112] Blank argued that there should be no "St Cyr system," which turned out young lieutenants with no experience in the lower echelons.[113] At first, the French resisted this initiative but finally agreed to it just before the treaty was signed. Many other points of dispute, however, were simply left open, pending full ratification of the EDC, when compromises presumably would be made.

Of course, that moment never came, and we will never know which views would have prevailed or how the proposed European army would have functioned in the field. We do know, however, that the much less ambitious Franco-German Brigade inaugurated in the 1980s suffered a host of problems in the realm of discipline and internal structure. Moreover, the history of common European institutions that *did* materialize, such as the European Community, the European Parliament, and the Exchange Rate Mechanism, suggests that the integrated army plan, inherently much bolder, would at the very least have suffered severe growing pains.

PART

3

NATO

AND THE

BUNDESWEHR

As Count von Baudissin was coming to the unhappy conclusion that plans for radical military reform in the FRG might be incompatible with Europe's scheme for full military integration, the four-year multinational effort to create a European army was approaching its futile culmination. In August 1954 the French Assembly shockingly killed the scheme by refusing to ratify the EDC treaty. Now some feared that a German defense contribution might never come to fruition. Yet within a mere seven months the powers would ratify a new treaty that provided for Bonn's integration into NATO. This was a momentous achievement. The speed with which it was accomplished, however, somewhat masked the fact that the "NATO solution" provoked deep controversy in Germany and new strains within the Western community. Moreover, though Bonn was now welcomed into the "Western Club," the invitation was extended partly to keep the invitee in line, and the terms of membership were not (whatever the club might say) entirely equal.

THE COLLAPSE OF THE EDC

There were many doubts from the outset about the viability of the European army concept. Churchill called it a "sludgy amalgam," JCS head Omar Bradley said it would never work; British defense minister Shinwell suggested it would provoke ridicule in the Soviet Union. The doubts were particularly strong in France, however, for the EDC would have cut the French army in two. The divisions stationed in Europe would operate under an international commissariat, while those serving in France's colonies would remain under direct French control. Few Frenchmen wanted to cede the primary responsibility for defending metropolitan France to an untested international agency, while retaining national authority only over colonial and Legionnaire forces. De Gaulle, ever the defender of *La Glorie*, warned that France's participation in the EDC would necessitate a sacrifice of its empire and national sovereignty to a nebulous European bureaucracy.[1] Speaking to Cyrus Sulzberger in January 1954, he called the EDC an *"enterprise manquée,* an error, a stupidity." It was a "fantasy to think you [could] suppress France and the French nationality," he huffed. He vowed to do everything he could against the plan: "I will work with the Communists to block it. I will make revolution against it. I would rather go with the Russians to stop it."[2] President Victor Auriol condemned the EDC as an idea that disregarded France in favor of West Germany, "on the pretext that [the latter] is getting its strength back—as if the aggressor deserved more encouragement than the victim."[3]

Reservations about the EDC were so strong in France that several premiers refused to bring it before the Assembly. After the treaty was signed in May 1952, three governments came and went before Pierre Mendès-France finally risked an attempt at ratification. During this period the chances for parliamentary approval continued to decline as successive cabinets grew increasingly dependent on the Gaullists. Foreign Minister Schuman, as the plan's primary backer, came under fierce attack. He was accused of wanting nothing less than to trade French interests for a European chimera behind which the Americans, supported by their German clients, would rule the Continent. Thus the Gaullists made Schuman's departure one of their conditions for supporting René Mayer's government, which assumed power in January 1953. Schuman was replaced by the Resistance hero Georges Bidault, who lacked his predecessor's dedication to Franco-German reconciliation and European unity. Bidault grudgingly supported EDC ratification, but only as a means to curb German rearmament, not to promote European unity.[4]

In March 1953, Mayer and Bidault brought the French case to America, combining demands for EDC revisions with pleas for American help in bailing France out of Indochina. This suit pointed up, once again, the contradiction between Paris's pretensions to Great Power status and her actual dependent condition. As Hervé Alphand observed disgustedly in his diary: "Bidault affirmed in a communiqué the determination of France that its adherence to the EDC must not compromise its position in the world. As if one could make great power real through a communiqué!"[5]

Mayer's cabinet fell on 21 May 1953, opening a new crisis characterized by the unwillingness of the major factions to form a government and face the host of problems confronting the Fourth Republic. Finally, a colorless Independent Party deputy, Joseph Laniel, secured the Assembly's endorsement by promising to square the circle: he would pursue an internationalist foreign policy while simultaneously demanding a "satisfactory solution" to the Saar question and additional Anglo-American troop commitments. His government believed that if it had any hope of securing a positive vote on the EDC, it would have to persuade France's Anglo-American partners to accept certain "indispensable guarantees" against what it saw as the ever-possible threat of German aggression.

At the Bermuda Conference of December 1953, which Washington and London had called to placate Paris, the French pleaded for a formal promise from Britain and America to keep their troops on the Continent for the full fifty-year life of the EDC treaty. The American delegation had anticipated this demand, noting that "of course [it was] impossible for both us and the British."[6] Churchill proposed to Eisenhower that if Paris continued to obstruct German rearmament, the Anglo-Saxon powers should consider an "EDC without France" or the "possibility of bringing Germany into NATO." Though Eisenhower still had hopes for the EDC, the Americans were now ready to threaten France with "alternative security arrangements." Douglas MacArthur II, counselor to the State Department, told Laniel that an EDC failure would cause Washington "to consider other programs and policies with respect to France and Germany." Dulles treated the French premier to a little homily on the responsibilities of power, reminding him "that any country which wishes to play a great role must act when necessity requires it to do so."[7]

France's reluctance to embrace the EDC and German rearmament was reinforced by developments on the international scene. The death of Stalin in March 1953 and the conclusion of a truce in Korea eased East-West tension and fueled new hopes for détente. At the same time, the emergence of hydrogen bombs made détente seem all the more imperative. Even that old Cold Warrior, Churchill, embraced this perspective. Presciently, he predicted that in a few years hugely destructive bombs could be (as he put it in a letter to Eisenhower) "delivered by rocket without even hazarding the life of the pilot." Not just London but New York and other great American cities were in danger. He added that he hoped Eisenhower still believed that war was not inevitable, despite some bellicose talk emanating from Washington. "I am glad that in your spirit, as in mine, resolve to find a way out of this agony of peril transcends all else."[8] Because Germany remained one of the chief sources of peril, Churchill proposed that the four wartime Allies sit down once again to discuss the problem. He now believed that German reunification within some form of neutrality might be acceptable because the Germans' hatred of Bolshevism would prevent them from siding with the Russians.[9]

Urged on by London and Paris, the four powers came together in early 1954 in Berlin. In agreement with Washington, London put forth the so-called Eden plan, essentially a warmed-over version of the West's earlier schemes for German reunification. The scheme called for free elections, the creation of an all-German government, and a peace treaty complete with (vaguely defined) guarantees for the Soviets. Its key feature was the insistence that the new German government must have the right to conclude "international agreements as it may wish." Obviously, this would allow Germany to join the EDC, a prospect that Dulles disingenuously insisted should not alarm Moscow because the pact was purely "defensive," whereas a *national* German army would be a threat to world peace.[10]

The Western powers could not have seriously believed that the Soviets would accept their plan, and indeed they did not. Restating the position that Moscow had taken since the abortive East German uprising in June 1953, Molotov insisted that the only safe way to reunify Germany was through a general European security framework, which would obviate the need for NATO, the EDC, or American troops on the Continent. The initial all-German government would be formed by merging the East and West German parliaments (thus guaranteeing parity for the smaller GDR). On the question of elections, Molotov proposed contests that excluded "fascist" participants who would undoubtedly "manipulate" the process for their own benefit. After all, he noted, Hitler had come to power through "parliamentary means."[11]

Molotov's counterproposal suggested that the Soviets were no more serious than was the West about negotiating German reunification under terms that were not stacked in their favor. In essence, they could countenance reunification only if it yielded a state more like the GDR than the FRG, a highly unlikely prospect. By the second half of 1953, then, Moscow's main concern was less to promote a neutral reunified Germany than to bolster the shaky GDR.[12]

Although Adenauer was pleased by the stalemate at Berlin, Erich Ollenhauer, the SPD leader, complained that the chancellor's determination to pursue rearmament would only force the Soviets to accord sovereignty to the GDR, thereby hardening the division of Germany. The *true* nature of Western policy, added Ollenhauer, was revealed when Dulles assured the Russians at Berlin that they had nothing to fear from the EDC because it was designed to protect Europe *from the Germans.* He doubted that Bonn could legitimately ask its citizens to join such an organization.[13]

Ollenhauer's protest notwithstanding, the confrontation at Berlin signaled no major intensification of the East-West rivalry. On the contrary, it showed how settled and ritualized the postwar arrangements were becoming. There were a few demonstrations in West Germany, but no widespread hue and cry. Though the citizenry was undoubtedly frustrated by the continuing failure to solve the German problem, their budding "national consciousness" seemed more aroused by West Germany's victory in the Football World Championships of 1954 than by this latest failure in the political arena.[14]

The failure of the Berlin conference also caused no great consternation in

France, whose Assembly did not even debate the results. Bidault did, however, appear before the legislative Foreign Affairs Commission to squelch rumors that he had promised Molotov to kill the EDC in exchange for Russian assistance in ending the Indochina war. Bidault declared: "I did not put the EDC in a hole in order to get a smile from Mr. Molotov. . . . You don't trade Adenauer for Ho Chi-minh."[15]

Nonetheless, the fate of the EDC and the conflict in Indochina were inextricably linked. Many Frenchmen believed that France would have difficulty fighting colonial wars while simultaneously retaining superiority over the resurgent Germans. As if to reinforce this concern, the devastating loss at Dien Bien Phu in May 1954 showed how vulnerable France's colonial enterprise was in an era of awakening Third World nationalism. Washington had not come to France's rescue in Indochina, and many Frenchmen were convinced that America could not be trusted to hold down the Germans either. To Paris, it seemed increasingly imperative either to get out of Indochina before joining the EDC or to abandon the army project altogether.

Here matters stood when Pierre Mendès-France became premier on 20 June 1954 with the brash announcement that he would quickly rid France of its three most pressing problems: colonial overextension in Indochina and Tunisia; economic instability; and finally the EDC, which he called "one of the most serious questions of conscience that has ever troubled the country."[16]

Despite a well-earned reputation for energy and brilliance, Mendès-France was widely distrusted. Aware that he was part Jewish, Adenauer feared that he would be automatically anti-German. Eden, a great snob, viewed him as a parvenu. Churchill found it hard to trust a man—and a Frenchman no less—whose favorite beverage was milk. The State Department worried that he would be willing to "sabotage" a united Europe in an effort to elevate France.[17] Many pro-EDC Frenchmen, for their part, doubted the sincerity of Mendès-France's occasional bows to European unity and Franco-German reconciliation. Their fears were heightened when, upon coming to power, he gave key cabinet posts to the Germanophobes Pierre Koenig and Jacques Chaban-Delmas. Equally ominous, in their view, was his statement that the EDC was a "national problem that required a national consensus."[18] Because the EDC, as one journalist put it, "divided French opinion as no other question since the war,"[19] there was little likelihood that the premier's demand for consensus could be realized.

Yet however ambivalent his position on the EDC, Mendès-France lived up to his promise to try to "liquidate" this and the other problems on his agenda as quickly as possible. He managed rapidly to extricate his country from Indochina and to deed this mess to the brash Americans, who would soon become bogged down there themselves. With that great achievement, he seemed to have amassed the political capital to work wonders elsewhere, perhaps even to save the EDC.

But how hard would he try? How much of his political capital would he invest in a project about which he had serious reservations and whose salvation—if such were even possible—might exhaust his resources? For all his reputation as an innovator, the approach he took to this problem was nothing if not orthodox: he proposed still more changes to the EDC treaty designed to make it more palatable to the parliament, but which stripped the scheme of the integrative features that had made it so attractive to the international "pro-Europe" faction.[20]

When he learned of Mendès-France's proposals, Dulles was "deeply shocked and disheartened." He instructed Ambassador Douglas Dillon to inform the premier that they were entirely unacceptable to the United States, where they would be viewed as "further proof of French unreliability." Churchill assured Dulles that he fully supported Washington's hard line. He noted that he had long "been wearied with this deeply injurious French procedure of delay" but reminded the American that there was a way out: "I hope . . . you will not fail to grip the NATO solution which I am sure can be arranged."[21]

One statesman who was not yet prepared to grasp alternative solutions was Adenauer. In an interview on 2 July 1954 he reaffirmed his commitment to the EDC, claiming still to have confidence that France would ratify it. But he also declared that if Paris killed this initiative, the Western powers would have "no choice" but to sanction a national military in Germany. "It would be a perverse irony of history and politics," he added, "if through a French veto of the EDC, that is through *France*, we were forced to establish a German national army."[22]

The chancellor understood that Mendès-France's proposals for "saving" the EDC had little chance of being accepted, but this hardly made them less worrisome, for he believed that Mendès-France must also see their hopelessness. Therefore, he thought Mendès-France's "real" reason for introducing them was to give France an opportunity to blame others, primarily the Germans, for the plan's collapse. "I was the main target," he later wrote. "I was the one who would be saddled with the odium of the EDC's failure."[23]

Adenauer also had domestic reasons to fear for the future of the EDC. In the spring of 1954 a group of nationalist politicians from the coalition parties and the SPD launched the Gesamtdeutsche Bewegung, which was designed to put German unity at the forefront of West German foreign policy. It also aimed to reorder Bonn's internal power structure by replacing Adenauer loyalists with an intraparty alliance embracing the likes of Jakob Kaiser, Thomas Dehler, Erich Ollenhauer, and Walter Freitag of the DGB. In May, moreover, Adenauer's FDP partners almost wrecked the coalition through an attempt to send a parliamentary delegation to Moscow to open independent negotiations on the German question with the Soviets.[24]

Meanwhile, Mendès-France brought his proposals before the Western diplomatic community at a meeting in Brussels on 19–22 August. Here he warned that the EDC would fail in the Assembly unless it were substantially modified and that this failure might bring in a "Popular Front" government that would pull France out of NATO. Though unimpressed by this threat, Belgian foreign minister Paul-Henri Spaak introduced a complicated formula that went partway toward accommodating Mendès-France's demands.[25] Yet he was not prepared to countenance any modifications fundamental enough to require resubmitting the treaty complex for parliamentary approval because this might put off German rearmament indefinitely.

America and Britain were even less inclined to dicker with the French premier. Dulles informed Spaak that Washington had no use for Paris's proposals. He added that if efforts to find a compromise failed, Washington would "not object" to an international meeting, without France, on "how best to associate Germany in sovereign equality with the West and to bring about German rearmament."[26] Churchill was more concerned about Adenauer's political fate than Mendès-France's. On 19 August he told Dulles: "I am distressed at Adenauer's position. I feel we owe him almost a debt of honor after all the risks he has run and patience he has shown."[27] He cabled Adenauer to assure him that regardless of what happened in Brussels, West Germany would be armed.

The Brussels conference dragged to a close on 22 August without reaching an acceptable compromise between the French and the other prospective EDC countries. Before returning to Paris to explain this failure, Mendès-France flew to England to meet Churchill and Eden at Chartwell. Here he hoped to feel out the British on alternative arrangements to the EDC, which he was now convinced would be rejected by the Assembly. Though insisting that the French people would never accept Germany's direct membership in NATO, he said they might tolerate a loose seven-power military association including the United Kingdom. This arrangement would be less ambitious than the EDC, eschewing its supranationality, which so many Frenchmen loathed.[28]

He might just as well have saved his breath. On the eve of the Chartwell meeting, Churchill had reassured Dulles that he would urge Mendès-France "to stake his political fame on getting EDC through." The British prime minister elected to call this maneuver "Operation Bite" because, "just like old times," it would give the Anglo-Saxon powers a chance to take a savory mouthful of French flesh. Dulles responded gleefully: "Let us bite hard!" Churchill and Eden accordingly used the Chartwell meeting to lecture Mendès-France one last time on the nasty consequences for France of an

EDC failure. To the premier's pleas of helplessness, Churchill testily replied that "we should not agree to be governed by the impotence of the French chamber."[29]

But Mendès-France had no intention of appeasing the Anglo-Saxons' appetite for French flesh with his own political skin. In the short period between the disappointments of the Brussels and Chartwell meetings and the fatal vote in the Assembly, he did his best to distance himself from the EDC. On 24 August he gave an account of the Brussels meeting which portrayed it as an attack on French interests, even on French dignity. "I could not," he said, "accept proposals that would have shocked the conscience of so many Frenchmen, and which were likely to be disavowed by their deputies."[30]

True to his determination to remain *au-dessus de la melée*, Mendès-France carefully avoided making the EDC a "question of confidence" when the matter finally came up for debate in the Assembly on 28–30 August. Instead of taking a specific position, he simply outlined the advantages and disadvantages of treaty ratification. Many deputies saw only the disadvantages. Jules Moch argued that the international situation no longer warranted German rearmament in any form. A delegate from the Republican-Social Party reminded his colleagues that Germany had "invaded us in 1792, in 1814, in 1815, in 1870, in 1914, and in 1940." Another shouted that the German problem went back to Attila the Hun. But the most devastating attack came from eighty-three-year-old Edouard Herriot, who thundered: "For me, the European Community is the end of France. It would not perhaps be the end of France to ally with a country that had not deceived us several times. But we have known and endured from [Germany] such deviations from right that I, an old man who is going to pass on, am justified in telling you affectionately: Beware of having to regret an act you would not be able to repair, an act you would not be able to take back."[31]

In the end, the vote that did in the EDC was not technically on the treaty itself but on a so-called *question préalable*, a parliamentary maneuver designed to kill a bill by tabling it without further debate. On 30 August the Assembly voted 319 to 264 to dispatch the European army plan in this fashion. After the historic vote, anti-EDC delegates celebrated by singing the "Marseillaise" and shouting "Vive la République! Vive la France!" Infuriated *Cedistes* screamed "Back to Moscow!" at their rivals.[32] Paul Reynaud complained that the treaty had been voted down without its author or signers being permitted to defend it. This was a fitting end, perhaps, for a grand scheme whose viability even some of its initial backers had come to doubt.

Widespread reservations about the EDC did not prevent its collapse from occasioning genuine consternation, even anguish, throughout the Western world. "The greatest tragedy since the war," declared French high commissioner François-Poncet.[33] The frustration generated much finger-pointing and name-calling. Alphand pointed his finger directly at Mendès-France, accusing him of having cold-bloodedly "murdered the EDC."[34] Churchill, though no friend of the plan, groused that Paris had behaved "in an unspeakable way, execrable . . . [full of] ingratitude and conceit." France had "forced Britain to go along" with the scheme, and now "the swine" had "wasted three years."[35] West German Catholics tended to blame the SPD for this debacle. *Mann in der Zeit* charged the Socialists with delaying German ratification long enough to allow the anti-EDC forces in France to get the upper hand. The paper also fingered the French Communists, who "under orders from Moscow and in league with World-Freemasonry, the Fifth Column of Satanocracy," had sabotaged the EDC.[36] America's chief Cold War crusader, John Foster Dulles, declared that "nationalism, abetted by Communism, has asserted itself so as to endanger the whole of Europe." He was so angry that he proposed the immediate suspension of American military aid to France.[37] Eisenhower was also appalled by the French decision but showed a greater willingness to pick up the pieces and push on. Upon hearing the news he declared: "America has never quit in something that was good for herself and the world. We will not quit now."[38]

Among the mourners of the EDC, no one was more shocked, more caught off balance, than Konrad Adenauer. On one level this is surprising. He had had ample warning that the EDC would likely be voted down in the Assembly. He deeply distrusted Mendès-France, believing that he intended to sabotage the treaty and shift the blame to Bonn. At the same time, however, he had come to see the EDC as pivotal to his foreign policy and the very future of Germany. He feared that if the project failed, the FRG might drift free of its Western moorings and fall victim to the dark powers of German nationalism. Thus when the final vote came in he was so distressed that he considered resigning. This moment was, he insisted later, "the bitterest disappointment and the greatest defeat" he had ever suffered.[39]

Characteristically, however, Adenauer did not let despair impede his search for the guilty parties, which he found readily enough. Within Germany, there was the SPD, and indeed the entire parliament, whose "obstructionist tactics" and long-winded debates had served as a lamentable "model" for the French.[40] Outside Germany, there was Mendès-France, whose behavior confirmed all the chancellor's suspicions regarding the Frenchman's "racial character." Not long after the fatal vote, when Adenauer was in London to discuss the NATO "ersatz solution," he confided to Spaak and Luxemburg prime minister Joseph Bech: "You see, Mendès-France is a Jew. We have had a lot of experience with the German Jews. They all suffer from a national inferiority complex, which they try to compensate for with displays of exaggerated nationalism. Mendès-France wants to be seen as a good patriot in France by holding down Germany, and this at the cost of Europe."[41]

The EDC's failure threatened to undercut what popular support Bonn had been able to muster for a defense contribution to the Western alliance. Rearmament, after all, had been justified as a significant step toward European unity; without the sugarcoating of Europeanism this pill was simply too bitter for many to swallow. Thus the Dienststelle Blank, which kept its finger on the fluttering pulse of popular sentiment, reported a dramatic decline in enthusiasm for an arms contribution. It seemed as if the West German people were fed up with trying to be "the only good Europeans in Europe."[42]

Yet the collapse of the EDC also produced quiet satisfaction in some quarters that had officially supported.it. At SHAPE there was secret "relief that the EDC [had] been torpedoed." Now the powers could concentrate on integrating German troops directly into the Atlantic alliance, which is what SHAPE had favored all along.[43] Even the Dienststelle Blank, which had invested thousands of hours in planning an EDC contribution, found silver linings in this dark cloud. Aware that political considerations had impeded crucial logistical arrangements for the deployment of German troops, Blank officials were relieved to escape (alas, only temporarily) what they feared would be an organizational disaster.[44] Those in the agency who had always harbored doubts about an integrated army's viability hoped that a less cumbersome route to rearmament might now be found. Even the military reformers, who regarded the EDC as a significant step toward European unity but an impediment to radical military innovation, wondered if the plan's failure was not a blessing in disguise.[45]

Konrad Adenauer, the European politician most devastated by the EDC's collapse, did not take long to recover his equilibrium. Soon he was busy examining the NATO alternative, which he found preferable to an EDC without France. Belatedly, he could even find merit in France's stance: "What the people there in Paris said is not entirely stupid," he told Walter Hallstein. "I've been looking over the treaty that you negotiated. Well, in fact it's not so good as you always maintained."[46]

No doubt this was true enough—the treaty *did* have severe deficiencies, above all its attempt to begin the European unity process with armies, those most crucial instruments of national sovereignty. Unquestionably, too, the final version of the EDC retained some anti-German features despite Bonn's largely successful assault on the original scheme.

Nevertheless, the subsequent London Agreements and Paris Treaties, which finally established the framework for German rearmament, were no substitute for the EDC in popular appeal, especially in Germany. Lacking association with the ideal of a united Europe, the substitute arrangements seemed too much like an extension of traditional alliance politics, which in fact they were. As one German diplomat told Charles Thayer: "When we were negotiating the EDC, we all seemed to be working together to build something new. But when we reconvened to negotiate the Paris Agreements, we suddenly moved back into that old familiar atmosphere of separate national groups horsetrading for our individual interests."[47]

EDEN TO THE RESCUE

The statesman usually credited with picking up the diplomatic pieces following the EDC debacle is Anthony Eden, the British foreign secretary.[48] Certainly Eden gave himself this credit. As he tells the story in his memoirs, he realized that France's action made an alternative arrangement for German rearmament urgently necessary if "Western unity was to be saved." Bonn had to become a member of NATO, but in a way that retained many of the safeguards devised for her entry into the EDC. But how might this be managed? Eden relates that while contemplating the problem in the bathtub at his Wiltshire cottage, he suddenly realized that he "might use the Brussels Treaty to do the job." This security pact, signed in 1948 by Britain, France, and the Benelux states, could be broadened to include West Germany and Italy. The expanded Brussels community (ultimately rechristened the Western European Union—WEU) would be part of NATO, thereby providing Bonn with a bridge to the Atlantic Pact. It would also constitute a framework under which German rearmament could be controlled. Though eschewing the EDC's ambitious military integration, it would crystallize the "vision of Europe" by embracing the losers of World War II and involving Britain more directly in Continental affairs.[49]

Whether Eden, like an Archimedes of modern diplomacy, indeed discovered this "solution" in his bath has been disputed by some of his contemporaries.[50] In fact, the evidence shows that other British officials, most notably Harold Macmillan, had been advancing this alternative well before Eden adopted it.[51] Indisputable, however, is that Eden hatched the idea of presenting the plan at a nine-power conference, for which he would lay the groundwork by touring the European capitals.

Eden began his diplomatic tour on 11 September in Brussels, where he met with the Benelux foreign ministers. They embraced his proposals in hopes both of preventing West Germany from "slipping over to the Russians" and Washington from "retreating to the peripheral defense of 'Fortress America.'" Eden next visited Adenauer, who professed "deep interest" in the Brussels Treaty, choosing to regard it as a lingering expression of the "European idea." The chancellor also said he was willing to accept some *self-imposed* limits on the size and arms of the German contingent in NATO.[52] This caveat was designed to further the illusion that Bonn was fully in control of its own destiny, which Eden was prepared to accept if it would bolster Adenauer's position at home.

As Eden was making his diplomatic rounds, his American counterpart, Dulles, hastened to Europe to intervene in the negotiations. Meeting with Adenauer on 16 September, Dulles sharply criticized Eden's proposal. According to the chancellor, the American worried that Eden intended to build up Europe as a "third force" that might pursue "neutralist tendencies." Adenauer assured Dulles that Eden had no such thing in mind. Both agreed that Bonn must be granted armed sovereignty soon if the unsavory forces of German nationalism and American isolationism were not to gain ground. Thus Adenauer proposed that Bonn be allowed to undertake certain "interim" steps toward rearmament, such as readying barracks and recruiting training cadres. If Paris objected to these measures, it should be kept out of the discussions.[53]

While Dulles conferred with Adenauer, Eden concluded his diplomatic tour in Paris, where he hoped to find support for his plan despite the untimely intervention of the American secretary. But his meeting with Mendès-France proved even more "tough and unsuccessful" than he had feared. The only point on which they could fully agree was that Dulles was a meddlesome bore. Mendès-France acknowledged that the Brussels Treaty might be a point of departure for German rearmament but insisted that it did not contain adequate "safeguards and controls." He also continued to oppose Bonn's participation in NATO. Eden responded that the safeguards could not be as tight as the abortive EDC's and "would have to give the *appearance* of being non-discriminatory." In any event, they must not constitute "a cage for the Germans."[54] But of course a cage is precisely what Paris had in mind for the aggressive German shepherd, convinced that if the beast were allowed to roam free he might, once again, chew up the French poodle next door.

Eden returned downhearted to London and to a conference with Dulles, which proved no more productive than his meeting with Mendès-France. Though claiming to be impressed with Eden's "statesmanlike efforts," Dulles complained bitterly about the Europeans' failure to realize the EDC. America, he reminded Eden, had placed great hopes in European integration; Congress had even tied European aid to the success of the EDC. He and Eisenhower hoped to "salvage as much as they could from the present situation," but he was not sure they could prevent Congress from leaving Europe to fend for itself.[55]

Faced with continued obstruction from Mendès-France and the gloomy prognostications of Dulles, Eden wondered whether there was much point in holding his projected nine-power conference at all. According to his memoirs, he now concluded that to save his plan, Britain might have to take an extraordinary step—that is, to make "a new commitment . . . to maintain our present forces on the Continent, and not to withdraw them against the wishes of the majority of the enlarged Brussels Treaty powers."[56]

THE LONDON AGREEMENTS

The London Nine-Power Conference opened in Lancaster House on 28 September 1954.[57] The conferees were quickly able to agree that West German sovereignty should be granted independent of final ratification of a rearmament plan, but Mendès-France adamantly opposed German remilitarization through the Brussels Treaty and NATO. He again insisted that this framework lacked adequate safeguards. This infuriated Eden, who reminded Mendès-France that their purpose was "not to discuss French security, but European security." Nonetheless, to keep the project alive, he unveiled to Dulles his contingency plan to guarantee the presence of British troops on the Continent. Dulles was delighted. This was just the gesture he needed to convince Congress that the Europeans were prepared to "do their share." On the following day, he announced that if the hopes originally invested in the EDC could be translated into "new arrangements," he would recommend that President Eisenhower "renew a pledge [of American commitment] comparable to that which was offered in connection with the EDC."[58]

Eden then publicly delivered his promise that Britain would maintain four divisions and a tactical air force on the Continent for as long as the majority of the Brussels Treaty powers desired it. Harping pompously on the historic implications of his offer, he declared that the English, "an island people in thought and tradition," were now making an extraordinary break with their insular customs to "show an example of unity to the world."[59] Responding to Eden's grandiloquence, Paris's ambassador to Britain, René Massigli, wept openly, saying that France had been waiting "fifty years for such an announcement!"[60] Adenauer solemnly observed that "we were all impressed with the obligation that this declaration placed upon us."[61]

Though Eden's initiative succeeded in pushing the conference to a fruitful conclusion, its significance should not be overstated. Eden was careful to qualify his offer with two crucial conditions. "This undertaking would be subject to the understanding that an acute overseas contingency might oblige Her Majesty's Government to omit this procedure." Moreover, "if the maintenance of U.K. forces on the mainland throws at any time too heavy a strain on the external finances of the United Kingdom, the U.K. will invite the North Atlantic Council to review the financial conditions on which the formations are maintained."[62] In other words, Britain would maintain troops on the Continent so long as they were not too expensive or needed elsewhere.

Seeing the flaws in Eden's gesture, Churchill huffed: "[It] can be cancelled at any time. . . . What is all the fuss about?" Indeed, Eden had "offered" something that Britain had no choice but to give. "No one in their senses thought we could bring our troops home from the Continent," Churchill observed. "No one imagined that if Russia decided to march to the West we could sit still and do nothing; if there is war we are bound to fight. We have always been better than our word. Now they are going to do exactly what I suggested in Strasbourg in August 1950. Never was the leadership of Europe so cheaply won."[63]

Anthony Nutting and Macmillan found it ironic that Eden, that "tepid European," was the one to promise a long-term British commitment in the name of "European unity." Even more ironic, from Macmillan's perspective, was that Britain's willingness to assuage French fears of Germany should later be rewarded by France's rejection of Britain's bid to join the Common Market. He wrote in his memoirs: "It has certainly been a bitter pill for us to swallow when, in later years, we [were] repelled by the French government which was almost a suppliant for our guarantees against their fears of a revived Germany."[64]

But all this bitterness came later. In the atmosphere of noble gestures at the Nine-Power Conference, Konrad Adenauer, not to be outdone by his colleagues, announced a noble gesture of his own. He renounced "quite voluntarily" any West German production of ABC weapons, as well as the manufacture of guided missiles, heavy warships, long-range artillery, and strategic bombers. Of course, he had renounced ABC weapons before, but this time he did so without reference to the "strategic exposure" argument that he had previously used to justify this gesture. His concession occasioned almost as much applause for statesmanlike vision as had Eden's. Spaak gushed to Count von Kielmansegg: "Tell your chancellor, he is a greater European than I."[65]

Yet here again, some historical reservations are necessary. In the first place, Adenauer's gesture was not really "voluntary" because the Western powers were insisting on it. Second, Adenauer, like Eden, qualified his offer in significant ways. He promised only that West Germany would not produce such weapons *on its own territory*, which of course did not rule out cooperative ventures with other countries. Moreover, Adenauer's vow that Bonn would not *produce* these weapons did not rule out its *possession* of them. In fact, the chancellor had previously insisted that West Germany's armaments must be equal to those of the other NATO powers, implying that Bonn would eventually want access to the heavy stuff, including nuclear weapons. Indeed, when Adenauer renewed his arms promise, Dulles asked him in a stage whisper: "Herr Chancellor, are we to understand that you have made this declaration—like all such international declarations—only *rebus sic stantibus* [under present conditions]?" Adenauer replied: "You have interpreted my declaration correctly."[66] With this piece of diplomatic theater, Adenauer and Dulles were openly suggesting that changes in the world situation might nullify the agreement and bring West Germany pushing on that nuclear door which the chancellor had so carefully left ajar.

Whatever its long-term import, Adenauer's concession came in the midst of a serious dispute over the way in which arms production and distribution within the alliance should be managed. On 29 September, Mendès-France informed Dulles that Paris would agree to German membership in NATO but wanted as compensation extensive intra-alliance controls over arms distribution and production. A centralized bureaucracy should have authority to prohibit production of certain kinds of arms, distribute available supplies among the allies, and inspect member nations for violations. The French plan also called for an expansion of the "strategically exposed area" in Central Europe to include virtually the entire Federal Republic.[67]

It took no great acumen to see that this proposal was designed primarily to circumscribe *German* arms production and secondarily to promote *French* economic and military interests. Dulles, indeed, suspected that what Mendès-France wanted was nothing less than the "prevention of any armament production in Germany and the concentration in France of the armament production of the entire community."[68] This was unacceptable to Washington, which had its own military aid program in Europe. The Joints Chiefs, moreover, complained that the "inhibitory and negative aspects" of the effort to arm Bonn could "detract seriously from the military effectiveness of any organization which might eventually be involved." The Chiefs believed that the "excessively rigid" French proposals "would fail to take advantage of German production facilities" and "inhibit the growth of an adequate mobilization base for NATO."[69]

The other NATO powers were no more enthusiastic about France's plan. Britain, which like America expected to help supply the German arms buildup, was unprepared to place any of its military production under the supervision of an outside bureaucracy.[70] The Benelux countries, for their part, agreed with Dulles that Paris's plan meant little more than the imposition of French standards and control.[71] Not surprisingly, Adenauer saw matters in a similar light. "Is the Federal Republic, according to Mendès-France's plan, supposed to remain perpetually without weapons factories of any kind?" he asked. This would hardly be acceptable to "those [Germans] who are to become soldiers."[72]

Rejecting Mendès-France's proposals, the conferees agreed that the task of meeting Bonn's initial military needs would be divided roughly as follows: America would supply 35 percent; Britain, France, and the Benelux states,

35 percent; and German domestic production, 30 percent. The British were pleased to have a part of the action, but they also welcomed Bonn's participation because it would force the FRG to shift some of its rapidly growing industrial capacity from the civilian export market to weapons production. Reflecting on this development, the American diplomat David Bruce declared (a little too rashly): "The era in which German industry can outmaneuver its British competition is over, as of today."[73]

It was further agreed that the German contribution to NATO would amount to twelve divisions totaling no more than five hundred thousand men. These units would all belong to NATO, which would have the primary responsibility for coordinating their deployment. Crucially, Bonn promised to refrain from any action inconsistent with the strictly defensive character of NATO and the WEU; nor would it ever "use force to achieve the reunification of Germany, or the modification of its present boundaries." The Western powers agreed further to liberalize the Contractual Agreements. Though they retained their rights on issues pertaining to German unification and Berlin, they altered the basis on which they stationed troops in Germany from a "reserved right" to a "treaty right." They further agreed that their right to take emergency measures for the protection of their troops would lapse when the "appropriate German authorities" had assumed "similar powers." They abandoned altogether the troublesome Binding Clause, which had struck many Germans as an intolerable infringement on their treaty-making powers. Finally, in a gesture important to Adenauer, they declared that Bonn would be recognized by its NATO partners as having "the only German government freely and legitimately constituted." Summing up these accomplishments, Dulles hailed the London Conference as "one of the greatest conferences of all time."[74]

Not surprisingly, the Soviets were less impressed. Moscow sent a new note to the Western powers complaining about the accords and warning of the dire consequences certain to attend a rearmament of West German "militarists and *revanchists.*" Russia (again) called for a four-power conference to discuss the possible restoration of German unity after German-wide elections, the removal of occupation troops from Germany, and the creation of a system of collective security for Europe.[75]

Temporarily ignoring the Soviet protest, the Western powers went ahead and formalized the London Agreements through the Paris Treaties in late October 1954. This done, the West told Moscow that the "essential basis" for a fruitful conference on German and European security did not exist because the Soviets had not clarified their position on free elections in Germany or signed the Austrian State Treaty. A meeting of the four powers might be held only when there was a "real prospect of finding solutions, and *after* the ratification of the Paris Treaties."[76]

BRITAIN AND FRANCE RATIFY THE PARIS TREATIES

"Our own vote in the House of Commons was overwhelming, 264 to 4 [actually, 264 to 6], the official Opposition being divided on the issue and deciding to abstain."[77] Anthony Eden's laconic description of Commons's ratification of the Paris Treaties in November 1954 hardly does justice to the acrimony occasioned by the Churchill government's endorsement of NATO membership for Bonn and its promise to keep British troops on the Continent for as long as they were needed. Though the final vote was indeed one-sided, it was achieved only because the left wing of the Labour Party had narrowly lost a bid to turn the party firmly against the government's policy. Labour was so divided on this issue that its parliamentary delegates were ordered to abstain. Thus in reality, the government's victory was less a foregone conclusion than—as Wellington said of Waterloo—"a damn close-run thing."[78]

The vote in Commons should not, moreover, obscure the fact that Britain as a whole remained sharply divided over the government's German policy. In January 1955, public opinion polls showed that only a slight majority of the population favored including West Germany in NATO. Furthermore, the debate over the Paris Treaties generated a new wave of German-bashing in the popular press. Ignoring Bonn's democratic successes, the British tabloids fell back on wartime clichés about the beastly Huns. They purveyed an image of West Germany as militaristic, re-Nazified, and bent on returning to the world of 1939. Chancellor Adenauer was shown sporting a Hitler mustache and strutting about among a menacing entourage of saber-scarred generals. The "quality" press was somewhat embarrassed by this campaign, which the *Observer* suggested might "lead one to suppose that Hitler was still alive and the Nazis back in power."[79]

In France, meanwhile, the London Agreements threw the parties into confusion. Many French politicians had thought that they had gotten rid of the German problem by killing off the EDC; now they were facing it all over again. Of course, the terms had changed, and this made matters even more confusing. Some Assembly delegates had opposed the EDC because it was supranational or because it was not administratively tied to Britain and America; now the supranational features were out and Britain was in. Mutatis mutandi, some had supported the EDC because it had promised to advance the cause of united Europe; the new arrangement made only feeble gestures in this direction. Each deputy would have to reassess his position in light of the new situation.[80]

Mendès-France's position had also changed since the death of the EDC. Fearing total diplomatic isolation and smarting from the international opprobrium heaped upon him as the "murderer of Europe," he had begun making speeches about the need for Franco-German reconciliation. On 20 September 1954, at the Council of Europe, he had embraced Eden's plan to include Bonn in the Brussels Treaty. In an Assembly debate on the London Agreements (7 October), he had presented the package as the best that France could expect under the circumstances. Here he had received a vote of confidence for his policy, but to get it he had had to argue out of both sides of his mouth, assuring the Assembly that under the new arrangement West Germany would be powerful as a friend but weak as an adversary and portraying the new Europe as more closely integrated but not supranational. No wonder many deputies, not buying Mendès-France's "tricky" performance, remained dead set against any pact embracing the Germans. "Instead of plague, they offer us cholera," grumbled Pierre Cot, a leading Progressive and old friend of the premier's.[81]

France's debates on the Paris Treaties, which were held in the last days of December 1954, were less passionate than the EDC donnybrook four months earlier. Perhaps the deputies were too tired of the rearmament question to whip themselves into their usual froth. At any rate, the opposition's attempts to generate hostility to the treaties by depicting them as the brainchild of the hated John Foster Dulles generated little excitement. The pro-treaty forces were no more animated: a parliamentary report called the package "a good solution, which scarcely arouses enthusiasm, but which makes a certain amount of sense."[82]

A new complication arose, however, when some Gaullist and MRP deputies joined the extreme leftists and rightists opposed to the treaties. While the Gaullists rejected the package *tout court*, a faction of the MRP was anxious to scuttle it to get revenge on Mendès-France for not having energetically pushed the EDC. This combined opposition was enough to achieve what most foreign diplomats had thought impossible: a second French "non" to German rearmament. On Christmas Eve the Assembly voted 280 to 259 (with 73 abstentions) to reject a modification of the Brussels Treaty allowing German and Italian membership. At the same time, however, the Assembly ratified protocols ending the occupation of Germany and providing for a referendum on the Europeanization of the Saar. Mendès-France, moreover, immediately made clear that he did not accept the first vote as final and would bring it up again as soon as possible.[83]

The Assembly's rejection of the Brussels Treaty bill moved NATO diplomacy into high hear. Upon hearing of the vote, Eisenhower exclaimed: "Those damn French! What do they think they're trying to do? This could really upset the applecart of Europe." (Even worse, the urgent need to consult with the British over this latest act of French perfidy upset Ike's sacred golf regimen. "The French have not only disturbed the whole free world," huffed the president, "they're cutting in on my [golf] lessons!")[84] Consultations with the British quickly yielded agreement not to issue a joint denunciation of the French action but to let Eden bully Paris into compliance. Churchill told his physician that he would like to "control the [French] business" himself, but that would mean "taking the bread out of Anthony's mouth after denying him the square meal he so much wanted."[85] Accordingly, Eden was allowed his bite of Frog; he issued a statement on 24 December containing the crucial (and distinctly threatening) provision: "The U.K. commitment, offered at the London Conference, to maintain British forces on the Continent of Europe, depends on the ratification of the Paris Agreements by all sides."[86]

Paris was effectively intimidated. When the Assembly reconvened after Christmas vacation, it voted 287 to 256 to approve NATO membership for West Germany and 287 to 260 to include West Germany and Italy in the Brussels Treaty. But this sudden reversal left many Frenchmen more dismayed than ever. Those who opposed German rearmament felt betrayed by leaders who for years had assured them that their troublesome eastern neighbor would remain militarily impotent. They felt humiliated by the Americans, who seemed to believe that upstart Bonn was a more valuable partner than France. They also felt abandoned by the British, who, like the Americans, appeared to have forgotten who their real friends were. They soon vented their frustration on Mendès-France, a convenient scapegoat for the failures and disappointments of the Fourth Republic. He was vilified as the sponsor of a "new Wehrmacht," the betrayer of French Indochina, and, perhaps worst of all, the enemy of the French wine industry because of his unpatriotic campaign against alcoholism. Abused from all sides, he was driven from office in February 1955.

WEST GERMANY AT THE RUBICON

The Adenauer government had decided not to attempt ratification of the Paris Treaties until the French Assembly had acted on them (thus reversing the EDC order of events), and the Bundestag did not hold its first reading on the treaty bills until mid-December and its final vote until February 1955. The plenum debates were preceded, however, by thorough discussions in the Bundestag Security Committee, where many revealing and significant objections were raised. Once again, a close examination of the committee's deliberations is in order.

On 10 November, Blank appeared before the committee to elucidate the treaty complex and to argue that Germany had again outmaneuvered France, this time even more tellingly. The FRG, he insisted, had achieved the best of all possible worlds: its admission to NATO would give it a voice in Western security policy, while its inclusion in the Brussels Treaty guaranteed it "automatic assistance" in the event of a Soviet attack. Bonn was, moreover, "much freer" now to build its military as it saw fit. With the exception of ABC weapons and certain heavy arms, West Germany could produce its own munitions. Bonn had achieved these successes, Blank gloated, by cleverly playing off the Anglo-Saxon and Benelux states against the French, who had perversely tried to prevent the Germans from "playing an equal role on the stage of international politics." Only in one area had Germany gone along with France: it had accepted Paris's insistence that the German contingent not exceed five hundred thousand men. But this was no real concession, Blank hastened to add, because it was going to be "hard enough" to reach that figure in any case, and Bonn had "no desire to go over the ceiling."[87]

The Socialist members of the committee, however, were by no means convinced that Bonn had gotten such a splendid deal. They remained skeptical that the NATO arrangement would give the FRG the "full equality" that had been so sorely missing in the EDC plan. Carlo Schmid objected that all German units would be under NATO command, which was not true for the other nations. "Only the Germans will be controlled," he complained. Moreover, because the German troops would lack a "strategic capacity," they would remain little more than "glorified foot soldiers"—nuclear cannon fodder. As for the prospective command structure, Schmid wondered at what level one might encounter "the first German general." In the realm of intelligence operations, he feared that Germany's partners would spend most of their time putting their new ally "under the microscope, checking into what [the Germans] were producing, finding out if what [they] claimed was a sewing machine was not some infernal instrument of war."[88]

Betraying a similar concern over equality, Fritz Erler asked whether Bonn's "freedom" meant that it was "free" to contribute fewer than five hundred thousand men—say none? Helmut Schmidt, the brilliant young SPD delegate from Hamburg, objected that the FRG was about to "buy the cat in the sack" by joining an alliance founded on "secret agreements" to which it was not privy. In the realm of grand strategy, he complained, the Germans were as uninformed as ever. As far as they knew, NATO still planned to establish its first line of defense on the Rhine, abandoning most of the FRG to the enemy. Ernst Paul noted that West Germany would be obliged to help defend the "free world." But what did this entail? Franco Spain? Tito's Yugoslavia? Restating concerns raised about Bonn's EDC contingent, he wondered if Germany's NATO units might be sent anywhere in the world where the Western powers saw their interests threatened.[89]

General Heusinger tried to calm such concerns in a report to the committee entitled "Germany's Strategic Situation in the Atomic Age." He argued that the atomic era did not render conventional weapons obsolete—a crucial point inasmuch as Germany's army would have no nuclear arms. Even if the next war eventually "went nuclear," declared Heusinger, Germany would have a vital role to play because the atomic exchange might remain "tactical," and tactical atomic weapons could not "wipe out the entire West German army and civilian population." No doubt this was reassuring news, but Heusinger's report raised a host of new questions. Who, asked Erler, would make the decision to deploy nuclear weapons? Would the Germans have a voice, or would a nod from Washington be sufficient to bring atomic Armageddon? Karl Mommer (SPD) asked if Bonn had demanded a "veto right" over the stationing of nuclear weapons on its soil, as the British had done. In another vein, Herbert von Bismarck (CDU) asked if NATO had given thought to the "strategic advantages" of hitting Moscow with a "preemptive nuclear strike." This last question shocked Heusinger, who gasped: "Do not even touch that idea!" He went on to reassure the committee that Germany would indeed have its finger on the nuclear trigger because any deployment of atomic weapons in the NATO theater required agreement of the NATO Council, of which the FRG would be a member. As for the danger that Russia might launch a "preventive war," Heusinger was equally reassuring. Why should the Soviets be frightened by 12 German divisions? he asked. After all, in the last war 250 German divisions had not been able to bring them to their knees![90] (Heusinger was apparently unaware that this argument nicely undercut the rationale for fielding a limited German contingent in the first place.)

Dienststelle Blank functionaries also defended the Paris treaties before the German public. Their task was onerous and sometimes even dangerous, as emotions on rearmament continued to run very high. A Dienststelle speaker appearing in Frankfurt was greeted by such comments as, "This time we'll finish off the Adenauer mercenary!" and "He won't come back here again!" During his presentation, the spokesman was heckled as an "American Foreign Legionnaire" and a "warmonger."[91] When Blank himself appeared at a political rally in Augsburg, youthful hecklers shouted "Sieg Heil" and "Niemals mehr Barras—lieber den Ivan!" As he was leaving, an angry pacifist hit him with a beer stein and a crippled war veteran struck him with his crutch. After this, Blank made sure he was well protected. When he spoke at the Technische Hochschule in Aachen the hall was guarded by hundreds of police. A couple of days later, roughly two thousand demonstrators tried to disrupt his appearance at a CDU rally in Freiburg, but local police, backed up by CDU bouncers, drove the dissidents out.[92]

That much of the opposition to rearmament came from the younger generation needs emphasis. Germany's young people, like the rest of the population, were divided on this issue, their attitudes varying considerably according to political affiliation, education, and social background. Some of the conservative and Christian youth groups accepted the principle of rearmament, though they often voiced reservations about the details.[93] Political and religious affiliations aside, men between the ages of sixteen and thirty were consistently less enthusiastic about rearmament than men over thirty, which was natural enough because the former group would provide Bonn's draft fodder.[94] Following the EDC collapse, several left-leaning youth groups came out strongly against remilitarization. Prominent among them were the youth organization of the Deutsche Gewerkschaftsbund (DGB) and the SPD's junior auxiliary, the Falken. Significantly, both groups assumed a less flexible stance than did their parent organizations. Blank functionaries trying to sell their program to younger audiences discovered that Germany's youth was very suspicious of government claims that the new military would be significantly more democratic or humane than past German armies. Even Baudissin encountered this distrust: at a meeting in Cologne his young audience shouted him down, disputing his promise that he and his associates would create a military structure devoid of "*Kommissköpfen.*"[95]

In mid-December 1954, against this volatile background, the Bundestag held its first debate on the Paris Treaties. Adenauer opened the session by stressing the added security, influence, and independence that Bonn would gain through the projected arrangement. He pointed out that the disputed Binding Clause had been abandoned, which improved prospects for re-unification. At the same time, he said, Bonn's inclusion in the Brussels Treaty and Britain's commitment to Continental defense were significant milestones on the way to European unity. He claimed that historic progress had also been made in the relationship between Germany and France, two old ene-mies who would now be joined in "equal partnership." Early fruits of this col-laboration could be seen in recent agreements on the Saar, where German citizens' political rights were now guaranteed and the future of that state made contingent on a free and open referendum.[96]

As usual, Adenauer's opening sally set the stage for a blistering counter-attack from the SPD. Ollenhauer condemned the Paris Treaties for putting rearmament before reunification. In maintaining this priority, he declared, the treaties confirmed "the tragedy of the Federal Republic's foreign policy" since 1949. Ollenhauer also called attention to the political and economic prerogatives which the Allied powers would retain. These *Vorbehaltsrechte* were so far-reaching, he insisted, that one "could not legitimately speak of sovereignty in the usual sense of the word." Indeed, instead of contemplating an "equal partnership in a free world," the Allies were still wallowing in the mind-set of the Morgenthau era. Finally, Ollenhauer warned of the economic and social costs of rearmament. Recent estimates placed the costs at DM 15.9 billion for each of the first three years of the military buildup. How could the German people carry such a burden? What social sacrifices would they be ex-pected to make? Of course, the government hoped that the Western powers would supply most of Germany's arms. But what kind of weapons would these be? He had the right to know, Ollenhauer shouted, whether his son, if he became a soldier, would be armed "with the best weapons available, or cast-off Allied junk."[97]

The FDP, though not opposing the Paris Treaties per se, also found much to fault in the proposed arrangement. There was nothing new in its reservations. Dehler, who had hailed the collapse of the EDC as the "end of Adenauer's dream of a Catholic Little Europe," believed that Eden's alternative plan should have been accompanied by a serious effort to bargain with the Russians. At a party conference in October, delegates had lamented Adenauer's "sterile" and "inflexible" foreign policy, insisting once again that it was based on the "illusion" that German unity could come through West integration.[98] Now, in the Bundestag debate, Dehler hedged his endorsement of rearmament within NATO with attacks on the Allied reserve rights in the General Treaty. He also condemned the Saar compromise, accusing Adenauer of selling out German rights in exchange for French support of Bonn's admission to NATO.[99]

As the Bundestag debated the Paris Treaties, the Soviets tried yet again to influence the outcome with a new démarche. On 15 January 1955, Moscow issued another proposal for all-German elections as an alternative to German rearmament. While permitting international supervision of the elections, the initiative insisted, as usual, that the GDR be included as an equal partner in the preparations. The SPD chose to interpret this offer as a "decisive new factor" in the diplomatic calculation. Claiming that the German question had reached a "watershed," Ollenhauer demanded that the West suspend rearmament preparations pending serious negotiations with Moscow.[100]

Adenauer acknowledged that West Germany faced a crucial decision but insisted that this political Rubicon must be crossed. He argued that Bonn's "moral-political rehabilitation" was dependent on its reliability as a partner of the Western powers; entertaining Soviet offers designed to neutralize Germany would hardly reassure the West. Indeed, he added, the Western powers had made German ratification of the Paris Treaties a prerequisite for their willingness to help Germany reunite in "peace and freedom." It was therefore "not in the German interest" to pursue the Soviet offer.[101]

These exchanges made clear, almost a half decade into the rearmament debate, that the major contenders had exhausted their rhetorical quivers. As far as the parliamentary standoff was concerned, all the factions had made their moves and were standing pat.

EXTRAPARLIAMENTARY OPPOSITION: THE PAULSKIRCHE INITIATIVE

Having received no satisfaction in the Bundestag debates, the SPD decided to take its case directly to the German people. The party hoped that an upsurge of grass-roots opposition to Adenauer's foreign policy would force the government to put off efforts to ratify the Paris Treaties until the possibility of productive negotiations with the Soviets had been fully explored. The SPD leadership had begun to consider resorting to extraparliamentary action in November 1954 and by early January 1955 had worked out a plan for a "spectacular" demonstration against the government's position.[102] Not all party leaders, however, were enthusiastic about this tactic. Willy Brandt and Karl Schiller, for example, were inclined to accept rearmament as inevitable and to try to influence it along Socialist lines. In addition, Security Committee members Fritz Erler, Carlo Schmid, and Helmut Schmidt were working behind the scenes with colleagues from the coalition parties to shape defense legislation. Such cooperation on security issues would soon become the SPD's official policy. But at this point the party executive was still partly guided by the Schumacher legacy of intransigence.

The SPD was not alone in concluding that something "spectacular" should be done to prevent rearmament. The DGB leadership, which like that of the SPD faced pressure from its rank and file, found itself swept into the extraparliamentary crusade. Walter Freitag tried to resist this, but at the annual congress in October he was outmaneuvered by antirearmament activists. The congress passed a resolution rejecting any "military contribution as long as all negotiation possibilities aiming at German unification have not been exhausted."[103]

Though the DGB did not specify what measures should be undertaken to stop ratification of the treaties, rumors began to circulate that the miners' union was considering a general strike. Hearing of this, Adenauer warned Freitag that he would "oppose any [strike] action with all measures at [his] disposal."[104] In the face of these conflicting pressures, Freitag met with Ollenhauer and Wilhelm Mellies to plan a public demonstration that might mobilize popular sentiment against the treaties without risking the disruption of a general strike. The avowedly peaceful demonstration would culminate with the proclamation of a "manifesto" against rearmament. But Freitag, who continued to have his doubts about extraparliamentary tactics, insisted that union figures appearing at the demonstration must do so as individual citizens, not as representatives of the DGB. He also urged that reunification—not rearmament—be emphasized.[105] Evidently he did not want the union movement to be overly exposed in this campaign, for that might endanger its ability to bargain with the government on other issues more directly relevant to the workers' welfare.

Important as SPD/DGB collaboration was in this enterprise, the real moving spirit behind it was Gustav Heinemann. He had welcomed the collapse of the EDC as a new opportunity to engage in "productive rethinking" of the German question. He thought that the 1954 Geneva settlement on Indochina, in which the contending parties had agreed to schedule free elections to determine the area's future, could serve as a model for Germany. But when the success of Eden's initiative made it clear that there would be no substantial rethinking of security policy, Heinemann concluded that only drastic measures could avert the "catastrophe" of rearmament. He was also convinced that existing parliamentary power relationships did not reflect the citizens' true views regarding the priority of reunification over rearmament. Certainly his own party, the newly formed Gesamtdeutsche Volkspartei, had too little influence to avert or even delay ratification. The only answer, then, was to go outside the parliamentary process, to create a new *Sammlungsbewegung* against rearmament. Heinemann envisaged a movement that would pull together the SPD, the unions, anti-Adenauer elements within the ruling coalition, pacifist theologians, and disaffected young people of all political stripes. The only constituency to be excluded were the Communists because Heinemann did not want his effort dismissed as a "front" for Moscow and the GDR.[106]

Heinemann tried to enlist the support of former chancellor Heinrich Brüning, to whom he offered titular leadership of the movement. Although Brüning had expressed sharp criticism of Adenauer's foreign policy, he chose to steer clear of this crusade. Heinemann then approached the SPD politicians Herbert Wehner and Ludwig Metzger, who embraced his cause and promised to win over Ollenhauer. But Heinemann realized that lining up prominent SPD figures would be inadequate; he needed additional support from within the government. Aware of Dehler's rift with Adenauer, he tried to bring him and the dissident wing of the FDP into the movement. Like Brüning, however, Dehler chose to keep his distance, as did the rest of the FDP leadership.

More successful was Heinemann's effort to recruit antirearmament theologians, particularly among the Protestants. His most important acquisition was Pastor Helmut Gollwitzer, who was known chiefly for his 1951 "letter" from a Russian prisoner of war camp, which had captured the anguish of millions of German prisoners and refugees. He was a man who had "seen through the Russians."[107] That he would join in a crusade to negotiate with them undoubtedly impressed many Germans, though it apparently confused some others. Heinemann was also assured of support from the dissident Protestants around Martin Niemöller and Karl Barth, as well as from the twenty-seven prominent pastors who had issued a declaration in Düsseldorf in mid-January insisting that since the "political, legal, and spiritual prerequisites" for German rearmament were not sufficiently developed, the country "had no right from God to take this step."[108]

This coalition of disaffected pastors, SPD politicians, union members, professors, and youth group leaders came together on 29 January 1955 at the

Saint Paul's Church in Frankfurt, where German liberals during the revolution of 1848 had drawn up their abortive blueprint for democratic unification. As in 1848, the historic church was festooned with black-red-gold flags. Speakers included Heinemann, Ollenhauer, union leader Ernst Reuter, the prominent sociologist Alfred Weber, the Catholic theologian Johannes Hessen, and the Protestant theologians Gollwitzer and Ernst Lange. Their speeches emphasized less the evils of rearmament than the disastrous impact this was likely to have on prospects for German reunification. Declared Heinemann: "Whoever pursues the perpetuation of military blocs through the integration of West Germany into the Atlantic Alliance may pay lip service to German reunification, but he in fact obstructs it." [109] Though Heinemann admitted that he was not speaking in the name of the Evangelical church, he made reference to the "crisis of conscience" suffered by Germany's Protestants in the face of their nation's division. Gollwitzer, too, could not resist sounding a spiritual note: "Not nationalism, not traditional allegiance to the nation-state, but our human duty toward 18 million [East] Germans, makes Germany's division unbearable for us. For them we are, as Martin Niemöller tellingly put it, 'our brothers' keepers.'" [110]

After the speeches were delivered, the participants jointly signed a "German Manifesto" that declared: "Commitment to a new Four-Power Agreement on reunification must have precedence over the construction of military blocs. We can and must find the conditions, acceptable to Germany and its neighbors, that would allow German reunification in peaceful coexistence with the other European nations." [111]

The Paulskirche meeting was unquestionably a significant event in the history of postwar Germany. For the first time since 1945, Socialists, union leaders, theologians, and leading representatives of the academic community had come together to take a public stand on a political issue of epochal importance. And yet this event was not all that its organizers had hoped it might be. Ecumenical though it was, it had not managed to show that a popular consensus opposed Adenauer's security policy (any more, for that matter, than the chancellor had been able to prove the opposite). The presence of one Catholic divine on the podium did not attest to widespread Catholic support, which indeed was not in evidence. The Union parties were entirely unrepresented, as were (more painfully) the FDP and the smaller nationalist parties, the DP and the BHE. Equally disappointing was the DGB's decision to send Ernst Reuter and not Walter Freitag, the chairman of the organization. And Reuter was careful to say that he was present not as a representative of the DGB but as "one citizen among millions of citizens." [112]

Various demonstrations ignited by the Paulskirche meeting were not especially impressive. In Munich twenty-five thousand union members demonstrated against the Paris Treaties on the day of their second reading in the Bundestag; elsewhere smaller marches and rallies took place. All were peaceful and all had a distinctly Socialist flavor. The DGB leadership gave the demonstrations its blessing but did little to promote them. It believed that these occasions might be useful as safety valves for pent-up frustrations, but it also saw them as potentially dangerous, for they might be taken over by the Communists and other extremists. At a time when the DGB leaders were struggling to prove their trustworthiness as bargaining partners with the government and employers, they could ill afford to be cast as agents of disorder.

But if the organizers of the Paulskirche demonstration hoped through their moderation to avoid being castigated as fomenters of disorder, they were singularly unsuccessful. Even before the event took place, representatives of the government were warning the SPD and DGB against their plan to move the antirearmament opposition into the nation's streets, union halls, and churches. Heinrich von Brentano declared that the unions had no business intervening in foreign policy, which was the prerogative of the government and parliament. He also insisted that the "overwhelming majority" of union members did not want their organizations "misused" for radical political purposes. His colleague Eugen Gerstenmaier made the same claim relative to the EKD. In a church publication, he insisted that the "majority" of German Protestants were not prepared to cast their lot with the "*Ohne-Mich* movement."[113]

In the wake of the Frankfurt meeting, attacks on the participants increased. One of the reasons was that the GDR weighed in on behalf of the Paulskirche enterprise, endorsing wholeheartedly its goals and tactics. This was grist in the mills of those who saw the movement's organizers as agents or dupes of Communism. Not surprisingly, Adenauer took this line. To him the Frankfurt demonstration smacked of a "red main dish with a few green salad leaves as garnish."[114] Dehler said he respected the "crisis of conscience" that had motivated the Paulskirche organizers but took them sharply to task for embracing "plebiscitary democracy." It was "dangerous poison," he said, to claim "that public opinion must determine the will of parliament, that the masses are the highest sovereign, supreme over the will of parliament."[115]

The Paulskirche demonstration also stimulated a new bout of bloodletting in the churches. Leading Catholics took this opportunity to attack the "Protestant pastor opposition" that was allegedly giving aid and comfort to the enemy. The bishop of Regensburg thundered against an unholy alliance of "pacifists, draft-dodgers, and soft-headed humanitarians forever touting their crises of conscience."[116] Progovernment Protestants sought to ward off these attacks by unleashing their own invective against the Heinemann-Niemöller faction, which did not, they stressed, represent the official position of the

EKD. The Evangelical Working Group within the CDU/CSU accused the Paulskirche people of overlooking "Soviet expansionism" and wondered aloud if these men truly acted "in good conscience when they claimed that rearmament would mean war."[117] An influential prorearmament lobby group, the Arbeitsgemeinschaft demokratischer Kreise, circulated an article by Pastor Hans Asmussen describing the Paulskirche demonstration as an "open crisis in the Evangelical church" and charging the antigovernment critics with threatening Evangelical traditions of individualism and spiritual freedom by turning their protest into a "collective movement."[118] Here was yet another statement of the old Lutheran thesis that Protestants had no business making public political issues out of their crises of conscience.

Heinemann learned at the EKD Synod of Elspekamp in March 1955 just how much he had offended his conservative Lutheran colleagues. Attacked for carrying "partisan politics" into the ranks of the church, he was stripped of his presidency of the synod. The EKD Council, deeply split on the issue of rearmament, clung to its position that the church must not pronounce officially on "questions of political insight."[119]

Yet a recent historian of postwar German Protestantism is surely correct when she argues that this rejection of any criticism of Adenauer's policies amounted to a tacit toleration of them.[120] In fact, the CDU/CSU Evangelical Working Group had no compunctions about openly expressing its support for rearmament. It applauded Heinemann's ouster from the synod presidency as a "clarification of the Christian view on rearmament." Passage of the Paris Treaties, it said, was a "necessary precondition for the restoration of sovereignty in the Federal Republic and full integration into the community of free peoples."[121]

The Paulskirche organizers had hoped to mobilize so much grass-roots opposition that the Bundestag would suspend its debate on ratification of the Paris Treaties. Instead, their efforts demonstrated the impotence of extraparliamentary populism in the early years of the Bonn Republic. Against the backdrop of the Paulskirche movement's obvious failure, the Bundestag opened its final two readings on the treaty complex. As in France, the debates displayed few oratorical pyrotechnics. Socialist delegates repeated their arguments against ratification, but almost pro forma, for they now realized the futility of their cause.

The Paris Treaties were duly passed on 27 February 1955, by a vote of 324 to 151, while the Saar Agreement made it through less impressively with 264 for, 206 against, and 9 abstentions. On 18 March the Bundesrat, having had its moment of defiance during the EDC debates, accepted the various agreements without opposition. President Heuss signed the treaty complex into law on 24 March. All the other powers had by now ratified the treaties so the diplomatic path was finally cleared for West Germany's rearmament as a full member of the NATO alliance.

On 5 May 1955, the Allied High Commission formally abrogated the Occupation Statute and thereby its own authority: henceforth the Western powers would be represented in Bonn by ambassadors. As Dulles put it, the Federal Republic had now become a "member of the club."[122] Konrad Adenauer regarded this moment as "one of the greatest in German history."[123] Typically, he wanted to commemorate it with an solemn ceremony in the Bundestag, highlighted by his own reading of a proclamation. But, as with the signing of the General Treaty in 1952, the chancellor was denied his pomp. Because the SPD and FDP strongly opposed Adenauer's commemoration plan, the Bundestag president simply read a short letter from the chancellor, and representatives of the various parties commented on the event according to their own political lights. Not surprisingly, the SPD insisted that this was no time for celebration. "We will be able to speak of German sovereignty only when Germany is reunified," said Ollenhauer.[124] Other Germans lamented the passage of the Paris Treaties as another blow to their hopes for a united Europe stretching from the Atlantic to the Urals. No doubt they would have agreed with Reinhold Maier's paraphrase of Bismarck's famous line about abusing the name of Europe: "I have always found the word Europe in the mouths of those who are asking of others something they don't dare to impose upon themselves."[125]

CHAPTER

10

THE

BUNDESWEHR

IS BORN

With its admission into NATO, Bonn was formally empowered, indeed required, to contribute to the security of Western Europe. But Germany's first soldiers, all volunteers, did not make their appearance for several more months, and then with such modesty that it seemed as if they hoped to slink unnoticed onto the historical stage. This was indeed a low-profile army, one that appeared to be embarrassed by its very existence.

Yet noticed the soldiers were: their historical entry, however belated and humble, caused almost as much controversy as the protracted diplomatic struggle that had made it possible. And once the Germans were "on the front," the trouble hardly subsided, for many Europeans still did not want them there, while many others, including many Germans, still could find no convincing justification for their presence. There were, moreover, bruising new battles over the legal foundation of the Bundeswehr (the Military Constitution) and the introduction of conscription. The internal debates and delays caused consternation within the NATO alliance, which openly fretted over the state of mind and strength of commitment of its newest member.

And yet there was no mistaking that the birth of the Bundeswehr was an epochal development in the history of the postwar era. On the one hand, more than any other event or action, it signaled the coming of age of the young Federal Republic of Germany. If, as Adenauer maintained, contributing to one's own defense was a natural part of being a nation, West Germany had taken a crucial step toward conventional nationhood. On the other hand, the difficult and acrimonious circumstances of the Bundeswehr's birth constituted yet another reminder that the Federal Republic was far from being a "normal" nation. By fielding an army of its own, Bonn ended the rearmament debate, but it did not end the more fundamental debates about the nature of the German state and its role in the divided postwar world.

A "PARLIAMENTARY VICTORY": THE VOLUNTEERS' LAW

On 7 June 1955, the Dienststelle Blank was transformed into the Ministry of Defense, and Theodor Blank was named West Germany's first defense minister.[1] Though Adenauer had promised Blank this post in 1953, his appointment was not a foregone conclusion, for the pressures of the long rearmament battle had taken their toll on him physically and mentally, and he had accumulated some influential enemies. The Allies, especially the British, harbored strong misgivings about him, as did the Bundestag Security Committee, which thought that he had not done enough to include parliament in military planning.[2] In the end, however, Blank's very weakness and unpopularity may have advanced his cause with Adenauer, who did not like having strong personalities around him, especially in posts he wanted to control himself. By naming Blank he could fend off the ambitious Franz Josef Strauss, whose headstrong independence he distrusted. ("Strauss will never become minister of defense while I am chancellor," he once predicted, all too boldly.)[3]

The transformation of the Dienststelle Blank into a Ministry of Defense also occasioned controversy. Characteristically, Adenauer had ordered the change without consulting the Bundestag Security Committee. This could not help but offend the amour propre of an agency increasingly determined to have its say in the decision-making process. Thus Helmut Schmidt called for a full debate on the new ministry. Richard Jaeger (CSU) complained that the ministry's first emissary to the committee was not Blank but a subordinate, the legal expert Elmar Brandstetter. "Just because [your office] is now a ministry," fumed Jaeger to Brandstetter, "don't think you can treat us so shabbily."[4] This contretemps was important, for it strained relations between parliament and the ministry just as the latter was attempting to establish itself on the political scene.

Blank's main task, of course, was to start assembling the army that Bonn had promised to NATO. He had always believed that a sound legal infrastructure, including a conscription law, should be in place before any soldiers were recruited. Yet this did not mesh with Adenauer's determination, now stronger than ever, to get an army in the field as quickly as possible. Having presided over the drawn-out battle over rearmament, Adenauer wanted to demonstrate to his new allies that the FRG was willing and able to live up to its ambitious commitment. This would give Bonn added credibility and strengthen its ties to the West at a time when a "thaw" in East-West relations—marked by the Austrian State Treaty and the impending Geneva Summit—threatened to undercut Bonn's Cold War foreign policy. Domestic political factors also dictated expedition. Adenauer was determined to have the first conscripts in uniform before the next Bundestag elections, which by law could be held no later than September 1957. This would prevent a debate over conscription from dominating the elections, which Adenauer believed would benefit the SPD. Finally, the more rapidly parliament was forced to deal with the necessary rearmament legislation, the less it could "tamper" with the government's program. Hence Adenauer forced Blank to replace his original buildup plan, which had called for eighteen months of legal preparations and a deployment period of almost six years, with a plan that eliminated the extensive legal preparations and promised a fully developed army by January 1959.[5]

The foregoing considerations help explain the genesis and fate of the Volunteers' Law, the FRG's first piece of military legislation. Immediately following Bonn's adherence to NATO, Adenauer had instructed the Dienststelle Blank to draw up a bill allowing recruitment of the first volunteers. He wanted the bill to go through the necessary parliamentary channels before the Bundestag recess at the end of the summer. As it happened, Blank's office had a skeleton bill already in hand, which it planned to introduce along with the legal framework regulating the rights and duties of the future soldiers. But Adenauer rejected this bill as too cumbersome and then turned the project over to Hans Globke, his gray eminence with a brown past, who was not likely to let democratic scruples stand in the way of efficiency and expedition.[6]

The bill that emerged from Globke's office in May 1955 was calculatedly vague; it authorized the government to recruit volunteers without specifying who would monitor their selection, and it sought to short-circuit potential legal difficulties by designating the first volunteers as "civil servants on probation." Moreover, it neither limited the number of recruits nor the functions they might perform. Only in one respect was it precise: it stipulated the exact wording of the soldiers' oath, including the phrase "So help me God." The bill was sent to the Bundestag for what Adenauer hoped would be expeditious passage.[7]

He was soon disappointed, for the Bundestag Judicial Committee declared that the law was so vague as to be unconstitutional. To this objection Adenauer reportedly snapped: "Don't be so legalistic!"[8] But parliament was in a legalistic mood. It understood that a failure to anchor the new army in the law of the land might undercut one of Bonn's signal advantages over Weimar: the luxury of having civilian institutions in place before the creation of a military.

After the Judicial Committee had registered its dissatisfaction with Adenauer's "Lightning Law," as it came to be called, the Bundestag Security Committee took the bill under advisement and subjected it to far-reaching criticism. Several members wanted to know why the government was in such a "big hurry" to get German citizens into uniform. They noted that Bonn's security seemed less threatened now than ever. They interpreted Adenauer's haste as an effort to solidify his policy of West integration before world tensions had ebbed even further. The bill's content also raised concerns. Carlo Schmid complained that it amounted to an open-ended "Enabling Law"—a reference to the legislation of March 1933 that allowed Hitler dictatorial powers. Moreover, he said, the designation "civil servants on probation" made no sense because civilian officials followed "directions," while soldiers obeyed "commands." More important, the bill allowed the defense ministry to start recruiting volunteers before parliament would have time to pass a Soldiers' Law defining the soldiers' rights and duties in a democratic society.[9]

As the debate progressed, it became clear that one of the main objections to the government's plan was its lack of a provision for a thorough political vetting of the first officers. Committee members agreed that a personnel screening board, independent of the government, needed to be created. There were differences among them, however, regarding the prospective agency's functions and scope. The Socialists argued that the board should begin its work as soon as the Volunteers' Law took effect. They also wanted the Bundestag itself to appoint board members, who should have the authority to propose (not just to veto) officer candidates, designate their ranks, and oversee their promotions. Justifying such far-reaching demands, Helmut Schmidt insisted that parliament must not be "conned" by the government's promise not to appoint any candidates of whom the board disapproved. If parliament was not vigilant, he added, Bonn's new army could become infested with unsavory characters like Kurt von Schleicher, that infamous "political general" of the Weimar era. Significantly, committee members from the coalition parties supported most of these proposals. Manteuffel (FDP) agreed that the board's functions should be anchored in law, while Bausch (CDU) and Jaeger believed that it should have the right to propose candidates to the ministry. Justifying this last idea, Bausch said that he had heard that former officers connected with the Twentieth of July movement were "not even being mentioned" by the ministry. This was a dangerous sign. His colleague Helmut Heye argued that while the screeners should establish the basic "guidelines" for officer selection, they should not control or monitor promotions, for that would alienate the military.[10]

Pressured by Adenauer, Blank resisted these demands, insisting that the screening board needed no specific legal foundation and objecting to "parliamentary interference" in military appointments. "It is *my* decision whether I take candidates whom the board has approved," he declared. "I don't have to take anyone I don't think is qualified. After all, I have to bear responsibility for my own personnel policies." Blank had reason to feel insecure about his prerogatives because he was not, whatever his protestations, his own man. This became painfully evident when, after getting assurances from the SPD that it would vote for a modified Volunteers' Law, he was unable to convince

Adenauer to accept parliament's demand for a special screening board bill. Reporting this news to the committee, Blank encountered a barrage of criticism and charges of bad faith: "We now see," huffed Wilhelm Mellies, "how seriously we should take your oft-repeated assurances that the government is anxious for cooperation with the Bundestag."[11]

Adenauer's intransigence succeeded in mobilizing the Security Committee against the hastily drafted Volunteers' Law. Despite persistent disagreements over the details of an alternative procedure, the committee, in cooperation with the Bundestag Judicial Committee, managed to come up with a compromise package which Adenauer would have to accept if he wanted to recruit any soldiers at all. Broadly formulated, the compromise involved the following stipulations: the Socialists would not insist on further constitutional amendments for rearmament or demand the passage of a Soldiers' Law before the Volunteers' Law came into effect; they would also cooperate with the coalition parties in working out the details of the military constitution; in return, the coalition deputies on the Security and Judicial committees would demand a separate Screening Board Law, to which an amended Volunteers' Law would allude.

The Personnel Screening Board Law that emerged from committee discussions was also a compromise. Members of the board would be nominated by the Ministry of Defense and approved by the Bundestag, with final power of appointment belonging to the federal president. The board itself would not propose or appoint military officers, but it would have absolute veto power over candidates recommended by the ministry for ranks of colonel and above. Unbound by any government directives, the board would be free to devise its own working rules. Furthermore, it would not be obliged to explain its decisions, which would not be subject to review or appeal. Though not empowering the board to supervise promotions, the law placed no limit on its life span.[12]

Taken together, these unprecedentedly broad provisions were perhaps, as one commentator later argued, unconstitutional.[13] Certainly no other public institution in the young state was subjected to such intense scrutiny. One positive result was that Bonn's new officer corps, though hardly without its problematical figures, turned out in general to be a reliable carrier of democratic values. Certainly it was "cleaner" with respect to the Nazi past than the judiciary or civil service, not to mention academia.

Like the Personnel Screening Board Law, the more comprehensive Volunteers' Law that eventually passed through committee review and the plenum debates in June–July 1955 represented a significant departure from the government's original draft. It allowed the ministry to recruit only six thousand volunteers and restricted their functions to staff, training, supply, and maintenance duties; the creation of regular military units was not permitted. Every volunteer position had to be specifically authorized by the Bundestag Security and Budget committees. Though the volunteers would be classed as "civil servants on probation," they would take no oath of office. This and the other restrictions were designed to ensure that the enlistment of volunteers would not constitute the standard for a permanent military force.[14]

The SPD hailed the institutionalization of a powerful Personnel Screening Board and the substantial revision of the Volunteers' Law as significant victories for parliamentary democracy over *Kanzlerdemokratie*. Outside observers agreed. The *New York Times* declared that the revised Volunteers' Law "represented the greatest victory of Parliament over the chancellor since he took office."[15] The chief political officer in the British embassy concluded that "the Federal Chancellor suffered a technical setback by [parliament's] refusal to accept the Volunteers' Bill in its original form." He added that the debate "provided a welcome and healthy sign that the Bundestag is prepared to scrutinize authoritarian tendencies in the organization of the armed forces themselves as well as in the parliamentary procedures adopted by the Chancellor." He regarded the SPD's collaboration on the legislation as "a welcome augury for the future."[16]

LOGISTICAL LOGJAM

Passage of the Volunteers' Law and the institution of the Personnel Screening Board cleared the way for the appearance of Bonn's first soldiers, but no officers were actually commissioned until November 1955 and no training cadres materialized until January 1956. The delays occurred because many of the logistical requirements for deployment were not in place when the last legal hurdles were cleared. For fear of alarming domestic and foreign opponents of rearmament, Bonn had postponed launching any military building projects until the Paris Treaties had been safely ratified. The Dienststelle Blank had also politely declined informal American offers secretly to train advance personnel at American bases in the use of NATO weapons. Any "premature actions," the Germans had explained, might "raise a lot of political dust."[17]

Once the defense ministry starting combing its list of prospective volunteers, it discovered an acute shortage of suitable personnel. It had hoped to staff the first training units exclusively with former Wehrmacht officers who had had distinguished military careers. *Ohne Mich* sentiment notwithstanding, this probably would have been possible had the army been created in 1951, as was originally envisaged. But with the postponement of recruiting, many veterans had gotten too old to start new military careers or had found lucrative jobs in the now-booming civilian economy. These difficulties had

become public in late 1954, when the press exposed the impending manpower shortage. Taking the cue, the Security Committee urged Blank to consider converting Bundesgrenzschutz units into military cadres, but Blank objected that the Border Guards were "ill-suited for military functions."[18]

Because of the long ban on securing military housing and training facilities, Blank's ministry faced difficulties here as well. The obvious candidates
for these functions—former Wehrmacht barracks and training centers—had
often been commandeered by the Western allies or expropriated by the states
for low-income and refugee housing. The construction of new *Kaserne*, air
bases, naval installations, and proving grounds required the cooperation of
the respective *Länder*, which was often not forthcoming. Blank did his best to
overcome these problems, but his solutions were not always happy ones.
For the first Bundeswehr officer training facility he chose a site—Sonthofen
in the Bavarian Allgäu—that had previously served as a Nazi *Ordensburg*. As
the elite training schools for Nazi Party cadres, the *Ordensburgen* were heavily freighted with political symbolism. They were literally freighted too: in
the case of Sonthofen, thousands of swastikas had to be sanded off beams and
walls to render the buildings politically suitable for their new occupants. (The
swastikas, incidentally, had not bothered the complex's previous tenants—the
American military.) Blank hoped that this scrubbing would be enough to ex-
orcise the past, but his selection aroused a storm of protest. Responding to
the criticism, Blank complained of a "crazy fear that the Nazi spirit still
haunted" physical structures connected to the Third Reich. Following the
logic of this "absurd fetishism," he fumed, one would not even be able to
drive on the *Autobahnen* because they too had been built by the Nazis.[19]

In a ham-handed attempt to still the swelling protest, Blank convinced the
Bavarian government to rename the Sonthofen complex after Ludwig Beck,
one of the anti-Nazi generals executed in the wake of the abortive Twentieth
of July coup. But Blank's critics remained unconvinced by this symbolic le-
gerdemain. As Fritz Erler put it: "The *Ordensburg* concept was developed by
a hideous regime, and it can hardly be salutary to pick precisely this symbol
for the beginning [of our new military]. . . . I would certainly understand it if
someone said, 'An *Ordensburg* as the beginning?—no, leave me out!'"[20]

Blank's critics soon found other, less symbolic reasons to question the minister's ability or willingness to start the new army off on a sound footing. In
August 1955 *Der Spiegel* published a "confidential memo" by Heinz Karst
that took Bonn's politicians to task for being so obsessed with political control over the military that they were undermining its self-respect, public status, and technical effectiveness. Though he did not question the "primacy of
politics," Karst complained that civilian officials were making all the important decisions, leaving officers to feel like pariahs. Hostility toward the officer
corps, he said, was evident in a recent decision to pay military men less than

their civilian counterparts. Bonn's apparent "distrust" of its own soldiers, combined with a "dilettantist distinction between 'civilian' and 'military,'" threatened to undermine the army's ability to serve as a credible tool against the nation's enemies. Much damage had already been done, he claimed, for many highly qualified former officers were refusing to volunteer for an institution that enjoyed so little official confidence. *Innere Führung*, too, was being undermined, for this ambitious ideal could hardly be actualized by men who were "poorly paid, poorly fed, and kept under the strictest controls." In short, Bonn seemed intent not so much on producing "citizens in uniform" as "soldiers in a ghetto."[21]

Karst was not the first official in the Dienststelle or defense ministry to say such things; von Bonin and de Maizière had articulated similar misgivings in 1953–54. More recently, in May 1955, Heusinger had sent a letter to Blank warning that a "denigration of the soldier's profession in its entirety" was creating an atmosphere "in which the efforts . . . to chart a new course and to justify [Bonn's] defense contribution were encountering skepticism and mistrust."[22] Blank had not responded to Heusinger's letter, which had inspired Karst to follow up with his own, more pointed, memo.

Many in the ministry applauded Karst's action, evincing sympathy with his views. Even Baudissin said he agreed in principle with Karst's perspective, though he criticized the sharpness of his tone.[23] Bonn's leading parliamentarians, however, were shocked and horrified to hear such views uttered by a defense ministry employee. The Bundestag Security Committee promptly called in Karst and Blank to explain themselves. Blank defensively reminded the politicians that Karst was the principal author of a brochure called *On Future German Soldiers*, which enshrined the basic ideals of *Innere Führung*. Without explicitly criticizing Karst's latest memo, he expressed outrage that the piece had been leaked to the press. Apparently convinced that Karst himself was behind the leak, Blank said that he would have fired him on the spot if he thought he could have gotten away with it. Karst, for his part, repeated his insistence that too much emphasis was being placed on civilian control and suggested that this misguided approach had its origins in a tendency to misapply the "Weimar analogy" to conditions obtaining in the Federal Republic. "I would regard it as problematic if backward glances at the Weimar Republic too strongly influenced the creation of our new military," he said. "One would thereby court the danger of freezing living realities in outmoded categories of the past." Overzealous efforts to prevent the new army from becoming a "state within the state" might perversely yield just that result by driving the soldiers into alienated isolation.[24]

The Karst case generated consternation in the press and parliament about a revival of "reactionary" attitudes among the officers working for Blank.[25] Though such dangers were overstated, Karst's memo and subsequent testimony, along with Blank's own performance, strengthened the Security Committee's determination to keep a close watch on the military planners. If Karst's views were typical of the defense ministry, declared Jaeger, then the military reform program was "in grave danger." To Fritz Erler, Karst's attitude indicated that "before there is a training course for future troop commanders, there ought to be a training course for members of the defense ministry."[26]

Before leaving the Karst case, we should note that Karst himself survived it well enough, staying in the ministry and continuing to be promoted. More important, his concerns about the "ghettoization" of the new army became a staple of conservative criticism of Bonn's military buildup. Within a year of his controversial memo, the Military Leadership Council, an influential body under the chairmanship of Heusinger, warned that Bonn's political leaders were not evincing adequate trust and support for the nation's new soldiers. "The soldier should certainly not have a privileged position in the state," said the council, "but he should also not be treated, as is now the case, as an orphan child."[27]

Meanwhile, as the political dust swirled around Karst, the Personnel Screening Board took up its appointed task of screening candidates for top ranks in the first training cadres. The board was larger than Blank had envisaged, and each of its thirty-eight members had been cleared by the Bundestag Security Committee. Nonveterans outnumbered former military officers thirty-one to seven. Ten members were affiliated with the SPD, eleven with the CDU/CSU, eight with the FDP, one with the DP, two with the BHE, and six had no party affiliation.[28] Two of the members, Fabian von Schlabrendorff and Annedore Leber (widow of the resistance martyr Julius Leber), had connections to the Twentieth of July conspiracy. Another member, former general Fridolin von Senger und Etterlin, had rebuffed Gestapo efforts to penetrate his command in Italy. The group's chairman, Wilhelm Rombach, had been removed from his post as mayor of Aachen by the Nazis in 1933.

On 10 October the Security Committee invited Rombach and the heads of the Screening Board subcommittees to discuss their work. Jaeger noted that the press had reported "disagreements" between the board and the defense ministry. Rombach and his colleagues confirmed the disagreements, complaining that Blank was denying them the information they needed to do their job. More specifically, the ministry had rejected the screeners' request for the entire list of officer corps applicants, which they needed to compare the men they were evaluating with those the ministry had chosen not to send on for review. The board had also not received the candidates' complete files, only the ministry's recommendations. Moreover, the defense ministry was pressing the board to hurry its evaluations, which flew in the face of Blank's claims to value a thorough screening process. It seemed, board members said, that Blank wanted to reduce the agency to a "rubber stamp." In response to such charges, the Security Committee reminded the board that it had an absolute veto on nominations for positions of colonel and above. It should not allow itself to be "intimidated or bamboozled" by the defense ministry, said Jaeger.[29]

FIRST SOLDIERS

Against this background of internal dispute and public skepticism, West Germany's first 101 senior officers—all employees of the defense ministry—received their commissions from Theodor Blank. The date, 12 November 1955, was symbolically significant, for it was the two hundredth anniversary of the birth of that great Prussian military reformer, Gerhard von Scharnhorst. According to ministry plans, the event was to be "very simple and entirely dignified," with a small number of guests and no newspaper, radio, or television coverage. Decorations at the site, the Ermekeilkaserne's cavernous motor pool, were limited to the federal flag "combined in an appropriate manner with the Iron Cross."[30]

What would the new organization be called? Like virtually everything associated with Bonn's army, the choice of an acceptable name was rife with controversy. In 1954 Blank had informed the foreign press that he was determined to avoid any names similar to "Reichswehr" or "Wehrmacht." These carried too much ballast from the past. Nor would he accept a CDU suggestion to name the twelve divisions of the new army after "lost" German cities like Danzig, Breslau, and Königsberg. The new military would "simply" be called Die Gesamtstreitkräfte der Bundesrepublik Deutschland (the Combined Armed Forces of the Federal Republic of Germany).[31]

Though appropriately unglamorous, this mouthful was virtually unpronounceable—Germany's new allies would never get it right. Taking up the question during discussion of the Volunteers' Law, the Security Committee insisted that it was parliament's job to name the new military. Accordingly, Hasso von Manteuffel suggested "Bundeswehr," which had already been advanced in some newspapers. Manteuffel admitted that he would have preferred to stick with "Wehrmacht," but the Americans had vetoed this suggestion. "Bundeswehr" at least had the advantage of sounding "provisional," allowing "Wehrmacht" to be saved for "the future army of united Germany." Accepting Manteuffel's proposal, Erler found it appropriate that a "provisional federation" like Bonn should have an army that also connoted provisionality; as for "Wehrmacht," this term just had "too many associations with the Third Reich." Other committee members, however, found "Bundeswehr" unacceptably pedestrian. Carlo Schmid thought it sounded too much like "Feuerwehr"; he preferred "Landwehr," which conveyed the "old Prussian militia ideal of 1813." Another member reported that "Bundeswehr" had provoked considerable mirth during the recent carnival season in Cologne. A straw vote in the committee yielded eighteen for Bundeswehr and eight for Wehrmacht. Nevertheless, Blank elected to stay with "Gesamtstreitkräfte" for the time being, and the term "Bundeswehr" did not come into formal use until passage of the Soldiers' Law in March 1956.[32]

Meanwhile, the commissioning ceremony came off as planned. Theodor Blank stood stiffly on a wooden platform beneath a large cardboard Iron Cross and handed out the appropriate documents. Afterward he gave a short speech pointing out the "historical parallel" between this moment and the accomplishments of Scharnhorst, whose goal had been the "union between people and army." But if Germany's contemporary reformers were successfully to emulate Scharnhorst's ideal, Blank cautioned, they would have to be decisive in applying the reform concepts that were now only on paper. This task, he added, was not just a "technical exercise" but a "human enterprise" that would succeed or fail according to the "spirit" with which it was addressed.[33]

Blank's ministry now began to recruit volunteers for the first training cadres, but this endeavor, like the swearing-in ceremony, was almost furtive. Revealingly, the ministry prohibited news photographers from taking pictures at recruiting stations on the grounds that prospective enlistees might suffer "difficulties" if their employers, wives, girl friends, or colleagues learned of their interest in joining the new army.[34]

Eventually, of course, the military had to show itself; and on a cold and windy day in mid-January 1956, some fifteen hundred freshly recruited troops were introduced to the world in Bonn's first military review. Despite hundreds of flags put out by the citizens of Andernach, the Rhineland village where the army was headquartered (naval personnel were sent to Wilhelmshaven and airmen to Nörvenich), the scene struck one observer as "very depressing . . . more like a funeral than a baptism."[35] There were a few hastily painted barracks and a cheap chain-link fence. The soldiers looked nervous and uncomfortable in their American-style tunics, which they derided as "mailman's jackets" or "monkey suits." Nor were they happy with their American-model helmets, so unimpressive compared to the old *Stahlhelme* of the Wehrmacht. And to add insult to injury, they were obliged to stand at attention not as German soldiers had traditionally stood, with fingers stretched smartly along pants seams, but with their hands in a balled fist—another American innovation that some troopers dubbed "the peeing stance" or the "SPD stance."[36]

When the soldiers paraded past the reviewing stand, representatives of the domestic and foreign press looked in vain for the man who had come to personify the new order of things: Count von Baudissin. It turned out that he was home with the flu, but *Der Spiegel* speculated that he had not been invited because he had alienated Blank and Adenauer by convincing President Heuss to forgo a military honor guard. In any event, Baudissin was not the only figure of note to miss the ceremony. It seems that Blank had forgotten to invite Bundestag president Eugen Gerstenmaier, a slight that did not improve the minister's troubled relationship with parliament.[37]

The "depressing" inauguration of the new army ushered in a host of other indignities and frustrations. Early recruitment goals could not be met because a high percentage of the applicants had to be rejected as unfit for service. In the first year, only 175,000 of the 260,000 would-be volunteers could be accepted, and only 9,500 Border Guards elected to transfer to the Bundeswehr.[38]

Yet there was insufficient housing to accommodate those who did join. By October 1956, commanders were urging the ministry not to send any more recruits, for they had no place to put them.[39] A few months later, several thousand soldiers had to be temporarily furloughed pending renovation of their quarters. The housing shortage was exacerbated by the unwillingness of many civilian landlords to rent rooms or apartments to soldiers. Even high officers had to live in cramped on-post quarters. Some towns declared that they wanted no bases anywhere near them.[40]

In addition to inadequate housing, soldiers complained that their pay fell far short of what they had been promised. "Bei Blank wirst Du blank!" ("With Blank you'll be broke!") they groused. Then there were those new uniforms, which were not only unstylish but also too thin for the cold winter months. Operation Barbarossa veterans groused that their first winter in Andernach reminded them of Hitler's Russian campaign. Some of their American-made weapons, moreover, were inferior to those they had used in the war. Their new machine guns did not fire as quickly as the old German models, and their gas-powered M-47 tanks were less efficient than the old German diesels.[41]

Bonn's new soldiers were also distressed by the treatment they experienced when they ventured outside their bases. Instead of the veneration traditionally accorded the uniform in Germany, military personnel were vilified, spat upon, and in some cases stoned. Now, instead of attracting women, their uniforms seemed a guarantee of celibacy. Bars put up signs saying "No Soldiers Allowed!" and some restaurants refused to serve "professional murderers." "Lepers in the middle ages probably had it better," insisted one veteran of the early Bundeswehr.[42]

As Karst had feared, such conditions hardly provided a healthy environment for nurturing the new army's ambitious program of military reform. There were, indeed, some signs that the ideals of *Innere Führung*—or "inner bullshit," as many soldiers called it—were being ignored or repressed in favor of reviving earlier practices and attitudes. Quickly, soldiers returned to the Wehrmacht style of saluting and standing at attention. More significantly, Bundeswehr units began informally assuming the lineage and honors of old German outfits such as the "Death Head Hussars."[43]

This does not mean, however, that the new Bundeswehr, either in its disciplinary regimen or in its guiding spirit, was becoming a Wehrmacht redivivus. The issue was much more complicated and nuanced. An experience reported by the American diplomat Charles Thayer is instructive on this score. Visiting a Bundeswehr officers' training center in 1956, Thayer found that the school was not, unlike the Wehrmacht cadet schools he had seen in 1937, similar in style and atmosphere to West Point. "Each room I looked into was arranged differently from the one before. The lockers even had locks to assure a little privacy. Inside, horror of horrors! civilian clothes hung next to uniforms and linen and underwear were neatly enough piled but in any order and on any shelf the owner saw fit." Thayer concluded, somewhat wistfully, that West Point, not the new German army, was now "the last stronghold of Frederick's Prussian discipline."[44]

And yet, if the nascent Bundeswehr was anything but an unqualified repository of the old spit and polish, let alone the old caste attitudes, it was also certainly not without its internal critics of the new reformist order. Again, Thayer is instructive. In his tour of Bundeswehr bases he encountered not just frustration over living conditions and uniforms but also, on occasion, rejection of the basic notion that the German military required fundamental reform. "The good old discipline of the Reichswehr had been good enough to produce the greatest Army Germany ever had," said some of the new troop commanders. "Why change it?"[45]

Why indeed? In a much-publicized display of reverence for the old ways, Captain Adolf Zenker, a former Kriegsmarine officer now heading the defense ministry's naval division, told the Bundeswehr's first naval training unit in January 1956 that Nazi admirals Erich Raeder and Karl Dönitz were models who ought to be emulated by Bonn's new sailors. In a Bundestag Security Committee hearing, Blank tried to downplay the significance of Zenker's comments, but many politicians found them disquieting to say the least. Erler demanded that Blank discipline Zenker, arguing that his views represented a "veneration for the Nazi past" hardly in keeping with the new military's mission or with Bonn's efforts to institutionalize democracy.[46]

The Zenker case focused attention on the newly instituted Personnel Screening Board, which had approved the captain's appointment. Critics on the left wondered how a man like Zenker could have slipped through the board's political screen. Writing to Erler, Otto Bleibtreu, a Socialist member of the board, acknowledged that the group had made a "mistake" and promised to be more vigilant in the future.[47] And in fact, the board promptly vetoed more than one hundred of the ministry's recommendations, including two of Blank's closest associates, former colonels Kurt Fett and Eberhard Kaulbach. Blank was particularly furious about the rejection of Fett, for Fett had been a member of the Dienststelle's EDC delegation in Paris and chief of military planning in the defense ministry. Though it did not explain its decision in this or any other case, the board may have rejected Fett because he had been promoted in the wake of the 20 July 1944 bloodletting.[48] No doubt the screeners also wanted to show their teeth and put Blank in his place.

In any event, the board's tactics generated a storm of criticism from veterans' groups, who accused it of conducting a "political inquisition" and practicing "collective judgment and defamation, just as the Allies had once done."[49] Particularly irate were the Waffen-SS veterans because former senior officers among them had not been allowed to join the new army, while junior personnel were subjected to particularly rigorous screening.[50] The Bundeswehr's difficulties in recruiting and fielding its first units, many former soldiers maintained, could largely be traced to its obsession with "civilian control" and its misguided efforts to produce "citizens in uniform."[51]

Though such charges are psychologically understandable, it would undoubtedly be fairer to argue that much of the chaos plaguing the early days of the Bundeswehr stemmed less from the reforms per se than from the government's overly ambitious buildup schedule. Not even Hitler, some critics noted, had tried to field so many men in so short a time.[52] Moreover, Hitler, unlike the Bundeswehr planners, had not been required to integrate his army into an international alliance system with priorities that did not always harmonize with German needs or ambitions.

THE MILITARY CONSTITUTION

The difficulties that bedeviled the Bundeswehr's early days were increased by confusion about the legal status of the new soldiers. The laws allowing the recruitment of the first volunteers were understood as temporary expedients that had to give way to a more comprehensive framework. As might be imagined, however, that system could not be thrown together overnight, especially because parts of it inspired sharp disagreement among the politicians responsible for turning the various proposals into law. Fortunately, the quarrels over diverse aspects of the Military Constitution eventually yielded to compromise on most of the key issues of contention. The informal intraparty coalition that had worked together successfully in some of the earlier negotiations held together long enough to work out agreements on a second series of military amendments to the Basic Law and also on a Soldiers' Law, which were enacted with bipartisan support in spring 1956. A conscription law, which came shortly thereafter, was passed over the vigorous objections of the SPD.[53]

After securing the first military amendments in 1954, which gave the government the right to recruit soldiers, Adenauer's administration maintained that conventional laws would suffice for the military buildup. But parliament demanded, on a bipartisan basis, that the army's place in the state needed to be thoroughly codified through new constitutional revisions. For Adenauer, this development was especially irksome because his coalition was coming apart at the seams and would probably not be able (as it had been in 1954) to muster the two-thirds majority necessary to push through any changes that the SPD decided to oppose. More than ever, the Socialists would have to be brought into the process. This prospect bothered the coalition politicians in the Bundestag much less than it did Adenauer, for many of them had already been working harmoniously with their counterparts in the SPD.

Among the welter of revisions proposed in this period, one of the most important involved the imposition of restrictions on the soldiers' constitutional rights. The defense ministry had argued that the military authorities themselves should decide what limitations on the soldiers' freedoms were necessary to maintain discipline.[54] But the Bundestag Security Committee, led by its SPD members, insisted that while some restrictions might be necessary, parliament must spell them out.[55] In proposing where these might lie and how far they should go, the committee followed Baudissin's dictum that the soldier was a citizen like any other and should therefore have his rights preserved as far as possible. The resulting legislation, which need not be recorded in detail here, ensured that the Bundeswehr soldiers were less circumscribed in their constitutional rights than any of their counterparts in past German armies had been.

Rather more divisive was the complex of issues relating to the *Oberbefehl*, which had resisted solution in earlier negotiations among the parties. For some time following the EDC collapse, the parties remained wedded to their respective visions, while the chancellor's office continued to offer its own solutions. The FDP stuck to its "presidential option"; the SPD pushed for a *Parlamentsheer* under the supervision of a defense minister responsible to the Bundestag; the Union parties held to the proposition that the chancellor should hold the supreme command, at least in wartime. What all the parties agreed upon, however, was that parliament must not allow the most important powers of military command to reside "outside the civilian realm." For this reason, they concluded that they could not look to the German past for solutions to this problem.[56]

Where then to look? The American model, which gave the president the powers of commander in chief, was unacceptable to the majority (excepting the FDP) because the Federal Republic had renounced a presidential system, which smacked of Weimar. A more attractive alternative was the so-called Churchill model, in which the prime minister (chancellor) assumed powers of military command during war or national emergency, while the defense minister held them during times of peace. The monarch (president) was reduced to essentially ceremonial functions. In effect, this was the solution offered by the Adenauer government and supported by the Union parties. Though the SPD preferred to see the defense minister maintain supreme command in war as well as in peace, it did not press this point.

Although many parliamentarians soon came to see this model as a useful framework in which to enclose the manifold powers of the old German *Oberbefehl*, specific details of the arrangement still needed to be defined. Most troublesome was the exact place of the defense minister in the government. As it turned out, it was only after other key ingredients in the Military Constitution were brought into play that the parties were able to find a satisfactory compromise on this and the rest of the *Oberbefehl* complex. The Security Committee, once again, provided the forum in which the crucial compromises were made.

In December 1955 Wilhelm Mellies (SPD) put before the committee a motion that restated his party's insistence upon "direct parliamentary responsibility" for the defense minister. This minister, said the motion, must (unlike the other cabinet members) be subject to recall by the Bundestag, which should be able to vote him out of office without having to topple the entire cabinet and offer a replacement government (the so-called Constructive Vote of No-Confidence provision). Mellies justified this measure as a way of ensuring that the defense minister would be responsible to the entire parliament. But he also claimed that the provision would strengthen the hand of the defense minister against abuses of power by the chancellor because the minister would have the full parliament behind him.[57]

Union party delegates denounced Mellies's concept as a "far-reaching violation of the system enshrined in the Basic Law." The constitutional framers, they argued, had ruled out direct parliamentary responsibility for individual cabinet members because the Weimar experience had shown this to be destabilizing. While embracing the principle of parliamentary control over the military, they said the SPD proposal would set parliament in an adversarial relationship to the army, rather than encourage cooperation.[58] The delegates were so far apart on this question that they decided to put it aside and turn to other issues.

When the committee returned to the knotty *Oberbefehl* question in its meeting of 11 January 1956, the SPD not only stuck to its position on the defense ministry but made its continuing cooperation in framing the Military Constitution dependent on this conception.[59] Its threat was made more potent by the addition of a new ally: the FDP. That party, having failed to curtail the chancellor's power by giving the *Oberbefehl* to the president, now supported the Socialists' call for direct parliamentary responsibility for the defense minister. This meant that the chancellor and his supporters had to find a modus vivendi with the opposition if the government wanted to proceed as scheduled with the military buildup. Time was running out, for the Volunteers' Law was scheduled to lapse on 31 March 1956. German troops might disappear from the front even before they had had a chance to break in their new uniforms.

Determined to avoid such a debacle, the CDU/CSU and SPD came together to fashion a comprehensive solution that must be regarded as one of the historic compromises of modern German history. On 23 February 1956, Heinrich Krone, head of the CDU's Bundestag delegation, and Fritz Erler of the SPD, agreed that the only way to solve the *Oberbefehl/*defense minister impasse was to strike a deal drawing in other elements of the prospective Military Constitution. In exchange for the SPD's withdrawing its insistence upon direct parliamentary control of the defense ministry, the Union parties would support the Socialists' repeated demands for a *Wehrbeauftragter* (parliamentary defense ombudsman) and the institutionalization of the Bundestag Security Committee as a permanent "constitutional organ" with full investigative powers. The SPD also received assurances that the provisions for employing the army during domestic crises would be subject to a constitutional law.[60]

These agreements, which eventually found their way into law, allowed the Security Committee to complete its work on the remainder of the new *Oberbefehl* system. The final arrangement necessitated additional smaller compromises among the parties. The Union parties agreed that the defense minister would supervise the military during peacetime, the chancellor in times of war and national emergency, as in the British system. Declaration of mobilization, as well as a "state of defense," would be the prerogative of the Bundestag, save in crisis situations when the parliament could not meet. The order then would be given by the federal president and countersigned by the chancellor. The decision to entrust the president with this power had been urged by Jaeger, who argued that it would endow the action with the necessary aura of national consensus. The president would have other powers as well, but they would be largely ceremonial. These included the right to commission (and dismiss) officers, to grant clemency to officers convicted of crimes, and to issue medals and military awards.[61]

This package, backed by the SPD because of the compromise outlined above, was sent to the Bundestag plenum for its second and third readings on 6 March 1956. As was inevitable with a compromise solution, it did not please everyone, and there was some spirited debate. Nonetheless, the package of amendments passed by a vote of 390 to 20.[62]

Enactment of the constitutional revisions was widely seen as a historic victory for parliamentary control over the military and a vital step toward full
integration of the new army into the democratic institutions of the state. The
same can be said for the Soldiers' Law, which Erich Mende aptly called the
"new German soldiers' Magna Carta."[63] The version of the bill that went
into effect on 1 April 1956 was the product of lengthy negotiations between
the government and the Bundestag Security Committee, which worked to
ensure the codification of the ideals of the "citizen in uniform." With this law
the army formally got its name, and the personnel who served in it received a
list of rights and duties whose comprehensiveness can only be considered
Germanic. They included, among others, the obligation faithfully to serve
the state and its constitution (see oath discussion below); the duties to display
comradeship, tell the truth, keep military secrets, and maintain discipline; assurance of the basic rights of citizenship, save as specifically restricted in the
constitutional revisions; preservation of human dignity; free expression of
personality; protection of physical person; equality before the law (a separate
military justice system was expressly forbidden in the constitutional revisions); freedom of religion; freedom of expression; active and passive fran-
chise; and the right to legal protection.[64]

Although the enshrinement of some of these rights provoked disagreement
among the parliamentarians, the most contentious issue by far was that of the
oath of allegiance, which had long been a source of hot dispute. The questions were manifold: Should there be an oath at all? If so, should it be the
same for draftees as for professional soldiers? Should any oath or oaths have a
religious component, or should they be strictly secular? The debates over the
military oath bear recounting in some detail, for they went to the heart of
basic questions about individual rights, freedom of conscience, the meaning
of Germany's military past (especially the role of the Wehrmacht and the
Twentieth of July resistance legacy), and the spiritual and political underpin-
nings of the new German army.[65]

During earlier discussions of the oath issue, Adenauer had demanded a religious oath for all soldiers. His view reflected the conviction, widespread
among Catholics, that swearing an oath before God would strengthen the
soldier's sense of duty. The officials in the legal division of the defense ministry also favored an oath (though not necessarily a religious one) because civil
servants were required to take one, and they wanted consistency between the
military and civil services. But the ministry's military reformers continued to
oppose an oath on the grounds that its recent abuse had shown it more dangerous than beneficial; they also argued that the nation's young people regarded the oath as a relic of the old military system that Bonn was claiming to
transcend. Baudissin therefore urged that instead of a conventional oath, soldiers should take a secular "pledge of obedience." But the count's voice was

not as strong as Adenauer's, and under pressure from the chancellor, the ministry drew up a proposal containing a religious oath for all soldiers, volunteers and draftees alike. It read: "I swear to protect and loyally to serve the Basic Law of this Federal Republic, and bravely to defend with my life my fatherland and its freedom, so help me God."[66]

Discussing the ministry's oath proposal, the Bundestag Security Committee sought to understand the issues at stake by calling in noted theologians. A Catholic prelate, Professor Hans Hirschmann, explained that his church had traditionally favored religious oaths for soldiers but also believed that a person "should never be forced to make a religious gesture that he regarded as immoral." An oath could have significance only if the person swearing it fully embraced its symbolism and unquestioningly accepted its terminology. But could West Germany's prospective soldiers be expected to identify fully with concepts like "fatherland" and "loyal service"? The recent abuse of such terms convinced Father Hirschmann that "we must be wary of similar abuses in the future." He nonetheless advocated retaining a religious oath as the norm, while allowing soldiers with conscientious objections to make some kind of secular pledge. This would, he believed, satisfactorily resolve potential conflicts of conscience.[67]

A representative of the EKD, Pastor Hermann Kunst, noted that the hierarchy had voted on 7 June 1955 to replace the traditional *Fahneneid* (formal oath to the flag) with a "solemn promise" to defend the constitution. The church had taken this position in light of the "shameful abuse" of the traditional gesture. But even if one overlooked the lessons of the past, he said, present political realities spoke against instituting an oath containing phrases like "defense of fatherland and freedom at the risk of life." Most Germans considered Dresden, Stettin, and Görlitz parts of their "fatherland" and understood that the new army could "defend" them only after a peaceful reunification had been achieved. Moreover, he added, West Germany's young people had been promised that no traditional oath would be reintroduced. Now they were up in arms to learn that this promise may have been no more than a *Lockvogel* (decoy) to entice their cooperation.

Kunst's comments sparked a lively discussion about the proper division between Caesar and God in the earthly realm. Fritz Berendsen (CDU) complained that Kunst's views were more "political" than theological, adding that the pastor "should leave the politics to us." To this Kunst countered that a sharp distinction between politics and theology "had also been recommended by Herr Rosenberg and Herr Goebbels." He wondered whether Berendsen would apply this rule also to the GDR. Would he tell the bishops there to leave politics to the secular authorities? "No," he concluded, "we do not plan for a minute to leave these questions exclusively to you."[68]

The committee did, however, wish to make a recommendation on this question, and one suspects that the theological input did not do much to alter any perspectives. After more discussion, in which members essentially re-stated old positions, the body voted to recommend a "ceremonial obligation" for all soldiers in place of the traditional oath. The suggested text read: "I swear loyally to serve the Federal Republic of Germany and bravely to defend the rights and freedom of the German people."[69]

Because the committee's proposal differed from the government's pro-posal, it was up to the Bundestag as a whole to reconcile the opposing drafts. In the second reading of the Soldiers' Law, a group of CDU/CSU delegates moved for different obligations for volunteers and draftees. Professional sol-diers and long-term volunteers would take a traditional oath, while conscripts would engage only in a "ceremonial obligation." Georg Kliesing (CDU) ar-gued that it made no sense to relieve professional soldiers of an oath when one was required for civil servants. After all, the soldiers were "the bearers of the strongest external powers of the state, and in crisis situations could deter-mine the life or death of many people. Especially in light of recent history, it must be in the interest of the state to bind the professional soldiers to it as closely as possible."[70] Although opposed by the SPD, this motion ultimately carried the day (221 for, 193 against, 2 abstentions). The divided approach was clearly a compromise between the old system and the aspirations of the military reformers. It was not necessarily a happy one, but it may have been the best that could have been expected under the circumstances.

Like the oath, conscription rekindled many of the fundamental antago-nisms surrounding West German security policy. This is hardly surprising, for, as Erich Mende observed, conscription affected the lives of German men "like no other issue since the foundation of the Republic."[71] Aside from the principle of a draft, controversy also attended the eighteen-month length-of-service requirement advanced by the government. Many parliamentarians thought this was too long, while most defense experts considered it too short.[72] Then there was the issue of conscientious objection: the bill provided for it, as was required by the Basic Law; but the criteria for qualification were considered much too narrow by many Germans.[73]

The government's conscription bill, introduced in spring 1956, was prob-lematical not only in its content but also in its timing. Following Khrush-chev's sensational denunciation of Stalinism at the Soviet Communist Party's Twentieth Congress in February 1956, a warmer political wind from the East threatened once again to melt away the Cold War foundations of Adenauer's security policy. Other auguries of a potential thaw included the dissolution of the Cominform, Molotov's resignation as foreign minister, and Soviet an-nouncements of unilateral arms reductions. Such developments prompted some German parliamentarians, particularly in the SPD, to question the wisdom of going ahead with conscription at this moment; instead, they wanted new negotiations with the Russians. As for the public at large, polls showed that opposition to full-scale rearmament was higher than at any time since 1950–51.[74] A number of youth organizations held news conferences to denounce conscription as an unnecessary concession to American pressure. To compound Adenauer's dilemma, the FDP split apart, and the Bundestag delegates who followed Dehler and Mende into opposition could not be counted on to support conscription. Meanwhile, the Bundesrat came out in opposition to the law's eighteen-month service requirement, insisting that for economic reasons it be reduced to twelve.

The SPD, not surprisingly, led the opposition to conscription. At a meeting in early March, party leaders commissioned their defense policy committee to examine how far the government's plan corresponded "to the current state of political and technical development."[75] When the committee convened on 24 March, Erler argued that conscription would "deepen the German division" because East Berlin could be expected to reply by forcing young East Germans to serve in a Communist army. He and other members of the committee were reluctant, however, to reject the government's bill without proposing an alternative of their own. In a major departure from traditional Socialist policy, Erler urged that the party call for a small professional army in place of the conscript system. Anticipating historically based objections, he argued that a professional army need not become a "second Reichswehr." On the contrary, he said, if it drew extensively from the working classes and included Socialists among its officers, it could be "a strong force for democracy."[76] A little later, Erler's colleague Fritz Beermann drew up a confidential memo arguing that the SPD's best hope to win the next federal election in 1957 lay in advocating a professional army. He claimed that this would allow the Socialists to attract a significant new constituency: middle-class males who wanted a military to "protect their standard of living" but who did not want to serve in an army themselves. If the SPD stuck to its "historic resentments" and stayed locked in its "Red tower," it could kiss the next election good-bye.[77]

Though the SPD's security committee endorsed the Erler-Beermann line, the party's executive strongly opposed it. Ollenhauer considered a *Berufs-armee* simply too foreign to Socialist traditions. Thus the party congress passed a resolution rejecting a draft and promising to revise Bonn's treaty obligations should the Socialists come to power.[78]

In its campaign against conscription, the SPD hoped to cooperate with the FDP, for this party, now outside the government coalition, seemed to be backing away from earlier commitments to a draft army. On 23 March 1956, the FDP's Federal Committee for Defense Questions issued a statement affirming the principle of conscription but proposing that the present moment, "especially in light of the reunification issue," was not opportune for its introduction.[79] The party's chief military expert, Mende, reinforced this line with nationalistic and Germany-first arguments. He claimed that the Western powers were willing to pursue détente at the expense of German reunification. Did it make sense to ask for sacrifices from German men when the West was prepared to write off German unity? Moreover, he noted, NATO was shifting to a greater emphasis on nuclear arms, and there was no meaningful place for a large German conscript army in that strategy. On the economic front, a draft would compound looming manpower shortages in industry and agriculture. Finally, technological changes in warfare demanded soldierly skills that only long-term professionals could master. If, nonetheless, Bonn were required to introduce conscription, it must at least wait until "injustices" of the de-Nazification era, such as the denial of pensions to Waffen-SS veterans, had been remedied. Impressed by these arguments but still wedded to the principle of conscription, the FDP's party congress in Würzburg (20–21 April) decided not to oppose the government's bill outright but to push for delays in implementing a draft.[80]

As the parties were wrestling with the conscription issue, the Security Committee was submitting the government's controversial bill to exacting scrutiny. The committee called in prominent former Wehrmacht generals for their perspective on the pros and cons of the draft under present conditions. Presenting a summary of the officers' position, Field Marshal Erich von Manstein declared that Bonn could meet its "obligation" to NATO only through a draft because "defamation of the Wehrmacht" had discouraged qualified veterans from enlisting. As for the time-of-service question, Manstein insisted that eighteen months was the "bare minimum"; twenty-four would be much better. General Friedrich Sixt added that a twelve-month obligation, as the Bundesrat was demanding, would "cripple" Bonn's army by providing too few soldiers who had been adequately trained.[81]

The committee got a much different perspective when it called in representatives from various professional groups and economic interest associations. An official of the academic Rectors' Conference, which formally opposed conscription, pleaded that students be exempt from the draft until they had finished their studies. Officials from the DGB pushed for a twelve-month obligation, along with exemptions for skilled workers. Arguing that there was "hardly an occupation with a more acute manpower shortage than agriculture," the Deutsche Bauernbund demanded exemptions for farmers and agricultural workers.[82]

Buffeted back and forth by conflicting arguments and aware that the Bundesrat's resistance to an eighteen-month service obligation could delay conscription indefinitely, the government coalition members of the Security Committee decided on a strategic retreat: they moved that the duration-of-

service issue be removed from the conscription law and presented in a separate bill once conscription was enacted. Though the SPD objected to this maneuver, it passed through the committee and was accepted by the government.
This was a crucial adjustment, for without it the conscription law might have
been voted down or extensively delayed. But it also ensured that the pot was
kept boiling when it came to the hotly disputed length-of-service question.

As it was, the run-up to the Bundestag's final vote on conscription in July
was rife enough with polemics and apocalyptic warnings about the effects of
this or that course. Deeply worried that his conscription bill might fail, Adenauer pulled out all the stops to force it through. To businessmen who feared
conscription's impact on the economy, he promised government credits and
tax relief. He also hinted that he might reduce the draft period. In other
speeches, he contended that the Soviets remained as aggressive as ever, despite a few propagandistic gestures. The Federal Republic, he cried, must
take care not to become "the first Western state to be swallowed by a tremen-
dously strong power that wants to dominate the world."[83]

In early summer 1956, Adenauer traveled abroad to gather ammunition to
use at home. In Paris he finalized the details for the integration of the Saar
into the Federal Republic, thereby clearing away a major impediment to
Franco-German understanding. In Rome he advocated the free migration of
labor, a policy designed to help ease West Germany's manpower shortage
through the importation of "guest workers" from the south. Most important,
in America he got new assurances from Bonn's chief protector that Washington would not abandon German unity in the name of détente. He considered
this especially urgent, for the White House had just made public an appeal
from Soviet premier Nikolai Bulganin for bilateral troop withdrawals from
Central Europe. Though the State Department quickly dismissed Bulganin's
letter as a propaganda stunt, Adenauer felt obliged to renew his warnings
against softheadedness. At the commencement exercises at Yale University,
where he received an honorary degree, he said that the Soviets, despite some
"new tactics playing on the longings for peace that live in all men," still aimed
at smashing the "mighty protective shield" of NATO "so that Europe will fall
like a ripe plum into the Soviet lap." German unity, he added pointedly, remained an epochal issue that could be resolved only by Western strength and
determination.[84]

Though, once again, Adenauer reaped good press notices at home for his
performances abroad, his achievements on the road did nothing to dampen
the acrimony of the final conscription debate in the Bundestag. In the second
reading (4 July 1956) SPD and FDP delegates introduced a host of amendments that the government majority promptly voted down with virtually no
discussion. This procedure so angered the amendments' sponsors that the entire SPD and BHE delegations, along with some from the FDP, stormed out

of the session.[85] During the third reading, which lasted from the morning of 6 July to the wee hours of the next day, government coalition members managed to work through all the sections of the long bill with only minor changes. The most important one involved draft exemptions for men who had next of kin in the East or who had lost close relatives (father or siblings) in the last war. An eloquent call by the CDU delegate Peter Nollen to expand the criteria for conscientious objection to include political objections to fighting in a *Brüderkrieg* were beaten down by his own party. Lacking a length-of-service provision, the bill passed by a margin of 269 to 166, with 20 (FDP) abstentions.

Watching the vote unfold, Fritz Erler shouted that parliament was approving a step that flew in the face of political trends. The East-West confrontation was ending, he said, and there would be no more "crusades in Europe." West Germany's soldiers would amount to no more than "the last tin soldiers of the ebbing Cold War."[86] Four months later, however, the Soviets crushed the Hungarian revolution, and few in the West were talking about an end to the Cold War. The complaint now was not about useless tin soldiers from Germany but about the continued delays in getting those soldiers to the front.

THE RADFORD PLAN AND LENGTH-OF-SERVICE CONTROVERSY

Ironically, Bonn's military buildup was partially undermined by its new allies, especially the impatient Americans. The problem had been sharply adumbrated by a week-long NATO air exercise called Carte Blanche, held in late June 1955.[87] As the alliance's first large-scale simulated air attack, this war game had divided Europe between North and South, with the Second Allied Tactical Air Force playing the North (Soviet) forces and the Fourth Allied Tactical Air Force playing the South (NATO). The idea was to explore several pressing issues: how effectively NATO's air forces could withstand a surprise air attack; whether command and control centers could function after the attack was over; whether radar was a useful countermeasure; and whether the Western forces could strike back with a massive attack of their own. Some three thousand aircraft participated, flying over twelve thousand sorties. They "dropped" 335 "A bombs" in a battle theater stretching from Norway to Italy. When the results were in, it turned out that some two-thirds of the "bombs" had fallen on German territory, "killing" an estimated 1.7 million people and "injuring" roughly 3.5 million more. While a military spokesman claimed that the exercise proved that a German air force could contribute effectively to NATO's defensive power, most Germans saw the grim results as more reason to question the logic of rearmament. The prominent journalist Adelbert Weinstein wrote: "The first billions which are ear-marked for rearmament would more wisely be spent securing the populace against a nuclear attack. If it is politically impossible to prohibit atomic bombs, then at least the protection of the populace against such warfare ought not to be treated as a negligible factor."[88]

The furor over Carte Blanche had barely subsided when public exposure of an American strategic concept known as the Radford Plan in mid-1956 fur-ther damaged the credibility of Adenauer's security program.[89] On 13 July 1956, only one week after the Bundestag had passed the bill authorizing con-scription, the *New York Times* gave credence to earlier speculations about an ongoing reorientation in American strategy toward a greater reliance on nu-clear weapons. According to the *Times,* JCS Chief Admiral Arthur Radford hoped that America's nuclear-strike capacity, enhanced by the addition of hy-drogen bombs, would allow Washington to pull some eight hundred thou-sand troops out of Europe in the next few years. Radford's plan was said to have the backing of President Eisenhower, who was anxious to reduce de-fense spending by cutting back American troop levels in Europe.

For Adenauer, who had heard nothing of this during his recent trip to America, the Radford initiative was a humiliating shock. If implemented, it would make a mockery of his oft-repeated assurances that Bonn's rearming would ensure a strong American presence on the Continent. America's switch to a largely nuclear deterrent would also undercut the logic of fielding a purely conventional force like the Bundeswehr. Trying to decipher Wash-ington's motives, Adenauer thought he detected a resurgence of dangerous isolationism and wishful thinking among top policy makers. Aware that this turn of events would also play into the hands of his domestic critics, he re-solved to do all he could to make Washington abandon the Radford scheme.[90]

On Adenauer's orders, Bonn's ambassadors to Washington, London, Paris, and Rome returned home for an urgent meeting with the chancellor's closest aides. They quickly issued a communiqué branding the Radford Plan as dan-gerous "not only for Germany and Europe, but for all humankind."[91] Next, Adenauer dispatched his press secretary and confidant, Felix von Eckardt, to Washington for confidential talks with key policy makers, including several Democrats. He turned to the Democrats because they controlled Congress and might also win the White House in the upcoming elections; moreover, Democrats Adlai Stevenson, Averell Harriman, George Kennan, and Mike Mansfield were known to be internationalists. Eckardt informed his inter-locutors of Adenauer's concerns, insisting that a reliance on the nuclear de-terrent would not stop the Soviets from pursuing localized conventional wars, possibly through their "satellites." Moscow would be especially tempted to do this if America reduced its force levels in Europe. At the same time, said

Eckardt, such reductions would make it very hard for Bonn to meet its man-power obligations to NATO.

Harriman assured Eckardt that he regarded Eisenhower's position on the Soviet Union as "weak." He promised that if the Democrats won the presidency, or even retained control of Congress, Washington would maintain existing troop levels in Europe and do its best to support Germany's military buildup. Robert Finletter (Stevenson's military expert) gave Eckardt similar assurances. Stevenson himself promised that in his presidential campaign he would "defend the policies of the Federal Chancellor as decisively as possible."[92]

Yet Adenauer could not be content with promises from the Democrats, who after all did not control America's foreign and defense policy. Thus he ordered Heusinger and Heinz Krekeler, his ambassador to Washington, to take Bonn's case directly to the State Department and Pentagon. Following a "stormy" session with Dulles, the Germans delivered their complaints against the Radford Plan to Defense Minister Charles Wilson. Wilson responded that, for now at least, America did not plan to reduce its forces in Europe. Shortly thereafter, Dulles sent Adenauer a personal letter claiming that America's commitment to "modernizing" its defenses did not necessarily entail "reducing" troop levels—a distinction Adenauer did not find terribly convincing. Nor was the chancellor impressed when Dulles's brother Allen assured him that the Radford Plan was just one idea among many that had been raised in connection with budget deliberations. Again hitting the apocalyptic note, Adenauer told Allen Dulles that if Washington reduced its troop levels in Europe, NATO was "done for." He also warned that if the German people lost confidence in America, his own government might fall. Washington would then have to work with the SPD, which everyone knew was a nest of neutralists.[93]

Though Adenauer's use of the Socialist bogey was a well-worn tactic, his warnings were taken seriously in Washington, and they helped prompt Eisenhower to back away from the Radford Plan. In early November 1955 his administration announced that it would not reduce American troop levels in Europe. Instead, it would continue to rely on the "shield" of large conventional forces combined with the "sword" of nuclear arms.[94]

In the meantime, however, Adenauer had decided to show his displeasure with Washington by formally abandoning Bonn's commitment to the eighteen-month conscription period in favor of a twelve-month obligation. In announcing this decision in mid-September, Adenauer said that America's possible pullback from Europe made it unlikely that the Bundestag would pass the longer commitment.[95] This was somewhat disingenuous, for though indignation over the Radford Plan had certainly increased parliamentary opposition to an extended draft, reservations about this policy stemmed also from long-standing economic objections. After all, many business leaders and politicians did not like the idea of removing young men from the civilian economy for extended periods. One aspect of this sentiment was colorfully articulated by a delegate of the Bayern Partei, who could "not understand why our farmer-sons should be drafted against their will, while imported Italian guest-workers sleep with their wives and girlfriends."[96] Thus the Radford Plan, threatening as it was to Bonn's military program, offered a convenient pretext for the chancellor to back away from a policy that had become a domestic liability.

Understandably, Adenauer's sudden announcement pleased local critics of an extended draft, but it alarmed his military advisers, who had repeatedly insisted that nothing short of an eighteen-month obligation would yield adequately trained soldiers. In fact, just before his announcement, a group of generals had privately urged Adenauer to retain the longer commitment. Yet this did not prevent the chancellor from telling the press that his military advisers uniformly endorsed his plan. Incensed, the generals pleaded with Blank to resign to demonstrate his ministry's dismay, but the minister decided to eat crow once again and to stay in office.[97]

As might have been expected, Adenauer's sudden change of course also alarmed Bonn's NATO partners. The NATO Permanent Council immediately warned that Germany's ability to meet its manpower commitment was in jeopardy. Indeed, it said Adenauer's decision imperiled European security because the complexities of modern warfare required longer training periods. In defense, the German representative on the NATO Standing Committee argued that Bonn could compensate for a shorter draft by recruiting more volunteers—a prospect he must have known was doubtful given low enlistment rates.[98]

NATO, and especially the Americans, were not pacified by Bonn's reassurances. Eisenhower sent his special ambassador to NATO, Senator Walter F. George, to Bonn on a protest mission. George told Adenauer that he was weakening NATO and that relations between the alliance and it newest member had already hit a "low." Back in Washington, Dulles let it be known that he thought Adenauer had "cynically" used the Radford Plan to drop an unpopular policy.[99]

Bonn's relationship with Washington had indeed reached a low. But the crisis had been brewing ever since 1954, when America had begun reorienting its strategic thinking toward the policy of massive retaliation in the event of a Soviet attack. From a distance, the clash can be seen as a product of the false sense of intimacy inherent in many alliances. Convinced of his rapport with Washington, Adenauer had recently told the Bundestag that he and the Americans thought alike on strategic questions. But in reality, Washington's strategic concept envisaged West Germany as little more than a protective "shield" behind which American air power could extend its nuclear "sword." The thicker the shield and the longer the sword, the faster America might be able to reduce its troop strength in Europe. But the Germans had always seen their willingness to rearm as a means of securing the American presence and gaining stature as an equal in the Western community. Despite Washington's eventual abandonment of the Radford Plan, knowledge that many Americans remained committed to the ideas behind it made Adenauer begin to recalculate the political costs of dutifully accepting the role Washington chose to assign its youngest "partner."[100]

EXIT BLANK, ENTER STRAUSS

Though Adenauer felt he had lost prestige and credibility as a result of the controversies and mishaps surrounding the Bundeswehr's birth, his defense minister, Theodor Blank, took most of the heat for the failures. Blank had long been under fire from many quarters, and the attacks mounted after his assumption of the ministry. Herbert Blankenhorn, Bonn's new ambassador to NATO, brought Adenauer "massive complaints" from the Western powers regarding Blank's apparent inability to realize Germany's military commitments.[101] Some Bundestag delegates, meanwhile, were accusing Blank of planning to "get rid" of Baudissin by shunting him off to a troop command. The count's continued presence in Bonn was essential, they said, to prevent Blank from backsliding on the military reform program.[102] In view of Blank's escalating image problems, Felix von Eckardt advised Adenauer to jettison his minister. But Adenauer was reluctant to do so, for this would be to acknowledge the inadequacies of his security policy and to lose the services of a loyal retainer with influential supporters in the left wing of the CDU. Even worse, Blank's ouster would open the way for his old rival, Franz Josef Strauss, who was being pushed by the majority of Union politicians as the only viable alternative to Blank. Nonetheless, as fiasco followed fiasco, Adenauer finally concluded that there was nothing to do but to fire Blank and bring in Strauss.

In contemplating this switch, Adenauer could at least console himself that the burly Bavarian, one of the Union's most effective spokesmen for rearmament, would be better able than Blank to defend the government's embattled security policy in parliament and in the corridors of NATO. Moreover, at this point in his career, Strauss still had a good press and was generally admired abroad, especially by the Americans, for whom he had worked after the war.[103]

When Adenauer asked Strauss in mid-October to take over Blank's job, the Bavarian, so he claims, reminded the chancellor of his recent pledge to keep him out of the defense ministry. Strauss says Adenauer replied: "Would you

deny an old man the right to change his mind?" Whether or not this exchange actually took place, Strauss would not have minded seeing the chancellor squirm; and he took this opportunity to extract concessions from him
in exchange for his acceptance of the job. As the leader of a "second opposition" in the Union parties and business circles to Adenauer's rapid buildup
program, he insisted that Bonn's plan to field 500,000 soldiers within three
years would have to be scaled back to roughly 350,000 men over five years.
The top leadership of the Bundeswehr must be reorganized through the appointment of a *Generalinspekteur* (chief of staff) responsible for all service
branches. Strauss also demanded that conscription be postponed, though he
consented to an early "symbolic draft" of 10,000 men as a sop to Bonn's
NATO partners. Above all, Strauss insisted on having a "free hand" to pull
the government's chestnuts out of the fire.[104]

Strauss lost no time in reorienting the Bundeswehr's buildup schedule.
Even before his official swearing-in, he ordered his staff to begin revamping
deployment according to his new projections. When Heusinger protested
that this would mean a loss of credibility abroad, Strauss told the general to
leave "politics" to him. He bragged that he would quickly put German security planning on a "realistic basis," even if this meant "dropping his pants" before Bonn's NATO partners.[105]

NATO's Annual Review in late October offered Strauss a fine opportunity
to drop his *Lederhosen*. Glorying in his advance billing as the "Bavarian
Siegfried," he immediately took the offensive, announcing plans to stretch
out the Bundeswehr buildup. He called this a "necessary adjustment" and
blamed it on the Western powers, whose "punitive demilitarization and re-
education measures" had "crippled" West Germany's chance to arm itself in
the early 1950s. Having partially recovered from the "Carthaginian Peace" of
1945, he said, Bonn would not be bullied into a deployment program that
might jeopardize its social and economic health. Nor would it rearm so fast
that it had to rely exclusively on hand-me-down Allied weapons. "We may
have lost the war," he declared, "but we have not lost our senses."[106]

Strauss continued on this tack when the NATO defense ministers assembled for a conference in late December. He chastised Sir Christopher
Steel for Britain's performance in the recent Suez Crisis, which he bluntly
called a "miserable debacle." He repeated that Bonn's revised deployment
schedule was the best that could be expected under existing circumstances but
added that the revisions in question would ensure "quality rather than mere
quantity" in the new German army. Still, to compensate for reduced numbers, Strauss proposed equipping the Bundeswehr with "the most modern weapons"—code for atomic arms. The Germans, he was widely quoted
as saying, would not remain content as "foot soldiers for American atomic
knights."[107]

Predictably, Bonn's NATO partners were highly alarmed by Strauss's blustering declarations. It seemed that Bonn had no sooner joined NATO than it was reneging on its promises to the alliance. The Anglo-Saxon powers were particularly distraught over this combination of backsliding and assertiveness, though the latter was hardly new, and the former—in the context of endless "burden-sharing" disputes—would remain a contentious issue throughout the history of the alliance. Complaining that the Germans were "not pulling their weight," Harold Macmillan, chancellor of the exchequer, said it was "paradoxical" that the Western powers had to bear "a great burden" defending Germany while West Germany itself, now a potent economic rival in the international marketplace, still had no armed forces or defense budgets to speak of. And he warned: "The British people, who after all won the war, cannot accept that the Germans are treating the U.K. like dirt while they have their own way. They will not agree to keeping British soldiers in Germany if the Germans do not play the game."[108] Speaking for the Eisenhower administration, Dulles declared that America too was getting a raw deal from its new German partner. In view of Bonn's policies, he said, he was "not at all sure that the large effort that the U.S. is making is justified."[109]

Yet Dulles's implied threat to reassess American backing for German rearmament had a hollow ring, for recent world events suggested that the need to bolster Western defenses was again critical. The Suez Crisis had revealed deep divisions between Washington and its traditional European allies, and Moscow's response to the Hungarian revolution showed that the Soviets were unprepared to release their grip on their Eastern European empire. This was no time to risk seriously alienating the Germans. Thus, though British foreign secretary Selwyn Lloyd urged his American colleagues to try to make Bonn toe the NATO line, Washington elected to swallow Bonn's "revisions" of its military program. Indeed, Admiral Radford and Secretary of Defense Wilson allowed themselves to be convinced by Strauss that Bonn's plans to reduce its draft period and stretch out its deployment were "sensible and clever." They accepted the Bavarian's contention that a leaner Bundeswehr, composed for the time being of volunteers, would be "a pretty good army" by the end of 1957.[110]

Another question altogether was whether the new German army would combine technical competence with a thorough institutionalization of the reform ideals that were supposed to revolutionize German military practice. Would Strauss be more effective in this regard than Blank had been? Early indications suggested that this might not be the case. In a report on *Innere Führung* prepared in November 1956, Baudissin complained that the reforms were being sabotaged by Wehrmacht veterans among the instructor corps who were reviving the old *Kommiss* methods.[111] The return to such methods, indeed, was widely held to be responsible for the young Bundeswehr's first

major training accident, the drowning of fifteen paratroop recruits in
Bavaria's Iller River on 3 June 1957. Citing the fact that the men had died
trying to complete a dangerous maneuver that they should not have been ordered to attempt, critics warned of a revival of "blind obedience."[112] But the
rightist *Deutsche Soldatenzeitung* attributed the Iller accident to inexperienced
noncommissioned officers and newfangled training techniques that "confused" enlisted men and officers alike. The tragedy would probably not have
occurred, the paper opined, if the Bundeswehr had been able to recruit the
best Wehrmacht veterans to teach the young men.[113]

For Strauss, who had to deal with the accusations and counteraccusations
arising from the Iller affair, the incident proved that his job was a "political
minefield." But his difficulties were just beginning. Soon he was lamenting
that his efforts to give the Bundeswehr more "self-respect"—his introduction, for example, of uniforms with a more military cut—were being
interpreted by his leftist critics as signs he was trying "to bring back the
Wehrmacht."[114]

This undoubtedly was not the case, but Strauss also proved somewhat ambivalent on the question of radical reform, electing to allow the new army to
flounder in a no-man's land between the aspirations of the reformers and the
restorationist practices of some local commanders. Such ambiguities, combined with the blossoming controversy over arming the Bundeswehr with nuclear weapons, made it difficult for the young military to achieve the popular
resonance its founders had hoped to secure. Though the comment is exaggerated, Baudissin was not entirely off the mark when he concluded that the
Bundeswehr had survived a "difficult birth" only to become an "unwanted
child."[115]

CONCLUSION

Looking back on the decade-long debate surrounding the decision to create a new army in the Federal Republic of Germany, we can see that the process was dominated by two overriding considerations. The first, operating primarily on the diplomatic level, involved the Western Allies' determination simultaneously to rearm and contain West Germany. The second, which profoundly affected the domestic debate, was the necessity to create an army from the ground up at the same time that the infant republic's first leaders, scrupulously watched over by the Allied occupiers, attempted to lay the foundations of a new democratic state. Both efforts took place under the dark political shadow cast by the Third Reich, and of course also amid the physical and economic wreckage left behind by the long and devastating war. Both began against the ominous backdrop of ideological division and a new outbreak of international tension that threatened to set Europe ablaze even before the ashes of the previous conflagration had been cleared away. No modern military had ever been born in such conflicted and challenging circumstances, and few states had had to face more trying tests in their first years of existence. There was no historical blueprint for what either the victors or the vanquished of World War II hoped to accomplish in building new security structures and defense institutions in a region haunted by the crimes of the past and torn asunder by the competing ideologies of the present. The road was as uncharted and the outcome as uncertain as are the present efforts to deal with the long legacy of division and to put back together what had grown apart for almost half a century.

It is hard to imagine a diplomatic decision taken with less enthusiasm than the one that called upon West Germans to take up military arms a mere half decade after they had been told that they must never possess such instruments again. Only the astoundingly rapid transformation of the wartime coalition against Germany into the competing blocs of the Cold War made this decision possible, let alone seem necessary. Even those in the Allied camp who favored German rearmament tended to see it as a "necessary evil"—a choice they would have been happy to avoid had conditions permitted. Considerations of controlling their new partner, therefore, ran like a red thread through all the Allied calculations regarding this endeavor. In the earliest ruminations, indeed, strategies of containment almost outweighed the imperative of getting the Germans to the front. Ironically and confusingly, the first talk of rearming Germany came amid continuing measures to keep the region permanently disarmed. Only as the negotiations over rearmament dragged on did Bonn win more leeway in its security policy and manage successfully to combine progress toward military equality with gains in the realm of political rehabilitation. On one level, then, the history of West German rearmament can be seen as a process of gradual and begrudging relaxation (though never complete abandonment) of the Allied restraints designed to keep the Germans from abusing the new powers and resources with which they were being entrusted.

The most elaborate of the postwar efforts to combine empowerment with constraint regarding Germany was the projected European Defense Community, whose ambitious scope testified to the complexities of the challenge and the willingness of the Western powers to conceive radical new solutions to the old problem of guaranteeing security in war-prone Europe. Yet in the end, of course, the EDC turned out to be too ambitious. Two of its sponsors, the United States and the United Kingdom, would not join it, for they did not want their own forces subordinated to its elaborate controls. The scheme's primary author, France, began to back away from the project when it saw that the envisaged restraints on Germany would not be as tight as originally planned. Even more important, Paris developed strong second thoughts about approving a program whose infringements upon traditional military sovereignty would apply to its own forces as well as to those of its rivals. Among other lessons, the fate of the EDC proved that even the universal desire to corral the Germans was not strong enough to overcome attachments to historic institutions of national sovereignty, especially in the military realm. Western Europe might have taken significant steps at this time toward economic unity, but when it came to security matters, Europe was not yet ready for Europe.

One European power, however, was considerably more ready for common institutions than the others, and that of course was the FRG. For Bonn, rearmament within the EDC meant much more than just enhanced security; it offered the most promising ladder yet out of the morass of the recent past.[1] We have seen that the Adenauer government understood very early that it could exchange its willingness to contribute to the security of Western Europe for the sovereign rights that the Federal Republic did not enjoy when it was born. West Germany, then, was in a unique position: unlike its neighbors, it could actually *gain* sovereignty by joining a supranational organization like the EDC. To the extent that this system was overtly discriminatory toward Bonn, German negotiators could (and did) demand revisions. For some Germans, of course, the revisions did not go nearly far enough, while others remained mired in nationalist resentments and feelings of persecution. There was also the very serious objection—advanced by the SPD as well as by elements of the nationalist Right—that the rearmament program as pursued by Adenauer and the Western powers spelled doom for German reunification. Nevertheless, Adenauer could count on considerable public support when he couched the FRG's security policy and political rehabilitation within the context of a unifying Europe.

The failure of the EDC—so shocking at the time—did not substantially alter the dynamics of West German rearmament. NATO, too, provided an international framework in which Bonn could be simultaneously armed and controlled. Through NATO, Europe would finally see Germans on the front, but none of those forces would stand outside the confines of the alliance. West Germany was empowered to contribute twelve divisions, but none would be armed with chemical, biological, or (most important) atomic weapons. The fact that Bonn was joining the NATO alliance just as the pact was emphasizing strategic nuclear defense—massive retaliation—caused many Germans to question the logic of rearming at all. Of what use would Bonn's conventional forces be in a nuclear exchange? many asked. Even more fundamentally, why rush to join NATO when the alliance seemed totally unwilling to protect Germany from the catastrophe of an atomic war? As Fritz Erler put the matter in July 1956: "The strategy of NATO leaves no room for doubting that an armed conflict in Europe—even with [the participation of] 500,000 German soldiers—will not remain a conventional conflict. NATO plans are based upon immediate and direct employment of atomic weapons in the event of a conflict in Europe."[2] Concerns that West Germany, NATO's very junior and not-quite-equal partner, could be pulled into a nuclear conflict over which it had no control competed with worries that the alliance might still pull back from the German front if push came to shove. "All alliances," wrote the political scientist Josef Joffe, "have been haunted by the twin specters of abandonment and entrapment."[3] From the German point of view, this was certainly true of NATO, and it would remain so over the course of the next generation.

But whatever anxieties the Germans might have harbored regarding NATO strategy and the Bundeswehr's place within it, on the political level NATO was crucial for Bonn: it was yet another ladder out of pit of the past— and this time one that was not snatched away at the last moment. Within NATO Bonn could not only pursue reconciliation with its old enemy France but cement its ties to its most important new ally, the United States. The American connection carried its own demands and burdens, but with Washington's support, Bonn gradually gained greater authority and leverage in the European/Atlantic arena. Thus, seen from our current perspective some forty years down the road, the treaties through which Bonn joined NATO and gained a larger measure of sovereignty were "the first great leap on the (West) German path back to independence."[4] The second leap came with the *Ostpolitik* of the early 1970s, and the third—now for the GDR as well as the old FRG—came with the German reunification in 1990.

The German rearmament question not only sharpened the East-West antagonism in the opening phases of the Cold War but severely strained relations among the Western powers. The French in particular did all they could to thwart or delay the rearmament of their "hereditary enemy," while the Americans, backed at first reluctantly, then more decisively, by the British, became the most insistent and impatient advocates of a German contribution to Western defense. But though quarrels over German policy produced plenty of rancor and bad feeling, they also helped to clarify the power relationships among the managers of the postwar order. With time they also helped to consolidate the Atlantic alliance.

Above all, the need to solve the protracted dilemma of German rearmament helped to keep the Americans thoroughly engaged in European affairs. One can say, in fact, that it was not just through it role in helping to defeat Nazi Germany, but also through its efforts to rearm the FRG, that America confirmed its political ascendancy in the mid-twentieth century. Though often so frustrated with their European colleagues that they were tempted to take their ball and go home, in the end Washington's statesmen remained determined not to repeat the "mistake" of the interwar era by abandoning the Europeans (especially the Germans) to their own devices.[5] Thus in the crucial early years of the Federal Republic, Washington led the Western Allies in efforts to ensure that Bonn succeeded in its democratic experiment. And if, down the line, the FRG, rather than France, became America's most important ally on the Continent, this was partly a result of the experiences the Americans went through in getting the Germans to the front.

Allied disputes over the rearmament of West Germany, especially over the degrees of control thought necessary to keep Bonn in line, undoubtedly contributed to the many delays in getting Germans into uniform. But that process was also complicated by the domestic side of the security equation— by all the difficulties attending the simultaneous construction of a new democracy and a new army. The delays were as frustrating to some Germans (particularly to Adenauer and his entourage) as to the Allied sponsors of rearmament. In the end, however, they worked out for the best because they allowed a level of public participation (via parliament, parties, churches, interest groups, and the like) that would have been impossible had the army come to life as soon as Adenauer wanted. The postponements also allowed for a thorough anchoring of the new army in the constitutional firmament of the new state. By taking their time, Bonn's parliamentarians and security planners were able to take advantage of the unique opportunities afforded by the complete collapse of the old German military establishment.

Nonetheless, many Germans—not to mention many foreign observers— inevitably argued that it was highly dangerous to start reviving military institutions before the new democratic order was fully established and tested by time. Aside from moral qualms about trying to rearm so soon after "God had struck the weapons of war from German hands," there was the practical concern that the new regime simply would not be strong enough to keep a revived military from assuming dominance or from withholding its support while sniffing around for political alternatives, as had been the case during Weimar. A related worry was that the financial costs of rearmament would overwhelm the infant nation's fragile economy, destabilizing the state before it could become firmly rooted.

These worries may seem exaggerated or even misplaced. As I have suggested, the absence of an entrenched military establishment gave Bonn a signal advantage over Weimar, and Germany's conquerors were now on hand to keep a close watch over the political scene. But it was precisely *because* the new system seemed so vulnerable to many contemporaries that West Germany was unprecedentedly careful in defining the nature of the military and its place in the state. Bonn's military planners and politicians devoted extraordinary efforts to creating a new kind of army that would reflect the nation's democratic credo and stay safely confined within the bounds allowed it by civilian authority. For some critics, both inside and outside the new army, the preoccupation with civilian control suggested an unseemly distrust of the new soldiers, who for their part often registered considerable disenchantment with the conditions of military life as the Bundeswehr made its rather inauspicious debut on the world stage.

If the early Bundeswehr had its troubles, the political process through which it was created was also no unambiguous demonstration of Bonn's democratic virtue. The German politician primarily responsible for the decision to rearm, Chancellor Adenauer, was anxious to control all aspects of security policy and to minimize the participation of parliament and the public. He had little patience with criticism, and he sought repeatedly to silence or circumvent his opponents, often with little regard for constitutional niceties. Those critics, especially the Social Democrats, were themselves not always models of democratic rectitude and were as prepared as the chancellor to use the rearmament debate for partisan political advantage. Former military men engaged in planning the new army complained that this enterprise was being treated as a political football.

It would be naive, however, to expect that an issue as crucial and controversial as rearmament could have avoided becoming an object of fierce partisan contention. Moreover, the battle that erupted over security policy helped clear the political air and was ultimately beneficial to the nation's health as a democracy. This was especially so because the process eventually involved intraparty cooperation and compromise as well as partisan posturing. It was through the long fight over rearmament that the SPD learned to work effectively and productively within the political system. The result of this experience was an ongoing and intensifying SPD role in the shaping of West German security policy. In light of this development, it is not surprising that Helmut Schmidt, Bonn's first Socialist defense minister (1969–72), got his start in defense policy as a member of the Bundestag Security Committee in the closing phase of the rearmament debate.

In the early phases of that battle, however, the advantages were all with Chancellor Adenauer, who was able to use Allied restrictions on the scope of the rearmament discussions to exclude unwanted interference. Moreover, Bonn's fledgling parliamentary institutions were at first unsure of how to operate on this terrain, or even if they wanted responsibility for making final decisions on so crucial an issue. It took time to overcome these inadequacies. Increasingly, however, the Bundestag (and to a lesser degree, the Bundesrat) effectively challenged Adenauer's *Kanzlerdemokratie* in matters of security policy. SPD politicians took the lead, but they were soon joined by figures from other parties, including the government coalition, in asserting the right of parliament to help lay the foundations for Bonn's new military. Indeed, we can see in retrospect that it was through the protracted duel over rearmament that the young Bonn Republic truly came into its own as a parliamentary democracy. And though there was never a consensus on either the necessity for rearmament or on its final modalities (conscription being especially controversial), the creation of an army gave the new nation a firmer sense of political identity. By 1956, when the Bundeswehr finally appeared, Bonn was still not a fully "normal" state, nor in every respect a sovereign one, but there was no question about where it stood on the political and ideological map of Europe.

NOTES

Abbreviations

In addition to the abbreviations used in the text, the following source abbreviations are used in the notes.

a.D.	ausser Dienst
AFES	Ausschuss für Fragen Europäischer Sicherheit
Af V	Ausschuss für Verteidigung
BAK	Bundesarchiv Koblenz
BA-MA	Bundesarchiv-Militärarchiv
DBPO	*Documents on British Policy Overseas*
FAZ	*Frankfurter Allgemeine Zeitung*
FES	Friedrich Ebert Stiftung
FNS	Friedrich Naumann Stiftung
FO	Foreign Office
FRUS	*Foreign Relations of the United States*
GAP	Deutsche Gesellschaft für Auswärtige Politik
GPO	Government Printing Office
HMSO	Her Majesty's Stationery Office
MGFA	Militärgeschichtliches Forschungsamt
MGM	*Militärgeschichtliche Mitteilungen*
NA	National Archives
NYT	*New York Times*
PA	Parlamentsarchiv
PRO	Public Records Office
RG	Record Group
VfZG	*Vierteljahrshefte für Zeitgeschichte*

Chapter One

1. Uwe Heuer, "Zur Perzeption der Bundeswehr in den Vereinigten Staaten von Amerika, 1963–1983. Deutsche Streitkräfte und deutsche Sicherheitspolitik im Urteil amerikanischer Experten" (Ph.D. dissertation, University of Bonn, 1989), 172–75.

2. Stalin quoted in Gerhard Wettig, *Entmilitarisierung und Wiederbewaffnung in Deutschland, 1943–1955* (Munich: R. Oldenbourg, 1967), 28.

3. Alexander Fischer, "Anfänge der Wiederbewaffnung in der SBZ/DDR (1945/46–1955/56)," in *Wiederbewaffnung in Deutschland nach 1945*, ed. Alexander Fischer (Berlin: Duncker & Humblot, 1986), 14–15.

4. *FRUS, Conferences at Cairo and Tehran, 1943* (Washington, D.C.: GPO, 1961), 511.

5. Quoted in Paul Hammond, "Directives for the Occupation of Germany," in *American Civil-Military Decisions*, ed. Harold Stein (University: University of Alabama Press, 1963), 389.

6. Lord William Strang, *At Home and Abroad* (London: Andre Deutsch, 1956), 211.

7. Ibid.

8. Robert Murphy, *Diplomat among Warriors* (Garden City, N.Y.: Doubleday, 1964), 294; Bernard Montgomery, *The Memoirs of Field Marshal and Viscount Montgomery of Alamein* (Cleveland: World, 1958), 298, 319.

9. Quoted in John L. Snell, *Wartime Origins of the East-West Dilemma over Germany* (New Orleans: Tulane University Press, 1959), 69.

10. Cordell Hull, *Memoirs of Cordell Hull*, 2 vols. (New York: Macmillan, 1948), 2:1603.

11. John Wheeler-Bennett and Anthony Nicholls, *The Semblance of Peace: The Political Settlement after the Second World War* (New York: Norton, 1972), 176.

12. Sir Llewellyn Woodward, *British Foreign Policy in the Second World War*, 5 vols. (London: HMSO, 1976), 5:223–24. See also D. C. Watt, *Britain Looks to Germany: British Opinion and Policy towards Germany since 1945* (London: Oswald Wolff, 1965), 41.

13. Hull, *Memoirs*, 2:1614.

14. Woodward, *British Foreign Policy*, 5:225.

15. Hull, *Memoirs*, 2:1617, 1621.

16. *FRUS, Conferences at Malta and Yalta, 1945* (Washington, D.C.: GPO, 1960), 143–44.

17. Among the large number of books on the Wehrmacht in the Nazi system, see especially Gordon A. Craig, *The Politics of the Prussian Army, 1640–1945* (New York: Oxford University Press, 1964); Manfred Messerschmidt, *Die Wehrmacht im NS-Staat: Zeit der Indoktrination* (Hamburg: R. von Decker's Verlag, 1969); Klaus-Jürgen Müller, *Das Heer und Hitler. Armee und nationalsozialistisches Regime, 1933–1945* (Stuttgart: Deutsche Verlags-Anstalt, 1969); Omer Bartov, *Hitler's Army: Soldiers, Nazis, and War in the Third Reich* (New York: Oxford University Press, 1991). On the issue of militarism in the German context, see Gerhard Ritter, "The Military and Politics in Germany," *Journal of Central European Affairs* 17 (Oct. 1957): 259–71.

18. Woodward, *British Foreign Policy*, 5:232.

19. Quoted in Earl F. Ziemke, *The U.S. Army in the Occupation of Germany, 1944–1946* (Washington, D.C.: Center for Military History, 1985), 142.

20. Lucius Clay, *Decision in Germany* (Garden City, N.Y.: Doubleday, 1950), 18. See also Wolfgang Krieger, *General Lucius D. Clay und die amerikanische Deutschlandpolitik, 1945–1949* (Stuttgart: Klett, Cotta, 1987), 98–101; and Jean Edward Smith, *Lucius Clay: An American Life* (New York: Henry Holt, 1990), 356–95.

21. *FRUS, Conferences at Malta and Yalta*, 571.

22. Ibid., 622, 621, 971.

23. Fraser J. Harbutt, *The Iron Curtain: Churchill, America and the Origins of the Cold War* (New York: Oxford University Press, 1986), 76–77.

24. Quoted in F. Roy Willis, *France, Germany and the New Europe* (New York: Oxford University Press, 1968), 14.

25. Montgomery, *Memoirs*, 321.

26. Wettig, *Entmilitarisierung*, 78–79; also "Besorgt um seinen Ruhm und Rang. Ein Hintergrund der sonderbaren Bemerkung Churchills," *Süddeutsche Zeitung*, 24 Nov. 1978.

27. Ziemke, *U.S. Army*, 241–43.

28. James Bacque, *Other Losses: An Investigation into the Mass Deaths of German Prisoners of War at the Hands of the French and Americans after World War II* (Toronto: Stod-

dart, 1989). See the review of Bacque's book by Stephen Ambrose, *NYT*, 24 Feb. 1991. See also Stephen Ambrose, *Eisenhower and the German POWs* (Baton Rouge: Louisiana State University Press, 1992).

29. James M. Diehl, *The Thanks of the Fatherland: German Veterans after the Second World War* (Chapel Hill: University of North Carolina Press, 1993), 55–56.

30. Friedrich Ruge, *Politik, Militär, Bündnis* (Stuttgart: Deutsche Verlags-Anstalt, 1963), 80.

31. Diehl, *Thanks of the Fatherland*, 58.

32. Ziemke, *U.S. Army*, 134–35; Edward N. Peterson, *The American Occupation of Germany: Retreat to Victory* (Detroit: Wayne State University Press, 1978), 166.

33. Quoted in Daniel Yergin, *The Shattered Peace: The Origins of the Cold War and the National Security State* (Boston: Houghton Mifflin, 1978), 82.

34. Harry S. Truman, *Memoirs: Year of Decisions* (Garden City, N.Y.: Doubleday, 1955), 102. For the views of Eisenhower and Clay, see Smith, *Clay*, 248–308.

35. Quoted in Kurt Tauber, *Beyond Eagle and Swastika*, 2 vols. (Middletown, Conn.: Wesleyan University Press), 1:258.

36. *FRUS, Conference of Berlin (Potsdam) 1945*, 2 vols. (Washington, D.C.: GPO, 1960), 2:1481.

37. Yergin, *Shattered Peace*, 90–97, 114.

38. Truman, *Year of Decisions*, 412.

39. Quoted in Willis, *France, Germany*, 15.

40. Walter Vogel, "Deutschland, Europa und die Umgestaltung der amerikanischen Sicherheitspolitik, 1945–1949," *VfZG* 19 (1971): 66.

41. Kenneth O. Morgan, *Labour in Power* (Oxford: Clarendon Press, 1984), 255.

42. Saki Dockrill, *Britain's Policy for West German Rearmament, 1950–1955* (Cambridge: Cambridge University Press, 1991), 6.

43. Dean Acheson, *Sketches from Life of Men I Have Known* (New York: Harper Brothers, 1959), 3.

44. U.S. Department of State, *Occupation of Germany, Policy and Progress, 1945–1946* (Washington, D.C.: GPO, 1947), 94–96.

45. Georg Meyer, "Zur Situation der deutschen militärischen Führungsschicht im Vorfeld des westdeutschen Verteidigungsbeitrages, 1945–1950/51," in *Anfänge westdeutscher Sicherheitspolitik, 1945–1956*, vol. 1: *Von der Kapitulation bis zum Pleven Plan*, ed. MGFA (Munich: R. Oldenbourg, 1982), 635–38. See also Sammlung Ritter von Schramm. Materiellen zu einer Geschichte der deutschen Berufssoldaten zwischen 1945 und 1955: Schicksale deutscher Berufssoldaten von 1945–1955, BA-MA, MSg 118/1. On the special problems of disabled veterans, see James M. Diehl, "Change and Continuity in the Treatment of German Kriegsopfer," *Central European History* 18 (June 1985): 170–87.

46. Dennis L. Bark and David R. Gress, *A History of West Germany*, vol. 1: *From Shadow to Substance, 1945–1963* (Oxford: Basil Blackwell, 1989), 126.

47. Thomas Griffiths, "Retrospect," *Yale Review* 34 (Sept. 1949): 101–2.

48. General a.D. Gerhard Müller quoted in Diehl, *Thanks of the Fatherland*, 63.

49. Strang, *At Home and Abroad*, 233.

50. *Akten zur Vorgeschichte der Bundesrepublik Deutschland, 1945–1949*, ed. Walter Vogel and Chrisoph Weiz, 5 vols. (Munich: R. Oldenbourg, 1976–81), 1:84. See also PRO, FO 1074/18 (Military Security Board).

51. Charles B. Burdick, "Vom Schwert zu Feder. Deutsche Kriegsgefangene im

Dienst der Vorbereitung der amerikanischen Kriegsgeschichtsschreibung über den Zweiten Weltkrieg. Die organisatorische Entwicklung der Operational History (German) Section," *MGM* 2 (1971): 73.

52. Reinhard Gehlen, *Der Dienst. Erinnerungen, 1942–1971* (Mainz: Hase & Koehler, 1971), 145.

53. On the foundation of the "Gehlen Organization," see Mary Ellen Reese, *General Reinhard Gehlen: The CIA Connection* (Fairfax, Va.: George Mason University Press, 1990), 3–100.

54. Wettig, *Entmilitarisierung*, 107–8; *The Papers of Lucius D. Clay, 1945–1949*, ed. Jean Edward Smith, 2 vols. (Bloomington: Indiana University Press, 1974), 2:965.

55. Fischer, "Anfänge der Widerbewaffnung," 20–21; Wettig, *Entmilitarisierung*, 113.

56. Thomas M. Forster, *NVA. Die Armee der Sowjetzone* (Cologne: Markus Verlag, 1965), 35–37.

57. For a detailed history of the Dienstgruppen in the three western zones, see Heinz-Ludger Borgert, Walter Stürm, and Norbert Wiggershaus, *Dienstgruppen und westdeutscher Verteidigungsbeitrag. Alternative Überlegungen zur Bewaffnung der Bundesrepublik Deutschland* (Boppard: Boldt, 1981).

58. Deutsche Labor Service in der U.S. Zone, BA-MA, BW9/3081.

59. Borgert, Stürm, and Wiggershaus, *Dienstgruppen*, 164–65. For estimate, see Arthur L. Smith, *Heimkehr aus dem Zweiten Weltkrieg. Die Entlassung der deutschen Kriegsgefangenen* (Stuttgart: Deutsche Verlags-Anstalt, 1985), 49–50.

60. See Tom Bower, *The Pledge Betrayed* (Garden City, N.Y.: Doubleday, 1982), 418, n. 59.

61. Yergin, *Shattered Peace*, 225.

62. For an analysis of the plan's reception, see John Gimbel, "Die Vereinigten Staaten, Frankreich und der amerikanische Vertragsentwurf zur Entmilitarisierung Deutschlands," *VfZG* 22(1974): 258–86.

63. Council of Foreign Ministers, Disarmament and Demilitarization of Germany, 11 Mar. 1947, Hoover Institution Archive, Stanford University, Robert Murphy Papers, Box 60.

64. *Clay Papers*, 1:220.

65. Clay quoted in Yergin, *Shattered Peace*, 314–15.

66. *Clay Papers*, 1:966.

Chapter Two

1. For a good summary of Allied security policy in the early postwar era, especially as it impinged on Germany, see Christian Greiner, "Die alliierten militärstrategischen Planungen zur Verteidigung Westeuropas, 1947–50," in *Anfänge westdeutscher Sicherheitspolitik*, vol. 1: *Von der Kapitulation bis zum Pleven Plan*, ed. MGFA (Munich: R. Oldenbourg, 1982), 119–323.

2. Hans-Jürgen Schraut, "U.S. Forces in Germany, 1945–1955," in *U.S. Military Forces in Europe: The Early Years, 1945–1970*, ed. Simon W. Duke and Wolfgang Krieger (Boulder, Colo.: Westview Press, 1993), 154, 159–60, 163.

3. Melvyn P. Leffler, *A Preponderance of Power: National Security, the Truman Administration, and the Cold War* (Stanford: Stanford University Press, 1992), 273.

4. Soviet Intentions and Capabilities, Joint Intelligence Committee 435/12, NA, RG 218, Records of the Joint Chiefs of Staff, GF 1948–50, USSR (3-27-45), section 34. See also Greiner, "Die allierten militärstrategischen Planungen," 195–206.

5. Functioning of the French High Command, 26 Oct. 1950, NA, RG 319, Records of Army Chief of Staff, G-3, 091 France TS (section 1), Box 20, number 97.

6. Walter S. Poole, "The History of the Joint Chiefs of Staff: The Joint Chiefs of Staff and National Policy," 4 vols., unpublished manuscript, NA, Historical Division, Joint Secretariat, JCS, Dec. 1979, 4:185.

7. Gregory F. Treverton, *America, Germany, and the Future of Europe* (Princeton: Princeton University Press, 1992), 43.

8. Leffler, *Preponderance*, 274. On HALFMOON, see also Greiner, "Die allierten militärstrategischen Planungen," 163–71.

9. Leffler, *Preponderance*, 274.

10. Ibid., 275.

11. Greiner, "Die allierten militärstrategischen Planungen," 176–78.

12. Poole, "History of the Joint Chiefs of Staff," 4:185.

13. Hans Buchheim, "Adenauers Sicherheitspolitik, 1950–1951," in *Aspekte der deutschen Wiederbewaffnung bis 1955*, ed. MGFA (Boppard: Boldt, 1975), 120–21.

14. Laurence W. Martin, "The American Decision to Rearm Germany," in *American Civil-Military Decisions*, ed. Harold Stein (University: University of Alabama Press, 1963), 646. For a more recent study of American calculations regarding German rearmament, see Thomas Alan Schwartz, *America's Germany: John J. McCloy and the Federal Republic of Germany* (Cambridge: Harvard University Press, 1991), 113–55. A somewhat dated treatment is Robert McGeehan, *The German Rearmament Question: American Diplomacy and European Defense after World War II* (Urbana: University of Illinois Press, 1971).

15. Martin, "American Decision," 646.

16. Harry S. Truman, *Memoirs: Years of Trial and Hope* (Garden City, N.Y.: Doubleday, 1957), 244–49.

17. Martin, "American Decision," 648.

18. Poole, "History of the Joint Chiefs of Staff," 4:25.

19. Liddell-Hart's views in *Picture Post*, 24 July 1948.

20. Bernard Montgomery, *The Memoirs of Field Marshal and Viscount Montgomery of Alamein* (Cleveland: World, 1958), 457. For the Chiefs of Staff, see German Association with the Defence of the West, 28 Aug. 1950, PRO, FO 371, File C5540/27/18 G.

21. Saki Dockrill, *Britain's Policy for West German Rearmament* (Cambridge: Cambridge University Press, 1991), 7.

22. Georges-Henri Soutou, "France and the German Rearmament Problem, 1945–1953," in *The Quest for Stability: Problems of West European Security, 1918–1957*, ed. R. Ahmann, A. M. Birke, and M. Howard (Oxford: Oxford University Press, 1993), 491.

23. Ibid., 497.

24. Georgette Elgey, *La république des contradictions* (Paris: Plon, 1968), 215.

25. Norbert Wiggershaus, "Die Entscheidung für einen westdeutschen Verteidigungsbeitrag 1950," in *Anfänge westdeutscher Sicherheitspolitik, 1945–1956*, vol. 1: *Von der Kapitulation bis zum Pleven-Plan*, ed. MGFA (Munich: R. Oldenbourg, 1982), 328.

26. Ibid.

27. Gorgette Elgey, *La république des illusions* (Paris: Plon, 1968), 381.

28. Soutou, "France and the German Rearmament Problem," 497.

29. *The Papers of Lucius D. Clay*, ed. Jean Edward Smith, 2 vols. (Bloomington: Indiana University Press, 1974), 2:1071–72.

30. "Defense Plan Offered," *NYT*, 21 Nov. 1949.

31. Gerhard Wettig, *Entmilitarisierung und Wiederbewaffnung in Deutschland, 1943–1955* (Munich: R. Oldenbourg, 1967), 277.

32. "Congressmen Ask West Bid Germans," *NYT*, 22 Nov. 1949; "Paris Gets Three Views on German Arming," ibid., 23 Nov. 1949; "Five Senators Oppose German Troop Use," ibid., 27 Nov. 1949.

33. *Joint Hearings before the Senate Committee on Foreign Relations and Committee on Armed Services*, 5 June 1950 (Washington, D.C.: GPO, 1950), 22; ibid., 6 June 1950, 54–55.

34. Byroade quoted in Leffler, *Preponderance*, 319.

35. On McCloy, see Schwartz, *America's Germany*, passim; Kai Bird, *The Chairman: John J. McCloy and the Making of the American Establishment* (New York: Simon and Schuster, 1992); and Walter Isaacson and Evan Thomas, *The Wise Men: Six Friends and the World They Made* (New York: Simon and Schuster, 1986).

36. Bird, *Chairman*, 327.

37. Schwartz, *America's Germany*, 123.

38. Bird, *Chairman*, 327–28.

39. Foreign Office Memos, 20 Jan., 30 Mar. 1950, PRO, FO 371/85087.

40. Kirkpatrick Memo, 1 Apr. 1950, ibid.

41. Position Paper, No. C2436, 5 Apr. 1950, ibid.

42. Ibid.

43. Wettig, *Entmilitarisierung*, 278.

44. "U.S.-German Pact Seen," *NYT*, 5 Dec. 1949.

45. Winster quoted in Wettig, *Entmilitarisierung*, 279.

46. *Winston Churchill: His Complete Speeches, 1897–1963*, ed. Robert Rhodes James, 3 vols. (New York: Chelsea House, 1974), 3:7972–73.

47. *House of Commons Debates*, H. C. Hansard, 472:1392, 1311.

48. Dockrill, *Britain's Policy*, 9–10.

49. Ibid., 10.

50. Quoted in F. Roy Willis, *France, Germany and the New Europe, 1945–1967* (New York: Oxford University Press, 1968), 56–58.

51. Quoted ibid., 68.

52. "Paris Gets 3 Views on German Arming," *NYT*, 23 Nov. 1949.

53. Wettig, *Entmilitarisierung*, 278–80.

54. Quoted in Ernst Nolte, *Deutschland und der Kalte Krieg* (Munich: Piper, 1974), 291.

55. *Allgemeine Zeitung*, 25 Nov. 1948.

56. T. W. Viggers, "The German People and Rearmament," *International Affairs* 2 (Apr. 1951): 152.

57. Charles Thayer, *The Unquiet Germans* (New York: Harper Brothers, 1957), 213.

58. Quoted in Roland G. Foerster, "Innenpolitische Aspekte der Sicherheit Westdeutschlands," in *Anfänge westdeutscher Sicherheitspolitik*, vol. 1: *Von der Kapitulation bis zum Pleven-Plan*, ed. MGFA (Munich: R. Oldenbourg, 1982), 431.

59. Heinz Guderian, *Kann Westeuropa verteidigt werden?* (Göttingen: Plesse Verlag, 1950), 49–53.

60. Augstein quoted in Foerster, "Innenpolitische Aspekte," 431.

61. "Remilitarisierung in Westdeutschland?" *Hamburger Allgemeine Zeitung*, 26 Nov. 1948.

62. "Remilitarisierung," *Westfalen Zeitung*, 27 Nov. 1948.

63. Quoted in Foerster, "Innenpolitische Aspekte," 432.

64. "So schnell schiessen die Preussen nicht mehr," *Wiesbadener Kurier*, 29 Nov. 1948.

65. "Der Verfassungskonvent von Herrenchiemsee, Protokolle und Unterausschüsse I, Auszug aus der 2. Sitzung von 18.8.1948," in *Der Kampf um den Wehrbeitrag*, ed. Institut für Staatslehre und Politik, 3 vols. (Munich: Isar Verlag, 1952–58), 2:39.

66. Foerster, "Innenpolitische Aspekte," 422.

67. Ibid., 424.

68. On the Lampheimer Circle, see ibid., 432–33. On Speidel, see Hans Speidel, *Aus unserer Zeit: Erinnerungen* (Berlin: Ullstein, 1977); "Der smarte General," *Der Spiegel*, 4 July 1956, 15–26.

69. For a copy of the memo, see *Sicherheitspolitik der Bundesrepublik Deutschland: Dokumentation, 1945–1977*, ed. Klaus von Schubert, 2 vols. (Cologne: Verlag Wissenschaft und Politik, 1978–79), 2:65–81; see also Speidel, *Aus unserer Zeit*, 255–57.

70. Speidel, *Aus unserer Zeit*, 253.

71. Text ibid., 468–71.

72. On Heusinger, see *Sicherheit und Entspannung. Zum siebzigsten Geburtstag von General a.D. Adolf Heusinger*, ed. Hans Herzfeld (Cologne: Markus Verlag, 1967); "Die tragische Laufbahn," *Der Spiegel*, 29 Feb. 1956, 24–31.

73. Text of memo in *Sicherheitspolitik der Bundesrepublik*, 2:67–71.

74. General a.D. Hasso von Manteuffel headed the Grossdeutschland Division in World War II. He represented the FDP in the first Bundestag but switched to the DP/FVP after 1956.

75. "Bekenntnis eines freimütigen Deutschen," BA-MA, BW9/3118.

76. For a discussion of the role of the resistance legacy in the rearmament debate, see David Clay Large, "'A Gift to the German Future'?: The Anti-Nazi Resistance Movement and West German Rearmament," *German Studies Review* 7 (Oct. 1984): 499–529.

77. Allied High Commission Decree Number 7, 19 Dec. 1949, *Information Bulletin*, Dec. 1949, Office of the United States High Commission for Germany, 72–74.

78. Hans-Peter Schwarz, *Die Ära Adenauer, 1949–1957* (Stuttgart: Deutsche Verlags-Anstalt, 1981), 47–48.

79. Arnulf Baring, *Aussenpolitik in Adenauers Kanzlerdemokratie* (Munich: R. Oldenbourg, 1969), 53.

80. Josef Foschepoth, "Westintegration statt Wiedervereinigung: Adenauers Deutschlandpolitik, 1949–1955," in *Adenauer und die deutsche Frage*, ed. Josef Foschepoth (Göttingen: Vandenhoeck and Rupprecht, 1988), 29–60.

81. Roscoe Drummond and Gaston Coblentz, *Duel at the Brink: John Foster Dulles's Command of American Power* (Garden City, N.Y.: Doubleday, 1960), 39–44; Anneliese Poppinga, *Konrad Adenauer: Geschichtsverständnis, Weltanschauung und politische Praxis* (Stuttgart: Deutsche Verlags-Anstalt, 1975), 88.

82. Dean Acheson, *Present at the Creation* (New York: Norton, 1969), 341–42.

83. Schwarz, *Die Ära Adenauer*, 109–10.

84. *FRUS, 1949*, vol. 3: *Council of Foreign Ministers, Germany and Austria* (Washington, D.C.: GPO, 1973), 360. See also Wettig, *Entmilitarisierung*, 284–85.

85. *L'Est Républicain*, 12 Nov. 1949.

86. Schwartz, *America's Germany*, 117.

87. Wettig, *Entmilitarisierung*, 288.

88. Ibid., 285.

89. Ivone Kirkpatrick, *The Inner Circle: Memoirs of Sir Ivone Kirkpatrick* (London: Macmillan, 1959), 228.

90. *Deutscher Bundestag. Verhandlungen*, 1. Wahlperiode, 24. Sitzung, 735–36.

91. Ibid., 736–37.

92. Ibid., 737–41.

93. Ibid., 741.

94. *NYT*, 22 Mar. 1950.

95. Report, Gerhard Graf von Schwerin, 9 Aug. 1950, PRO, FO 371/85088; on Schwerin's appointment, see his own comments in *Aspekte der deutschen Wiederbewaffnung*, ed. MGFA (Boppard: Boldt, 1975), 133–35; Foerster, "Innenpolitische Aspekte," 456–58; Dieter Krüger, *Das Amt Blank. Die schwierige Gründung des Bundesministerium für Verteidigung* (Freiburg: Rombach, 1993), 17.

96. This, at least, was how the British interpreted Adenauer's appointment of Schwerin. See Report, 22 Mar. 1950, PRO, FO 1005/1126a.

97. Marion Dönhoff, *Von Gestern nach Übermorgen* (Hamburg: Knaus, 1981), 75.

98. Aktennotiz Schwerin, 25 May 1950, BA-MA, BW9/3105.

99. Text of Schwerin's memo in BA-MA, BW9/3105.

100. See Gerhard Buss to Schwerin, 17 June 1950, BA-MA, BW9/3109.

101. On the personnel structure of the Zentrale, see BA-MA, BW9/3109, 50–52.

102. Unterrichtung des Führers der Opposition, BA-MA, BW9/3118; also comments of Schwerin in *Aspekte der deutschen Wiederbewaffnung bis 1955*, ed. MGFA (Boppard: Boldt, 1975), 112.

103. Bericht Oster, BA-MA, BW9/3108.

104. Schwerin to Globke, 17 July 1950, BA-MA, BW9/3111; BW9/3108, 23–24; Foerster, "Innenpolitische Aspekte," 467–68.

105. "Betrachtung über die Schaffung einer Nachrichtenstelle für die Bundesregierung," BA-MA, BW9/3108.

106. Foerster, "Innenpolitische Aspekte," 469.

107. Hansa-Haus Godesberg, BA-MA, BW9/3118, 57.

108. "Richtlinien," BA-MA, BW9/3111, 31–32.

109. For copies of letters, see BA-MA, BW9/3105, 164–68.

110. Vorschläge zur Sprachregelung Graf Schwerin—Vertretung der ehemaligen Berufssoldaten, BA-MA, BW9/3118, 21–22.

111. Foerster, "Innenpolitische Aspekte," 554.

112. Gerhard Brandt, "Rüstung und Wirtschaft in der Bundesrepublik," in *Studien zur politischen und gesellschaftlichen Situation der Bundeswehr*, ed. Georg Picht, 3 vols. (Witten: Eckart, 1966), 3:75–104.

113. See report on meeting of interior and economic ministries, BA-MA, BW9/3106, 126.

114. Tätigkeitsbericht der Abteilung I/w, BA-MA, BW9/3116.

115. On Schumacher's background, see Lewis Edinger, *Kurt Schumacher: A Study in Personality and Political Behavior* (Stanford: Stanford University Press, 1965), 20–50. On his commitment to German reunification, see Ulrich Buczylowski, *Kurt Schumacher und die deutsche Frage. Sicherheitspolitik und strategische Offensivkonzeption von August 1950 bis September 1951* (Stuttgart: Seewald, 1973), 30–47; and Gordon D.

Drummond, *The Social Democrats in Opposition: The Case against Rearmament* (Norman: University of Oklahoma Press, 1982), 21–25.

116. Der Standpunkt von Herrn von Schumacher in der Frage der Einschaltung der BRD in die militärische Abwehrfront Europas, BA-MA, BW9/3105, 31.

Chapter Three

1. For discussions of the Korean War's impact on the West German rearmament debate, see Gunther Mai, *Westliche Sicherheitspolitik im kalten Krieg. Der Korea-Krieg und die deutsche Wiederbewaffnung, 1950* (Boppard: Boldt, 1977); Christian Greiner, "Die allierten militärstrategischen Planungen zur Verteidigung Westeuropas, 1947–1950," in *Anfänge westdeutscher Sicherheitspolitik*, vol. 1: *Von der Kapitulation bis zum Pleven-Plan*, ed. MGFA (Munich: R. Oldenbourg, 1982), 287–91; Norbert Wiggershaus, "Die Entscheidung für einen westdeutschen Verteidigungsbeitrag 1950," ibid., 325–402; Thomas Alan Schwartz, *America's Germany: John J. McCloy and the Federal Republic of Germany* (Cambridge: Harvard University Press, 1991), 124–35; Ernst Nolte, *Deutschland und der kalte Krieg* (Munich: Piper, 1974), 287–330; Wilfried Loth, "The Korean War and the Reorganization of the European Security System," in *The Quest for Stability: Problems of West European Security, 1918–1957*, ed. R. Ahmann, A. M. Birke, and M. Howard (Oxford: Oxford University Press, 1993), 465–86; Norbert Wiggershaus, "Bedrohungsvorstellungen Bundeskanzler Adenauers nach Ausbruch des Korea-Krieges," *MGM* 1 (1979): 79–122.

2. Robert S. Griffith, *The Politics of Fear: Joseph R. McCarthy and the Senate* (Lexington: University Press of Kentucky, 1970), 58–60.

3. Melvyn P. Leffler, *A Preponderance of Power: National Security, the Truman Administration, and the Cold War* (Stanford: Stanford University Press, 1992), 345.

4. Ibid., 326; also Ernest R. May, "The Impact of Nuclear Weapons on European Security, 1945–1957," in *The Quest for Stability: Problems of West European Security, 1918–1957*, ed. R. Ahmann, A. M. Birke, and M. Howard (Oxford: Oxford University Press, 1993), 522–23.

5. May, "Impact," 522; Leffler, *Preponderance*, 350.

6. NSC/68, United States Objectives and Programs, 14 Apr. 1950, *FRUS, 1950*, 1:283–87.

7. May, "Impact," 523.

8. Laurence Martin, "The American Decision to Rearm Germany," in *American Civil-Military Relations*, ed. Harold Stein (University: University of Alabama Press, 1963), 651.

9. See comments of Secretary of the Navy Francis P. Matthews, *Washington Post*, 10 Sept. 1950. The U.S. military service secretaries sent Secretary of Defense Louis Johnson a memo suggesting that the Western allies consider waging "an aggressive war for peace." See Service Secretaries to Secretary of Defense, 17 Aug. 1950, NA, RG 330, Records of the Secretary of Defense, CCS 092 (Western Europe), section 55.

10. Omar Bradley to A. C. Davis, 30 June 1950, NA, RG 330, CCS 092 (Germany), section 2; Johnson memo, 14 Aug. 1950, ibid., section 3.

11. Minutes of meetings of Under Secretary of State, 5 July 1950, NA, RG 59, Records of Executive Secretariat, Box 13.

12. Ibid. See also McCloy's comments in *NYT*, 28 June 1950.

13. Charles Thayer, *The Unquiet Germans* (New York: Harper Brothers, 1957), 210–12; Ivone Kirkpatrick, *The Inner Circle* (London: Macmillan, 1959), 238.

14. Thayer, *Unquiet Germans*, 210–11.

15. *Kölnische Rundschau*, 8 July 1950; *Münchner Merkur*, 28 June 1950.

16. *Die Zeit*, 29 June 1950.

17. *Jahrbuch der öffentlichen Meinung, 1947–1955*, ed. Peter Neumann and Elisabeth Noelle (Allensbach: Verlag für Demoskopie, 1957), 53, 350, 354.

18. Quoted in Nolte, *Deutschland und der Kalte Krieg*, 288.

19. Wiggershaus, "Bedrohungsvorstellungen," 79–82. See also Arnulf Baring, *Aussenpolitik in Adenauers Kanzlerdemokratie* (Munich: R. Oldenbourg, 1969), 81–82.

20. Wiggershaus, "Bedrohungsvorstellungen," 82.

21. Heinz reports in BA-MA, BW9/3109; and BW9/3108, 52–59, 137–41.

22. BA-MA, BW9/3108, 145.

23. See Schwerin recollections in *Aspekte der deutschen Wiederbewaffnung bis 1955*, ed. MGFA (Boppard: Boldt, 1975), 134.

24. Kurzprotokoll über das Zusammentreffen zwischen General Hays, Graf Schwerin, und Herbert Blankenhorn, 22 July 1950, BA-MA, BW9/3105, 67–73. British Military Intelligence came to the same conclusion regarding the dangers of a Communist offensive in Central Europe following the Korean War. See report of Lt. Col. R. H. Keenlyside, 28 Nov. 1950, PRO, FO 371/85090.

25. Aufzeichnungen, Gespräch am 17 Juli 1950, BA-MA, BW9/3105. A copy of this protocol can also be found in BAK, Nachlass E. Wildermuth, 251/7a.

26. Kurzprotokoll, Hays, Schwerin, Blankenhorn, 22 July 1950, 70.

27. See his report, 19 July 1950, BA-MA, BW9/3105, 60–64.

28. Roland G. Foerster, "Innenpolitische Aspekte der Sicherheit Westdeutschlands (1947–1950)," in *Anfänge westdeutscher Sicherheitspolitik, 1945–1956*, vol. 1: *Von der Kapitulation bis zum Pleven-Plan*, ed. MGFA (Munich: R. Oldenbourg, 1982), 510–11.

29. *NYT*, 18 Aug. 1950.

30. For a strong statement of this view, see Karl Kaiser, "Germany's Unification," *Foreign Affairs* 70 (1991): 181.

31. Konrad Adenauer, *Erinnerungen, 1945–1953* (Stuttgart: Deutsche Verlags-Anstalt, 1965), 350–54.

32. Foerster, "Innenpolitische Aspekte," 515.

33. For a text of the conference, see *Sicherheitspolitik der Bundesrepublik. Dokumentation, 1945–1977*, ed. Klaus von Schubert, 2 vols. (Cologne: Verlag Wissenschaft und Politik, 1978–79), 1:71–74.

34. BA-MA, BW9/3106, 102.

35. Foerster, "Innenpolitische Aspekte," 517.

36. Texts of memos in *Sicherheitspolitik*, 1:79–83, 84–85.

37. BA-MA, BW9/3108, 153–54, 137–41.

38. *Sicherheitspolitik*, 1:83.

39. Ibid., 84.

40. Adenauer, *Erinnerungen, 1945–1953*, 361.

41. *Sicherheitspolitik*, 1:74–79.

42. On Heinemann, see Diether Koch, *Heinemann und die Deutschlandfrage* (Munich: Kaiser, 1972); Hans-Erich Volkmann, "Gustav W. Heinemann und Konrad Adenauer," *Geschichte in Wissenschaft und Unterricht* 1 (1989): 10–31.

43. Koch, *Heinemann*, 168–91; Baring, *Aussenpolitik*, 166–67.

44. *Schweizer National-Zeitung*, 6 Sept. 1950.

45. Koch, *Heinemann*, 170–76.

46. Ibid., 175.

47. "Memorandum über die deutsche Sicherheit," *Europa-Archiv*, 20 Dec. 1950, 3594–96.

48. *Essener Allgemeine Zeitung*, 27 Sept. 1950.

49. *Die Neue Zeitung*, 10 Oct. 1950.

50. Koch, *Heinemann*, 194–97.

51. Quoted in Anselm Doering-Manteuffel, *Katholizismus und Wiederbewaffnung: Die Haltung der deutschen Katholiken gegenüber der Wehrfrage, 1948–1955* (Mainz: Matthias-Grünewald, 1981), 76.

52. Ibid., 83.

53. *Kirchenzeitung für das Erzbistum Köln*, 17 Sept. 1950.

54. *Bonifatiusbote* 61 (27 Aug. 1950).

55. *Kettler-Wacht* 44 (1 Sept. 1950).

56. Doering-Manteuffel, *Katholizismus*, 86–89.

57. See Wilfried Loth, "Die Europa-Bewegung in den Aufbaujahren der Bundes-republik," in *Vom Marshallplan zur EWG. Die Eingliederung der Bundesrepublik in die westliche Welt*, ed. Ludolf Herbst (Munich: R. Oldenbourg, 1990), 63–77.

58. Doering-Manteuffel, *Katholizismus*, 105–8.

59. Quoted in Heinz Josef Varain, "Die Auseinandersetzung innerhalb der Evangelischen Kirche wegen der deutschen Wiederaufrüsting," *Geschichte in Wissenschaft und Unterricht* 9 (1958): 411.

60. Quoted in Dennis L. Bark and David R. Gress, *A History of West Germany*, vol. 1: *From Shadow to Substance* (Oxford: Basil Blackwell, 1989), 151.

61. Johanna Vogel, *Kirche und Wiederbewaffnung. Die Haltung der Evangelischen Kirche in Deutschland in den Auseinandersetzungen um die Wiederbewaffnung der Bundesrepublik 1949–1956* (Göttingen: Vandenhoeck and Rupprecht, 1978), 52–54.

62. Koch, *Heinemann*, 110.

63. Varain, "Die Auseinandersetzung," 413.

64. See the report on this meeting by one of its participants, Josef Iwand, in FES, Nachlass Ollenhauer, 114.

65. Ibid. See also Vogel, *Kirche und Wiederbewaffnung*, 131.

66. Koch, *Heinemann*, 210.

67. Ibid., 221.

Chapter Four

1. JCS, Memo for the Secretary of Defense, 30 Aug. 1950, NA, RG 330, 09107 (Europe), Box 175. See also *FRUS, 1950*, vol. 3: *Western Europe* (Washington, D.C.: GPO, 1977), 1077; Laurence Martin, "The American Decision to Rearm Germany," in *American Civil-Military Decisions*, ed. Harold Stein (University: University of Alabama Press, 1963), 653. A recent treatment of rearmament diplomacy in 1950 is Rolf Steininger, *Wiederbewaffnung. Die Entscheidung für einen westdeutschen Verteidigungsbeitrag: Adenauer und die Westmächte 1950* (Erlangen: Straube, 1989).

2. Quoted in Melvyn P. Leffler, *A Preponderance of Power: National Security, the Truman Administration, and the Cold War* (Stanford: Stanford University Press, 1992), 386.

3. Ibid.

4. *NYT*, 6 Sept. 1950.

5. Thomas Alan Schwartz, *America's Germany: John J. McCloy and the Federal Republic of Germany* (Cambridge: Harvard University Press, 1991), 129–31.

6. JCS Memo for Secretary of Defense, 30 Aug. 1950, NA, RG 330; see also JCS Survey Committee to JCS, 27 July 1950, NA, RG 218, Records of the Joint Chiefs of Staff, CCS-092 (Germany), Box 19.

7. *Congressional Record, Senate,* 1950, 12743.

8. Martin, "American Decision," 656–57; Harry S. Truman, *Memoirs: Years of Trial and Hope* (Garden City, N.Y.: Doubleday, 1956), 253.

9. *FRUS, 1950,* vol. 4: *Central and Eastern Europe: The Soviet Union* (Washington, D.C.: GPO, 1980), 711–12.

10. Peter Jones, "Labour-Regierung, deutsche Wiederbewaffnung und die EVG 1950–51," in *Die Europäische Verteidigungsgemeinschaft. Stand und Probleme der Forschung,* ed. MGFA (Boppard: Boldt, 1985), 54–57. See also Bevin's memo "German Association with Defence of the West," *FRUS, 1950,* 3:265–66; Bevin to Harvey, 5 Sept. 1950, *DBPO,* ser. 2, vol. 3, *German Rearmament, September–December 1950* (London: HMSO, 1989), 13; Saki Dockrill, *Britain's Policy for West German Rearmament, 1950–1955* (Cambridge: Cambridge University Press, 1991), 24–28.

11. *NYT,* 13 Sept. 1950.

12. *DBPO,* ser. 2, vol. 3, 21.

13. Jules Moch, *Histoire du réarmement allemand depuis 1950* (Paris: Robert Laffont, 1965), 45–47.

14. *FRUS, 1950,* 3:1193, 1207, 1208; also *DBPO,* ser. 2, vol. 3, 54–55.

15. *FRUS, 1950,* 3:1201. For a British report on the New York meeting, see Cabinet Papers, 6 Oct. 1950, PRO, Cab/129/42, CP223, 103–5.

16. *FRUS, 1950,* 3:1200. See also Dean Acheson, *Present at the Creation* (New York: Norton, 1969), 442.

17. *FRUS, 1950,* 3:1204. Also *DBPO,* ser. 2, vol. 3, 47–50.

18. *FRUS, 1950,* 3:1204, 1206.

19. Ibid., 1230–31.

20. Ibid., 1296–99, 1231.

21. *NYT,* 13 Sept. 1950.

22. Moch, *Histoire,* 63.

23. Strang Memo, 15 Sept. 1950, PRO, FO 371/85054.

24. *FRUS, 1950,* 3:310; *DBPO,* ser. 2, vol. 3, 76–77.

25. M. A. Fitzsimmons, *The Foreign Policy of the British Labour Government* (South Bend, Ind.: Notre Dame University Press, 1953), 150.

26. National Union of Furniture Trade Operatives to Attlee, 8 Nov. 1950, PRO, FO 371/85090; Amalgamated Engineering Union Protest, 26 Nov. 1950, ibid.

27. Union of Jewish Ex-Service Men and Women to Secretary of State, Foreign Office, 27 Nov. 1950, ibid.

28. Dean Acheson, *Sketches from Life of Men I Have Known* (New York: Harper Brothers, 1959), 27; *FRUS, 1950,* 3:311–12.

29. *FRUS, 1950,* 3:314–15; Moch, *Histoire,* 57.

30. *FRUS, 1950,* 3:337, 338.

31. Ibid., 353, 342.

32. Ibid., 344, 354.

33. Ibid., 1296–99.

34. Ibid., 352.

35. Konrad Adenauer, *Erinnerungen, 1949–1953* (Stuttgart: Deutsche Verlags-

Anstalt, 1965), 365–73. See also "Die Diskussion über den deutschen Verteidigungsbeitrag," *Europa-Archiv*, 20 Dec. 1950, 3576–78.

36. Adenauer, *Erinnerungen, 1945–1953*, 373.

37. Dieter Koch, *Heinemann und die Deutschlandfrage* (Munich: Kaiser, 1972), 200.

38. Radio Address, 11 Oct. 1950, Adenauer-Haus Rhöndorf, File StB KAH, RI-I.

39. *FRUS, 1950*, 3:362–63.

40. Moch, *Histoire*, 93–94.

41. *FRUS, 1950*, 3:377–79.

42. Ibid., 379–80, 385. See also Acheson, *Present at the Creation*, 457.

43. For good analyses of the Pleven Plan, see Norbert Wiggershaus, "Die Entscheidung für einen westdeutschen Verteidigungsbeitrag 1950," in *Anfänge westdeutscher
Sicherheitspolitik, 1945–1956*, vol. 1: *Von der Kapitulation bis zum Pleven-Plan*, ed.
MGFA (Munich: R. Oldenbourg, 1982), 390–400; Schwartz, *America's Germany*, 141–
44; Gerhard Wettig, *Entmilitarisierung und Wiederbewaffnung in Deutschland, 1943–
1955* (Munich: R. Oldenbourg, 1967), 363–69; Edgar J. Furniss, *France, Troubled Ally:
De Gaulle's Heritage and Prospects* (New York: Harper Brothers, 1960), 64–71.

44. Wettig, *Entmilitarisierung*, 369.

45. Groener quoted in Gordon A. Craig, *The Politics of the Prussian Army* (New
York: Oxford University Press, 1964), 367.

46. Georges-Henri Soutou, "France and the German Rearmament Problem, 1945–
1955," in *The Quest for Stability: Problems of West European Security, 1918–1957*, ed.
R. Ahmann, A. M. Birke, and M. Howard (London: Oxford University Press, 1993),
498.

47. F. Roy Willis, *France, Germany and the New Europe, 1945–1967* (New York: Oxford University Press, 1968), 130.

48. A. G. Gilchrist to Foreign Office, 25 Oct. 1950, PRO, FO 371/85089.

49. Schwartz, *America's Germany*, 142.

50. *FRUS, 1950*, 3:411–12.

51. *DBPO*, ser. 2, vol. 3, 206; *FRUS, 1950*, 3:405, 413–14; see also Jones, "Labour-
Regierung," 60–62.

52. Quoted in Schwartz, *America's Germany*, 143.

53. *NYT*, 5 Nov. 1950; Wettig, *Entmilitarisierung*, 370.

54. *FRUS, 1950*, 3:420.

55. Pierre Guillen, "Die französische Generalität, die Aufrüstung der Bundesrepublik und die EVG," in *Die Europäische Verteidigungsgemeinschaft. Stand und Probleme
der Forschung*, ed. MGFA (Boppard: Boldt, 1985), 132–33.

56. Moch, *Histoire*, 93; *FRUS, 1950*, 3:413–21; *DBPO*, ser. 2, vol. 3, 234–35.

57. *FRUS, 1950*, 3:430–31, 433, 441–42.

58. Ibid., 382.

59. Ibid., 419, 518. See also Wiggershaus, "Die Entscheidung," 398.

60. Burns memo for Secretary of Defense, 5 Dec. 1950, NA, RG 330, Records
of Secretary of Defense, CD 091.7 (Europe) 1950, Box 176; *FRUS, 1950*, 3:471,
517–18.

61. *DBPO*, ser. 2, vol. 3, 291–96, 298, 305.

62. Wilfried Loth, *Sozialismus und Internationalismus. Die französischen Sozialisten
und die Nachkriegsordnung Europas, 1940–1950* (Stuttgart: Deutsche Verlags-Anstalt,
1977), 288.

63. *FRUS, 1950*, 3:497.

64. It was so labeled by Count Schwerin in *Aspekte der deutschen Wiederbewaffnung*

bis 1955, ed. MGFA (Boppard: Boldt, 1975), 142. On the Himmeroder Denkschrift, see Roland G. Foerster, "Innenpolitische Aspekte der Sicherheit Westdeutschlands (1947–1950)," in *Anfänge westdeutscher Sicherheitspolitik*, vol. 1: *Von der Kapitulation bis zum Pleven-Plan*, ed. MGFA (Munich: R. Oldenbourg, 1982), 562–66; Hans-Jürgen Rautenberg and Norbert Wiggershaus, "Die Himmeroder Denkschrift von Oktober 1950," *MGM* 21 (1977): 135–206; Hans Speidel, *Aus unserer Zeit. Erinnerungen* (Berlin: Ullstein, 1977), 272–75.

65. BA-MA, BW9/3105, 94–95.

66. Interview with Johann Graf von Kielmansegg, May 1983. See also Speidel, *Aus unserer Zeit*, 272–75.

67. For complete texts of the memorandum, see BA-MA, BW9/3119; and Rautenberg and Wiggershaus, "Himmeroder Denkschrift," 168–89. Quotations in the following paragraphs are from these sources.

68. On this, see Donald Abenheim, *Reforging the Iron Cross: The Search for Tradition in the West German Armed Forces* (Princeton: Princeton University Press, 1988), 47–63.

69. A good discussion of German military justice in World War II is Manfred Messerschmidt, *Die Wehrmachtjustiz im Dienste des Nationalsozialismus* (Baden-Baden: Nomos Verlag, 1987).

70. Baudissin later related that the former officers soon began treating the monks who served them like "orderlies." See interview with Baudissin in *Die zornigen alten Männer*, ed. Axel Eggebrecht (Reinbek: Rowohlt, 1979), 208.

71. Schwerin, Stellungnahme zur Himmeroder Denkschrift, BA-MA, BW9/3102, 181–87.

72. Denkschrift des militärischen Expertenausschuss von 9 Okt. 1950, BA-MA, BW9/3102, 177–78.

73. *Stuttgarter Nachrichten*, 24 Oct. 1950; *Frankfurter Rundschau*, 25 Oct. 1950.

74. *Die Welt*, 28 Oct. 1950. See also Foerster, "Innenpolitische Aspekte," 567.

75. *FAZ*, 30 Oct. 1950.

76. Hans-Peter Schwarz, *Die Ära Adenauer, 1949–1957* (Stuttgart: Deutsche Verlags-Anstalt, 1981), 119.

77. Adenauer, *Erinnerungen, 1945–1953*, 388–90.

78. See report on this discussion by Britain's ambassador to France, Harvey, in *DBPO*, ser. 2, vol. 3, 244.

79. *Deutscher Bundestag. Verhandlungen*, 1. Wahlperiode, 8 Nov. 1950, 3565–67.

80. Quoted in Ulrich Buczylowski, *Kurt Schumacher und die deutsche Frage* (Stuttgart: Seewald, 1973), 115–19.

81. On the Prague Resolution, see Department of State, *Documents on Germany, 1944–1985* (Washington, D.C.: GPO, 1985), 345–47.

82. Adenauer, *Erinnerungen, 1945–1953*, 377.

83. Ibid., 395.

84. Ibid.; *Neue Zeitung*, 12 Dec. 1950.

85. *FRUS, 1950*, 3:531–32, 538–39, 566–68.

86. Secretary of Defense Memo, 5 Dec. 1950, NA, RG 330, Office of Secretary of Defense, 09107 (Europe), 1950, Box 175.

87. *FRUS, 1950*, 3:571–72, 584.

88. Acheson, *Present at the Creation*, 483.

89. Ibid., 487.

90. Robert McGeehan, *The German Rearmament Question: American Diplomacy and European Defense after World War II* (Urbana: University of Illinois Press, 1971), 77.

91. Ivone Kirkpatrick, *The Inner Circle* (London: Macmillan, 1959), 241–42.

92. McGeehan, *German Rearmament Question*, 90.

93. *FRUS, 1950*, 3:579.

Chapter Five

1. On the EDC's importance for the evolution of Bonn's relations with the West, see David Clay Large, "Grand Illusions: The United States, the Federal Republic of Germany, and the European Defense Community, 1950–1954," in *American Policy and the Reconstruction of West Germany, 1945–1955*, ed. Jeffry M. Diefendorf, Axel Frohn, and Hermann-Josef Rupieper (New York: Cambridge University Press, 1993), 375–94.

2. "Wer ist Theo Blank?" *Deutsche Korrespondenz*, 23 Aug. 1951. See also "Der härteste Schädel in Bonn," *Der Spiegel*, 10 Dec. 1950, 6–12.

3. "Wer ist Theo Blank?" *Deutsche Korrespondenz*, 23 Aug. 1951.

4. Christian Greiner, "Die Dienststelle Blank," *MGM* 1 (1975): 103–4.

5. "Ebenfalls grosse Schweiger," *Der Spiegel*, 25 Dec. 1950, 9–10.

6. For discussions of the Twentieth of July legacy's place in West German rearmament, see David Clay Large, "'A Gift to the German Future'?: The Anti-Nazi Resistance Movement and West German Rearmament," *German Studies Review* 7 (Oct. 1984): 499–529; Wolfgang von Groote, "Bundeswehr und 20. Juli," *VfZG* 14 (1966): 285–99; Norbert Wiggershaus, "Zur Bedeutung und Nachwirkung des militärischen Widerstandes in der Bundesrepublik Deutschland und in der Bundeswehr," in *Der militärische Widerstand gegen Hitler und das NS-Regime, 1933–1945: Vorträge zur Militärgeschichte*, ed. MGFA (Herford: E. S. Mittler, 1984), 501–28.

7. Greiner, "Die Dienststelle Blank," 104–5. For an excellent monograph on Blank's office, see Dieter Krüger, *Das Amt Blank. Die schwierige Gründung des Bundesministeriums für Verteidigung* (Freiburg: Rombach, 1993).

8. "Ebenfalls grosse Schweiger," *Der Spiegel*, 25 Dec. 1950, 10; "Bonner Quartiermacher für alliierte Soldaten," *Süddeutsche Zeitung*, 20 Jan. 1951.

9. See comments of Kielmansegg in *Aspekte der deutschen Wiederbewaffnung bis 1955*, ed. MGFA (Boppard: Boldt, 1975), 150.

10. Charles Thayer, *The Unquiet Germans* (New York: Harper Brothers, 1957), 232.

11. Stephen E. Ambrose, "Eisenhower and the Germans," unpublished conference paper, 13.

12. Thayer, *Unquiet Germans*, 232–33.

13. *FRUS, 1951*, vol. 3: *Western Europe* (Washington, D.C.: GPO, 1977), 446. Also Hans Speidel, *Aus unserer Zeit: Erinnerungen* (Berlin: Ullstein, 1977), 286.

14. *FRUS, 1951*, 3:447.

15. Manfred Messerschmidt, "Hitlers ehrenhaften Komplizen," *Die Zeit*, 5 Feb. 1993.

16. Among the large number of studies on the Wehrmacht in the National Socialist system, see Gordon Craig, *The Politics of the Prussian Army, 1640–1945* (New York: Oxford University Press, 1964), 468–503; John W. Wheeler-Bennett, *The Nemesis of Power: The German Army in Politics, 1918–1945* (New York: Viking, 1964); Manfred Messerschmidt, *Die Wehrmacht im NS-Staat. Zeit der Indoktrination* (Hamburg: R. v. Decker's Verlag, 1969); Klaus-Jürgen Müller, *Das Heer und Hitler: Armee und nationalsozialistisches Regime, 1933–1945* (Stuttgart: Deutsche Verlags-Anstalt, 1969).

17. War Minister von Blomberg and Army Chief Fritsch questioned Hitler's war plans in 1937. In January 1938 Blomberg was suddenly dismissed—allegedly for having married a prostitute. Shortly thereafter, Fritsch was accused of homosexuality and dismissed as well. The rest of the military leadership did nothing to protest these travesties. They now accepted Hitler as commander in chief of the armed forces. For a recent study of this affair, see Karl-Heinz Janssen, *Der Sturz der Generäle: Hitler und die Blomberg-Fritsch Krise, 1938* (Munich: Beck, 1994).

18. On the Wehrmacht's crimes in Russia and the Balkans, see Theo Schulte, *The German Army and Nazi Policies in Occupied Russia* (Oxford: Berg, 1989); Omer Bartov, *The Eastern Front, 1941–1945: German Troops and the Barbarization of Warfare* (New York: St. Martin's, 1986); Christian Streit, *Keine Kameraden: Die Wehrmacht und die sowjetischen Kriegsgefangenen, 1941–1945* (Stuttgart: Deutsche Verlags-Anstalt, 1978); Christopher Browning, "Wehrmacht Reprisal Policy and the Mass Murder of Jews in Serbia," *MGM* 1 (1983): 31–47.

19. For a good account of the apologetic perspective of former German top officers, see Gotthard Breit, *Das Staats- und Gesellschaftsbild deutscher Generäle beider Weltkriege im Spiegel ihrer Memoiren* (Boppard: Boldt, 1973). On Bitburg, see *Bitburg in Moral and Political Perspective*, ed. Geoffrey Hartman (Bloomington: Indiana University Press, 1986).

20. Thomas Alan Schwartz, *America's Germany: John J. McCloy and the Federal Republic of Germany* (Cambridge: Harvard University Press, 1991), 165.

21. Thayer, *Unquiet Germans*, 234–35.

22. Schwartz, *America's Germany*, 168.

23. Thayer, *Unquiet Germans*, 235; *NYT*, 1 Feb. 1952.

24. Achenbach to McCloy, 27 Nov. 1951, FNS, Nachlass Thomas Dehler, Box 172.

25. McCloy to Achenbach, 8 Dec. 1951, ibid.; McCloy to Karl Brandt, 27 Feb. 1952, FES, Nachlass Schumacher, Bestand J102.

26. Ridgway's remarks recorded in PA, Stenographische Protokolle, Sonderausschuss zur Mitberatung des EVG-Vertrages und der damit zusammenhängenden Abmachungen, 6. Sitzung, 37.

27. Quoted in Kai Bird, *The Chairman: John J. McCloy and the Making of the American Establishment* (New York: Simon and Schuster, 1992), 364.

28. Gerhard Wettig, *Entmilitarisierung und Wiederbewaffnung in Deutschland, 1943–1955* (Munich: R. Oldenbourg, 1967), 402–3.

29. Ibid., 404. See also Edward Fursdon, *The European Defense Community: A History* (New York: St. Martin's, 1980), 107.

30. *FRUS, 1951*, vol. 3: *European Security and the German Question* (Washington, D.C.: GPO, 1981), 991, 999, 1024.

31. Ibid., 1045–46.

32. See "Eine untragbare Belastung der Bundesrepublik," *FAZ*, 30 Nov. 1951; Rüdiger Proske, "Die Kosten unserer Sicherheit," *Frankfurter Heften* 1 (Jan. 1950): 58–65.

33. *FRUS, 1951*, 3:1028.

34. Ibid., 1066–67.

35. See undated Dienststelle Blank report in BAK, B136 (Bundeskanzleramt), 2160.

36. *FRUS, 1951*, 3:1027.

37. Ibid., 994, 1003.

38. Ibid., 997–98.

39. Ibid., 1027.

40. Ulrich de Maizière, "Zur Planung und Vorbereitung eines westdeutschen Wehrbeitrages," in *Entmilitarisierung und Aufrüstung in Mitteleuropa, 1945–1956*, ed. MGFA (Herford: E. S. Mittler, 1986), 82.

41. Ulrich de Maizière, *In der Pflicht. Lebensbericht eines deutschen Soldaten im 20. Jahrhundert* (Herford: E. S. Mittler, 1989), 144.

42. The "principle" in question was proposed by the SPD politician Fritz Erler. See PA, Stenographische Protokolle, Sonderausschuss zur Mitberatung des EVG-Vertrages, 8. Sitzung, 17.

43. Niederschrift über die Besprechung über den Pleven Plan, 5 June 1951, BA-MA, BW9/3066.

44. Hervé Alphand, *L'étonnement d'être. Journal, 1939–1973* (Paris: Fayard, 1977), 229–30.

45. Pierre Guillen, "Die französische Generalität, die Aufrüstung der Bundesrepublik und die EVG (1950–1954)," in *Die Europäische Verteidigungsgemeinschaft. Stand und Probleme der Forschung*, ed. MGFA (Boppard: Boldt, 1985), 132–34.

46. For a study of French parties, public opinion, and German rearmament, see Jean-Pierre Rioux, "Französische öffentliche Meinung und die EVG: Parteienstreit oder Schlacht der Erinnerungen," ibid., 159–76.

47. *FRUS, 1951*, 3:598.

48. Albert E. Kersten, "Niederländische Regierung, Bewaffnung Westdeutschlands und die EVG," in *Die Europäische Verteidigungsgemeinschaft. Stand und Probleme der Forschung*, ed. MGFA (Boppard: Boldt, 1985), 199.

49. Ibid., 198–99.

50. See record of General Mathon's conversation with Speidel, 21 Mar. 1952, BA-MA, BW9/2048, 26.

51. See David Reynolds, *Britannia Overwhelmed: British Policy and World Power in the Twentieth Century* (London: Longman, 1991), 195.

52. Peter Jones, "Labour-Regierung, deutsche Wiederbewaffnung und EVG 1950–1951," in *Die Europäische Verteidigungsgemeinschaft. Stand und Probleme der Forschung*, ed. MGFA (Boppard: Boldt, 1985), 79, 64. See also D. C. Watt, "Die konservative Regierung und die EVG, 1951–1954," ibid., 86.

53. *FRUS, 1951*, 3:763; Jones, "Labour-Regierung," 71–76.

54. *FRUS, 1951*, 3:760–61.

55. *Congressional Record*, 14 Mar. 1951, 2470–71.

56. Dean Acheson, *Present at the Creation* (New York: Norton, 1969), 557.

57. *FRUS, 1951*, 3:801–3.

58. Ibid., 802–3, 806.

59. Stephen Ambrose, *Eisenhower*, 2 vols. (New York: Simon and Schuster, 1988), 1:508.

60. Quoted in Schwartz, *America's Germany*, 222.

61. Walter Isaacson and Evan Thomas, *The Wise Men: Six Friends and the World They Made* (New York: Simon and Schuster, 1986), 68.

62. Quoted in Robert McGeehan, *The German Rearmament Question: American Diplomacy and European Defense after World War II* (Urbana: University of Illinois Press, 1971), 128–29.

63. Ibid., 129.

64. Schwartz, *America's Germany*, 223–24.

65. Ambrose, *Eisenhower*, 1:506.

66. Ibid., 508.

67. *Department of State Bulletin*, 12 Feb. 1951, 247.

68. Ambrose, *Eisenhower*, 1:504.

69. *Department of State Bulletin*, 26 Mar. 1951, 488.

70. Ramcke statement, 6 Feb. 1951, FNS, Nachlass Thomas Dehler, Box 169.

71. Hermann Bernhard Ramcke, *Fallschirmjäger. Damals und Danach* (Frankfurt: Lorsch Verlag, 1951), 264–65.

72. See Large, "'A Gift to the German Future'?" 514–15. In 1952 Remer was tried in Braunschweig for insulting the memory of the Twentieth of July resisters. The court concluded that he was still living in the mental world of 1944 and engaging in "unreconstructed defiance" of the new democratic order. See Georg Meyer, "Zur Situation der deutschen militärischen Führungsschicht im Vorfeld des westdeutschen Verteidigungsbeitrages, 1945–1950/51," in *Anfänge westdeutscher Sicherheitspolitik, 1945–1956*, vol. 1: *Von der Kapitulation bis zum Pleven-Plan*, ed. MGFA (Munich: R. Oldenbourg, 1982), 668–69. In 1992 he was convicted by the Schweinfurt regional court of instigating racial hatred by denying the existence of the Holocaust.

73. Hans-Peter Schwarz, *Die Ära Adenauer, 1949–1957* (Stuttgart: Deutsche Verlags-Anstalt, 1981), 132.

74. Heinz Guderian, *Kann Westeuropa Verteidigt Werden?* (Göttingen: Plesse Verlag, 1950), 23, 28–73.

75. *Information Bulletin Monthly* (Monthly Magazine of the United States Military Government in Germany), Sept. 1951, 75.

Chapter Six

1. Arnulf Baring, *Aussenpolitik in Adenauers Kanzlerdemokratie* (Munich: R. Oldenbourg, 1969), 108.

2. *FRUS, 1951*, vol. 3: *European Security and the German Question* (Washington, D.C.: GPO, 1981), 825.

3. Stehlin Gespräch, BA-MA, BW9/2048, 53–54.

4. Ulrich de Maizière, *In der Pflicht. Lebensbild eines deutschen Soldaten im 20. Jahrhundert* (Herford: E. S. Mittler, 1989), 153; Gerhard Wettig, *Entmilitarisierung und Wiederbewaffnung in Deutschland, 1943–1955* (Munich: R. Oldenbourg, 1967), 441.

5. *FRUS, 1951*, 3:869.

6. Antwort des Herrn Bundeskanzlers auf die von United Press am 10 Sept. 1951 gestellten Fragen, Speech Collection, Adenauer Haus, Rhöndorf.

7. Bundeskanzler Dr. Adenauer vor dem Deutschlandtag der Jungen Union am 28 Sept. 1951, ibid.

8. *NYT*, 4 Aug 1951.

9. *NYT*, 11 Sept. 1951.

10. Aufzeichnung über das Gespräch zwischen Herr Blank and Herr Alphand vom 11 Okt. 1951, BA-MA, BW9/2048, 12.

11. William G. Carleton, "Germany Seven Years after Defeat," *Yale Review* 16 (Mar. 1952): 325.

12. Aufzeichnung über das Gespräch zwischen Herr Blank und Herr Alphand vom 11 Okt. 1951, BA-MA, BW9/2048, 16–18.

13. Blank Besprechungen, BA-MA, BW9/2048, 21–23.

14. Ibid.

15. Baring, *Aussenpolitik*, 114.

16. Saar-Frage, BA-MA, BW9/2048, 42.

17. *FAZ*, 1 Feb. 1952.

18. Baring, *Aussenpolitik*, 115.

19. *Deutscher Bundestag. Verhandlungen*, 1. Wahlperiode, 190. Sitzung, 8099–8104.

20. Otto Lenz, *Im Zentrum der Macht. Das Tagebuch von Staatssekretär Lenz, 1951–1953* (Düsseldorf: Droste, 1989), 249.

21. *Deutscher Bundestag. Verhandlungen*, 1. Wahlperiode, 190. Sitzung, 8108–12.

22. Innenpolitische Berichte, 24 Jan. 1952, 8 Jan. 1952, 25 Jan. 1952, 5 Feb. 1952, BAK, B136 (Bundeskanzleramt) 2160.

23. Parlamentärischer Ausschuss für Spitzenbesetzung, 26 Sept. 1951, BA-MA, BW9/2123, 88.

24. Innenpolitischer Bericht, 2 Feb. 1952, BAK, B136, 2160.

25. *Deutscher Bundestag. Verhandlungen*, 1. Wahlperiode, 190. Sitzung, 8118–21.

26. Lenz, *Zentrum*, 187.

27. Erich Mende, "Die innere und äussere Sicherheit Deutschlands," *Freideutsche Korrespondenz*, 23 Oct. 1951, 5.

28. *Deutscher Bundestag. Verhandlungen*, 1. Wahlperiode, 190. Sitzung, 8132–33.

29. *FAZ*, 14 Feb. 1952.

30. *Deutscher Bundestag. Verhandlungen*, 1. Wahlperiode, 190. Sitzung, 8144.

31. The phrase comes from Timothy Garton Ash, *In Europe's Name: Germany and the Divided Continent* (New York: Random House, 1993).

32. *Deutscher Bundestag. Verhandlungen*, 1. Wahlperiode, 191. Sitzung, 8184–95.

33. *Die Welt*, 12 Feb. 1952; Lenz, *Zentrum*, 249.

34. *Deutscher Bundestag. Verhandlungen*, 1. Wahlperiode, 191. Sitzung, 8239.

35. *Mannheimer Morgen*, 12 Feb. 1952.

36. Quoted in F. Roy Willis, *France, Germany and the New Europe, 1945–1967* (New York: Oxford University Press, 1968), 138.

37. René Massigli, *Une comédie des erreurs, 1943–1956* (Paris: Plon, 1978), 308.

38. Willis, *France, Germany*, 141–44.

39. Jules Moch, *Histoire du réarmement allemand depuis 1950* (Paris: Robert Laffont, 1965), 283.

40. Willis, *France, Germany*, 143.

41. Massigli, *Une comédie des erreurs*, 309.

42. Hervé Alphand, *L'étonnement de'être* (Paris: Fayard, 1977), 227.

43. Paul Weymar, *Adenauer: His Authorized Biography* (New York: Dutton, 1957), 424, 426.

44. Baring, *Aussenpolitik*, 120.

45. On this see Gerhard Brandt, "Rüstung und Wirtschaft in der Bundesrepublik," in *Studien zur politischen und gesellschaftlichen Situation der Bundeswehr*, ed. Georg Picht, 3 vols. (Witten: Eckart, 1965), 3:75–104.

46. *Die Neue Zeitung*, 20 Feb. 1952.

47. Speidel Gespräch mit General Larminat, 4 Mar. 1952, BA-MA, BW9/2048, 49–52.

48. *FRUS, 1952–1954*, vol. 5: *Western European Security* (Washington, D.C.: GPO, 1983), 250–51.

49. Ibid., 142–45.

50. Ibid., 160; Dean Acheson, *Present at the Creation* (New York: Norton, 1969), 624.

51. Acheson, *Present at the Creation*, 626.

52. Text of Stalin Note in *Documents on Germany, 1944–1985* (Washington, D.C.: Office of the Historian, Department of State, 1986), 361–64.

53. Bernd Pröll, *Bundeswehr und Nationale Volksarmee in Staat und Gesellschaft* (Bonn: Haag & Herchen, 1983), 13–18. See also Manfred Messerschmidt, "Aus der Geschichte lernen—Vom Umgang mit der Erblast des Nationalsozialismus in der Bundeswehr und in der NVA," in *Die Nationale Volksarmee. Beiträge zu Selbstverständnis und Geschichte des deutschen Militärs von 1945–1990*, ed. Detlef Bald (Baden-Baden: Nomos, 1992), 13–14.

54. See Hermann Graml, "Die Legende von der verpassten Gelegenheit. Zur sowjetischen Notenkampagne des Jahres 1952," *VfZG* 29 (1981): 307–41; Rolf Steininger, *Eine vertane Chance: Die Stalin-Note vom 10. März 1952 und die Wiedervereinigung* (Bonn: Verlag Neue Gesellschaft, 1986); Gerhard Wettig, "Die sowjetische Deutschland-Note vom 10. März 1952—Wiedervereinigungsangebot oder Propagandaaktion?" *Deutschland Archiv* 15 (1982): 130–48; Alexander Fischer, "Anmerkungen zur sowjetischen Deutschlandpolitik in der Phase der EVG," in *Die Europäische Verteidigungsgemeinschaft. Stand und Probleme der Forschung*, ed. MGFA (Boppard: Boldt, 1985), 221–38; Hermann-Josef Rupieper, "Zu den sowjetischen Deutschlandnoten 1952. Das Gespräch Stalin-Nenni (Dokumentation)," *VfZG* 33 (1985): 547–57; Dietrich Staritz, "Zur sowjetischen Deutschland- und Sicherheitspolitik," in *Zwischen Kaltem Krieg und Entspannung. Sicherheits- und Deutschlandpolitik der Bundesrepublik im Mächtesystem der Jahre 1953–1956*, ed. MGFA (Boppard: Boldt, 1988), 35–49.

55. Fischer, "Anmerkungen," 233.

56. For a survey of the Western response to the Stalin Note, see Klaus A. Maier, "Die internationalen Auseinandersetzungen um die Westintegration der Bundesrepublik und um ihre Bewaffnung im Rahmen der Europäischen Verteidigungsgemeinschaft," in *Anfänge westdeutscher Sicherheitspolitik, 1945–1956*, vol. 2: *Die EVG-Phase*, ed. MGFA (Munich: R. Oldenbourg, 1990), 109–19.

57. Charles Bohlen, *Witness to History, 1929–1969* (New York: Norton, 1973), 297.

58. George Kennan, *Memoirs, 1950–1963* (Boston: Little, Brown, 1972), 108–9.

59. *FRUS, 1952–1954*, 5:176; Acheson, *Present at the Creation*, 630.

60. Gespräch Speidel, Blank, Gruenther am 2 Mai 1952, BA-MA, BW9/2048, 67–69.

61. Quoted in Steininger, *Eine vertane Chance*, 132.

62. German Rearmament and the Four-Power Talks, 22 Feb. 1951, PRO, FO 1008/9.

63. Acheson, *Present at the Creation*, 631. The British were especially concerned that a reunited Germany have the right to join the EDC. See Shuckburgh to Colville, 24 June 1952, PRO, PREM 11 (168).

64. Baring, *Aussenpolitik*, 146; Lenz, *Zentrum*, 299–300.

65. Andreas Hillgruber, "Adenauer und die Stalin-Note," in *Konrad Adenauer und seine Zeit*, ed. Dieter Blumenwitz, 2 vols. (Stuttgart: Deutsche Verlags-Anstalt, 1976), 2:114–15. See also Hans-Peter Schwarz, *Adenauer. Der Aufstieg* (Stuttgart: Deutsche Verlags-Anstalt, 1986), 910–12.

66. Baring, *Aussenpolitik*, 148.

67. Ibid. See also Schwarz, *Adenauer*, 911–12.

68. For Schumacher, see letter dated 22 Apr. 1952 in *Documents on International Affairs, 1951*, ed. Denise Folliot (London: Oxford University Press, 1954), 94–95; on

the EKD, see Diether Koch, *Heinemann und die Deutschlandfrage* (Munich: Kaiser, 1972), 309–32.

69. Baring, *Aussenpolitik*, 150.

70. Blücher's letter quoted in Georg Vogel, *Diplomat unter Hitler und Adenauer* (Düsseldorf: Econ, 1969), 189–91. On Blücher's rebellion, see also Dietrich Wagner, *FDP und Wiederbewaffnung. Die wehrpolitische Orientierung der Liberalen in der Bundesrepublik Deutschland, 1949–1955* (Boppard: Boldt, 1978), 96–97.

71. Acheson, *Present at the Creation*, 645–46; Vogel, *Diplomat*, 209; Baring, *Aussenpolitik*, 409–10, n. 153.

72. Wettig, *Entmilitarisierung*, 482–83.

73. See "Entschliessung," undated, BA-MA, BW9/758.

74. Acheson, *Present at the Creation*, 644–45.

75. Gerstenmaier to Adenauer, 2 May 1952, BAK, B136 (Bundeskanzleramt) 2160.

76. Adenauer speech, 7 Apr. 1952, Südwestfunk. Text in BA-MA, BW9/764.

77. Quoted in Baring, *Aussenpolitik*, 153.

78. *Deutscher Bundestag. Verhandlungen*, 1. Wahlperiode, 204. Sitzung, 8768.

79. Baring, *Aussenpolitik*, 154–55.

80. *Deutscher Bundestag. Verhandlungen*, 1. Wahlperiode, 214. Sitzung, 9415.

81. *Die Neue Zeitung*, 26 May 1952.

82. Quoted in Weymar, *Adenauer*, 439.

83. Acheson, *Present at the Creation*, 645; *The Times* (London), 24 May 1952.

84. Acheson, *Present at the Creation*, 647; Mitteilung an die Presse, 27 May 1952, BPA Sammlung, 1952, Adenauer Haus Rhöndorf.

85. Innenpolitischer Bericht, 8 Jan. 1952, BAK, B136 Bundeskanzleramt 2160.

86. *FAZ*, 30 Apr. 1952.

87. See Pierre Guillen, "Frankreich und die NATO-Integration der Bundesrepublik," in *Vom Marshallplan zur EWG. Die Eingliederung der Bundesrepublik in die westliche Welt*, ed. Ludolf Herbst (Munich: R. Oldenbourg, 1970), 429–31.

88. On Pfleiderer's speech, see Baring, *Aussenpolitik*, 177–78; Hans-Erich Volkmann, "Die innenpolitische Dimension Adenauerscher Sicherheitspolitik in der EVG-Phase," in *Anfänge westdeutscher Sicherheitspolitik*, vol. 2: *Die EVG-Phase*, ed. MGFA (Munich: R. Oldenbourg, 1990), 342–48.

89. "Mit Pfleiderer nicht einverstanden," *Freideutsche Korrespondenz*, 8 Oct. 1952, 6.

90. Reinhold Maier, *Erinnerungen* (Tübingen: R. Wunderlich, 1966), 456–58.

91. On the peace movement, see Jeffrey Herf, *War by Other Means: Soviet Power, West German Resistance, and the Battle of the Euromissiles* (New York: Free Press, 1991); *Sicherheitspolitik contra Frieden? Ein Forum zur Friedensbewegung*, ed. Hans Apel (Berlin: J. H. W. Dietz, 1981); Kendall Baker, Russel J. Dalton, and Kai Hildebrandt, *Germany Transformed: Political Culture and the New Politics* (Cambridge: Harvard University Press, 1981).

Chapter Seven

1. For a convenient guide to the high court, see *Das Bundesverfassungsgericht*, ed. Bundesverfassungsgericht (Karlsruhe: C. F. Muller, 1963). Good surveys of the constitutional battles over rearmament can be found in Arnulf Baring, *Aussenpolitik in Adenauers Kanzlerdemokratie* (Munich: R. Oldenbourg, 1969), 221–61; Dieter

Gosewinkel, *Adolf Arndt. Die Wiederbegründung des Rechtsstaats aus dem Geist der Sozialdemokratie* (Bonn: J. H. W. Dietz, 1991), 296–346; Karl Loewenstein, "The Bonn Constitution and the European Defense Treaties," *Yale Law Journal* 64 (1955): 804–39; and Mark Cioc, "Reforging the Basic Law: *Wehrgewalt* and the European Defense Community Treaty," in *A Framework for Democracy: Forty Years of Experience with the Grundgesetz of the Federal Republic of Germany*, ed. Thomas Childers (Cambridge: Cambridge University Press, forthcoming).

2. Konrad Adenauer, Pressetee, 24 Jan. 1952, in *Teegespräche, 1950–1954*, ed. Hans Jürgen Kusters (Berlin: Siedler, 1986), 186.

3. Justice Minister Dehler and the FDP believed that constitutional amendments might have been necessary for a national army but not for a German contribution to the EDC. See *Die Welt*, 17 Jan. 1952.

4. "Die Stellungnahme der Bundesrepublik," in *Der Kampf um den Wehrbeitrag*, ed. Institut für Staatslehre und Politik, 3 vols. (Munich: Isar Verlag), 2:5–37. See also Hans-Erich Volkmann, "Die innenpolitische Dimension Adenauerscher Sicherheitspolitik in der EVG-Phase," in *Anfänge westdeutscher Sicherheitspolitik*, vol. 2: *Die EVG-Phase*, ed. MGFA (Munich: R. Oldenbourg, 1990), 373–74.

5. "Stellungnahme der SPD-Bundestagfraktion vom 28. Okt. 1952 zur verfassungsrechtlichen Frage der Vereinbarkeit eines bewaffneten Beitrages mit dem Grundgesetz," *Kampf um den Wehrbeitrag*, 2:289–311. For an excellent discussion of Arndt's role in the SPD's legal battle against rearmament, see Gosewinkel, *Adolf Arndt*, 296–362.

6. There is some confusion in the literature over whether Adenauer went to see Heuss himself or sent Dehler. Baring, *Aussenpolitik*, 224, says Dehler told him that Adenauer acted alone; Eberhard Pikart, *Theodor Heuss und Konrad Adenauer. Die Rolle des Bundespräsidenten in der Kanzlerdemokratie* (Stuttgart: Belser, 1976), 106, says that Dehler did the negotiating.

7. Pikart, *Theodor Heuss*, 104–6. See also Loewenstein, "Bonn Constitution," 810.

8. Baring, *Aussenpolitik*, 226.

9. *Kampf um den Wehrbeitrag*, 1:227–28.

10. Ibid., 446.

11. Loewenstein, "Bonn Constitution," 810.

12. Arndt to Höpker-Aschoff, 14 Aug. 1952, *Kampf um den Wehrbeitrag*, 2:831.

13. Quoted ibid., 231.

14. Quoted in Volkmann, "Die innenpolitische Dimension," 378.

15. Paul Weymar, *Adenauer: His Authorized Biography* (New York: Dutton, 1957), 446.

16. Quoted ibid., 448.

17. Ibid.

18. Loewenstein, "Bonn Constitution," 812, 813.

19. *Kampf um den Wehrbeitrag*, 3:812–15.

20. "Rücknahme-Erklärung des Bundespräsidenten," ibid., 2:811. See also Reinhold Maier, *Erinnerungen, 1948–1953* (Tübingen: R. Wunderlich, 1966), 463; Pikart, *Theodor Heuss*, 109–11; Baring, *Aussenpolitik*, 247.

21. The German press coverage of the Heuss affair is discussed in *NYT*, 10 and 11 Dec. 1952.

22. Loewenstein, "Bonn Constitution," 815; Maier, *Erinnerungen*, 463–65.

23. Quoted in Loewenstein, "Bonn Constitution," 813.

24. For a scholarly study of this committee, which was later called the Ausschuss für

Fragen der europäischen Sicherheit (AFES), then the Ausschuss für Verteidigung (AfV), see H. J. Berg, *Der Verteidigungsausschuss des deutschen Bundestages: Kontrollorgan zwischen Macht und Ohnmacht* (Munich: Bernard & Graefe, 1982).

25. Stenographische Protokolle, Sonderausschuss zur Mitberatung des EVG-Vertrages und der damit zusammenhängenden Abmachungen, PA, 2. Sitzung, 8; 3. Sitzung, 37; 5. Sitzung, 31–38.

26. Ibid., 11. Sitzung, 62; 3. Sitzung, 25–30.

27. Ibid., 2. Sitzung, 21; 3. Sitzung, 24.

28. Ibid., 4. Sitzung, 2–5; 3. Sitzung, 12.

29. Ibid., 5. Sitzung, 39; 6. Sitzung, 44; 9. Sitzung, 24.

30. For discussions of the nuclear arms question, see Dieter Mahncke, "Nuclear Participation: The Federal Republic of Germany and Nuclear Weapons, 1954–1966" (Ph.D. dissertation, Johns Hopkins University, 1968); Catherine Kelleher, *Germany and the Politics of Nuclear Weapons* (New York: Columbia University Press, 1975); Mark Cioc, *Pax Atomica: The Nuclear Defense Debate in West Germany during the Adenauer Era* (New York: Columbia University Press, 1988); Detlef Bald, *Die Atombewaffnung der Bundeswehr* (Bremen: Edition Temmen, 1994).

31. Protokolle, Sonderausschuss, 9. Sitzung, 51–53.

32. Ibid., 22, 64–67; 8. Sitzung, 97–98.

33. Ibid., 9. Sitzung, 14–15.

34. Quoted in Baring, *Aussenpolitik*, 269.

35. Maier, *Erinnerungen*, 45–51, 447, 458–60.

36. "Nicht Drücken, Nicht Drängen," *Der Spiegel*, 29 Apr. 1953, 7–9.

37. Vierter Bundesparteitag der FDP zu Bad Ems, 1952, FNS, A1 Bundesparteitag, Bd. 30.

38. Baring, *Aussenpolitik*, 264–65.

39. *Bundesrat. Sitzungsberichte*, 87. Sitzung, 271.

40. Maier, *Erinnerungen*, 464.

41. Konrad Adenauer, *Erinnerungen, 1945–1953* (Stuttgart: Deutsche Verlags-Anstalt, 1965), 564–89. See also Zusammenfassender Bericht über den Aufenthalt in Washington, BA-MA, BW9/50, 4–9. For an analysis of Adenauer's image in America, see Peter H. Merkl, "Das Adenauer Bild in der öffentlichen Meinung der USA," in *Konrad Adenauer und seine Zeit*, ed. Dieter Blumenwitz, 2 vols. (Stuttgart: Deutsche Verlags-Anstalt, 1976), 2:220–28.

42. Quoted in Volkmann, "Die innenpolitische Dimension," 401.

43. Quoted ibid., p. 402. Adenauer's entourage during the Washington trip warned him not to "overestimate" the Americans' willingness to help the Federal Republic. Assistance would be forthcoming only if Bonn ratified the EDC.

44. Maier, *Erinnerungen*, 480.

45. Ibid., 482.

46. Ibid., 482–83.

47. Hans-Peter Schwarz, *Die Ära Adenauer, 1949–1957* (Stuttgart: Deutsche Verlags-Anstalt, 1981), 178.

48. For details of this operation, see Volkmann, "Die innenpolitische Dimension," 408–14.

49. Maier, *Erinnerungen*, 485; Schwarz, *Die Ära Adenauer*, 179.

50. Maier, *Erinnerungen*, 490.

51. "Der Antrag von 11. Mai (1953) und seine Begründung," *Kampf um den Wehrbeitrag*, 3:166–81.

52. Loewenstein, "Bonn Constitution," 817.

53. For analyses of the elections, see Volkmann, "Die innenpolitische Dimension," 419–32.

54. Herbert Blankenhorn, *Verständnis und Verständigung. Blätter eines politischen Tagebuchs 1949–1979* (Frankfurt: Propylaen, 1980), 170.

55. Entwurf eines Gesetzes zur Ergänzung des Grundgesetzes der CDU/CSU, GB/BHE, DP-Fraktion, 4 Dec. 1953, *Deutscher Bundestag. Drucksachen*, 1953, vol. 26, No. 124.

56. Volkmann, "Die innenpolitische Dimension," 443–44.

57. Adenauer, *Erinnerungen, 1953–1955* (Stuttgart: Deutsche Verlags-Anstalt, 1966), 271.

58. Loewenstein, "Bonn Constitution," 837.

59. Ibid.

60. Ibid., 839.

61. Lübke, whose job involved representing Germany abroad, was unfortunately a terribly clumsy speaker. On one occasion he translated the phrase *gleich geht's los* (something's about to start) as "equal goes it loose." See Dennis L. Bark and David R. Gress, *A History of West Germany*, vol. 2: *Democracy and Its Discontents* (Oxford: Basil Blackwell, 1989), 25.

62. Loewenstein, "Bonn Constitution," 837.

63. The phrase is from Volkmann, "Die innenpolitische Dimension," 386.

Chapter Eight

1. Lamentably, there is as yet no biography of Baudissin. For insights into his life and career, see Dietrich Genschel, *Wehrreform und Reaktion. Die Vorbereitung der Inneren Führung* (Hamburg: R. v. Decker's Verlag, 1972), passim; Donald Abenheim, *Reforging the Iron Cross: The Search for Tradition in the West German Armed Forces* (Princeton: Princeton University Press, 1988), 88–104; *Die zornigen alten Männer*, ed. Axel Eggebrecht (Reinbek: Rowohlt, 1977), 203–24; "Träumer in zu schweren Stiefeln," *Ruhr Nachrichten*, 13 Nov. 1954.

2. "Niederschrift eines Interviews von Diane Tridoux mit Graf Baudissin am 5. Mai 1980 in Hamburg," unpublished manuscript in possession of author. See also Baudissin's interview with Charles Schüddekopf in *Die zornigen alten Männer*, 206; and Baudissin, "Die Bedeutung der Reformen aus der Zeit der deutschen Erhebung für die Gegenwart," *Wehrkunde* 7 (Feb. 1958), Heft 2:3–8.

3. For a history of this regiment, see Wolfgang Paul, *Das Potsdamer Infanterie-Regiment 9, 1918–1945: Preussische Traditionen in Krieg und Frieden* (Osnabruck: Biblio, 1985).

4. Abenheim, *Reforging the Iron Cross*, 90; author's interview with Baudissin, 30 May 1983.

5. This was certainly the view of two of Baudissin's closest colleagues, Johann Graf von Kielmansegg and Heinz Karst (author's interviews, 13, 27 May 1983).

6. Abenheim, *Reforging the Iron Cross*, 91.

7. *Die zornigen alten Männer*, 204. In January 1955, the official East German newspaper, *Neues Deutschland*, insisted (with no proof) that Baudissin had been a zealous Nazi and a war criminal. See "Den Mörder von Tobruk aus Berlin vertrieben," *Neues Deutschland*, 15 Jan. 1955.

8. "Keine Angst vor den Soldaten," *Deutsche Soldatenzeitung*, Jan. 1955, 2–3.

9. Diane Tridoux interview with Baudissin, 5 May 1980.

10. Author's interview with Baudissin, 30 May 1983.

11. Primarily because of his role in the Third Reich, Foertsch was later denied a commission in the Bundeswehr. See Norbert Wiggershaus, "Zur Debatte um die Tradition künftiger Streitkräften, 1950–1955/56," in Hans-Joachim Harder and Norbert Wiggershaus, *Tradition und Reform in den Aufbaujahren der Bundeswehr* (Herford: E. S. Mittler, 1985), 54.

12. Before Baudissin joined the Dienststelle, Kielmansegg worked on an investigation into the legal status of future soldiers. See Hans-Jürgen Rautenberg, "Zur Standortbestimmung für künftige deutsche Streitkräfte," in *Anfänge westdeutscher Sicherheitspolitik, 1945–1956*, vol. 1: *Von der Kapitulation bis zum Pleven-Plan*, ed. MGFA (Munich: R. Oldenbourg, 1982), 486.

13. See Kielmansegg's comments in *Aspekte der deutschen Wiederbewaffnung bis 1955*, ed. MGFA (Boppard: Boldt, 1975), 216.

14. See Ulrich de Maizière, *In der Pflicht. Lebensbild eines deutschen Soldaten im 20. Jahrhundert* (Herford: E. S. Mittler, 1989), 142.

15. On Karst, see the provocative profile, "Not am Mann," *Der Spiegel*, 16 June 1969, 75–76. In 1969 Karst condemned Baudissin's reform approach as a "contradiction in terms" because it "sought to create an unsoldierly army." See "General Karst kritisiert 'unsoldatische Armee,'" *Die Welt*, 28 Apr. 1969.

16. On the organizational structure of the Dienststelle Blank, see Christian Greiner, "Die Dienststelle Blank," *MGM* 1 (1975): 99–124.

17. Rautenberg, "Zur Standortbestimmung," 799.

18. Ibid., 799–801.

19. Among Baudissin's many writings and speeches, see especially "The New German Army," *Foreign Affairs* 34 (Oct. 1955): 1–13; *Soldat für den Frieden. Entwürfe für eine zeitgemässe Menschenführung* (Munich: Piper, 1969); "Aufgaben und Bedeutung der Inneren Führung zukünftiger deutscher Streitkräfte," Radio text, Südwestfunk, Sendenreihe "Politik von Morgen," 10 Jan. 1955.

20. Baudissin, "New German Army," 1–4.

21. See "Interview Alfred Fischer mit Graf Baudissin über die neuen deutschen Streitkräfte," 7 May 1956, Dänischer Rundfunk, Radio text, Baudissin file, Biographisches Archiv, Bonn.

22. Baudissin, "New German Army," 5–10; Baudissin, "Wollen Sie wieder Soldat werden?" Radio address, 8 Nov. 1954, Baudissin file, Biographisches Archiv, Bonn.

23. On the oath issue, see Rautenberg, "Zur Standortbestimmung," 824–29; Abenheim, *Reforging the Iron Cross*, 169–70; and Peter Dade, *Fahneneid und feierliches Gelöbnis* (Darmstadt: Wehr und Wissen Verlag, 1971).

24. For a recent and very thorough discussion of these issues, see Georg Meyer, "Zur inneren Entwicklung der Bundeswehr bis 1960/61," in *Anfänge westdeutscher Sicherheitspolitik, 1945–1956*, vol. 3: *Die NATO Option*, ed. MGFA (Munich: R. Oldenbourg, 1993), 885–919.

25. Rautenberg, "Zur Standortbestimmung," 779.

26. *Deutscher Bundestag. Verhandlungen*, 1. Wahlperiode, 240. Sitzung, 1132–33.

27. "Die Leute hören's gern," *Der Spiegel*, 18 Oct. 1954, 8.

28. "Soldaten ohne Eid?" *Rheinischer Merkur*, 21 Nov. 1952.

29. Quoted in Wiggershaus, "Zur Debatte," 17.

30. Innenpolitischer Bericht, 25 Jan. 1952, BAK, B136 (Bundeskanzleramt) 2160.

Other critics also believed that Blank was "too weak" to resist pressures toward a restoration of the old ways. See Hans Speier interview with Adelbert Weinstein and Karl Helfer in Speier, *From the Ashes of Disgrace* (Amherst: University of Massachusetts Press, 1981), 269–76.

31. "Hat sich Blank den Generälen gefügt?" *Badischer Tageblatt*, 26 Feb. 1952; see also "Dienststelle Blank breitet sich aus," *Westdeutsche Allgemeine Zeitung*, 8 Oct. 1952.

32. "Der härteste Schädel in Bonn," *Der Spiegel*, 10 Dec. 1952, 6–12; "Die Krise im Amt Blank geht weiter," *Die Zeit*, 20 Nov. 1952; "Auseinandersetzung um Graf Baudissin," *Süddeutsche Zeitung*, 25 June 1956.

33. This is one of the main arguments of Genschel, *Wehrreform und Reaktion*.

34. Ibid., 120–40; Innere Führungshilfen—Inneres Gefüge, 11 Dec. 1952, BA-MA, BW9/5016.

35. Genschel, *Wehrreform und Reaktion*, 136; "Träumer in zu schweren Stiefeln," *Ruhr Nachrichten*, 13 Nov. 1954.

36. On Bonin, see Heinz Brill, *Bogislav von Bonin im Spannungsfeld zwischen Wiederbewaffnung — Westintegration — Wiedervereinigung* (Baden-Baden: Nomos Verlagsgesellschaft, 1987), passim; Hans Speier, *German Rearmament and Atomic War: The Views of German Military and Political Leaders* (Evanston, Ill.: Row, Peterson, 1957), 75–84; Meyer, "Zur inneren Entwicklung," 892–900, 1025–27; "Was sag' ich meinem Sohn?" *Der Spiegel*, 30 Mar. 1955, 7–12; and obituary in *Münziger-Archiv*, 15 Nov. 1980.

37. Brill, *Bogislav von Bonin*, 61–64, 118–22; Mark Cioc, *Pax Atomica: The Nuclear Defense Debate in West Germany during the Adenauer Era* (New York: Columbia University Press, 1988), 25–28, 35–36.

38. On this, see Abenheim, *Reforging the Iron Cross*, 107; Meyer, "Zur inneren Entwicklung," 892–98.

39. Dienststelle Blank, Tagebuch, Unterabteilung II/1, 7 Oct. 1952, BA-MA, BW9/2571-1. See also Genschel, *Wehrreform und Reaktion*, 141–43; "Bürger in Uniform," *Der Spiegel*, 15 Dec. 1954, 10.

40. "Bürger in Uniform," 9–10; Abenheim, *Reforging the Iron Cross*, 108; Genschel, *Wehrreform und Reaktion*, 143; "Die Krise im Amt Blank geht weiter," *Die Zeit*, 20 Nov. 1952.

41. For protocols of the Ausschuss meetings, see BA-MA, BW9/1291. The background of the Ausschuss is discussed in Meyer, "Zur inneren Entwicklung," 892–98.

42. Kurzprotokoll über die 10. Sitzung des Ausschusses Innere Führung, 14 Apr. 1953; 25. Sitzung, 16 June 1953, BA-MA, BW9/1291.

43. Author's interview with Baudissin, 30 May 1983.

44. See Karst's memo, "Leitsätze für die Erziehung des Soldaten," 15 June 1953, BA-MA, BW9/2527-56.

45. Heinz Karst, "Von '08/15' zum Verteidigungsbeitrag," *Der Monat* 6 (1954): 532–38; Karst, "Staatsbürger in Uniform," *Soldat im Volk* 3 (June 1954): 1.

46. On the postwar veterans' groups, see Kraft Freiherr Schenck zu Schweinsberg, "Die Soldatenverbände in der Bundesrepublik," in *Studien zur politischen und gesellschaftlichen Situation der Bundeswehr*, ed. Georg Picht, 3 vols. (Witten: Eckart, 1965), 1:96–177; Georg Meyer, "Zur Situation der deutschen militärischen Führungsschicht im Vorfeld des westdeutschen Verteidigungsbeitrages, 1945–1950/51," in *Anfänge westdeutscher Sicherheitspolitik, 1945–1956*, vol. 1: *Von der Kapitulation bis zum Pleven-Plan*, ed. MGFA (Munich: R. Oldenbourg, 1982), 578–735; Manfred Janke, *Verschwörung von Rechts?* (Berlin: Colloquium Verlag, 1961), 302–21; "German

Veterans' Associations and the Defense Contribution," Rand Corporation Study, RM-928, unpublished manuscript, GAP Archive; James Diehl, *The Thanks of the Fatherland: German Veterans after World War II* (Chapel Hill: University of North Carolina Press, 1993), passim.

47. See Diehl, *Thanks of the Fatherland*, 171.

48. Schenck zu Schweinsberg, "Die Soldatenverbände," 132–33; Hans-Helmuth Knutter, "'Nein—aber . . .' zur Wiederbewaffnung," in Carl-Christoph Schweitzer, *Eiserne Illusionen. Wehr- und Bündnisfragen in den Vorstellungen der extremen Rechten nach 1945* (Cologne: Markus Verlag, 1969), 57–64.

49. Hansen to General a.D. Pickert, 18 Sept. 1951, Karl Weigand Papers, Box 13, Hoover Institution, Stanford, Calif.

50. Kurt Tauber, *Beyond Eagle and Swastika: German Nationalism since 1945*, 2 vols. (Middletown, Conn.: Wesleyan University Press, 1967), 1:293.

51. Ibid., 293–94.

52. Diehl, *Thanks of the Fatherland*, 212–21.

53. "Schickt deutsche Männer," *Der Spiegel*, 2 May 1951, 7.

54. Adelbert Weinstein, *Armee ohne Pathos. Die deutsche Wiederbewaffnung im Urteil ehemaliger Soldaten* (Bonn: Köllen Verlag, 1951), 85.

55. Mosbach to Deutsche Presse-Agentur, 22 June 1953, BA-MA, BW9/757.

56. Erfahrungsbericht über 11 Veranstaltungen mit dem Film 'Wehrhaft und frei' vor Kreisverbänden des VdS in Bayern während der Zeit von 14.1 bis 30.1.54, BA-MA, BW9/778.

57. On this see David Clay Large, "'A Gift to the German Future'?: The Anti-Nazi Resistance Movement and West German Rearmament," *German Studies Review* 7 (Oct. 1984): 499–529.

58. Declaration quoted in "10. Jahre: 20 Juli 1944," *Soldat im Volk*, July 1954, 4.

59. Quoted in Tauber, *Beyond Eagle and Swastika*, 1:294.

60. Wiggershaus, "Zur Debatte," 44.

61. *FAZ*, 1 Oct. 1951; Schenck zu Schweinsberg, "Soldatenverbände," 144.

62. Diehl, *Thanks of the Fatherland*, 181–82.

63. Wiggershaus, "Zur Debatte," 46.

64. Hansen to Pickert, 18 Sept. 1951, Weigand Papers, Hoover Institution.

65. Quoted in Tauber, *Beyond Eagle and Swastika*, 1:268.

66. See reports on meetings between Dienststelle Blank personnel and veterans' leaders in BA-MA, BW9/754.

67. Strauss speech to Kyffhäuserbund reported in memo by British high commissioner Kirkpatrick, PRO, FO 1074/23.

68. "Vom künftigen deutschen Soldaten," *Soldat im Volk*, Nov. 1954, 1.

69. Stellungnahme zu dem Ergebnis der Beratung des Sechser-Ausschusses des VdS/BvW und des Kyffhäuser am 25.6.53, FNS, Thomas Dehler Nachlass, 56 (Ehemalige Berufssoldaten).

70. Memo, United Kingdom Office of High Commissioner, 9 June 1952, PRO, FO 1074/23. See also "The Coordination of German Ex-Servicemen's Activities," PRO, FO 1074/22.

71. Bericht über die Grossdeutschland Tagung am 2. Juni in Kassel, BA-MA, BW9/2122, 138.

72. Der Stahlhelm. Bund der Frontsoldaten. Stand 20. Okt. 1953, BA-MA, BW2/1259.

73. Rautenberg, "Zur Standortbestimmung," 806.

74. Quoted in Hartmut Soell, *Fritz Erler. Eine politische Biographie*, 2 vols. (Berlin J. H. W. Dietz, 1976), 1:193.

75. "The West German Parties and Rearmament," *World Today* 9 (1953): 53–64.

76. Dietrich Wagner, *FDP und Wiederbewaffnung. Die wehrpolitische Orientierung der Liberalen in der Bundesrepublik Deutschland, 1949–1955* (Boppard: Boldt, 1978), 112–16.

77. Bericht über die erste Sitzung des Ausschusses für Sicherheitsfragen, 30 Sept. 1952, FNS, Bundesverteidigungsausschuss, File 904.

78. "Orden und Ehrenzeichen—Kein heikles Problem," *Freideutsche Korrespondenz*, 6 Sept. 1951, 7; "Kein Streit um den Eid," ibid., 11 Sept. 1951, 3; "Ein ehrendes Andenken," ibid., 20 July 1954, 3–4.

79. Stenographische Protokolle, Sonderausschuss zur Mitberatung des EVG Vertrages, PA, 38. Sitzung, 7.

80. "Wer soll Oberbefehlshaber sein?" *Freideutsche Korrespondenz*, 15 Dec. 1953, 5–6.

81. Klaus Hornung, *Staat und Armee. Studien zur Befehls- und Kommandogewalt und zum politisch-militärischen Verhältnis in der Bundesrepublik Deutschland* (Mainz: Hase & Koehler, 1975), 59–64.

82. Hans-Erich Volkmann, "Die innenpolitische Dimension Adenauerscher Sicherheitspolitik in der EVG-Phase," in *Anfänge westdeutscher Sicherheitspolitik*, vol. 2: *Die EVG-Phase*, ed. MGFA (Munich: R. Oldenbourg, 1990), 433.

83. Hornung, *Staat und Armee*, 62–63.

84. Innenpolitischer Bericht, 8 Jan. 1952, BAK, B136 (Bundeskanzleramt) 2160, 2–6.

85. Sonderausschuss, 8. Sitzung, 128–31.

86. Ibid., 135.

87. Ibid., 26. Sitzung, 6, 19–29.

88. Ibid., 8. Sitzung, 138, 41.

89. See Abenheim, *Reforging the Iron Cross*, 126–35.

90. Sonderausschuss, 39. Sitzung, 51–52. See also ibid., 129.

91. Rautenberg, "Zur Standortbestimmung," 797.

92. Blank to Hays, 15 Apr. 1951; Hays to Blank, 28 Apr. 1951, BA-MA, BW9/502.

93. Pinckney to Wirmer, 29 Sept. 1951; Pinckney to Blank, 20 Aug. 1951, ibid.

94. Rautenberg, "Zur Standortbestimmung," 802.

95. Charles Thayer, *The Unquiet Germans* (New York: Harper Brothers, 1957), 246–47.

96. Upton quotation in Peter S. Michie, *The Life and Letters of Emory Upton* (New York: Arno Press, 1979), 386–87.

97. For a good analysis of American military views of the Wehrmacht, see Uwe Heuer, "Zur Perzeption der Bundeswehr in den Vereinigten Staaten von Amerika, 1963–1983. Deutsche Streitkräfte und deutsche Sicherheitspolitik im Urteil amerikanischer Experten" (Ph.D. dissertation, University of Bonn, 1989), 197–224.

98. Ibid., 213.

99. In April 1951 the U.S. Historical Division sought advice from former German General Staff officers regarding the establishment of "commando units" for use in Korea. See Akten Oster, BA-MA, BW9/2122, 76–78. In late 1952, President-Elect Eisenhower declared that the U.S. Army would be reorganized partly along lines suggested by General Heinz Guderian in a memo he wrote in 1948. See "Mit Guderians

Anregungen," *Der Spiegel*, 3 Dec. 1952, 14. The American army's field manual of the late 1970s and early 1980s was full of praise for the Wehrmacht.

100. "Gruenther Takes Precautions," *Foreign Report* (published by the *Economist*), 21 Oct. 1954, 5–6.

101. Bericht über die Reise in die USA von 30 Juni bis 29 August 1955, BA-MA, BW9/626.

102. Quoted in Wiggershaus, "Zur Debatte," 17.

103. F. R. Hoyer-Millar memos, 23 Feb., 22 Apr. 1955, PRO, FO 371/11824.

104. Kurzprotokoll, Ausschuss Innere Führung, 24 June, 26 May 1953, BA-MA, BW9/1291.

105. See Speidel's comments in BA-MA, BW9/3376, 525.

106. Kurzprotokoll, Ausschuss Innere Führung, 26 May 1953.

107. Sonderausschuss, 4. Sitzung, 56.

108. *Die zornigen alten Männer*, ed. Eggebrecht, 218.

109. Das Problem der Kriegsdienstverweigerung im Blicke der Streitkräften, 11 Feb. 1953, BA-MA, BW9/1318.

110. 1. Bericht des Sachverständigen Ausschusses "Uniform" im Militärausschuss des Interimausschusses, 23 June 1953, BA-MA, BW9/1311.

111. Wilhelm Meier-Dörnberg, "Die Planung des Verteidigungsbeitrages der Bundesrepublik Deutschland im Rahmen der EVG," in *Anfänge westdeutscher Sicherheitspolitik*, vol. 2: *Die EVG-Phase*, ed. MGFA (Munich: R. Oldenbourg, 1990), 683–84.

112. Deutscher Vorschlag über die Ausbildung zum aktiven Offizier der EVG, BA-MA, BW9/1318.

113. Meier-Dörnberg, "Die Planung," 684.

Chapter Nine

1. Edgar S. Furniss, *France, Troubled Ally: De Gaulle's Heritage and Prospects* (New York: Harper Brothers, 1960), 80.

2. Quoted in C. L. Sulzberger, *A Long Row of Candles* (Toronto: Macmillan, 1969), 950.

3. Quoted in F. Roy Willis, *France, Germany and the New Europe, 1945–1967* (New York: Oxford University Press, 1968), 162.

4. Hervé Alphand, *L'étonnement d'être. Journal, 1935–1973* (Paris: Fayard, 1977), 139.

5. Ibid., 234.

6. *FRUS, 1952–1954*, vol. 5: *Western European Security* (Washington, D.C.: GPO, 1983), 1728.

7. Ibid., 1740–43, 1843–44.

8. *The Churchill-Eisenhower Correspondence, 1953–1955*, ed. Peter G. Boyle (Chapel Hill: University of North Carolina Press, 1990), 122–24.

9. Josef Foschepoth, "Churchill, Adenauer und die Neutralisierung Deutschlands," *Deutschland Archiv* 17 (Dec. 1984): 1286–1301.

10. On the Eden Plan, see *FRUS, 1952–1954*, vol. 7: *Germany and Austria* (Washington, D.C.: GPO, 1986), 1170–80, 899–900, 933–34. For a good discussion of the diplomatic background of Eden's initiative, see Bruno Thoss, "Der Beitritt der Bundesrepublik Deutschland zur WEU und NATO im Spannungsfeld von Blockbildung

und Entspannung," in *Anfänge westdeutscher Sicherheitspolitik, 1945–1956*, vol. 3: *Die NATO Option*, ed. MGFA (Munich: R. Oldenbourg, 1993), 3–31.

11. Molotov proposal in *FRUS, 1952–1954*, 7:956–57.

12. For analyses of the Soviet position at this stage, see Dietrich Staritz, "Zur sowjetischen Deutschland- und Sicherheitspolitik, 1953–1954," in *Zwischen Kaltem Krieg und Entspannung. Sicherheits- und Deutschlandpolitik der Bundesrepublik im Mächtesystem der Jahre 1953–1956*, ed. MGFA (Boppard: Boldt, 1988), 43–47; Hermann-Josef Rupieper, "Die Berliner Aussenministerkonferenz von 1954," *VfZG* 34 (1986): 427–53.

13. Ollenhauer speech to Social Democratic editors and publishers, text in FES, Nachlass Schumacher, J77.

14. Hans-Peter Schwarz, *Die Ära Adenauer, 1949–1957* (Stuttgart: Deutsche Verlags-Anstalt, 1981), 220.

15. Quoted in Willis, *France, Germany*, 167.

16. Quoted in Jean Lacouture, *Pierre Mendès-France* (New York: Holmes & Meier, 1984), 266.

17. Peter Koch, *Konrad Adenauer. Eine politische Biographie* (Reinbek: Rowohlt, 1985), 284–85; Edward Fursdon, *The European Defense Community: A History* (New York: St. Martin's, 1980), 267; Alexander Werth, *Lost Statesman: The Strange Story of Pierre Mendès-France* (New York: Abelard-Schuman, 1958), 89.

18. René Massigli, *Une comédie des erreurs, 1943–1956* (Paris: Plon, 1978), 431.

19. Janet Flanner, *Paris Journal* (New York: Atheneum, 1965), 230. A still very useful summary of the French debate of the EDC is *France Defeats the EDC*, ed. Daniel Lerner and Raymond Aron (New York: Frederick Praeger, 1957).

20. Willis, *France, Germany*, 180.

21. *FRUS, 1952–1954*, 5:1029–37. Some Foreign Office officials, however, worried that the Americans were too impatient and that their attempt to force the EDC down France's throat would cause Paris to cough it up. See Evelyn Shuckburgh, *Descent to Suez: Diaries, 1951–1956* (London: Weidenfeld and Nicolson, 1986), 137.

22. Text of interview in *Bulletin des Presse- und Informationsamtes der Bundesregierung*, 3 July 1954, 1085–88.

23. Konrad Adenauer, *Erinnerungen, 1953–1955* (Stuttgart: Deutsche Verlags-Anstalt, 1966), 274.

24. Schwarz, *Die Ära Adenauer*, 225.

25. Paul-Henri Spaak, *The Continuing Battle: Memoirs of a European, 1936–1966* (Boston: Little, Brown, 1971), 167–68.

26. *FRUS, 1952–1954*, 5:1059.

27. Ibid., 1051.

28. Pierre Guillen, "Frankreich und die NATO-Integration der Bundesrepublik," in *Vom Marshallplan zur EWG. Die Eingliederung der Bundesrepublik Deutschland in die westliche Welt*, ed. Ludolf Herbst (Munich: R. Oldenbourg, 1990), 453.

29. *FRUS, 1952–1954*, 5:1071, 1077.

30. Quoted in Werth, *Lost Statesman*, 128.

31. Quoted ibid., 183.

32. Flanner, *Paris Journal*, 242.

33. Quoted in Charles Thayer, *The Unquiet Germans* (New York: Harper Brothers, 1957), 216.

34. Alphand, *L'étonnement*, 248.

35. Lord Charles Moran, *Churchill: The Struggle for Survival, 1940–1965* (Boston: Houghton Mifflin, 1966), 634.

36. *Mann in der Zeit* 7 (Oct. 1954): 2.

37. *FRUS, 1952–1954,* 5:1120–22.

38. Dwight D. Eisenhower, *Mandate for Change* (Garden City, N.Y.: Doubleday, 1963), 403.

39. Adenauer, *Erinnerungen, 1953–1955,* 298.

40. Ibid., 271.

41. Quoted in Koch, *Adenauer,* 285.

42. See correspondence between Baudissin and Ernst Egon Schutz in BA-MA, BW2/4026.

43. "SHAPE Prepares for Germans," *Foreign Report,* 8 Oct. 1954, 6–7.

44. Wilhelm Meier-Dörnberg, "Die Planung des Verteidigungsbeitrages der Bundesrepublik Deutschland im Rahmen der EVG," in *Anfänge westdeutscher Sicherheitspolitik, 1945–1956,* vol. 2: *Die EVG-Phase,* ed. MGFA (Munich: R. Oldenbourg, 1990), 753.

45. Author's interview with Baudissin, 30 May 1983.

46. Quoted in Koch, *Adenauer,* 283–84.

47. Quoted in Thayer, *Unquiet Germans,* 216.

48. Gerhard Wettig, *Entmilitarisierung und Wiederbewaffnung in Deutschland, 1943–1955* (Munich: R. Oldenbourg, 1967), 596–98; Anthony Nutting, *Europe Will Not Wait: A Warning and a Way Out* (New York: Frederick A. Praeger, 1960), 69–75; Fursdon, *European Defense Community,* 305–10; Roscoe Drummond and Gaston Coblentz, *Duel at the Brink: John Foster Dulles's Command of American Power* (Garden City, N.Y.: Doubleday, 1960), 101–9.

49. Anthony Eden, *Full Circle: The Memoirs of Anthony Eden* (Boston: Houghton Mifflin, 1960), 168.

50. Eden's claim was disputed by Harold Macmillan and Pierre Mendès-France. See Harold Macmillan, *Tides of Fortune, 1945–1955* (New York: Harper Brothers, 1969), 481; Pierre Mendès-France, *Choisir* (Paris: Stock, 1974), 77.

51. Rolf Steininger, "Das Scheitern der EVG und der Beitritt der Bundesrepublik zur NATO," *Aus Politik und Zeitgeschichte* 85 (27 Apr. 1985): 15.

52. Eden, *Full Circle,* 173–74.

53. Adenauer, *Erinnerungen, 1953–1955,* 309–11.

54. Eden, *Full Circle,* 179.

55. *FRUS, 1952–1954,* 5:1213–21.

56. Eden, *Full Circle,* 184–85. See also Eden memo, 27 Sept. 1954, PRO, Cab 129/70, C(54)298. Eden's aide Anthony Nutting claimed that he and Gladwyn Jebb, London's ambassador to Paris, came up with this solution and that when they put it to Eden he "reacted like a kicking mule." See Nutting, *Europe Will Not Wait,* 71.

57. For a complete record of the London Conference, see Nine Power Conference, Lancaster House, 28 Sept. 1954, Verbatim Record, Secret, PRO, FO 371/109774. The London and Paris conferences are discussed in Thoss, "Der Beitritt der Bundesrepublik," 32–134. For the British perspective, see David Carlton, "Grossbritannien und die Gipfeldiplomatie, 1953–1955," in *Zwischen Kaltem Krieg und Entspannung,* ed. MGFA (Boppard: Boldt, 1988), 51–69.

58. *FRUS, 1952–1954,* 5:1301; Eden, *Full Circle,* 188. For a general discussion of European security issues from the Eisenhower administration's perspective, see Ste-

phen E. Ambrose, "Die Eisenhower-Administration und die europäische Sicherheit, 1953–1956," in *Zwischen Kaltem Krieg und Entspannung*, ed. MGFA (Boppard: Boldt, 1988), 25–34.

59. Eden, *Full Circle*, 188–89.

60. Nutting, *Europe Will Not Wait*, 74.

61. Adenauer, *Erinnerungen, 1953–1955*, 340.

62. Quoted in Fursdon, *European Defense Community*, 321.

63. Moran, *Churchill*, 640.

64. Macmillan, *Tides of Fortune*, 483.

65. Fursdon, *European Defense Community*, 324.

66. Adenauer, *Erinnerungen, 1953–1955*, 347.

67. *FRUS, 1952–1954*, 5:1308–11.

68. Ibid., 1309.

69. Radford Memo, 22 Sept. 1954, NA, RG 218, CCS 092 (Germany), Section 25.

70. Aide Memoire, Supply of British Equipment and Training Aid for the Future German Forces, 18 Nov. 1954, PRO, FO 371/118319.

71. "Die Sparbüchse verstopft," *Der Spiegel*, 20 Oct. 1954, 8–12.

72. Adenauer, *Erinnerungen, 1953–1955*, 332–33.

73. "Die Sparbüchse verstopft," *Der Speigel*, 20 Oct. 1954, 8.

74. Dulles quoted in Louis J. Halle, *The Cold War as History* (London: Chatto & Windus, 1967), 258. The terms of the London Agreement can be found in *FRUS, 1952–1954*, 5:1339–66.

75. For a text of the Soviet note, see *Department of State Bulletin*, 13 Dec. 1954, 902.

76. Fursdon, *European Defense Community*, 331.

77. Eden, *Full Circle*, 191.

78. D. C. Watt, *Britain Looks to Germany* (London: Oswald Wolff, 1965), 129. On the Labour Party's debate, see *The Backbench Diaries of Richard Crossman*, ed. Janet Morgan (New York: Holmes & Meier, 1981), 343–46; Hugh Dalton, *Memoirs, 1945–1955: High Tide and After* (London: Muller, 1962), 405–6.

79. Watt, *Britain Looks to Germany*, 128.

80. Willis, *France, Germany*, 188.

81. Quoted in Worth, *Lost Statesman*, 189.

82. Ibid., 191.

83. Willis, *France, Germany*, 191–93.

84. *FRUS, 1952–1954*, 5:1520–21.

85. Moran, *Churchill*, 634.

86. *FRUS, 1952–1954*, 5:1525.

87. For Blank's testimony, see PA, AFES, 20. Sitzung, 13–16.

88. Ibid., 17–19.

89. Ibid., 25. Sitzung, 20–24, 51; 27. Sitzung, 22–23.

90. Ibid., 32. Sitzung, 13–48, 67, 52, 70–74.

91. Seminar für Politik im Bund für Volksbildung, Frankfurt, 9 Oct. 1954, BA-MA, BW9/740.

92. For accounts of these incidents, see "Die Tumulte um Blank," *FAZ*, 26 Nov. 1954; "Lehren der Blank Tumulte," *Bremen Nachrichten*, 27 Nov. 1954; "Foes of Bonn Arms Beat Defense Aide," *NYT*, 25 Nov. 1954; "Wasserwerfer decken Blank," *Abendpost* (Frankfurt), 14 Feb. 1955; "Keine Freiheit ohne Opfer," *Badische Zeitung* (Freiburg), 16 Feb. 1955; "Wieder Tumulte um Blank," *FAZ*, 17 Feb. 1955.

93. Hans-Adolf Jacobsen, "Zur Rolle der öffentlichen Meinung bei der Debatte um die Wiederbewaffnung, 1950–1955," in *Aspekte der deutschen Wiederbewaffnung bis 1955*, ed. MGFA (Boppard: Boldt, 1975), 84.

94. "Bonn Tries to Stir Interest in Army," *NYT*, 9 Dec. 1954; "Der Wille der Zwanzigjährigen," *FAZ*, 10 Nov. 1954.

95. "Heftige Diskussion um den Wehrbeitrag," *Frankfurter Rundschau*, 17 Nov. 1954; "Zwanzigjährigen wollen nicht Soldat werden," *Weser-Kurier* (Bremen), 5 Nov. 1954.

96. *Deutscher Bundestag. Verhandlungen*, 2. Wahlperiode, 61. Sitzung, 3123–28.

97. Ibid., 3127, 3142, 3144. On the weapons issue, see also "08/15," *Der Spiegel*, 13 Oct. 1954, 7–8.

98. Kurzprotokoll von der Sitzung des Bundeshauptausschusses am 9. Okt. 1954, Bonn, FNS, Bundeshauptausschuss file.

99. *Deutscher Bundestag. Verhandlungen*, 2. Wahlperiode, 61. Sitzung, 3159–63.

100. Text of Ollenhauer letter in *SPD Jahrbuch, 1954–55* (Bonn: Vorstand der SPD, 1956), 330–31.

101. For a text of Adenauer's reply, see FES, PV-Bestand Ollenhauer, Korrespondenz Ollenhauer-Adenauer, 9152–61.

102. *Vorwärts*, 21 Jan. 1955. For examinations of the SPD and the Paulskirche movement, see Gordon D. Drummond, *The German Social Democrats in Opposition: The Case against Rearmament* (Norman: University of Oklahoma Press, 1982), 133–39; Kurt Klotzbach, *Der Weg zur Staatspartei. Programmatik, praktische Politik und Organisation der deutschen Sozialdemokratie 1945 bis 1965* (Berlin: J. H. W. Dietz, 1982), 343–46.

103. Quoted in Ernst-Dieter Köpper, *Gewerkschaften und Aussenpolitik. Die Stellung der westdeutschen Gewerkschaften zur wirtschaftlichen und militärischen Integration der Bundesrepublik in die Europäische Gemeinschaft und in die NATO* (Frankfurt: Campus, 1982), 208. Also on the unions and rearmament, see Gerhard Braunthal, "West German Trade Unions and Disarmament," *Political Science Quarterly* 73 (1957): 82–99; "German Labor Unions and the Question of German Participation in Western Defense," Rand Corporation Study, RM-929, GAP Archive.

104. Theo Pirker, *Die SPD nach Hitler. Die Geschichte der Sozialdemokratischen Partei Deutschlands, 1945–1964* (Munich: Rütten & Loening, 1965), 208.

105. Köpper, *Gewerkschaften und Aussenpolitik*, 320.

106. Dieter Koch, *Heinemann und die Deutschlandfrage* (Munich: Kaiser, 1972), 437–52.

107. Johanna Vogel, *Kirche und Wiederbewaffnung. Die Haltung der Evangelischen Kirche in Deutschland in den Auseinandersetzungen um die Wiederbewaffnung der Bundesrepublik, 1949–1956* (Göttingen: Vandenhoeck & Rupprecht, 1978), 194.

108. Koch, *Heinemann und die Deutschlandfrage*, 443.

109. Quoted ibid., 446.

110. Quoted in Heinz Josef Varain, "Die Ausseinandesetzung innerhalb der Evangelischen Kirche wegen der deutschen Aufrüstung," *Geschichte in Wissenschaft und Unterricht* 9 (1958): 417.

111. Text of manifesto in *Sicherheitspolitik der Bundesrepublik Deutschland: Dokumentation, 1945–1977*, ed. Klaus von Schubert, 2 vols. (Cologne: Verlag Wissenschaft und Politik, 1978–79), 1:196–97.

112. See Köpper, *Gewerkschaften und Aussenpolitik*, 323.

113. "Schärfe Auseinandersetzung über die Wehrfrage," *FAZ*, 19 Jan. 1955.

114. Adenauer, *Erinnerungen, 1953–1955*, 421.

115. Thomas Dehler, "Antwort auf die Paulskirche," *Freideutsche Korrespondenz*, 16 Feb. 1955, 1.

116. Quoted in Anselm Doering-Manteuffel, *Katholizismus und Wiederbewaffnung. Die Haltung der deutschen Katholiken gegenüber der Wehrfrage, 1948–1955* (Mainz: Matthias Grünewald, 1981), 243.

117. Koch, *Heinemann und die Deutschlandfrage*, 488.

118. Ibid.

119. Ibid., 449.

120. Vogel, *Kirche und Wiederbewaffnung*, 205.

121. "In protestantischer Sicht," *Die Rheinpfalz* (Ludwigshafen), 18 Apr. 1955.

122. Thomas Alan Schwartz, *America's Germany: John J. McCloy and the Federal Republic of Germany* (Cambridge: Harvard University Press, 1991), 294.

123. Adenauer, *Erinnerungen, 1953–1955*, 430.

124. Ollenhauer quoted ibid., 432.

125. Quoted in Willis, *France, Germany*, 197.

Chapter Ten

1. For a good discussion of the transformation of the Dienststelle Blank into the ministry of defense, see Dieter Krüger, *Das Amt Blank. Die schwierige Gründung des Bundesministeriums für Verteidigung* (Freiburg: Rombach, 1993), 149–70.

2. For Adenauer's promise to Blank, see his United Press interview, Oct. 1953, BAK, B 145/718. *Der Spiegel* speculated in early 1955 that Adenauer would appoint an "American style" manager or industrialist to the post, perhaps the banker Hermann Abs. See "Der Zügel schiessen," 1 Jan. 1955, 6. The British Foreign Office believed that Adenauer would take the post himself. See Dean report, 14 Jan. 1955, PRO, FO 371/118319. For British misgivings about Blank, see Dean meeting with Heusinger, 14 Jan. 1955, PRO, FO 371/118319. At the time of his appointment, Blank was reported to have a drinking problem and to be "a bundle of nerves." See "Der Kanzler blieb sitzen," *Der Speigel*, 16 June 1955, 10–11.

3. Franz Josef Strauss, *Die Erinnerungen* (Berlin: Siedler, 1989), 272. Regarding Adenauer's attitude toward subordinates, *Der Spiegel* wrote: "The weakest defense minister is also the most attractive to the old man." See "Wo die Mängel zu suchen sind," *Der Spiegel*, 11 Dec. 1955, 17.

4. PA, AFES, 37. Sitzung, 15–17.

5. Hans-Peter Schwarz, *Die Ära Adenauer, 1949–1957* (Stuttgart: Deutsche Verlags-Anstalt, 1981), 288.

6. "Seien Sie nicht so juristisch!" *Der Spiegel*, 8 Aug. 1955, 7.

7. Charles Robert Naef, "The Politics of West German Rearmament, 1950–1956," 2 vols. (Ph.D. dissertation, Rutgers University, 1979), 2:578.

8. "Seien Sie nicht so juristisch!" *Der Spiegel*, 8 Aug. 1955, 8.

9. PA, AFES, 39. Sitzung, 18–19.

10. Ibid., 37. Sitzung, 86, 44–45, 53, 63.

11. Ibid., 63; 40. Sitzung, 18–20.

12. For a text of the Screening Board Law, see *Deutscher Bundestag. Anlagen*, 2. Wahlperiode, Band 36, Drucksache 1620.

13. Ulrich de Maizière, *In der Pflicht. Lebensbild eines deutschen Soldaten im 20. Jahrhundert* (Herford: E. S. Mittler, 1989), 193.

14. For provisions of the Volunteers' Law, see Gerhard Loosch, "Die gesetzlichen Grundlagen der Bundeswehr und ihrer Organisation," *Die öffentliche Verwaltung* 14 (Mar. 1961): 206–10. For a recent discussion of the law, see Hans Ehlert, "Innenpolitische Auseinandersetzungen um die Pariser Verträge und die Wehrverfassung 1954 bis 1956," in *Anfänge westdeutscher Sicherheitspolitik, 1945–1956*, vol. 3: *Die NATO Option*, ed. MGFA (Munich: R. Oldenbourg, 1993), 441–42.

15. *Jahrbuch der SPD, 1954–1955* (Bonn: Vorstand der SPD, 1956), 21; *Times* article quoted in John L. Sutton, "The Personnel Screening Committee and Parliamentary Control of the West German Armed Forces," *Journal of Central European Affairs* 19 (Jan. 1960): 21.

16. Dispatch, 1 July 1955, PRO, FO 371/118326; Dispatch, 19 July 1955, ibid.

17. For correspondence relative to these offers, see BA-MA, BW9/1337.

18. PA, AFES, 47. Sitzung, 26.

19. Ibid., 13–14.

20. Ibid., 14.

21. "Soldat im Ghetto," *Der Spiegel*, 24 Aug. 1955, 11–12. For a cogent analysis of the memo, see Georg Meyer, "Soldat im Ghetto? Eine Denkschrift der Gruppe Innere Führung im Bundesministerium für Verteidigung," *Militärgeschichtliche Beiträge* 5 (1991): 63–68. See also "Unzufriedenheit im Blank Ministerium," *Frankfurter Rundschau*, 25 Aug. 1955.

22. Meyer, "Soldat im Ghetto?" 63–64.

23. Ibid.

24. PA, AFES, 46. Sitzung, 4–7, 21, 23–30.

25. See "Der Fall Karst wird behandelt," *FAZ*, 14 Sept. 1955; "Die vertrauliche Denkschrift," *Frankfurter Rundschau*, 19 Sept. 1955; "Wir sind gebrannte Kinder," *Stuttgarter Zeitung*, 28 Sept. 1955.

26. PA, AFES, 46. Sitzung, 44, 62.

27. Quoted in Meyer, "Soldat im Ghetto," 66.

28. For a political breakdown of the board's membership, see Gliederung der PGA, 2 Sept. 1955, FES, Nachlass Erler, 140. A detailed discussion of personnel issues is to be found in Georg Meyer, "Zur inneren Entwicklung der Bundeswehr bis 1960/61," in *Anfänge westdeutscher Sicherheitspolitik, 1945–1956*, vol. 3: *Die NATO Option*, ed. MGFA (Munich: R. Oldenbourg, 1993), 1020–1119.

29. PA, AFES, 50. Sitzung, 2–3, 6–12, 20–25.

30. Feierliche Verpflichtung und Überreichung der Urkunden an die ersten Soldaten der Bundeswehr, 3 Nov. 1955, BA-MA, BW9/218, 5–7. On the problems associated with the appearance of the first soldiers, see Christian Greiner, "Die militärische Eingliederung der Bundesrepublik Deutschland in die WEU und die NATO 1954 bis 1957," in *Anfänge westdeutscher Sicherheitspolitik, 1945–1956*, vol. 3: *Die NATO Option*, ed. MGFA (Munich: R. Oldenbourg, 1993), 786–844.

31. "Streitkräfte," *Der Spiegel*, 24 Oct. 1954, 3–4.

32. The Ausschuss für Fragen Europäischer Sicherheit changed its name to Ausschuss für Verteidigung (AfV) in January 1956. See PA, AfV, 37. Sitzung, 28; 42. Sitzung, 4; 82. Sitzung, 13–16. See also Erich Mende, *Die neue Freiheit, 1945–1961* (Munich: Herbig, 1984), 373.

33. Text of Blank's speech in Archiv der CDU, St. Augustine, Pressepolitik, File I-088-001.

34. "Rekrutierung," *Der Spiegel*, 14 Dec. 1955, 11.

35. Gerd Schmückle, *Ohne Pauken und Trompeten* (Stuttgart: Deutsche Verlags-Anstalt, 1982), 103.

36. Donald Abenheim, *Reforging the Iron Cross: The Search for Tradition in the West German Armed Forces* (Princeton: Princeton University Press, 1988), 153.

37. "Guten Morgen Soldaten!" *Der Spiegel*, 25 Jan. 1956, 13–14.

38. Schwarz, *Die Ära Adenauer*, 299.

39. "Rat in dem Wind," *Der Spiegel*, 10 Dec. 1956, 16–17.

40. PA, Af V, 69. Sitzung, 4–8. Thirty-five years later, as the defense ministry was beginning to close down unneeded bases, mayors pleaded for the retention of posts in their towns. See "Erst mal das Maul halten," *Der Spiegel*, 4 Dec. 1990, 26–27.

41. Schmückle, *Ohne Pauken*, 109; Abenheim, *Reforging the Iron Cross*, 171.

42. Author's interview with Heinz Karst, 27 May 1983.

43. Abenheim, *Reforging the Iron Cross*, 174–84.

44. Charles Thayer, *The Unquiet Germans* (New York: Harper Brothers, 1957), 243–47.

45. Ibid., 246.

46. PA, Af V, 67. Sitzung, 56.

47. Bleibtreu to Erler, 17 Jan. 1956, FES, Nachlass Erler, 143.

48. So speculated *Der Spiegel*. See "Wo die Mängel zu suchen sind," *Der Spiegel*, 14 Dec. 1955, 18.

49. "Personalgutachterausschuss eine Monstrosität," *Deutsche Soldaten-Zeitung*, Aug. 1955, 2.

50. On the Waffen-SS veterans' frustrations with the Screening Board, and indeed with rearmament in general, see David Clay Large, "Reckoning without the Past: The HIAG of the Waffen-SS and the Politics of Rehabilitation in the Bonn Republic," *Journal of Modern History* 59 (Mar. 1987): 79–113.

51. "So geht es nicht, Graf Baudissin!" *Deutsche Soldaten-Zeitung*, Jan. 1955, 1.

52. For such criticism, see Schmückle, *Ohne Pauken*, 103; Strauss, *Erinnerungen*, 271; and Fritz Erler's comments in *Deutscher Bundestag. Verhandlungen*, 2. Wahlperiode, 143. Sitzung, 7494.

53. A summary of the new laws can be found in *Verteidigung im Bündnis. Planung, Aufbau und Bewährung der Bundeswehr, 1950–1972*, ed. MGFA (Munich: Bernard & Graefe, 1975), 104–16. See also Schwarz, *Die Ära Adenauer*, 292–99. An extensive discussion of the entire *Wehrverfassung* deliberations can be found in Ehlert, "Innenpolitische Auseinandersetzungen," 430–560.

54. Vorentwürf einer Regierungserklärung, BA-MA, BW9/1316.

55. PA, AFES, 53. Sitzung, 22. Also, for the SPD view, see Kurzprotokolle, 1. Sitzung, Sicherheitsausschuss beim Parteivorstand, FES, Nachlass Ollenhauer, 113; and Gordon D. Drummond, *The German Social Democrats in Opposition: The Case against Rearmament* (Norman: University of Oklahoma Press, 1982), 159–63.

56. See Hans Herzfeld, "Die Bundeswehr und das Problem der Tradition," in *Studien zur politischen und gesellschaftlichen Situation der Bundeswehr*, ed. Georg Picht, 3 vols. (Witten: Eckart, 1965), 1:42–43. See also Horst Ehmke, "Militärischer Oberbefehl und parlamentärische Kontrolle," *Zeitschrift für Politik* 1 (1954): 337–56.

57. Klaus Hornung, *Staat und Armee: Studien zur Befehls- und Kommandogewalt und zum politisch-militärischen Verhältnis in der Bundesrepublik Deutschland* (Mainz: Hase & Koehler, 1975), 68.

58. Ibid.

59. PA, Af V, 64. Sitzung, 1–3.

60. Hornung, *Staat und Armee*, 72–73.

61. Ibid., 76–100.

62. *Deutscher Bundestag. Verhandlungen*, 2. Wahlperiode, 132. Sitzung, 2823–36.

63. See Naef, "Politics of West German Rearmament," 2:646.

64. *Verteidigung im Bündnis*, 107–12.

65. Peter Dade, *Fahneneid und feierliches Gelöbnis* (Darmstadt: Wehr und Wissen Verlag, 1971), 51–67; Abenheim, *Reforging the Iron Cross*, 169–70.

66. *Deutscher Bundestag. Drucksachen*, 2. Wahlperiode, vol. 37, Drucksache 1700.

67. PA, Af V, 65. Sitzung, 6–18.

68. Ibid., 68. Sitzung, 2–18, 19–25.

69. Ibid., 69. Sitzung, 77.

70. *Deutscher Bundestag. Verhandlungen*, 2. Wahlperiode, 132. Sitzung, 6831–32.

71. Ibid., 143. Sitzung, 7515.

72. Studie zur Frage der Dienstdauer, BA-MA, BW9/1316; also, de Maizière, *In der Pflicht*, 191.

73. On conscientious objection and draft resistance, see "Macht es wie Adenauer," *Der Spiegel*, 16 Jan. 1957, 14–19.

74. *Jahrbuch der öffentlichen Meinung, 1956*, ed. Erich-Peter Neumann and Elisabeth Noelle (Allensbach: Institut für Demoskopie, 1957), 301.

75. *Vorwärts*, 16 Mar. 1956. On the SPD and conscription, see Drummond, *German Social Democrats in Opposition*, 163–73.

76. Protokoll über die Sitzung der Sicherheitsausschuss beim Parteivorstand, 24 Mar. 1956, FES, Nachlass Ollenhauer, 113.

77. Wehrfrage und Wahlkampf, 7 June 1956, FES, Nachlass Erler, 139.

78. Naef, "Politics of West German Rearmament," 2:684.

79. Protokolle, 7. ordentlicher Bundesparteitag der FDP, 20/21 Apr. 1956, FNS, Bundesparteitag Handakt, 96.

80. Protokoll der Arbeitstagung der Bundesausschuss für Verteidigungsfragen, 19 Apr. 1956, FNS, Bundesverteidigungsausschuss Handakt, 892.

81. Af V, 99. Sitzung, 17–32.

82. Ibid., 97. Sitzung, 11–24.

83. Quoted in Paul Sethe, *Zwischen Bonn und Moskau* (Frankfurt: Scheffler, 1957), 54–55.

84. *Facts on File*, 6 Dec. 1956, 189–90.

85. *Deutscher Bundestag. Verhandlungen*, 2 Wahlperiode, 157. Sitzung, 8633–39.

86. Ibid., 159. Sitzung, 8775.

87. On Carte Blanche, see Mark Cioc, *Pax Atomica: The Nuclear Defense Debate in West Germany during the Adenauer Era* (New York: Columbia University Press, 1988), 28–30; Schwarz, *Die Ära Adenauer*, 300–301; Hans Speier, *German Rearmament and Atomic War: The Views of German Military and Political Leaders* (Evanston, Ill.: Row, Peterson, 1957), 140–47; "Carte Blanche," *Wehrkunde* 4 (July–Aug. 1955): 308–10. For recent discussions of the strategic context of which Carte Blanche was a part, see Greiner, "Die militärische Eingliederung," 603–29; Johannes Steinhoff and Reiner Pommerin, *Strategiewechsel: Bundesrepublik und Nuklearstrategie in der Ära Adenauer-Kennedy* (Baden-Baden: Nomos Verlag, 1992); and Klaus A. Maier, "The Federal Republic of Germany as a 'Battlefield' in American Nuclear Strategy, 1953–1955," in

American Policy and the Reconstruction of West Germany, 1945–1955, ed. Jeffry M. Diefendorf, Axel Frohn, and Hermann-Josef Rupieper (New York: Cambridge University Press, 1993), 395–409.

88. Quoted in Cioc, *Pax Atomica,* 30.

89. On the Radford Plan, see ibid., 33–34; Schwarz, *Die Ära Adenauer,* 343; *Verteidigung im Bündnis,* 83; Hans-Gert Pöttering, *Adenauers Sicherheitspolitik, 1955–1963: Ein Beitrag zum deutsch-amerikanischen Verhältnis* (Düsseldorf: Droste, 1975), 62–64; Johannes Fischer, "Militärpolitische Lage und militärische Planung bei Aufstellungsbeginn der Bundeswehr," in *Militärgeschichte: Probleme — Thesen — Wege,* ed. MGFA (Stuttgart: Deutsche Verlags-Anstalt, 1982), 452–77; Felix von Eckardt, *Ein unordentliches Leben* (Düsseldorf: Econ, 1967), 451–60; Konrad Adenauer, *Erinnerungen, 1955–1959* (Stuttgart: Deutsche Verlags-Anstalt, 1967), 197–214.

90. Adenauer, *Erinnerungen, 1955–1959,* 205.

91. Quoted in Pöttering, *Adenauers Sicherheitspolitik,* 73–74.

92. Eckardt, *Ein unordentliches Leben,* 459.

93. Adenauer, *Erinnerungen, 1955–1959,* 214. See also Pöttering, *Adenauers Sicherheitspolitik,* 78–79.

94. Adenauer, *Erinnerungen, 1955–1959,* 244.

95. *Europa-Archiv* 20 (1956): 9267. On the length-of-service controversy, see Ehlert, "Innenpolitische Auseinandersetzungen," 538–52.

96. "Mir san blass Infanterie," *Der Spiegel,* 15 Feb. 1956, 45.

97. De Maizière, *In der Pflicht,* 192.

98. Text of declaration in *Europa-Archiv* 1 (1957): 9521–22. See also Pöttering, *Adenauers Sicherheitspolitik,* 82–83.

99. "Avec tristress," *Der Spiegel,* 10 Oct. 1956, 11.

100. Catherine Kelleher, *Germany and the Politics of Nuclear Weapons* (New York: Columbia University Press, 1975), 48–56.

101. "Der Kasseler Despeche," *Der Spiegel,* 17 Oct. 1956, 16; Strauss, *Erinnerungen,* 273.

102. "Auseinandersetzung um Graf Baudissin," *Süddeutsche Zeitung,* 25 June 1956.

103. Eckardt, *Ein unordentliches Leben,* 440–41; Adenauer, *Erinnerungen, 1955–1959,* 246. On Strauss's career up to his appointment as defense minister, see the biographical profile, "Der Primus," *Der Spiegel,* 2 Jan. 1957, 11–25. For a discussion of the transition from Blank to Strauss, see Krüger, *Das Amt Blank,* 171–75.

104. Strauss, *Erinnerungen,* 274.

105. Ibid., 276; "Tote auf dem Felde," *Der Spiegel,* 24 Oct. 1956, 13–16.

106. "Der Primus," *Der Spiegel,* 2 Jan. 1957, 11; Strauss, *Erinnerungen,* 301–2. Strauss's views were echoed by his colleague the CDU defense expert Fritz Berendsen, who told NATO representatives in November that West Germany could not risk jeopardizing its living standard by carrying too heavy a defense burden. His comments were not well received. See "NATO: Vieles hat sich geändert," *Der Spiegel,* 28 Nov. 1956, 11–12.

107. Strauss, *Erinnerungen,* 303; Kelleher, *Germany and the Politics of Nuclear Weapons,* 61–88; Cioc, *Pax Atomica,* 34–35.

108. *FRUS, 1955–1957,* vol. 4: *North Atlantic Treaty Organization* (Washington, D.C.: GPO, 1986), 127.

109. Ibid., 126.

110. Ibid., 132.

111. Abenheim, *Reforging the Iron Cross,* 172.

112. On the Iller accident, see ibid., 173; Strauss, *Erinnerungen*, 290–92; Schmückle, *Ohne Pauken*, 143–53.

113. "Das Illerunglück," *Deutsche Soldaten-Zeitung*, July 1957, 1.

114. Strauss, *Erinnerungen*, 292–96.

115. Author's interview with Count Baudissin, 30 May 1983.

Conclusion

1. See Timothy Garton Ash, *In Europe's Name: Germany and the Divided Continent* (New York: Random House, 1993), 21.

2. Quoted in Hans Speier, *German Rearmament and Atomic War: The Views of German Military and Political Leaders* (Evanston, Ill.: Row, Peterson, 1957), 207.

3. Josef Joffe, *The Limited Partnership: Europe, the United States, and the Burdens of Alliance* (Cambridge, Mass.: Ballinger, 1987), 45.

4. Ash, *In Europe's Name*, 45.

5. Thomas Alan Schwartz, *America's Germany: John J. McCloy and the Federal Republic of Germany* (Cambridge: Harvard University Press, 1991), 295.

J